CONCEPT
AND
DESIGN
IN
MUSIC

A COMPREHENSIVE APPROACH TO THEORY

CONCEPT AND DESIGN IN MUSIC

A COMPREHENSIVE APPROACH TO THEORY

ROBERT WM SHERMAN

Ball State University

Harcourt Brace Jovanovich, Publishers

San Diego   New York   Chicago   Austin   Washington, D.C.
London   Sydney   Tokyo   Toronto

ISBN: 0-15-512835-3
Library of Congress Catalog Card Number: 88-80630

Printed in the United States of America

Credits appear on pages 494–95, which constitute a continuation of the copyright page.

Preface

> It is implied, I think, that the act of
> a man creating is the act of a whole man,
> that it is this rather than the product
> that makes it good and worthy.
> —Jerome S. Bruner in *On Knowing*

Concept and Design in Music: A Comprehensive Approach to Theory is a course of study in which the student experiences and comes to know the underlying principles of the musical art through the creative act of making music. The course incorporates the best features of apprenticeship training, independent study, creative invention, experimental and exploratory research, repetitive drill, and the guidance of the instructor.

As a course of study, *Concept and Design in Music* relies on personal discovery, experimentation, and invention, rather than on prescriptive, stylistic imitation. This approach to teaching the "theory" of music deals directly with the materials and principles of the musical art. The course cultivates each student's need to come to grips personally with the materials and craft of music in ways that reflect his or her own assessments and decisions.

The content of this course of study is arranged in seven study units, each consisting of six to ten creative learning experiences that lead to several mini projects and one or more unit projects. Each creative learning experience is in the form of a chapter, and the number of chapters in a particular study unit depends upon the materials and concepts required for completing the respective mini projects and unit projects.

The Mini Projects

The mini projects provide independent study and creative exercise of specific aspects of music. They serve as preparation for the unit projects, as the means of dealing creatively with materials and procedures that could be used in a unit project but that are too numerous for a single unit project, and as the means of pursuing special interests in independent research.

The Unit Projects

The unit projects are final, culminating projects that demonstrate the students' understanding of the materials and principles of the study units. As such, they serve as the focus of all other activities in each unit. These projects offer students the means of understanding concepts and principles that can be understood only through the process of composition, and they provide artistic projects that can be evaluated and graded.

Whenever possible, the unit projects should be performed in public. In any case, the unit projects and the compositionally oriented mini projects should be performed, and evaluated, in class. Without the experience of realizing their unit projects in *sound*—that is, relating the *results* to their *expectations*—students cannot fully benefit from their efforts.

The Workbook

Concept and Design in Music: A Comprehensive Approach to Theory includes a workbook that provides drill in those elements of music study for which drill is essential. Throughout the textbook, applicable workbook exercises are referenced by a simple code: **W8** refers the student to exercise number 8; **W2–5**, to exercises 2 through 5.

It is unreasonable to assume that any one unit project or mini project can require the full use of all of the materials presented in the study unit. Although the unit project provides valuable experience in using materials and concepts, it is obvious that each study unit presents more material than can be utilized immediately, and that the nature of some material requires repetitive drill. For this reason, the workbook is designed to give students exposure to the full range of notation, nomenclature, terminology, and compositional procedures presented in the textbook. And because the primary function of the workbook is to provide drill, it contains a large number of exercises on the recognition and notation of pitch and durational relationships—for example, intervals, scale materials, chords, transposition, and temporal patterns. Most instructors will assign the workbook exercises according to the specific needs of their classes, but students should take it upon themselves to complete additional exercises as needed to improve their speed and accuracy and for review.

ACKNOWLEDGMENTS

I am much indebted to my good friends Morris Knight, Jr., and Cleve Scott for their moral support and technical assistance in writing this book. Their contributions have been many and substantial. I also acknowledge my indebtedness to my students, whose individual and collective successes in learning and applying the concepts and design principles presented herein have made this book a personal imperative.

Without the reviewers' critical and forthright evaluations of the original manuscript, the book would have remained a manuscript. My thanks go to professors Arthur Campbell of St. Olaf College, John Fonville of the University of California at San Diego, and Douglas Phillips of Millikin University.

Transforming the manuscript into a physically attractive, readable book has been the task of an HBJ bookteam. Their professionalism, support, and graciousness have made this experience a highlight of my career. I extend my gratitude to Julia Berrisford (acquisitions editor), Carole Bailey Reagle (manuscript editor), Cathy Reynolds (designer), Caty Van Housen (production editor), Cindy Robinson (art editor), and Lynne Bush (production manager).

Finally, I thank my wife, Joan, whose patience and support have made it possible to bring this work to a happy conclusion.

Robert Wm Sherman

Contents

U N I T

ONE

FUNDAMENTALS OF
CONVENTIONAL NOTATION

1 Systems

What is a system?

A **system** is an arrangement or network of like elements or things that are connected so as to form an integrated, specialized field within which particular conditions may exist, particular activities take place, particular functions are performed, or particular commodities are delivered. We are all familiar with the solar system, transportation systems, the cardiovascular system, the nervous system, school systems, electrical systems, sewage systems, irrigation systems, and many, many others. Each of the systems is a highly developed organism that is limited to one particular state of being or purpose. A number of systems exist in music. Those we will discuss in this chapter are the staff system, the clef system, and the diatonic system.

What is the function of a staff?

When used in conjunction with a clef, a **staff** functions as a visual frame of reference for indicating pitches. The five-line staff (Figure 1-1), the most prominent form of the staff in use, is

1-1

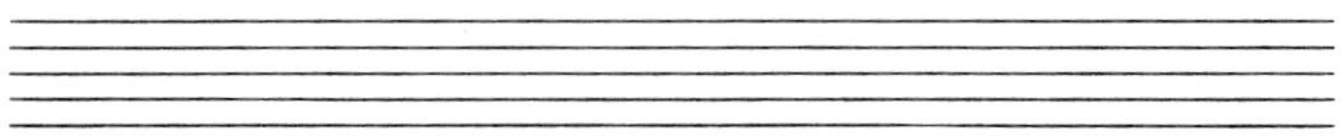

the product of a long evolutionary development. The nomenclature of the five-line staff and the extensions made possible by leger lines are shown in Figure 1-2.

1-2

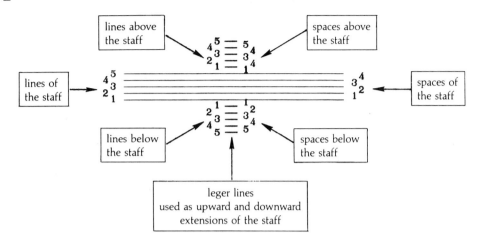

What is a staff system?

A **staff system** is a combination of two or more **staves** (plural) usually joined by a **bracket**, a **brace**, or a combination of the two. Such a system is used for the notation of music for a particular instrument or group of instruments. **Measure bars** (**barlines**) in a staff system are placed in a manner that best facilitates visual orientation by joining various subgroupings of instruments.

Systems with two staves are used for harp, keyboard instruments, and combinations of voices and single-line instruments. The staves of harp and keyboard systems are connected with curved braces, as shown in Figure 1-3; the staves of systems used for duets are connected by brackets. Observe the differences in barring; some barlines join the staves, some do not.

1-3

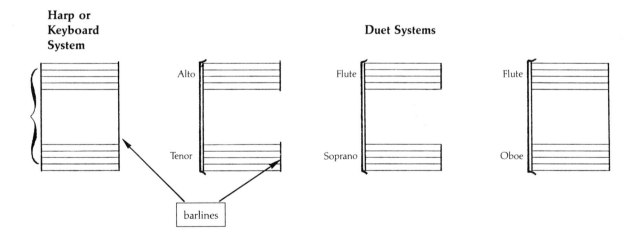

Systems with three staves are used for organ, occasionally for piano, solo voice or solo instrument with keyboard or harp accompaniment, and for combinations of voices and single-line instruments. Take particular note of the braces, brackets, and barlines in the examples of Figure 1-4.

1-4

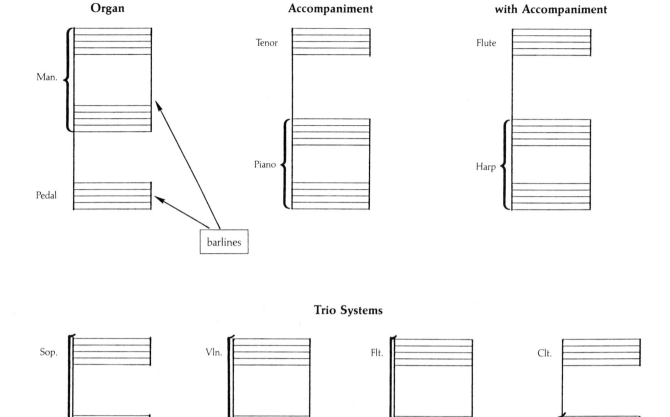

Systems having from four to forty or more staves are used for scores calling for combinations of voices and instruments. Examples of multistaved systems are shown in Figure 1-5. For additional examples of staff systems and the use of braces, brackets, and barlines, consult scores for full orchestra, band, chorus with instruments, and the various conventional and unconventional systems used in chamber music.

1-5

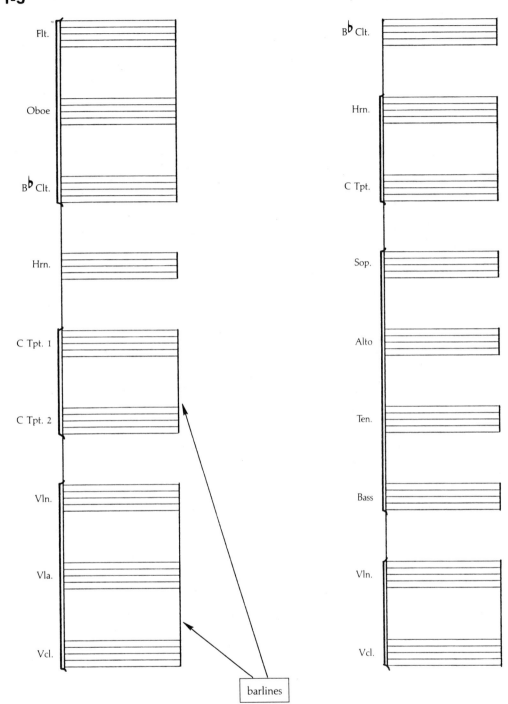

barlines

What should be the order of instruments in a score?

     In conventional layouts of scores for band and orchestra, instruments are grouped as families; that is, as **woodwinds**, **brass**, **percussion**, miscellaneous **keyboard instruments**, and **strings** (Figure 1-6). Such families as the woodwinds, brass, and strings cover approximately the same general pitch range. Although the order in which instruments within a given family are scored is generally related to the instruments' high/low pitch ranges, this relationship is interrupted when more than one size of a given type of instrument is used. For example, the

1-6   STAFF SYSTEMS

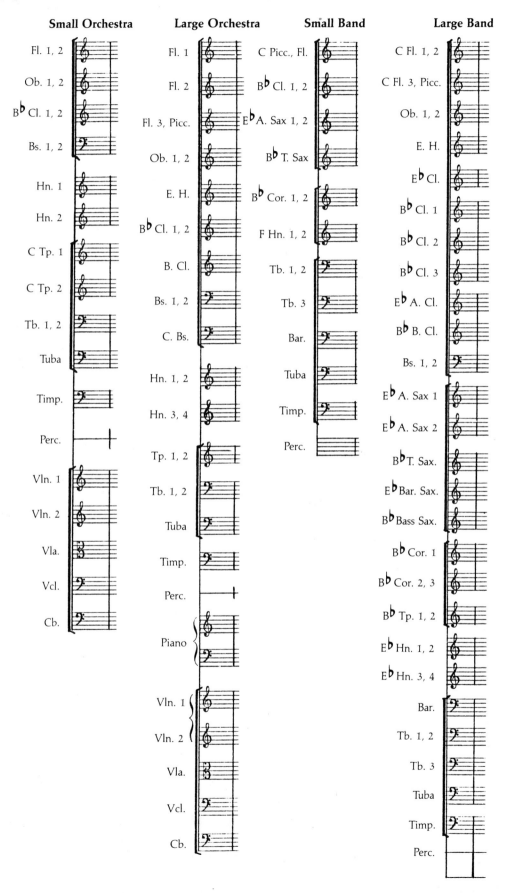

usual positioning of the flute, oboe, B-flat clarinet, and bassoon lines would be interrupted if a bass flute were added to the score. The bass flute line would be placed above the oboe line, even though its pitch range is considerably below that of the oboe.

When developing a staff system for the score of a small, heterogeneous group of instruments, the order of instruments might very well be a compromise between the prevailing conventional positioning of instruments in a full score for band or orchestra and what seems practical. If entire families of instruments are not used, the conventional practice of placing woodwinds at the top, brass next, and so on, as in a score for full orchestra, might not be the best solution. It might be more practical to position the instruments according to their ranges, the nature of the music, or such a purely physical aspect as the space available for leger lines. If two instruments of a given family are used, they may be separated under certain conditions. A quintet for flute, two horns, violin, and 'cello might appear in a score—depending, of course, on the nature of the music—either as flute, violin, two horns, and 'cello or as violin, flute, two horns, and 'cello. There is a logical reason for separating the violin and 'cello in this case; there would be no logic in separating the two horns.   **W1–2**

What is the function of a clef?

As stated at the beginning of this chapter, the staff, in conjunction with a **clef**, provides a visual frame of reference for the indication of pitch. The function of the clef is to designate one line of the staff, depending on the clef used, as pitch-name F, C, or G. Historically, the C clef appeared first, the F clef next, and the G clef last.

What is the clef system?

The **clef system** is an arrangement of three clefs that, because of the clefs' placement on a staff and their relationship to each other, provides an on-the-staff frame of reference for the notation of pitches extending approximately three octaves. Figure 1-7 illustrates how the

1-7

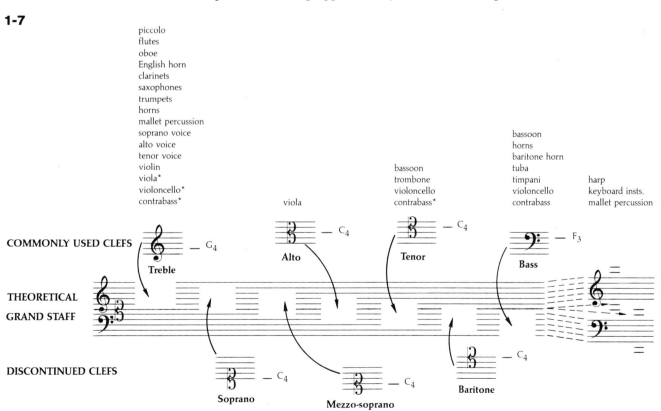

*Occasionally used

various clefs of the clef system are related, how the five-line staff is related to the theoretical **grand staff**, and which clefs are used by voices and instruments in current use. Theoretically, the five clefs denoting "middle C" are all on the same line of the grand staff, but they appear on different lines when placed on a five-line staff. A five-line staff represents a particular five-line portion of the fixed grand staff, a portion denoted by the clef that is placed on it.

Vocal music was the first music to appear in notation. The pitch ranges of the voices used in the medieval and Renaissance periods are modest in comparison to present-day vocal ranges. Using C clefs for the five voices for which they are named (soprano, mezzo-soprano, alto, tenor, and baritone) and the F clef (bass voice) made it possible to notate the music for each voice directly on the staff with but few exceptions.

What is the diatonic system?

The **diatonic system** is a series of seven pitch classes* arranged in an ordered succession of half steps and whole steps. The half steps are placed so that the whole steps are separated into a group of two whole steps alternating with a group of three whole steps.

How is the natural diatonic system expressed on the staff?

Though it serves as a frame of reference for the pitch content of the diatonic system, the staff, appearing as a set of equally spaced, parallel lines, does not provide any visual means of representing the pitch relationships of the diatonic system. What is illustrated in Figure 1-8, for example, is simply a series of notes on alternate lines and spaces of the staff. No actual pitches are represented; the relationships, at face value, would have to be considered equal. If we add a clef

1-8

(Figure 1-9), we gain the benefit of knowing the pitch names and the location of the half steps and whole steps of the **natural diatonic system**. However, we still have not changed the visual relationship of any line to another line, any space to another space, or of any line to any space; the relationships still appear equal visually.

1-9

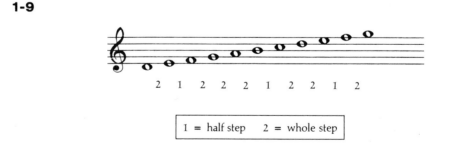

The inability of the staff to provide a visual impression of the half-step/whole-step relationships of the natural diatonic system, though a seemingly troublesome imperfection, is what makes the combined staff and clef systems an extremely workable and flexible framework for the notation of pitch. Because there are no visual differences in the staff, the location of half steps and whole steps can be changed. The natural diatonic system must be learned and

*A **pitch class** is any and all of the pitches represented by a given pitch name.

understood as an ordered series of half steps and whole steps with neither a beginning pitch nor an ending pitch. This aspect of the system may be more easily observed when the system is presented as a circle, as in Figure 1-10.

1-10

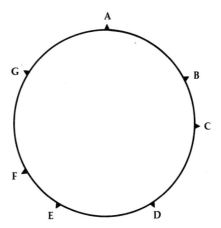

The term *diatonic* is used to describe the notation of any pitch relationship, or set of pitch relationships, within the framework of the natural diatonic system or any of its transposed versions. These basic relationships may be perceived more handily by an examination of the visual and aural relationships expressed by the white keys of the piano. The natural diatonic system, with pitch members identified by the letters A, B, C, D, E, F, and G, is shown in Figure 1-11. **W3**

1-11

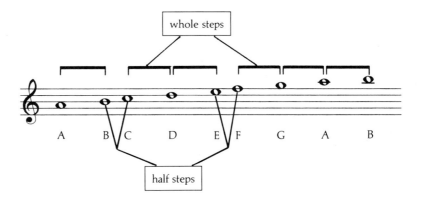

MINI PROJECT 1

As a means of gaining some historical perspective about how the conventional **systems** presented in this chapter came into being, research and write a brief paper on one of these topics:

1. The establishment of the diatonic system

2. The evolutionary development of the staff

3. The evolutionary development of clefs

4. The evolutionary development of score systems for the orchestra

5. The evolutionary development of score systems for the band

2 | Pitch

What is pitch?

Pitch is a perceptual term used in music to denote the aspect of a sound that results from the fundamental frequency of vibration of the waveform producing it. We most generally refer to a pitch in terms of a specific pitch name, such as C_4 or "middle" C. A pitch represented by a specific **pitch name** is called a **discrete pitch**. We may also use the term *pitch* to express such vague generalities as high pitch, low pitch, or indefinite pitch. Pitch is thus a relative, comparative dimension of sound for us to utilize; we can relate pitches to each other in various ways to achieve various purposes. Our ultimate joy in exercising this capacity to relate pitches is to produce the kinds of sound complexes we call music.

What is the significance of the octave?

When the frequency of a given pitch is doubled or halved an interesting phenomenon occurs: we recognize that the second pitch duplicates the first pitch but sounds in a higher or lower pitch range. This duplication of a pitch is called an **octave**. A pitch name representing any one or all octave repetitions of a given pitch is called a **pitch class**.

If we were to sound the pitch A-440, a frequency of 440 Hz*, and then sound a pitch having the frequency of 880 Hz, we would recognize the two pitches as being the same with the exception that the second pitch would be perceived as sounding an octave above the first pitch. Likewise, if the frequency of the pitch A-440 were halved (220 Hz), a duplicate pitch would result and it would be perceived as sounding an octave below the A-440. The phenomenon of the octave is a built-in-by-nature repetition that provides a framework within which our comprehension of pitch and pitch relationships may be achieved.

* Hz is an abbreviation of the last name of Heinrich Rudolph Hertz, a German physicist. Hz has replaced the older CPS, for cycles per second.

On the staff, the octave of a notated pitch is located on the eighth degree of the staff above or below it, counting the original notated pitch as one and each line and space of the staff as one degree. Figure 2-1 is a visual expression of the octave repetitions within the pitch range of the piano. Figure 2-1 also provides a suitable terminology for the verbal and written references to a given pitch by pitch name and **register**. By custom, each octave register begins on the pitch name "C." **W4**

2-1

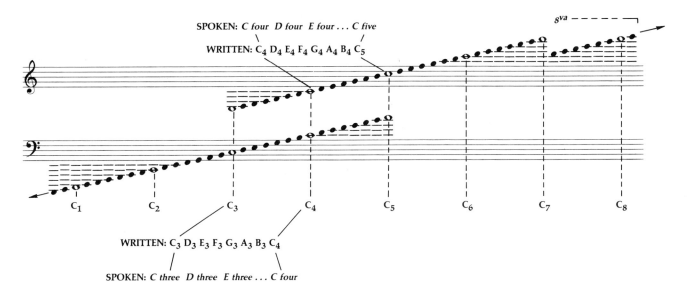

Pitch Registers

How is pitch represented in notation?

When referring to pitch, we are accustomed to using a convenient form of language which, if taken literally, is misleading. For example, in referring to the notated pitches in Figure 2-2, we would conveniently identify the pitches as D sharp, G sharp, E, F, A flat, and E flat. The fine distinction that can be lost by this "convenience" is that D sharp, G sharp, E, F, A flat, and E flat are really not pitches; they are "names" given to pitches.

2-2

The notation of pitch is simply achieved by placing the appropriate symbol on the appropriate line or space of the staff. The appropriate symbol, of course, is a note indicating the desired duration preceded by a qualifying "accidental" (a sharp, flat, or natural) if needed. When a sharp or flat is used within the music rather than in a signature, it is customary that the sharp or flat pertains only to the notes on that particular line or space in that particular measure (Figure 2-3). If we wish to cancel a sharp or flat (whether the sharp or flat is in a signature or within a

2-3

line of music) we simply place a natural sign before the appropriate note (Figure 2-4 a and b). The natural sign would apply to all of the notes that follow on that particular line or space in that particular measure.

2-4

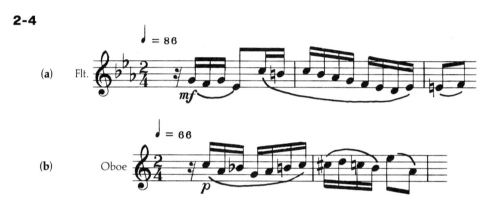

What is meant by the enharmonic notation of pitch?

The **enharmonic** notation of pitch refers to the availability of more than one pitch name and notation for a given pitch, especially those pitch names and notations that require a sharp or flat. In Figure 2-5 are shown some common enharmonic notations. What should be

2-5

understood about enharmonic pitch names and their notations is that, in each case, an audio frequency is perceived as a pitch. In using this pitch in the making of music, we can name and notate it in more than one way. The particular name and notation we use is determined by its relationship to other pitch names and their notations. Enharmonic pitch names and notations are much the same as homonyms; that is, words that sound alike but have different spellings and definitions. Words such as *to, too,* and *two* or *hear* and *here* are examples of homonyms.

As an example of how we choose which pitch name and notation to use, let us assume we have a pitch that we can notate as either A sharp or B flat. It is expected that our choice will form the best relationship with the notation of the pitches that precede and follow it. In such cases, the circumstances of usage require a selection that recognizes one of them as the preferred notation and the other as a second choice, or "enharmonic" notation. If the needed pitch occurs between a notated A and a C (Figure 2-6a), B flat is the preferred notation because the relationship of A to B flat and B flat to C is, in each case, a diatonic relationship. The A sharp would not form a diatonic relationship with either the A or C. If, on the other hand, the needed pitch occurs between a notated A and a B, a diatonic relationship is possible with either the A or the B but not with both at the same time. As shown in Figure 2-6b, A sharp would be the preferred notation for practical reasons: the use of B flat would require a natural sign before the

2-6

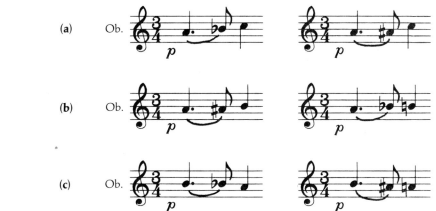

B to cancel the previous flat. Similarly, as shown in Figure 2-6c, B flat would be the preferred notation because the use of A sharp would require a natural sign before the A to cancel the previous sharp.   **W5—6**

What is a chromatic relationship?

Two different pitches that are notated on the same line or space of the staff form a **chromatic** relationship; the same two pitches can also be notated as a diatonic relationship (Figure 2-7). These two notations indicate a chromatic half step and a diatonic half step,

2-7

chromatic   diatonic

respectively. It is interesting to note the difference between an enharmonic notation and a chromatic notation. An enharmonic notation provides two notations on two different degrees of the staff for the same pitch, whereas a chromatic notation provides two notations on the same degree of the staff for two different pitches.

What is an interval?

An **interval** is a measured relationship between the notations of two pitches. Intervals occur between the notations of pitches that sound **simultaneously** (Figure 2-8a) and those that sound **consecutively** in ascending or descending motion (Figure 2-8b).

2-8

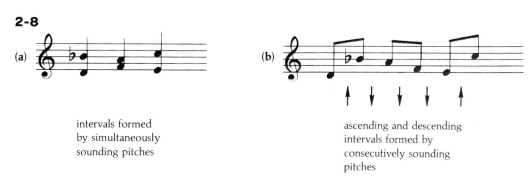

intervals formed
by simultaneously
sounding pitches

ascending and descending
intervals formed by
consecutively sounding
pitches

How do we name and notate intervals?

The intervallic relationships of the diatonic system provide the positive, one-to-one matching of name with notation and sound that is used as a standard for the aural identification of sounding pitch relationships and the auralization* of notated pitch relationships. Therefore, insofar as possible, we should notate pitches so that the resulting intervallic relationships fit within the framework of the natural diatonic system or one of its transpositions.**

The staff, which was developed for the notation of the natural diatonic system, implies a fixed framework within which the ordering of the half steps and whole steps of the system may be notated. Through the use of accidentals, the staff becomes equally serviceable as a framework within which the eleven transpositions of the natural diatonic system may be notated and chromatic alterations within the diatonic system may be made. Music composed within the **dodecaphonic** system (a system incorporating all twelve pitches within the octave) may also be notated on the staff. Pitch names and notations that are considered members or chromatic alterations of members of the natural diatonic system and any of its transpositions are considered separate and distinct, having equal status with all other pitch names and notations in the dodecaphonic system. For example, the notated G sharp in Figure 2-9a is a chromatic alteration of G, which is a member of a diatonic system. However, the notated G natural in Figure 2-9b is a chromatic alteration of G sharp, which is also a member of a diatonic system. The dodecaphonic system, which contains twelve pitches, has no transpositions; therefore, G natural and G sharp would be notations of separate and distinct pitches at all times in that system.

2-9

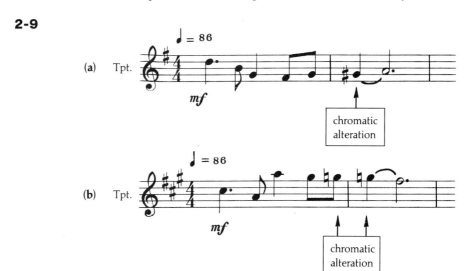

How are the ordinal and cardinal numbering systems used in naming intervals?

The naming of intervals in the diatonic system is based on the **ordinal system** of numbering: 1st (first),*** 2nd (second), 3rd (third), 9th (ninth), and 12th (twelfth) are examples of ordinal numbers. An ordinal number identifies a member of a series in terms of its position in the series. The members of a series need not be equal to one another; a member may be a single item or several items. Both the half-step and whole-step relationships formed by the

---

*The mental realization of a notated pitch. Auralization is to hearing what visualization is to seeing. The term is attributed to Morris Knight.

**A transposed diatonic system is a duplication of the half-step/whole-step ordering of pitch relationships of the natural diatonic system at any one of the eleven other possible pitch levels.

***In naming intervals, *prime* is used instead of *first*.

adjacent line-to-space and space-to-line degrees of the staff are considered individual members of an ordinal series. To arrive at the proper ordinal number for an interval, call the first of the notated pitches "one," and count the lines and spaces up (or down) to and including the second notated pitch (Figure 2-10a). Ordinal names for intervals formed by two simultaneously sounding pitches are calculated from the notation of the lower member of the interval to that of the higher.

2-10

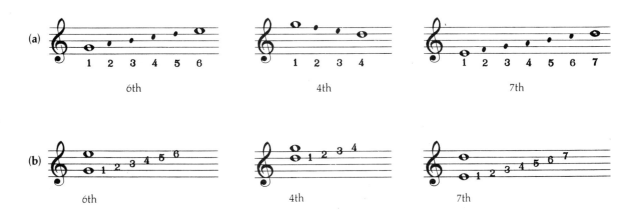

For some purposes we need only to know that an interval is, for example, a 3rd, a 6th, or a 2nd. For other purposes it is necessary to know what kind of 3rd, 6th, or 2nd the interval is. Ordinal numbers are used for naming intervals in terms of scale degrees or degrees of the staff for general purposes; however, additional qualifying terms are needed for naming intervals precisely. For example, the two kinds of 3rds found in the natural diatonic system; see Figure 2-11. Thirds containing a natural diatonic half step plus a whole step are *minor thirds* and are

2-11

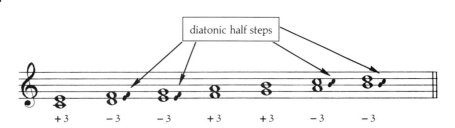

labeled -3 (or m3). The -3 naming label may be read as "minus three"; both -3 and m3 may be read as "minor third." Thirds containing two whole steps are *major thirds* and are labeled $+3$ (or M3). The $+3$ naming label may be read as "plus three," and both $+3$ and M3 may be read as "major third." Regardless of how we label it and read it, the number is still regarded as an ordinal number.

The naming of intervals in the dodecaphonic system is based on the **cardinal system** of numbering: 1, 2, 3, and 4 are examples of cardinal numbers. In the cardinal system, an **integer** (a whole number) expresses a one-to-one relationship between the integer and whatever it is the integer represents. Each of the eleven half steps of the dodecaphonic system represents the integer 1 (one). Therefore, 3 represents three half steps, 9 represents nine half steps, and so on.

To use the cardinal system, we first assign an integer (using 0 through 11) to each member of the dodecaphonic system. In accord with the custom established in the diatonic system and continued in the chart of pitch registers, we begin with 0 (zero) for the pitch name C (Figure 2-12). Each succeeding integer in the series represents a pitch name as well as the number of half steps above C. The integer 8, for example, serves as the pitch name for a notated

G sharp as well as for a notated A flat; it also indicates that both G sharp and A flat are eight half steps above the pitch name C. Using integers as pitch names eliminates the need for enharmonic naming of pitches but not the enharmonic notation of pitches.

2-12

How can the ordinal and cardinal systems of numbering be combined to serve both the diatonic and dodecaphonic systems?

Because we use the same symbols to notate pitch in both the diatonic and dodecaphonic systems, there are possibilities for some mutually beneficial trade-offs between the systems in the notating and naming of intervals. For example, the music reading habits of most performers are developed within the context of conventionally notated diatonic music. For this reason, it is wise to notate the adjacent pitches of dodecaphonic music so that the resulting relationships conform to what is possible within the diatonic system. For example, the diatonic notations of the intervals in Figure 2-13a are easier to read than the nondiatonic notations of the same pitches in Figure 2-13b.

2-13

Because cardinal numbers can be added and subtracted, they can be used to determine the ordinal names of discrete intervals. The chart in Figure 2-14 presents: (a) the diatonic notation of the eleven discrete pitch relationships within the octave C_4 and C_5, (b) the discrete interval names of the diatonic intervals expressed in ordinal nomenclature, and (c) the discrete

2-14

(a)												
(b)	P	−2	+2	−3	+3	P4	4+ 5°	P5	−6	+6	−7	+7	P8
	P	m2	M2	m3	M3	P4	A4 d5	P5	m6	M6	m7	M7	P8
(c)	0	i1	i2	i3	i4	i5	i6	i7	i8	i9	i10	i11	i12
													0

interval names of the same diatonic intervals expressed in cardinal nomenclature. From the chart, we can see, for example, that the notated interval C_4 to E_4 is called a $+3$ (M3) in ordinal nomenclature. The same notated interval is also called i4 ("interval four") in cardinal nomenclature. If a $+3$ (M3) is the same as an i4, the difference of four half steps between the integer notations of any two notated pitches will also form an i4, hence a $+3$ (M3) or 4°, a diminished fourth.* The difference between the notated interval E_4 and $G\sharp_4$ in cardinal nomenclature is the difference between p4 and p8 which is i4, or $+3$ (M3) in ordinal nomenclature.

What is the procedure for using cardinal nomenclature to determine the ordinal name of an interval?

Instant recognition and application of the relationships between ordinal nomenclature for intervals and their notations is required if success in theory studies is to be achieved. On the way to this goal, however, a number of obstacles appear, such as the ordering of half steps and whole steps in the diatonic system resulting from the apparent sameness in the appearance of half steps and whole steps on the staff—a problem compounded by the use of accidentals. For example, the three $+3$ (M3) intervals in Figure 2-15 appear different because of the differences in notation. The following procedures are given to assist students who cannot overcome these

2-15

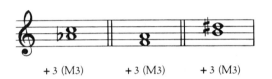

$+3$ (M3) $+3$ (M3) $+3$ (M3)

initial difficulties. Two things are required to make them work: (1) memorized cardinal nomenclature of notated pitches and the interval equivalents and (2) the ability to add and subtract. These procedures may also be used to check any uncertainty concerning particular intervals.

The first of the procedural steps is to determine the ordinal number of the interval (Figure 2-16a). As was shown in Figure 2-10, this is done by counting the lines and spaces from and including the first note (or lower note in the case of pitches sounding together) to and including the second note (or upper note). Initially, therefore, we know that $D\flat_4$ up to $B\flat_4$ is a 6th of some kind. The second step (Figure 2-16b) is to assign the appropriate integer nomenclature—whole-number names—to the notated pitches: D flat is p1 and B flat is p10. The lower integer in this case is the smaller of the two. The third step (Figure 2-16c) is to

2-16

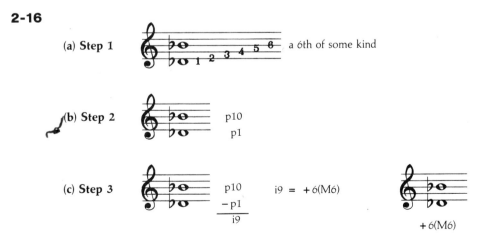

(a) Step 1   a 6th of some kind

(b) Step 2   p10 / p1

(c) Step 3   p10 / −p1 / i9   i9 = +6(M6)   +6(M6)

Reproduced through the courtesy of Dr. Cleve Scott

*This nondiatonic equivalent of $+3$ will be studied later.

subtract the lower integer from the upper integer. The difference (p10 minus p1) provides the discrete interval integer, i9. Referring to Figure 2-14, we find that i9 is the same as the discrete ordinal interval, +6 (M6).

When the integer of the lower notated pitch is larger than the upper integer, we may use either of the two variations of step 3 shown in Figure 2-16. In step 3 (Figure 2-17c), we can add i12 (the octave) to the upper integer and then subtract the lower integer to produce the discrete interval integer i9, which is the same as +6 (M6). Or, as shown in step 3 (Figure 2-17d), we can subtract the upper integer from the lower integer to arrive at a difference of 3, which is the discrete interval integer i3. To arrive at the discrete cardinal interval, we must find the *reciprocal* of i3 by subtracting i3 from i12. This gives us the cardinal interval i9, which, in turn, translates to the ordinal interval +6 (M6).   **W7—18**

2-17

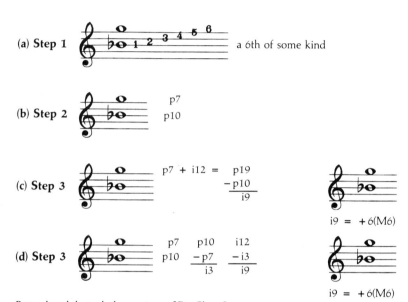

Reproduced through the courtesy of Dr. Cleve Scott

MINI PROJECT 2

For the purpose of focusing attention on aspects that go beyond the identification, notation, and recognition of intervals, research and write a brief paper on one of these topics:

1. The expressive (for example, aesthetic, psychological, religious) connotations of intervals during a particular historical period

2. The association of intervals with colors

How can the procedure outlined in Figure 2-16 be used to notate discrete diatonic intervals?

The procedure presented in Figure 2-16 used three elements: two discrete notated pitches and one discrete interval. If we know any two of those three elements, we can determine the third one. In Figure 2-16 we were given the two discrete pitch names and used them to identify the discrete interval.

In Figure 2-18a we are to provide the notated pitch that is a +6 (M6) above the given notated pitch D flat. The first step is to convert +6 (M6) to i9 and the notated pitch D flat to p1. The second step is to count up six degrees of the staff to find the particular line or space on which the notated pitch will be placed. In this case it is on the third line, so it will be a B of some kind. In step 3 we simply add i9 and p1; the resulting sum gives us p10, which is B flat.

In Figure 2-18b we are to provide the notated pitch that is a +6 (M6) below the given B flat. The first step is to convert +6 (M6) to i9 as before and B flat to p10. The second step is to count down six degrees of the staff to find the particular line or space on which the notated pitch will be placed. In this case it is on the first space below the staff, so it will be a D of some kind. In step 3 we simply subtract i9 from p10; the resulting difference gives us p1, which is D flat.

2-18

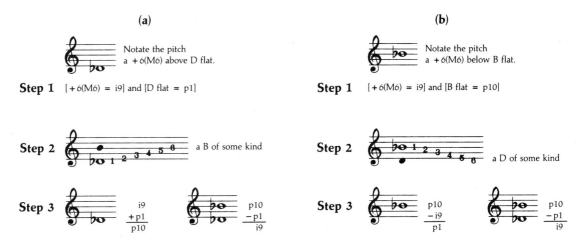

Reproduced through the courtesy of Dr. Cleve Scott

Figure 2-19 illustrates a modification of the procedure used in Figure 2-18; it is intended to accommodate situations in which the integer name of the lower notated pitch is larger than the integer name of the upper notated pitch. In Figure 2-19a we are to provide a notated pitch that is a −6 (m6) above the given notated pitch A. The first step is to convert −6 (m6) to i8 and the notated pitch A to p9. The second step is to count up six degrees of the staff to find the line or space on which the notated pitch will be placed. In this case it is the top line of the staff, so it will be an F of some kind. In step 3 we encounter the modification: as before, we will add the integers representing the given pitch name and the discrete interval—that is, p9 and i8. Because the resulting sum, p17, exceeds the octave, we must subtract an octave (i12) to arrive at p5, which is the notated pitch F.

In Figure 2-19b we are to provide a notated pitch that is a −6 (m6) below the given notated pitch F. The first step is to convert −6 (m6) to i8 and the notated pitch F to p5. The second step is to count down six degrees of the staff to find the line or space on which the

2-19

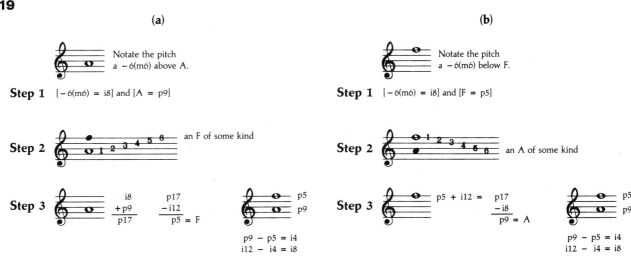

Reproduced through the courtesy of Dr. Cleve Scott

notated pitch will be placed. In this case it is the second space, so it will be an A of some kind. In step 3 we must add an octave to p5 because we cannot subtract i8 from p5. We can subtract i8 from p17 (p5 plus i12) to yield p9, which is the notated pitch A.

What is an interval class (ic)?

The concept of **interval class** is bound to the concept of pitch class. A **pitch class** refers to any and all possible octaves of any given pitch name. The pitch class B flat, for example, refers to any and all of the B flats in the pitch spectrum. The relationship of the pitch class C (pc C) to the pitch class A (pc A), for example, provides the discrete ordinal intervals -3 (m3) and $+6$ (M6). However, even though these two pitch classes will sound different when sounded as A_4 and C_5 than when sounded as C_4 and A_4, if the pc A (all A's) and the pc C (all C's) were sounded, the -3 and $+6$ distinction could not be made. Such an intervallic relationship is best described as an interval-class 3 (ic3).

The table in Figure 2-20 gives the ordinal nomenclature with alternative discrete interval names, the cardinal nomenclature, and the interval-class name of each intervallic relationship in the natural diatonic system. The table also indicates whether one, both, or neither of the natural diatonic half steps (E–F and B–C) are contained in the diatonic intervals.

W19–26

2-20   Intervals of the Natural Diatonic System

General Type	Written (preferred)	Spoken	Written (alternate)	DIATONIC HALF STEPS	Discrete Interval	Interval Class
prime*	P	prime	P	—	—	—
2nd (second)	-2	minor second	m2	1	i1	ic1
	$+2$	major second	M2	0	i2	ic2
3rd (third)	-3	minor third	m3	1	i3	ic3
	$+3$	major third	M3	0	i4	ic4
4th (fourth)	P4	perfect fourth	P4	1	i5	ic5
	4^+	augmented fourth	A4	0	i6	ic6
5th (fifth)	$5°$	diminished fifth	d5	2	i6	ic6
	P5	perfect fifth	P5	1	i7	ic5
6th (sixth)	-6	minor sixth	m6	2	i8	ic4
	$+6$	major sixth	M6	1	i9	ic3
7th (seventh)	-7	minor seventh	m7	2	i10	ic2
	$+7$	major seventh	M7	1	i11	ic1
8va (octave)	P8	perfect octave	P8	2	i12	—

The columns above are grouped: ORDINAL NOMENCLATURE (General Type, Written (preferred), Spoken, Written (alternate)); CARDINAL NOMENCLATURE (Discrete Interval, Interval Class).

*Technically not an interval
Note: -3, $+3$, -6, and $+6$ were first used by Morris Knight, Jr.

How does a discrete pitch relationship relate to the notation of pitch?

The preferred notation of a given pitch is the notation that best suits the particular pitch configuration in which it is used. In most cases, the preferred notation will form intervallic relationships that conform to the intervals of the diatonic system. This preference is supported by what we are able to hear and identify as pitch relationships. In whatever manner a configuration is notated, we can hear only one thing: the pitches that make up the configuration. What these pitches are called or how they are notated is a matter of what will be the most useful to the performer. Therefore, notational relationships that conform to the diatonic system, although the most desirable, cannot always be used; the inner design of a configuration may need to contain enharmonic notations of intervals.

What constitutes the enharmonic notation of an interval?

We know that many pitches can be notated in two or more different ways through the use of sharps and flats.* For example, G sharp and A flat represent two different notations and names of the same pitch. The intervallic relationship of this pitch to a pitch notated as F obviously can be notated in two different ways. When two forms of notation are possible, one is diatonic and the other enharmonic; when four forms are possible, two are diatonic and two are enharmonic (Figure 2-21). We are assuming that the diatonic notation of an interval is accepted

2-21

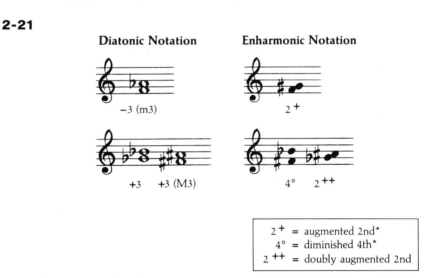

Diatonic Notation   Enharmonic Notation

−3 (m3)   2 +

+3   +3 (M3)   4°   2 ++

2 +	= augmented 2nd*
4°	= diminished 4th*
2 ++	= doubly augmented 2nd

*To be studied at a later time

as the standard notation in the sense that it represents the identifiable pitch relationships we hear. Other notations—that is, nondiatonic notations of intervals—are enharmonic. Neither type of notation is more correct than the other; they should be used with respect to their relative suitability for achieving particular and instructive musical goals. Such choices are akin to our selecting words in order to achieve a particular verbal nuance. Figure 2-22 provides some examples. In (1a) the D flat is best suited to the collection of pitches, whereas in (2a) the C sharp is best suited. The D flat in (1a) and the C sharp in (2a) each form a diatonic relationship with the preceding and succeeding notated pitches. The C sharp in (1b) and the D flat in (2b) each form an enharmonic relationship with the preceding and succeeding notated pitches; these are not suitable for expressing the inner relationships of the configuration.

*Use of the double sharp and double flat in composition should be avoided except when they are appropriate; for example, the F double sharp (leading tone) in the key of G sharp minor.

2-22

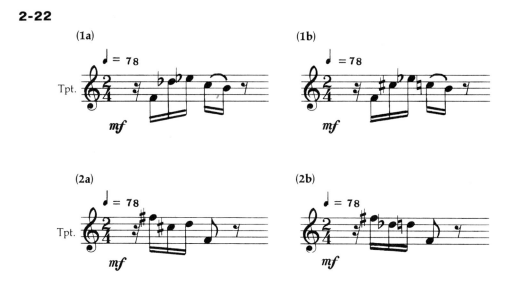

In some cases the preferred notation of a given pitch configuration requires a choice between two different enharmonic notations of an interval. A number of situations occur in both diatonic and dodecaphonic music that will not permit the diatonic notation of an interval. In Figure 2-23, the preferred notation must be one of two nondiatonic notations. The notation

2-23

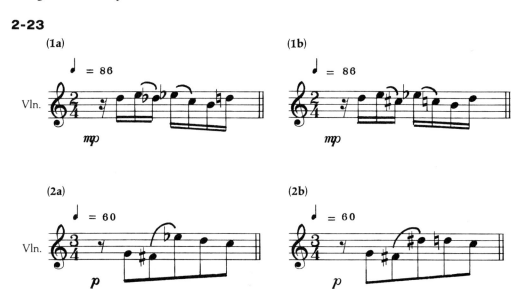

in (1b) might easily be preferred over that of (1a) because the configuration seems to emphasize the −3 intervals expressed by E to C sharp, E flat to C, and B to D. Also, the relationship of C sharp to E flat of (1b) is probably seen more commonly than is that of the E to D flat in (1a). If, on the other hand, the configuration were to begin on the beat and the +2 and −2 intervals of (1a) were considered more important than the −3 interval, the notation of (1a) would be the preferred notation. In (2a), the F sharp–E flat relationship might better support the diatonic character of the configuration than would the D sharp–D relationship in (2b), even though both notations use a nondiatonic notation of a pitch relationship. Even though the F sharp–D sharp notation is diatonic, the E flat better expresses the inner design characteristics of the configuration.

<table>
<tr><td>

**MINI
PROJECT
3**

</td><td>

Using no more than three melodic, diatonic intervals (for example, −2, +2, −3; −2, +3, P4; +2, −3, P5) deemed suitable for achieving the expressive intent you desire, complete one of these projects:

</td></tr>
</table>

1. Select a short poem about which you have some expressible feelings and produce a musical setting for unaccompanied voice (preferably your own voice).

2. Select a painting or other artwork about which you have some expressible feeling or select an expressive word (for example, *joy, grief, anger, mystery*) and produce an unaccompanied melody for a brass, woodwind, or stringed instrument. The melody should reflect the expressive quality of the artwork or word.

Conditions

1. Your melody will very likely not be contained in the diatonic system.

2. The intervals may be used in any order and in any direction, but they may not be repeated in succession; for example, if you elect to use intervals +2, −3, and P4, no two +2, −2, or P4 intervals should appear in succession.

3. A pitch may be reiterated as needed within the melody.

4. The rhythmic content of the melody will be what you believe is conducive to achieving the expressive quality you desire.

5. The melodies will be performed in class, and each will be discussed in terms of its success in achieving the expressive intent of the composer.

3 Transposition

What is transposition?

Transposition is the process by which a given pitch configuration is reproduced at a higher or lower pitch level. The concept of transposition is used to achieve such "mechanical" procedures as (1) the reproduction of the natural diatonic system at another pitch level, (2) the raising or lowering of an entire musicwork to a different pitch level, and (3) the production of performance parts for transposing instruments.

How do we transpose the natural diatonic system?

Because of its particular arrangement of half steps and whole steps, the natural diatonic system is asymmetrical. Each octave segment of the natural diatonic system—beginning on any one of the seven pitch names of the system—yields a unique arrangement of half steps and whole steps. Any one of these arrangements can be reproduced at another pitch level through the process of transposition. This is achieved by altering the position of the basic half-step/whole-step relationships of the system by means of one or more appropriately placed sharps or flats. In Figure 3-1, for example, any octave segment D to D is shown to have a unique arrangement of half steps and whole steps. This same arrangement can be reproduced within

3-1

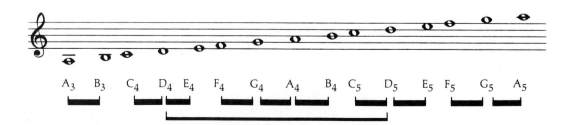

any G to G segment of the natural diatonic system by changing the notated B to B flat, as shown in Figure 3-2.

3-2

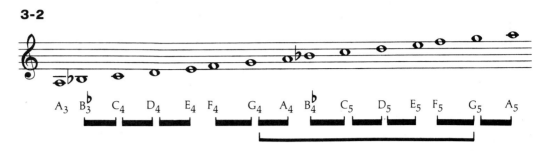

What is the function of a "transposing" signature?

The practice of placing sharps or flats on the staff immediately following the clef sign to form signatures became standard at about the time music printing became a practical reality. The use of the signature very likely evolved from the desire of copyists and printers to simplify and codify the conventional practices in which the use of a B flat, for example, was intended to lower the pitch range of a mode for the purpose of accommodating lower voices as well as to exploit the expressive qualities of lower tones. The signature as a music symbol, without regard to the various conventions associated with its use throughout history, serves the fundamental purpose of indicating the transposition of the diatonic system from its natural position to another pitch level.

What a signature "means" should not be carelessly confused with "special usage" descriptors related to the various conventions having to do with the tonal organization of music. A signature of one sharp (Figure 3-3), for example, indicates or "means" that the diatonic system has been transposed to a different pitch level. Hence, the series of half-step/whole-step relationships of the octave segment A to A of the transposed version is the same as that in the D to D segment of the natural diatonic system.

3-3

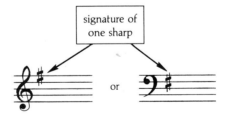

If we wonder why the sharp in a signature of one sharp must be an F sharp, we need but observe that only an F sharp serves to transpose the diatonic system. If a different single notated pitch were sharped, the system would not be transposed; it would be transformed. See Figure 3-4. Similarly, a signature of one flat intended to transpose the diatonic system requires that B be flatted (Figure 3-5). The flatting of a different notated pitch would transform the system rather than transpose it. All of the signatures using sharps and flats placed on the staff in accordance with correct order using the G clef and F clef are shown in Figure 3-6. The locations of the resulting diatonic half steps are indicated for each signature.

3-4

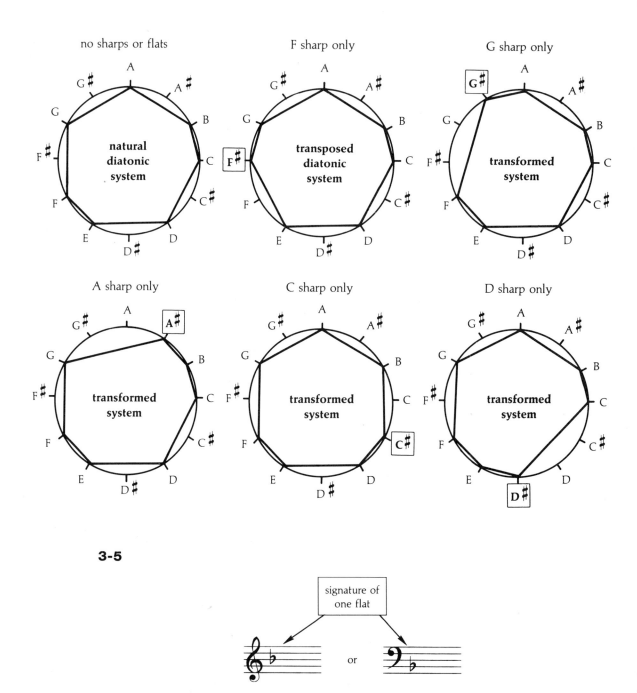

3-5

For the sake of clarity, a signature should be referred to in terms of the number of sharps or flats used to form it rather than in terms of "keys" or "modes," which serve to imply a special case usage. Thus a signature of three sharps should be referred to as "the signature of three sharps" rather than "the key of A major." The music having such a signature might be in A major; on the other hand, it might have a pitch organization utilizing the resources of the Dorian mode on B, the Phrygian on C sharp, or any of the remaining modes. The music might have an organization that is not related to either "key" or "mode." It is appropriate, however, to say the key of A major has a signature of three sharps or that the Dorian mode on B has a signature of three sharps. The concepts of "key," "mode," and other kinds of pitch organization are separate issues that should not be confounded with the concept of "signature."

3-6

diatonic half steps

What are transposing instruments?

How do we know whether or not an instrument is a transposing instrument? And what *is* a transposing instrument? Judging from their names, you might assume that a number of instruments—the E-flat tuba for example—are transposing instruments. Name alone, however, does not make an instrument a transposing instrument. For an instrument to be a transposing instrument, according to present conventions, it must conform to three specifications:

1. It is either a woodwind or brass instrument.

2. It is pitched on a fundamental other than C.

3. It requires performance parts that are principally notated (we will use the term WRITTEN for transposed notation) in the G (treble) clef.

The E-flat tuba, which requires performance parts to be WRITTEN in the F (bass) clef, is not a transposing instrument. On the other hand, the E-flat alto saxophone, a woodwind that is pitched on E flat and requires performance parts to be WRITTEN in the G clef, is a transposing instrument. The difference is this: when the performance part is WRITTEN in the F clef, it is WRITTEN as it SOUNDS and the transposing is done by the instrument; when the performance part is WRITTEN in the G clef, the transposing is done by the person who WRITES the part.

What is the distinction between WRITTEN and SOUNDING pitch?

Pitch, as already defined, is the perceived aspect of sound that is the result of the frequency of vibration of the waveform that produces it. Pitch is thus an aural phenomenon; its representation in the notation of music—our present concern—is a matter controlled by other, sometimes whimsical considerations.

A convention has developed in the notation of music for some of the instruments pitched on fundamentals other than C. This music is written with pitch designations that differ from those that are actually sounded. Because of this, we must distinguish between WRITTEN pitch and SOUNDING pitch when dealing with transposing instruments.

Sounding pitch, as the term implies, refers to pitch as it actually sounds in accordance with the standards of the time. The frequency of A-440—that is, a waveform with a fundamental frequency of 440 Hz that is represented by the pitch name A—is the standard by which all pitches of the diatonic system are determined and all instruments are tuned. The present standard of A-440 has evolved over a number of years from a standard believed to have been as low as A-435 at one time.

Certain aspects of the conventional notation of music for instruments pitched on fundamentals other than C seem to defy reason. Why tubas, trombones, and baritone horns are *not* considered transposing instruments, whereas trumpets, cornets, and horns *are*, is a distinction musicians simply accept as an inherited condition. Any explanation we might attempt in support of why some instruments are "transposing" instruments breaks down when we consider why other instruments are not.

The following principle can serve as a guide for determining the relationship between the WRITTEN pitch for a transposing instrument and the SOUNDING pitch:

A WRITTEN C for a transposing instrument, when played on the instrument, SOUNDS the fundamental pitch of the instrument.

Thus, a WRITTEN C for the B-flat trumpet SOUNDS a B flat; a WRITTEN C for the A clarinet SOUNDS an A; a WRITTEN C for the G flute SOUNDS a G.

The following guidelines should help you to understand the conventions and avoid confusion in preparing performance parts for transposing instruments:

1. When referring to the transposing process as it relates to transposing instruments, always use the term WRITTEN when referring to a pitch as notated for the instrument in the performance part and the term SOUND (SOUNDS, SOUNDING) when referring to a pitch as heard. Avoid such ambiguous and meaningless phrases as "the trumpet plays a G," "the soprano saxophone transposes up," and so on.

2. To determine whether a transposing instrument SOUNDS higher or lower than WRITTEN, observe the instrument's length. The flute, a nontransposing instrument pitched on a fundamental of C, is roughly two feet long and produces C_4 (middle C) as its lowest SOUNDING pitch. Instruments longer than the flute will SOUND lower than the flute; instruments shorter than the flute will SOUND higher. A WRITTEN C_4 for the E-flat soprano clarinet—which is a few inches shorter than the flute—will SOUND the $E\flat_4$, which is above the WRITTEN C_4 (Figure 3-7a). Similarly, a WRITTEN C_4 for the E-flat alto saxophone—which is longer than the flute—will SOUND the $E\flat_3$, which is below the WRITTEN C_4 (Figure 3-7b).

3-7

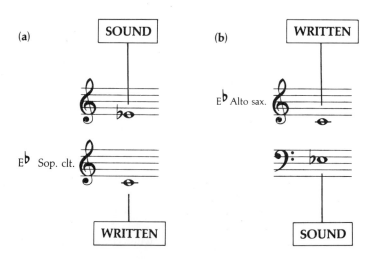

3. When transposing music that is composed in a "key" or "mode" and notated with the appropriate signature, the same relationship exists between the WRITTEN and SOUNDING key (or mode) as exists between the WRITTEN C and SOUNDING pitch of a transposing instrument. As an example, Figure 3-8 shows the relationship between a WRITTEN C and a SOUNDING A on the A clarinet; music WRITTEN in the key of C for the A clarinet in its performance part SOUNDS in the key of A. Or, to put it in the form we will most likely deal with when preparing performance parts: music SOUNDING in the key of A must be WRITTEN in the key of C for the A clarinet. It would follow from this that music SOUNDING in the key

3-8

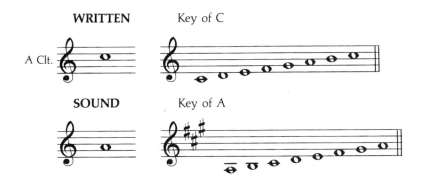

of D with a signature of two sharps must be WRITTEN in the key of E with a signature of four sharps for the B-flat clarinet (Figure 3-9).

3-9

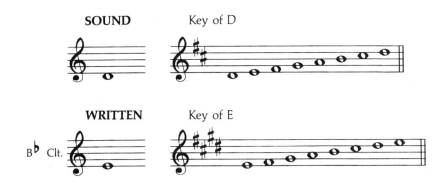

4. A number of nontransposing instruments, though pitched on a fundamental of C, do not SOUND in the octave in which the music is WRITTEN. Typically, these are instruments that SOUND in the relatively extreme ranges of the total pitch range covered by instruments. For example, the contrabass SOUNDS an octave below its WRITTEN pitch, and the piccolo SOUNDS an octave above its WRITTEN pitch. Among the voices, the tenor voice SOUNDS an octave lower than WRITTEN. Figure 3-10 shows the common variations of the G clef used for the tenor voice. The simple G clef is sufficient; however, the other three clefs shown attempt to indicate that the SOUNDING pitch is an octave lower than WRITTEN. The last clef shown is the least desirable.

3-10

When communicating verbally in classes, rehearsals, and similar situations, it is customary to refer to pitch in terms of SOUNDING pitch. This eliminates the confusion of one person thinking WRITTEN pitch while another is thinking SOUNDING pitch. It also eliminates the need for making qualifying statements every time a pitch name is used during rehearsals and classes.

The charts in Figure 3-11 give the relative WRITTEN and SOUNDING pitches for the more common instruments pitched on the fundamentals of A, B flat, D, E flat, E, F, and G. Also included in the figure are those instruments that are pitched on C (nontransposing instruments) that SOUND in octaves above or below their WRITTEN pitches.   **W27—52**

3-11

Instruments Pitched on a Fundamental of B Flat

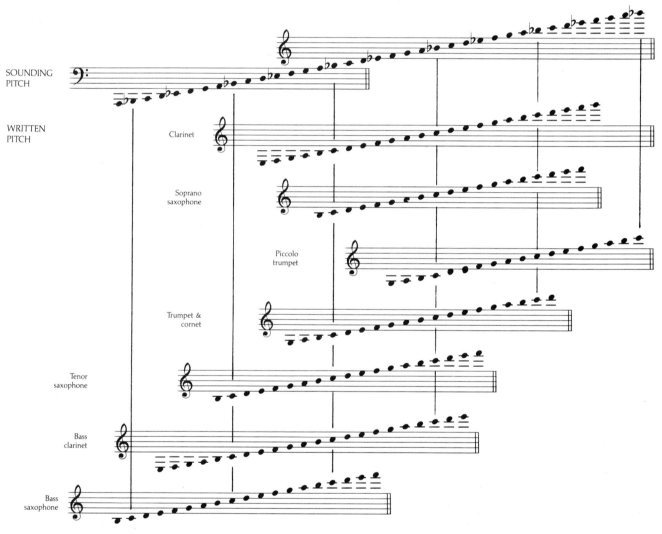

3-11, *continued*
Instruments Pitched on a Fundamental of A

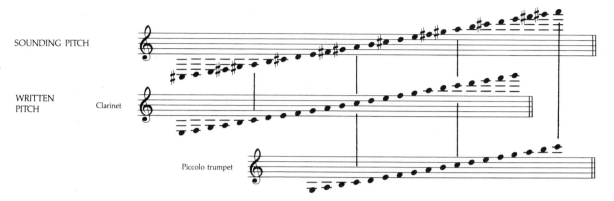

Instruments Pitched on a Fundamental of E Flat

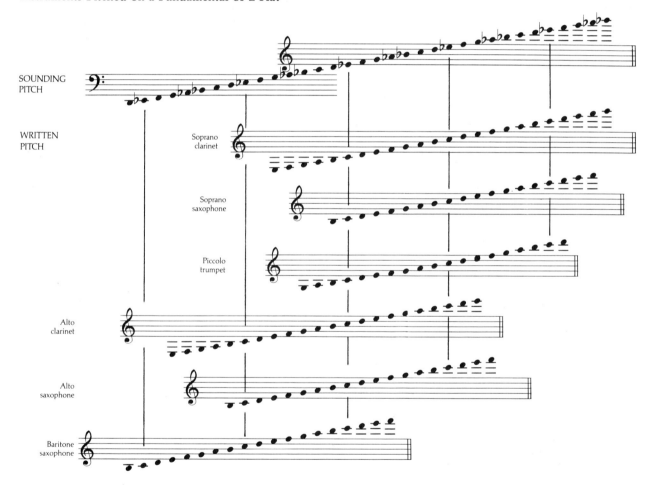

continued

3-11, *continued*

Instruments Pitched on a Fundamental of D

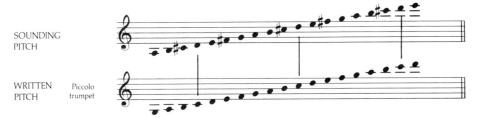

Instruments Pitched on a Fundamental of G

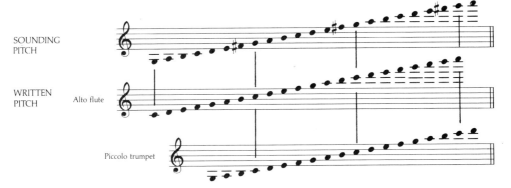

Instruments Pitched on a Fundamental of F

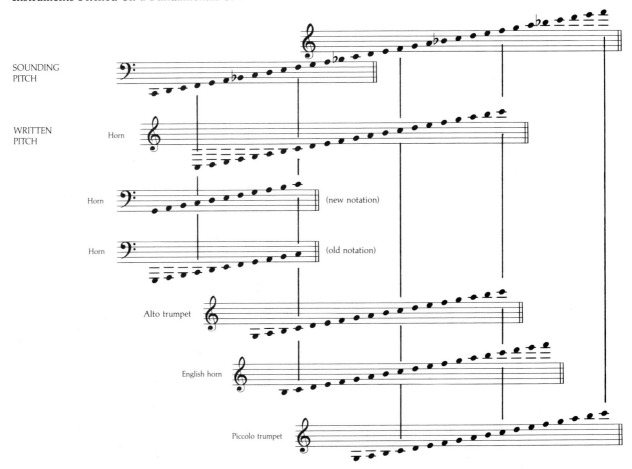

3-11, *continued*
Instruments Pitched on a Fundamental of C

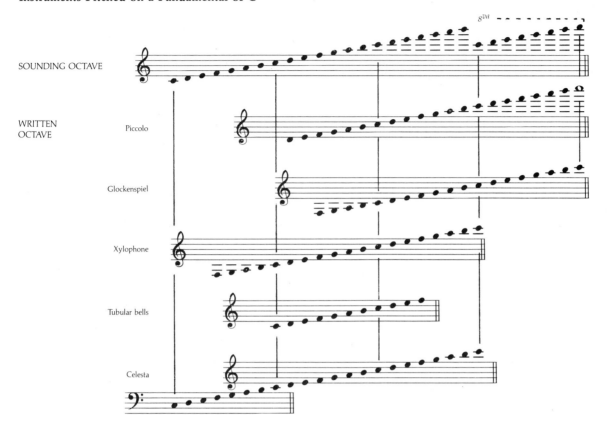

Instruments Pitched on a Fundamental of C

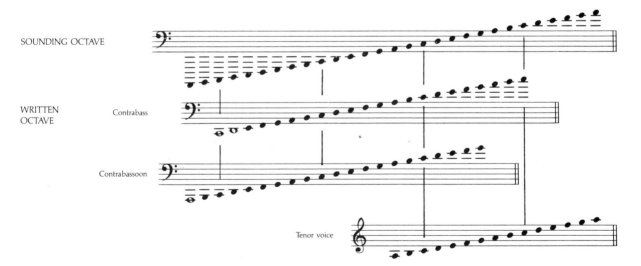

<table>
<tr><td>

**MINI
PROJECT
4**

</td></tr>
</table>

As an exercise in transposition in preparation for Unit Project 1, complete one of these projects using the melody you created for Mini Project 3:

1. If the original melody is for voice or for an instrument pitched on C, rewrite the melody to be played in unison or octaves by two or three instruments (pitched on something other than C) so that the result will sound on a different pitch level than the original. The first interval used in the melody can be used as an arbitrary interval of difference between the sound of the original and the new level of sound.

2. If the original melody is for an instrument pitched on something other than C, rewrite the melody to be played by two or three instruments (pitched on something different from the three instruments used) so that the resulting sound will be the sounding pitch produced by the instrument for which the melody was originally composed.

Meter, Tempo, and Measure

What is meter?

Meter in music is simply measurable temporal ordering. All music is metered in the sense that the durations and occurrences making up its various sound events are related and measurable by some temporal unit, even though the temporal unit may be too small to perceive aurally. Whether or not meter must be notated depends on the nature and organization of the music being produced. If a musicwork is so conceived as to reveal a dependence on meter as a discernable factor that is necessary for the control of performance and the listener's aural comprehension, meter must be expressed by the notation used. Conversely, if a musicwork is so conceived as to reveal no dependence at all on meter for controlling performance or making the work comprehensible to the listener, meter does not need to be expressed in notation. In some forms of "chance" music, for example, perceptible metric control is antithetical to the aesthetic intent of the music. In a sense, meter is necessary to achieve temporal ordering as the composer's option; it need not be used when temporal ordering is to be the performer's option.

In measured music, meter is the all-embracing system within which all proportions and temporal values function. The typical levels of measurement are the measure, the basic metrical unit, and the divisions of the basic metrical unit. In some cases the measure is coincidental to the basic metrical unit, as for example, in a Beethoven scherzo. Sometimes the basic metrical unit is the smallest note value used; there is no division of the basic metrical unit in such a case.

What is tempo?

Tempo is an expression of the relative rate at which the various durations and occurrences making up the sound events of a musicwork take place in time. As a secondary but illusory expression, tempo is associated with movement. A rapid tempo produces an illusory expression of rapid movement; a slow tempo, the illusion of slow movement.

What is a tempo marking (or indicator)?

In the past it was the practice to use certain words—generally Italian but also French and German—denoting a particular mood (*grave, allegro*) or rate of motion (*andante, presto, adagio*) to indicate tempo. At the time, this convention was an effective, sufficient means of indicating tempo. However, such verbal tempo indicators are relatively meaningless today because they are not sufficiently precise. There are occasions in which the use of English words is appropriate: *fast as possible, slow and dragging, light and spirited.* In such cases, tempo is a natural by-product of the expressive intent of the words, much as it was during the time Italian was in conventional use.

The tempo of a musicwork is now more commonly indicated in terms of how many notes of a particular value occur within a minute's time. In the early nineteenth century, Mälzel developed a device called the metronome that enabled composers to indicate tempo more precisely. Mälzel's metronome, featuring a double pendulum with a sliding weight that can be set to mark off any number of pulses per minute, is still used today though it is being replaced by an electrical device that serves the same purpose. A tempo marking, or metronome marking as it is sometimes called, usually contains the letters **M.M.** or just **M.** to give reference to Mälzel's metronome.

Figure 4-1 shows some examples of tempo markings. In (a) the quarter note may occur 72 times within one minute's time. In (b) the eighth note may occur **circa** (Latin "around," abbreviated c.) 72 times per minute. In (c) the quarter note may occur circa 66 to 76 times within one minute's time. These examples show that various degrees of specificity are possible. Whether we use M.M., M., or no letter at all is of no consequence; it is purely a matter of choice.

For best results, the kinds of tempo markings shown in Figure 4-1 are combined with a verbal descriptor, which, by describing the general character of the music, tempers the rigidity of the tempo marking and contributes to a more musically appropriate tempo.

4-1

What is a measure?

If a musicwork has a discernible meter, it is measurable. Music has been considered measurable (by historians) since about 1250. This convenient date marks the beginning of **mensural (measured) notation**, a form of notation that prevailed until around 1600. Mensural notation was used in achieving a variety of measurable systems. Before 1250, music was considered to be unmeasured; after 1600, music was considered composed in **measures**. Figure 4-2 shows musical examples from these three historical periods: (a) is an example of Gregorian

4-2

(a) Gregorian chant   ***Missa Orbis factor*, Kyrie**

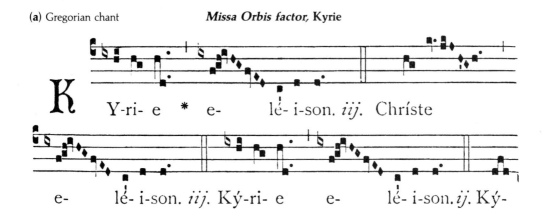

(b)   ***Rex quem metrorum***

Philippe de Vitry (1291–1361)

(c)   **Sonata in A major, K. 331**

W. A. Mozart

chant, (b) an example from Phillipe de Vitry (1291–1361), and (c) an example from Wolfgang A. Mozart (1756–1791). Though the Mozart example is the only one that is composed in "measures," upon hearing either of the other two we would be fully aware of intelligible groupings of pitches. These groupings would provide the same effects aurally as do the "measures" in the Mozart example.

What is the function of the barline?

Historically, the concept of measure preceded the use of **barlines**. As music became more complex—especially due to the increased use of instruments during the fifteenth and sixteenth centuries—barlines began appearing in music scores to facilitate easier reading of the music. The use of barlines did not become a standard practice until about the end of the sixteenth century.

It should be noted, however, that at the time of its introduction in the fourteenth century, the barline did not necessarily coincide with the "measuring" of music, as shown in the example in Figure 4-3. Even into the seventeenth century the barline was used at times as a pure

4-3

Messe Petri de la Rue, Kyrie

Pierre de la Rue

convenience, having nothing to do with the marking off of measures; see Figure 4-4. From the eighteenth century through the nineteenth century, the barline could be depended upon to mark off what was perceived aurally as a measure. Now again in the twentieth century we find a return to some of the same ambiguities between the concept of measure and the practical use of the barline; see for example the music of Igor Stravinsky in Figure 4-5. Some composers of the

4-4

Recitative from *Orfeo*

Claudio Monteverdi (1567–1643)

4-5

from the ballet *Petroushka*

Igor Stravinsky

twentieth century have reverted to the practice of using no barlines at all or of using only an occasional barline, as exemplified by the work of Charles Ives (Figure 4-6a) and Ernesto Pellegrini (Figure 4-6b).

4-6

(a)

from *The Cage*

Charles Ives

(b)

from Movement II for Solo Double Bass

Ernesto Pellegrini

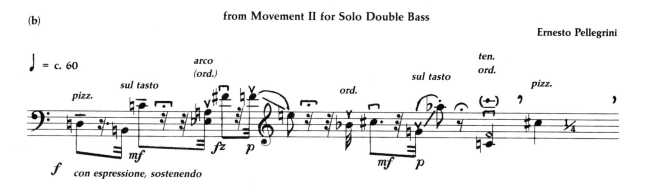

How did the "signatures" of measured music evolve?

Since the introduction of **mensural notation**, composers have used signatures of one sort or another to indicate the manner in which the temporal aspect of notation is to be understood. Though the conventions have changed considerably over the years, the signatures used can be categorized into three types: time signatures, meter signatures, and measure signatures. The differences in these signatures are subtle but conceptually important.

Though there have been a variety of understandings about how the **time signatures** of the Renaissance functioned in relation to "real" time—that is, clock time—it is presently understood that the signature indicates the note value that serves as the **tactus**. The tactus, by general consensus, has a relatively fixed duration. With the amount of time allotted the tactus established, all other note values bear a proportional relationship to it and to one another. (See the notation comparison chart in Figure 4-7.) For example, if the tactus is the **breve**, it may be equal to two or three **semibreves**; the semibreve, in turn, may be equal to two or three **minims**. Renaissance notation, therefore, is appropriately called "proportional" notation, because time

4-7

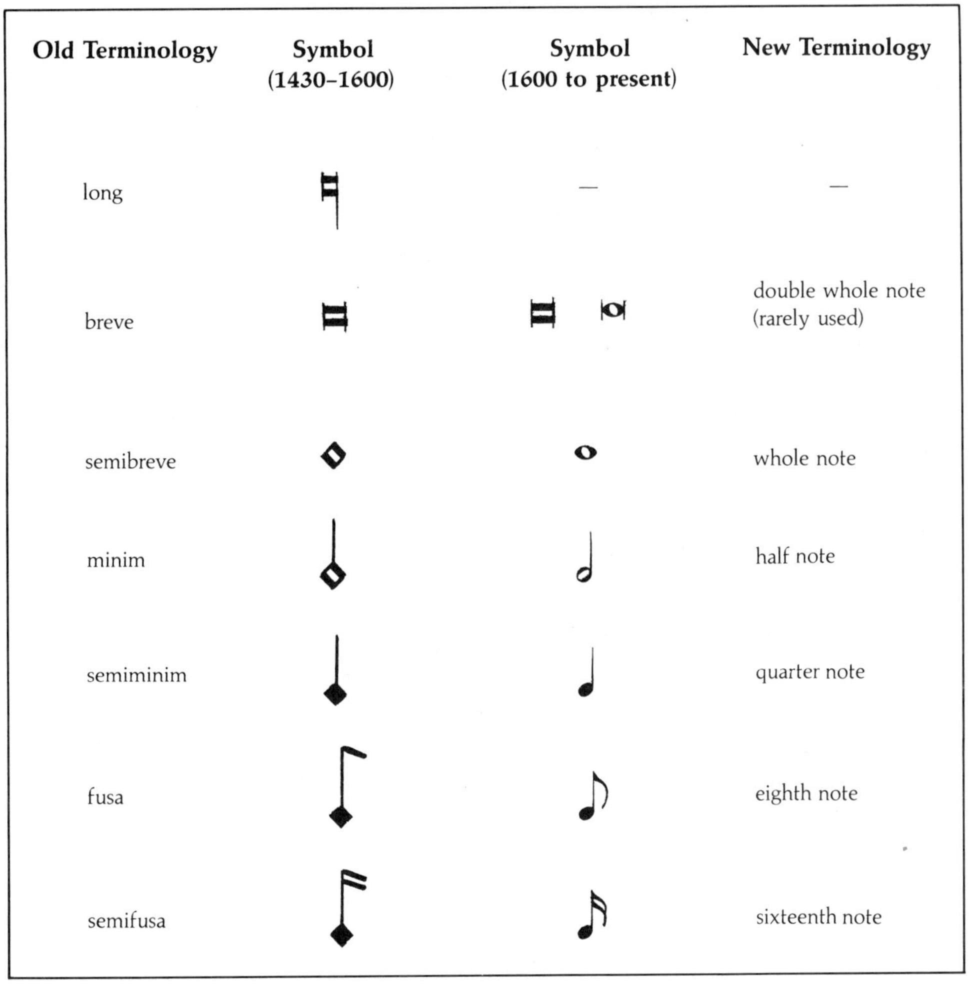

Old Terminology	Symbol (1430–1600)	Symbol (1600 to present)	New Terminology
long	𝄷	—	—
breve	𝄶	𝄶 𝅜	double whole note (rarely used)
semibreve	◆	𝅝	whole note
minim	♩◆	𝅗𝅥	half note
semiminim	♩◆	♩	quarter note
fusa	♪	♪	eighth note
semifusa	♬	♬	sixteenth note

signatures dating from that period express particular proportions. Figure 4-8 lists the signatures of the Renaissance and the terms that identify the respective proportions.

4-8

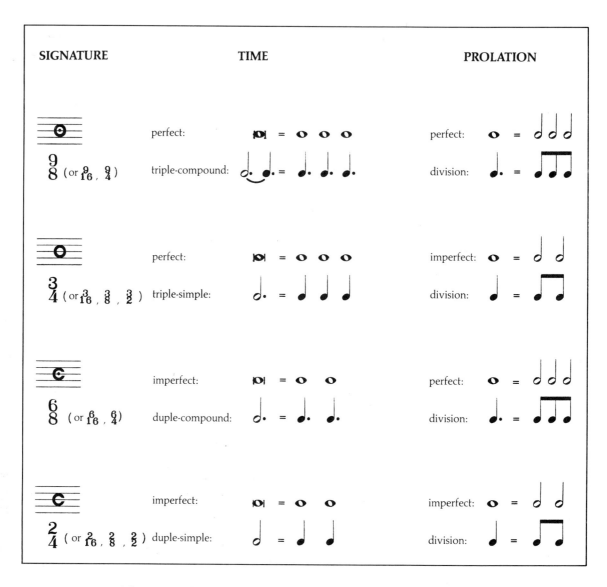

The **meter signature** indicates which note value represents the metric unit and how many of the units are contained in a measure. By the time the meter signature was established, the basic proportional relationship between note values was two to one. Examples of common meter signatures with two-to-one proportions are shown in Figure 4-9. The three-to-one

4-9

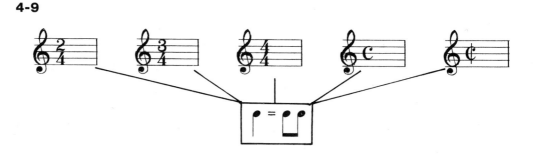

proportion of Renaissance music is achieved in conventional modern notation by using dotted note values as beat units. By this system, the beat unit is divided into three of the next-smaller note value (Figure 4-10). A category of signature, shown in Figure 4-11, provides for the combining of the metric units into groups of twos and threes to form beat units of differing durations. These signatures, commonly used in twentieth-century music and referred to as **measure signatures**, are seldom used as meter signatures; however, one or two of them can be

4-10

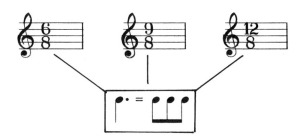

4-11

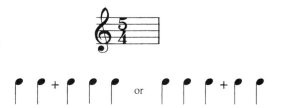

found in some late-nineteenth-century music. The excerpt from the Sixth Symphony of Tchaikovsky (Figure 4-12) is an example of a meter signature with a mixed beat unit. The term *measure signature* was made necessary by the practice of many twentieth-century composers of making numerous signature changes within a musicwork.   **W53**

4-12

from Symphony No. 6, Mov. II

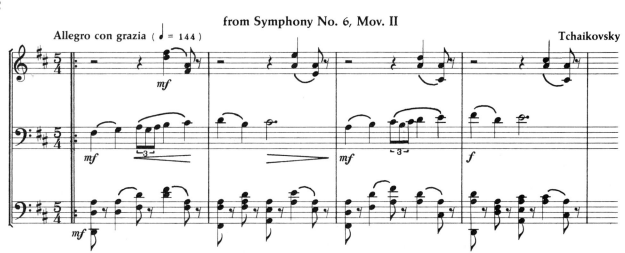

The time signatures of the Renaissance and the proportional notation they imply are more easily understood when we translate their intended effect into the meter signatures of modern conventional notation. All temporal relationships expressed by Renaissance notation can also be expressed with modern conventional notation (Figure 4-13).*

4-13

Numerical signatures were used during the Renaissance to express changes in proportion within the context of a musicwork. See Figure 4-14. The signature $\frac{3}{2}$ indicates that three semibreves are to be performed in the time of two. As a meter signature, $\frac{3}{2}$ indicates that the half-

*In regard to all discussion about Renaissance signatures and notation in this chapter, it should be remembered that this period of approximately two hundred years was not a static period. There was then and is yet some ambiguity and contradiction about the workings of Renaissance signatures and notation. The explanations and comparisons presented here provide yet another attempt to present a means for understanding a few of the "best entrenched" practices in use around the year 1600 as described by Robert Donington in *The Interpretation of Early Music* (London: Faber and Faber, 1975).

note value is the metric unit and that there are three of them in the measure. This alteration in the signature's meaning was certainly a source of ambiguity and contradiction; such a drastic change could not have occurred overnight.

4-14

Missa Fortuna desperata, Gloria

Jacob Obrecht

Two other signatures carried over from the Renaissance originally had to do with tempo. They are **diminution** (halving the previous note values) and **augmentation** (doubling the previous values). Figure 4-15 demonstrates their use then and now by comparing them with numerical meter signatures. The *alla breve* signature in part a is described as "the more" because the tactus is represented by the breve, the note value represented by "the stroke" (the conductor's beat today). There would be two conductor's "strokes" and thus two breves in what constituted a measure of music (barlines were not used to mark off measures until after 1600). The *alla semibreve* signature in part b is described as "the less" because the tactus is represented by the semibreve, the note value represented by "the stroke." There would be two conductor's "strokes" and thus two semibreves per measure of music. Theoretically, music sung in alla semibreve would be sung twice the tempo of that sung in alla breve. In practice, however, "the more" would be sung in a relatively slow tempo and "the less" would be sung in a moderately fast tempo; the relationship between the two would not be two-to-one. The tempos would, in fact, relate to the musical sense of the musicworks rather than to an exact two-to-one ratio. In some cases the signatures would be reversed, but the music would still be performed in a manner reflecting musical sense.

4-15

THE RENAISSANCE   **TODAY**

(a) *alla breve*   *common time**
(the more)   4 beats per measure

                                                            same as

(b) *alla semibreve*   *cut time**
(the less)   2 beats per measure

                                                            same as

*colloquialism

In modern conventional notation, the alla breve signature is conducted and felt in four beats per measure within a variety of tempos rather than in two relatively slow "strokes." The alla semibreve signature is still conducted and felt in two beats in a variety of tempos, many of which are comparable to the two "strokes" of the Renaissance conductor. Though these two signatures were often used as meter signatures in the nineteenth and early twentieth centuries, they are not regarded as useful measure signatures in twentieth-century music.

UNIT PROJECT 1

Transcribing a Renaissance Motet

Introduction

Typically, composers, transcribers, and arrangers produce music for performance by specific individuals or performance groups. A composer's music, for example, is often intended for performance at a particular time, place, and event. Also, with exceptions of course, music is designed to reflect the capabilities of the performers and the nature of the occasion for which it is originally made. On some occasions, the one producing the music may even consider the person or the organization that is providing the financial support for a commissioned work. These historical realities are usually obscured by the aura of mystery and romance that has come to surround the making of music. Though such seemingly mundane considerations may seem trivial when compared to the wonderousness of the art of music, they are among the most practical and important considerations prior to and during the process of making music. Those who disregard the abilities of performers or who make music for no one in particular for performance nowhere in particular stand a good chance of having a very poor first performance or possibly no performance at all.

With few exceptions, we can assume that the membership of the class in which you presently find yourself will remain intact for the academic year. However constituted, the class members will make up the body of musicians for whom each student will produce music unless cooperative arrangements are made with the members of other classes. As a practical circumstance, the bond of mutual dependence among the members of a class must be recognized by each member. The degree of success achieved by the class will depend in large part on the individual members' sense of responsibility and cooperation.

The best intentions—if success is to be assured—must be based on a kind of "talent" assessment that will enable the class to know its individual and collective abilities. Such an assessment must provide you and other class members with a "feel" for each other's performance capabilities and with the knowledge of what you each must do personally and quickly to prepare yourselves to be effective contributors to this newly formed body of talent. Each of these assessment goals can be achieved through this first unit project of transcribing a fifteenth- or sixteenth-century motet, or similar musicwork, for performance by the members of the class.

The music selected for use in this unit project offers a simple, transparent, and predictably consistent type of material that lends itself easily and effectively to the treatments described in the unit projects. These qualities balance well with the unpredictability of the assessment being made. The problems encountered in making the transcription offer each student the opportunity to begin learning the mechanics of the "craft" of music making in a situation that favors success but yet readily reveals errors in transposition, balance, range, copying, and performance.

Description

Select one of the following options and complete it in accordance with the specifications given in the general instructions. Time permitting, more than one project may be completed.

OPTION 1. Transcribe one of the suggested vocal compositions* for all of the instruments available in the class, and conduct a performance of the work in class.

---

*A variety of suggested compositions are listed in the appendix at the end of Unit One; similar compositions selected and approved by the instructor will serve as well (see page 71).

OPTION 2. Transcribe one of the suggested vocal compositions (see footnote to option 1) for any mixed combination of woodwind, brass, stringed, and mallet percussion instruments available in the class—using one instrument per line—and conduct a performance of the work in class.

OPTION 3. Transcribe one of the suggested vocal compositions (see footnote to option 1) for any mixed combination of woodwind, brass, stringed, and mallet percussion instruments available in the class. Use instruments on all but the most prominent line, which should be sung by the remaining members of the class. Conduct a performance of the work in class.

Instructions

1. Prepare a score for whatever instruments are used—voices, also, in the case of option 3—arranged in the most practical score system using conventional practice as a guide. The score should be notated in SOUNDING pitch except for instruments pitched on a fundamental of C that do not sound in the octave in which their parts are written; these should be notated in WRITTEN pitch. Use either pencil or ink as directed by your instructor.

2. Prepare a set of parts for the performing instruments, and for the singers if option 3 is used. All parts should be neatly copied on full sheets of paper *in ink*. Parts for transposing instruments must be properly transposed. Proofread all copy. Proofreading one another's work is recommended as a second check, because people often fail to see their own errors.

3. Arrange the seating of the players in a location that best suits the nature of the instruments, the balance of sound, and the visual needs of the performers.

4. Prepare to conduct the performers in a clear and musical manner. Consider yourself responsible for the accuracy and musicality of the performance. The use of a text or neutral syllable by singers in option 3 is left to the discretion of the instructor.

Notes

In producing a transcription, the purpose is to prepare a musicwork for a different performance medium than the one for which it was originally made. We may transcribe a piano work for performance by an orchestra, for example, or an orchestral work for performance by a band.

In making a transcription, do only what is necessary to adapt the music to a different performance medium. In adapting a piano work to the orchestral medium, the tonal range of the work will probably have to be expanded to accommodate the broader spectrum of sound that is characteristic of an orchestra. This might require that certain configurations idiomatic to the piano be altered or changed to configurations more idiomatic to the orchestra. If we were transcribing an orchestral work for performance on the piano, the process would be reversed.

A transcription is different from an arrangement. The basic objective in making a transcription is to change the performance medium without changing the integrity of the original version of the musicwork. Whether or not there is an intended change in the performance medium, the basic objective in making an arrangement is to change the musicwork so as to conform to a new purpose, new aesthetic values, and possibly new conventions.

The portion of *Virgo salutiferi* by Josquin des Prez shown in Figure 4-16 presents a number of the problems typically encountered in completing this project. Most of the materials and concepts needed for making a transcription have been presented in the first four chapters of this book. What has not been presented is a "feel" for the style of the period from which your selected musicwork is taken and for the selected musicwork itself. You can acquire this in part by listening to good-quality recordings of musicworks from the period on your own and in class and through class discussions. The class discussion should help you to an expressive intent that is clear and aesthetically in sympathy with what you heard on the recordings. What is additionally required for the successful completion of the project is presented in chapters five through eight. As much as possible, the materials and concepts in Unit One are presented in the order in which you are most likely to need them as you make your transcription. However, some related materials and concepts are discussed more thoroughly than specifically required for this project.

4-16

Virgo salutiferi

Josquin des Prez

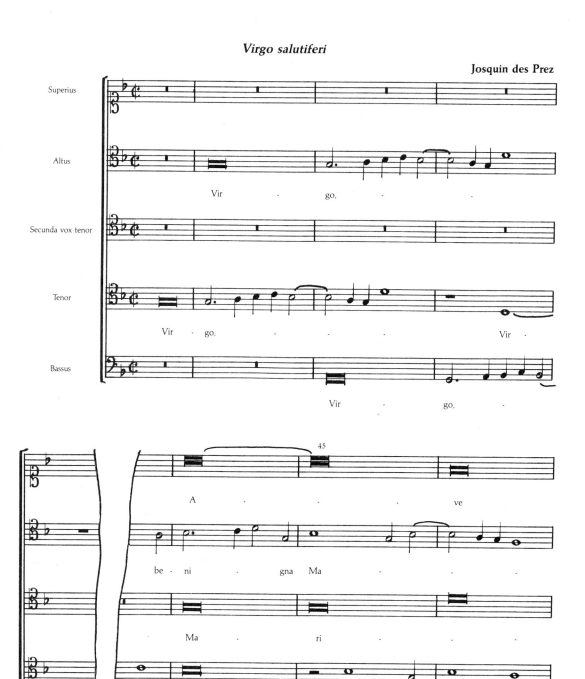

5 Selecting Instruments

What are the characteristics of the instruments and voices available to you: range, tessitura, and timbre?

Because you are limited to selecting instruments from among those available in the class, the obvious first step in making your transcription is to learn all you can about the instruments your classmates play and your classmates' performance abilities. Each student should be prepared to give a brief demonstration of his or her instrument or voice and to discuss its range, tessitura, and timbre.

An instrument's **range** is the total range of pitches it can produce, from the lowest pitch to the highest. The ranges of many instruments—especially the upper limits of them—are partly determined by the playing ability of the performer. General ranges are given for voices, but these, too, are limited by individual capabilities of singers.* *Range* may also refer to the total pitch range in a particular melodic line or the total pitch range of an entire musicwork.

The **tessitura** of an instrument or voice is the portion of the total pitch range that is the most comfortable, least tiring, and least difficult to use in performance. The tessitura of a melodic line or an entire musicwork refers to the portion of the melody or musicwork having the greatest concentration of pitches.

Timbre refers to tone color or tone quality. The timbre of a tone is determined in great part by the number (how many), distribution (which ones), intensity (strength), and phase relations (relative support or interference) of the harmonics that make it up. Other factors such as attack and release contribute greatly to the distinguishing characteristics of a tone. Timbre and the attack transients are what enable us to distinguish particular instruments and voices from each other.

*For the purpose of this project, individual players and singers should indicate their practical performance ranges.

How do we create a good match between the available instruments and the selection of a musicwork to be transcribed?

If you selected option 1, your basic problem will be to make the best use of all of the instruments. If one of the other two options is selected, the combination of instruments selected will be a purely arbitrary choice. However, whimsy is not untutored; an arbitrary choice must incorporate the exercise of good judgment. Therefore, if you wish to avoid raising or lowering the pitch level of the entire musicwork or requiring instrumentalists to perform in awkward areas of their ranges, a preliminary examination of several vocal scores is in order. It is a good idea to scan the ranges and tessituras of each line of a number of musicworks and compare them with the ranges and tessituras of the available instruments. This leads to a wiser though nonetheless arbitrary choice of music and instrumental use.

An examination of the complete musicwork from which the excerpt in Figure 4-16 is taken shows the range and tessitura of each line of music to be as indicated in Figure 5-1. If

5-1

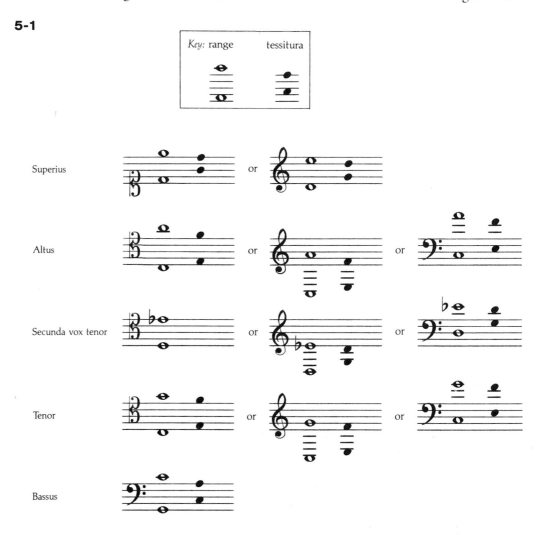

you were using *Virgo salutiferi* for the transcription, any of the instruments and voices shown in Figure 5-2 could be used for the top voice line (the superius), but their effectiveness would vary. Such factors as the relative ease of tone production, characteristic tone quality (timbre), and relative weight of sound within a texture of other instruments and voices determine the effectiveness of an instrument or voice. Symbols denoting the instruments' effectiveness— (V) very effective, (M) moderately effective, (N) not effective—follow the instruments in the listing.

5-2

WOODWINDS	flute (M–V), oboe (M–V), English horn (M), E-flat soprano clarinet (M), B-flat clarinet (V), B-flat bass clarinet (N), bassoon (N), B-flat soprano saxophone (M), E-flat alto saxophone (V), B-flat tenor saxophone (N)
BRASS	F horn (N), C trumpet (V), B-flat trumpet (V), trombone (N)
STRINGS	violin (V), viola (M), violoncello (M)
VOICE	soprano (V), mezzo-soprano (V), alto (M)
PERCUSSION	marimba (V), vibraphone (M) (Both would have to roll sustained tones.)

There is no effective substitute for the knowledge of instruments and voices gained through extensive aural experience. In the absence of such experience, you should consult the chart in Figure 5-3; it provides generalized information concerning the effective range, tessitura, tone quality, and dynamic profiles of the common orchestral and band instruments. The information there is based only on the natural tendencies of instruments; it does not consider individual players' ability (or lack of it) to overcome the instruments' limitations in tone quality and dynamic profile. Whenever possible, therefore, supplement the information in Figure 5-3 by having a classmate play what you have written.

5-3

Key: Written range: encompassed by **O**

Tessitura: encompassed by ●

Tone Quality: ↑ or ↓ expresses an increased tendency to become the quality expressed by the term that follows; for example, ↑ thinner indicates that the tone becomes thinner toward the top of the range.

Dynamic profile: Louder at the top of the range, softer at the bottom

Softer at the top of the range, louder at the bottom

Relatively even throughout the range

Flute   ↑ brilliant   ↓ velvety

Piccolo   ↑ shrill   ↓ mellow

continued

5-3, *continued*

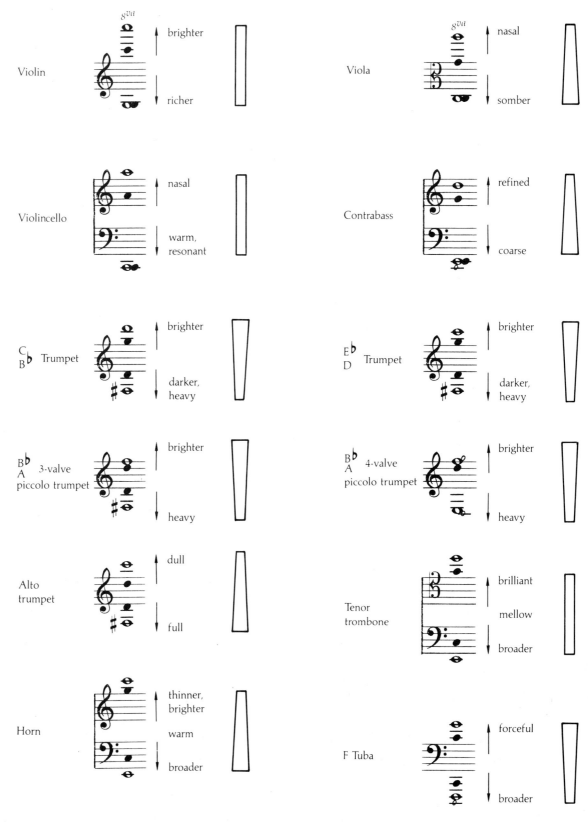

5-3, *continued*

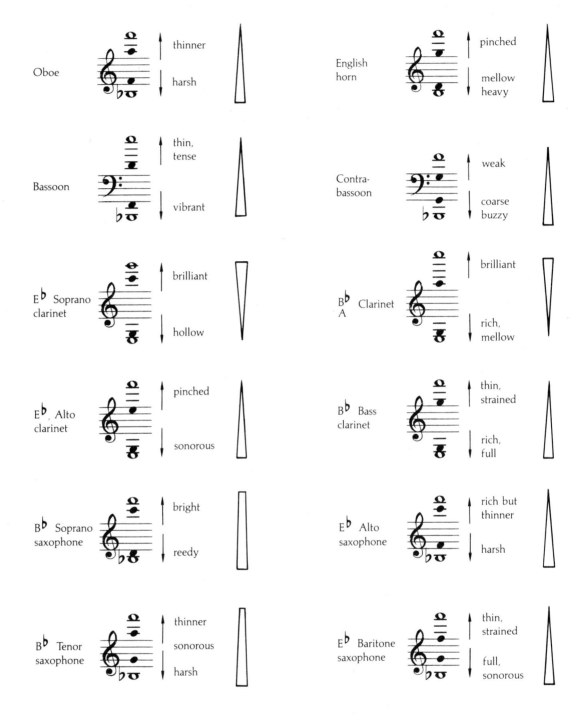

6 Preparing the Score and Parts

Is a change of pitch level desirable?

After selecting the musicwork to be transcribed with consideration for the instruments available, you may still find it advantageous to transpose the entire work up or down by a particular interval. The purpose of such a transposition, of course, is to place the musicwork in a range that is better-suited to the instruments being used. A musicwork sounding in the ranges most desirable for the human voice may be too high or too low for some instruments.

If the musicwork shown in Figure 4-16 were the one to be transcribed, for example, we might consider the work pitched too low for most upper woodwinds and strings to play as is but yet too high to be transposed an octave higher. The highest pitch of the upper voice is only E_5; it would be appropriate, therefore, to raise the pitch level of the work at least the interval of a -3 (m3). The top voice would still be well within the range of the soprano voice for option 2 or 3.

Is expansion of the pitch range desirable?

The primary objective in making an instrumental transcription of a vocal work is to produce an instrumental version that is as suitable for the selected instruments as the original is for voices. You may find, therefore, that the total pitch range of a vocal work may be too restricted for a convincing, literal transcription. For this reason, if only one instrument is to be used for each vocal line, it may be desirable to expand the pitch range upward, downward, or in both directions depending on the instruments used. This may be done by displacing some of the voices by transposing them an octave higher or lower as shown in Figure 6-1. Note that in all five examples of expansion shown, the soprano voice remains the soprano voice and the bass voice remains the bass voice.

6-1

Expanding the Pitch Range by Octave Transposition

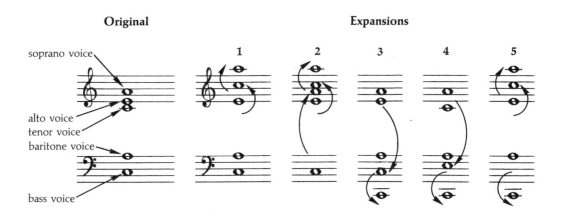

Are unison and octave doubling of voices desirable?

If more than one instrument is to be used for any or all of the voice lines of the original vocal score, as would be probable in doing option 1, the effectiveness of doubling voices at the unison or octave will depend on factors of range, tessitura, quality of sound, and ease of performance. Octave doubling serves to expand the pitch range of a transcription and produce a fuller body of sound. The octave doublings shown in Figure 6-2 are typical of what will produce effective acoustical results with an appropriate selection of instruments. Note that in each case there are no intervening pitches between the soprano or bass voices and their octave doublings.

6-2

Expanding the Pitch Range by Doubling of Voices

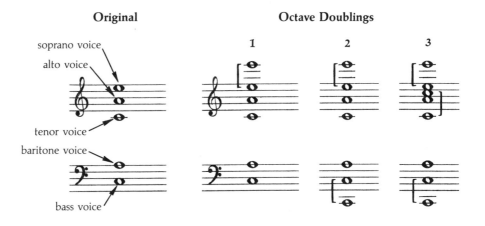

What are a performer's expectations with regard to hand-copied notation?

Calligraphy is the art of producing clear and stylistically consistent hand-copied music. Because even seasoned performers tend to be a bit skittish when confronted with a hand-copied performance part, the unseasoned performer may most certainly be apprehensive about reading manuscript. The problem of reading manuscript is essentially that of the uncertainty associated with the possibility of errors and the vagaries of calligraphic styles in hand-copied music: we are never certain that the parts are accurate.

The performing musician is generally conditioned to respond predictably to the shapes and placements of the symbols of modern conventional notation. Your primary concern at this point, therefore, is to produce a hand-copied score and set of parts that are as clear and effective as your calligraphic skills will permit. Practice in calligraphy involves developing skill in the use of tools and in the accurate placement of properly drawn music symbols on the staff.

The differences in the notational conventions of fifteenth- and sixteenth-century music and that of today were briefly discussed in chapter 4. This discussion, focused as it is on but a few of the pertinent aspects of the notation of Renaissance vocal music, provides little of the vast body of information that makes up the conventions of twentieth-century notation. The remainder of this chapter discusses some of the more common elements of conventional notation.

What are the conventional forms and uses of the common music symbols?

Though most of what we need to learn about making music symbols can be deduced from printed music, Figures 6-3 through 6-9 present a number of special considerations concerning the proper form of the most commonly used symbols. Figure 6-3 shows the forms and relative positions of the clef, the transposing signature, and the measure signature.

6-3

Figure 6-4 shows the general practice to be observed concerning the length of the **note stem** and the direction of the stem from the notehead.

6-4

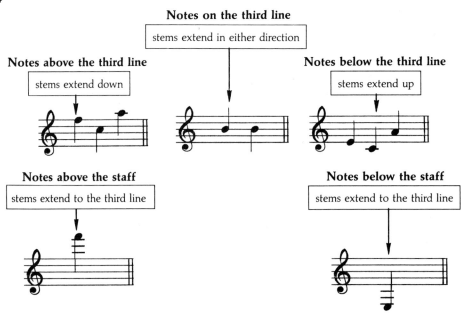

Figure 6-5 shows the correct positioning of the sharp, flat, and natural sign before a note when used within the context of a musicwork.

6-5

Figure 6-6 shows the location of the **tie** in relation to noteheads.

6-6

Figure 6-7 shows a few applications of the **slur**.

6-7

Figure 6-8 shows the use of the phrase indicator, the **bow**. The bow is not a slur; therefore, various forms of articulation may be used within it.

6-8

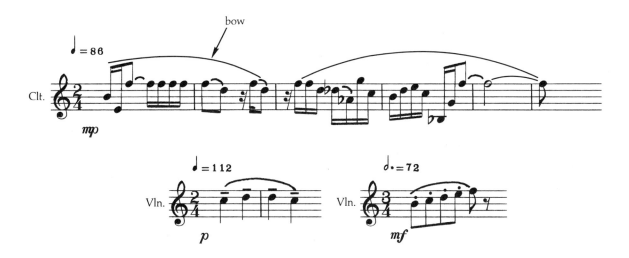

Figure 6-9 shows the placement of dynamic marks.

6-9

INSTRUMENT:

VOICE:

What consideration must be given to the spacing of notes and rests on the staff?

When placing notes, rests, and other symbols on prepared manuscript paper, you need to consider (1) the total space available on the staff, (2) the relative spacing of the notes and rests with respect to their durations, and (3) the overall clarity and unified appearance of the page. The second of these considerations involves making spacing adjustments to fill the available space on each staff and provide effective visual representation of the temporal aspects of the music. With experience, you will learn to envision the layout of each line of music so that you can make the necessary adjustments from line to line without it being visually noticeable. Figure 6-10 illustrates four ineffective uses of space and gives an example of good spacing.   **W54**

6-10

1. *Symbols equally spaced:* wasteful of space, poor visual impression.

2. *Symbols proportionally spaced:* wasteful of space, exaggerates what is visually necessary.

3. *Symbols irregularly spaced:* Symbols too close at the beginning of the line, leaving too much space at the end.

6-10, *continued*

4. *Symbols irregularly spaced:* symbols too far apart at the beginning of the line, leaving too little space at the end.

5. *Symbols relatively well spaced:* conserves space and gives an effective representation of durations and occurrences.

What governs vertical alignment in an instrumental score?

It is absolutely necessary that all simultaneous occurrences in a score be aligned vertically. This takes precedence over spacing considerations. Effective spacing is still important, but it is expressed in whatever portions of melodic lines contain the smallest temporal divisions. The bracketed portions in Figure 6-11 indicate the temporal divisions that govern spacing. Note that all simultaneous occurrences are properly aligned.

6-11

from Quartet No. 29 in G major, Op. 17 No. 5, Mov. I

What governs vertical alignment in a vocal score?

All simultaneous occurrences are vertically aligned in a vocal score as they are in an instrumental score, except that varying lengths of words in the text often necessitate irregular spacing. Thus, the regulating elements of vertical alignment in a vocal score are first the text and then the smallest divisions in notation whenever the text permits. Figure 6-12 illustrates this.

6-12

What is a ligature and how is it used?

Whenever two or more adjacent notes within a metric unit are eighth notes or notes of smaller divisions, they are generally combined by the use of **beams** to form a **ligature**. This method of organizing the contents of a measure into patterns within the limits of the metric unit simplifies reading and enables the player to remain metrically and visually oriented. Figure 6-13 illustrates the simplification of a difficult-to-read line by the use of ligatures.   **W55—60**

6-13

What are some exceptions to the conventional use of ligatures?

Although ligatures are sometimes used to create combinations that exceed the limits of the metric unit, it should not be done without good reason; clarity and ease of reading must be the criteria in making exceptions. Examples of some easy-to-read ligatures and familiar exceptions are shown in Figure 6-14. In a scherzo, in which the dotted half note is the metric unit, the ligature shown in (a) is appropriate. If the music in (a) were slower and the quarter note were the metric unit, the ligature would be an exception based on a familiar and logical precedent. The ligature formed by four eighth notes in (b) is appropriate, because the half note is the metric unit. The ligatures in (c) are familiar exceptions. A measure in $\frac{3}{4}$, in which the quarter

6-14

note is the metric unit, would be just as confusing with a ligature such as shown in Figure 6-15 as it would with a flag on each of the note stems. Such a case is, therefore, beyond exception. Using a ligature for each quarter-note value is an effective solution for this notation problem.

6-15

Whether or not you elect to make exceptions, keep in mind that visual clarity and your intent should govern your notation when you are preparing parts for players and singers.* A score or performance part that does not express the music in the simplest and clearest terms is pretentious and self-defeating; it fails to perform the basic function of notation.

What are dynamics?

The term **dynamics** refers to the relative loudness and softness of music. The change from one dynamic level to another can be abrupt or gradual. Figure 6-16 lists the common dynamic markings used in conventionally notated music of the last few centuries.

The music in Figure 4-16, as well as the music you have selected (unless it has been edited), contains no dynamic markings, because dynamic markings were not used in notation until after the sixteenth century. Control over the volume (amplitude, relative loudness and softness) is mandatory if musical performance is to be effective. Therefore, you will need to

*Contrary to a long-standing convention, ligatures are now being used in notating vocal music.

6-16

SYMBOL	TERM	MEANING
fff	*fortississimo* or *triple forte*	extremely loud
ff	*fortissimo* or *double forte*	very loud
f	*forte*	loud
mf	*mezzo-forte*	moderately loud
mp	*mezzo-piano*	moderately soft
p	*piano*	soft
pp	*pianissimo* or *double piano*	very soft
ppp	*pianississimo* or *triple piano*	extremely soft
<	*crescendo*	becoming louder
>	*diminuendo*	becoming softer

specify the dynamics for the performance of your transcription. Reason would tell us that the music of the fifteenth and sixteenth centuries had varying dynamic levels, but reason would also tell us that the differences were modest. For obvious stylistic reasons, the dynamics you specify should reflect the general character of the music and text and serve to achieve an appropriate balance of sound and projection of the melodic lines.

What is articulation?

Articulation refers to the manner in which a performer initiates a tone and follows one tone with another. A tone may be initiated by a great variety of attacks, ranging from the strongest possible accent to the imperceptible. The movement from one tone to another may be marked by distinct separation or by an extremely smooth motion with no separation at all.

What is phrasing?

Phrasing refers to the manner in which a performer gives intelligible shape to music. Though composers have used phrasing symbols for more than two hundred years, such symbols are seldom taken literally by performers; they are generally accepted only as guides. Although a bow or other phrasing symbol marks off or gathers up a particular collection of notes that are to be phrased as a unit intelligible to listeners, a phrasing symbol does not indicate precisely how it is to be done. This is perhaps the most nebulous aspect of notation. Because phrasing is, for all practical purposes, the responsibility of the performer, familiarity with style and tradition is essential to intelligent musical phrasing. A musician's phrasing, dynamics, and articulation are akin to an actor's "delivery" of his or her lines.

What are some common articulation and phrasing symbols?

The articulation and phrasing symbols shown in Figure 6-17 are typical of those used in conventional notation over the last one hundred years or so. Though some of the articulation symbols were originally applicable to specific types of instruments (strings generally), they have come to be used for most other instruments as well. When articulation symbols intended for bowed instruments are used for woodwinds and brass, the players simply try to imitate the effect of the particular articulations on a bowed string.

6-17

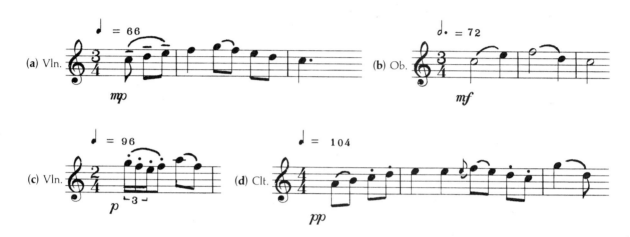

What are the articulation and phrasing needs of the transcription being made?

Articulation and phrasing of fifteenth- and sixteenth-century vocal music is determined by the pronunciation, enunciation, and meaning of the text. Since no special articulation and phrasing symbols were used at that time, the sample score (Figure 4-16) and the music you have selected (unless it has been edited) contain no articulation or phrasing symbols. Consequently, you will need to indicate the articulation and desired phrasing for the kinds of instruments you are using. The articulation and phrasing should reflect the intent of the original music insofar as it can be determined by the setting of the text and the nature of the melodic lines. If two or more notes are used for one syllable, for example, these notes should be slurred when they are scored for instruments to reflect the effect of the voice.

7 Performing the Transcription

Why should the transcription be performed?

The culminating act of producing a musically convincing performance will help you to achieve the final "shaping" of your transcription. You will gain some acquaintance with the music and a number of musical skills by making the transcription and preparing the score and parts. However, until the work is performed and your musical and aesthetic judgments are subjected to the reality of performance, the transcription is merely a speculative, theoretical exercise. Things you have read and discussed about calligraphy, transposing, and other important skills are certainly necessary to the success of this first project. However, the supreme test of transcribing a musicwork that was composed in one medium for performance in another is in the hearing. Learning what works and what does not work in transcribing is a primary objective of this unit, and you can learn this only by *doing* it.

What considerations must be given to the seating of players?

Because the instruments for which the transcription is made are more likely than not to form something other than a typical or conventional ensemble, some consideration should be given to the seating of the players. Among the many things that must be considered if a fair hearing is to be had are the following:

1. If the performance is to be recorded—and it should be if at all possible—the placement of instruments in relation to microphones is important. This is a matter that cannot be predetermined; the variables demand a certain amount of experimentation and testing.

2. Determine which direction the various instruments should face to obtain the best balance of sound and the best visual contact between the players and conductor. This matter is particularly important with respect to strings, flutes, and some brass instruments.

3. Be concerned about seating players too close to walls if the performance is to take place in a classroom or other relatively small space. Some instruments are affected very little by this; others, the horn for example, are greatly affected if the player's back is toward and close to the wall.

What are the functions of the conductor and the conductor's beat?

The primary function of the conductor's beat is to provide a group of musicians with a common tempo for the beat unit of the measure. Through the manner in which beat patterns are executed, the conductor may indicate elements of style and character, duration, rhythmic shape, articulation, and other temporal and aesthetic values. The conductor's beat is but one of the many, extremely varied aspects of his or her demeanor that supply the visual effects to which the musicians respond throughout a performance.

How are conductor's beat patterns formed?

Conducting an ensemble of players is probably a completely new experience for you. If so, it is important that you prepare yourself at least to the extent that you are able to produce a clear beat pattern with enough authority to lead a group rather than follow it. Practicing these exercises—in the privacy of your room or a practice room if you like—will help you to prepare:

1. Using a felt marker or crayon to make the numerals large enough to be seen at a distance, prepare four sheets of paper (at least as large as the pages of this book) as shown in Figure 7-1.

7-1

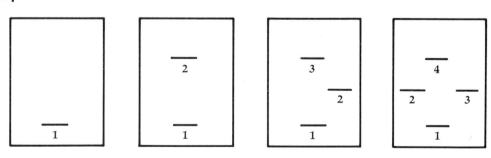

2. Tape one of the prepared sheets at a time to a door or wall with the top of the paper at just below eye level; then complete the following two steps:

   a. Stand approximately five to six feet from the paper; extend your right arm comfortably; close one eye; while sighting with the other eye, form the beat patterns with a baton or pencil, seemingly touching the lines above the numbers on the paper lightly with the tip of the baton in doing so. Use the motions indicated in Figure 7-2 for the respective beat patterns without making a hitting or striking gesture or exerting any muscular strain. If you are left-handed, simply reverse the patterns shown.

7-2

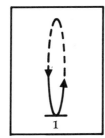 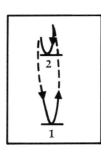 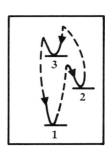 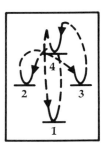

b. With both eyes open and keeping the character and proportions of the beat patterns as practiced, enlarge them gradually to a fuller, more comfortable size.

What is a preparatory beat?

A **preparatory beat** is simply the beat that precedes the one on which the players (or singers) are to begin. If the players are to begin on the fourth beat of a measure of four, a normally executed third beat is sufficient preparation. In moderate or slow tempos, music beginning on the second half of a beat (or the last quarter of a beat) needs no more preparation than the beat itself. The preparatory beat should express the character and tempo of the music to be performed. The practice of "giving an entire measure for nothing" should be avoided; it leads to confusion and reduces preparedness by giving the tempo without consideration for character.

How can flexibility and mobility be achieved in conducting?

Ideally, through the conductor's eye contact, natural body gestures, and positioning of the baton, each member of a performing ensemble feels that he or she is receiving much if not all of the conductor's attention. The conductor is conducting players and singers, not music, but music is being made because of it. All motions, therefore, must be directed at members of the ensemble for the purpose of getting them to do something at a particular moment, in a particular manner, and for a particular period of time. An effective conductor's visual contact with the score is fleeting and not particularly noticeable to the players or singers.

Keeping the manner and direction of approach used in producing the beat patterns, do the following exercises:

1. Practice the beat patterns while facing, looking at, and pointing the baton at a different object on each beat as if each object were a performer. You should be able to face left, center, and right without changing your stance. The basic pattern in Figure 7-3a might thus become one of the patterns in Figure 7-3b. In relation to the direction in which the conductor is facing, each beat will appear normal to the performer or group of performers.

7-3

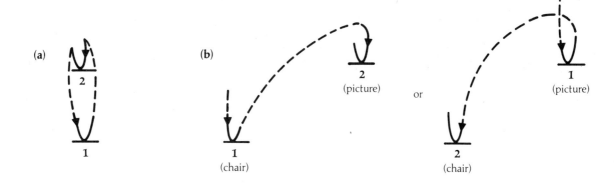

2. Repeat the process using the patterns for measures of three and four. In practicing mobility, use objects in your room in a manner similar to what is shown in Figure 7-4a and b.

7-4

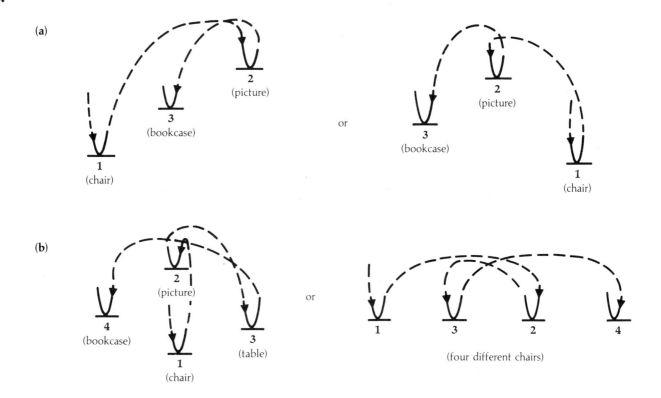

What can be done to increase flexibility and mobility in conducting while using a score?

The following exercise can help you increase your flexibility and mobility. It can be repeated any number of times with increasingly complex scores and increasingly greater numbers of pages.

1. Using a relatively simple orchestral score that uses a moderately small instrumentation, learn the exact instrumentation and general location of solo instruments and sections in accordance with one of the standard seating arrangements.

2. Place the score on a conductor's stand so that it lays flat and is raised to a level no higher than your waist. If the stand is raised higher, your movements will be inhibited and the performers' vision obstructed.

3. Study a page of the score for as long as it takes to determine where in the imaginary orchestra you must direct your attention. DO NOT MARK THE SCORE WITH DIRECTIONS OF ANY KIND!

4. Conduct the imaginary orchestra through the page you have studied and keep your attention on the players. As you move your eyes from one player or section of the imaginary orchestra to another, catch a passing glimpse of the score. If few shifts of attention are demanded by the nature of the music, repeated glances at the score can be made as needed. As a rule, the conductor's eyes should never remain fixed on anything for more than a moment.

8 Evaluating the Unit Project

What should be the terms of an evaluation?

Much of what is to be evaluated in this unit project involves the "mechanics" of producing music. Among these are a few things that must be regarded in terms of accuracy and, as such, are not really a part of an evaluation. Correct transposition and correct notation of durations and pitch, for example, are *not* factors about which we make a judgment; they are either correct or not correct. An **evaluation**, on the other hand, should be concerned primarily with the elements of the mechanics that can be judged as *effective* or *ineffective*. These elements might involve such mechanical aspects as the selection of instruments, voicing of instruments, doubling of parts, articulations, phrasing, instrumental balance, and similar matters. The seating of players and the execution of the conducting pattern also can be regarded in terms of their effectiveness.

How does musicality relate to the mechanics?

The second general category of evaluation includes things pertaining to the musicality of the project. In judging musicality, we will, in some instances, be concerned with the same things we consider from the standpoint of "mechanics." That is, it is possible to succeed at the mechanics of a thing but, because of other circumstances, be less than successful musically. You may produce a conducting pattern with mechanical clarity, for example, but yet fail to do what is necessary with the pattern to produce a musical result.

What factors are beyond a student's control?

An evaluation should take into consideration the degree to which the individual student is able to control those aspects of the project that require his or her dependence on others. We should consider whether there were such factors as a malfunctioning instrument, a student who is absent, and a substitute player who is less capable than the one who was supposed to play. Other situations involving dependence on others, however, should be evaluated in terms of (1) how well the student utilized performers whose playing abilities are limited, (2) how well the student utilized the available instruments, and (3) how well the student, during the act of conducting, handled any of the many problems that can occur in performance.

How do we produce an evaluation instrument?

If the students are to be involved in the evaluation of the unit projects, an evaluation form should be produced for the purpose. The form should indicate which aspects of the project are to be evaluated and whether they are to be evaluated in terms of mechanical effectiveness, musicality, or both. An identifiable scale indicating the number of increments to be used in the evaluation should be provided for each aspect to be considered. The outer limits of the scale might simply be designated "poor" and "excellent" and the scale consist of five to ten increments along which the evaluator places a check to indicate where a student's effectiveness or musicality falls. Because most if not all of the students are going to be involved in the performance of each project, the evaluation form should be simple enough so that each student can evaluate the project immediately after the performance. The evaluation instrument should facilitate honest appraisals and not contain too many items. The last item on the form should ask the student to evaluate the overall impression of the transcription and performance.

Appendix to Unit One: Sources of Compositions for Unit One Projects

The following are commonly available collections of fifteenth- and sixteenth-century vocal music that contain compositions suitable for use in the projects described in Unit One.

Agricola, Alexandri. *Complete Works*, 5 vols., ed. Edward R. Lerner. Rome: American Institute of Musicology, 1961.

Arcadelt, Jacob. *Complete Works*, 10 vols., ed. Albertus Seay. Rome: American Institute of Musicology, 1965.

Asola, Giovanni Matteo. *Sixteen Liturgical Works*, ed. Donald M. Fouse. New Haven: A-R Editions, Inc., 1964.

des Pres, Josquin. *Achttiende Aflevering Motetten, Bundel VII*, ed. A. Smijers. Amsterdam: Vereeniging voor Nederlandsche Muziekgeshiedenis, 1938.

Gombert, Nicolas. *Complete Works*, 7 vols., ed. Joseph Schmidt. Rome: American Institute of Musicology, 1951.

Goudimel, Claude. *Complete Works*, 11 vols., transcriptions by Henri Gagnebin. New York: Institute of Medieval Music, 1967.

Lassus, Orlando de. *Samtliche Werke, Neue Reihe: Motetten, Canons, Madrigals*, 10 vols. Wiesbaden: Berenreiter, 1956.

Monte, Philippi de. *Complete Works*, 30 vols., ed. Julius Van Nuffel. New York: Broude Brothers, 1965.

Nanino, Giovanni Maria. *Fourteen Liturgical Works*, ed. Richard J. Schuler. Madison: A-R Editions, Inc., 1969.

Obrecht, Jacob. *Werken*, ed. Johannes Wolf. England: Gregg International Publishers Ltd., 1968.

Palestrina, Giovanni P. da. *Complete Works*, 31 vols., ed. Casimi. Roma: Fratelli Scalera, 1939.

Rogier, Philippe. *Eleven Motets*, Vol. II., ed. Lavern J. Wagner. New Haven: A-R Editions, Inc., 1966.

Senfl, Ludwig. *Complete Works*, 8 vols., ed. Edwin and Otto Ursprung. Wolfenbüttel und Zürich: Moseler Verlag, 1962.

Sweelinck, Jan Pietersz. *Complete Works*, 10 vols., ed. Max Seiffert. Leipzig: Breitkopf und Härtel, 1898.

Tinctoris, Johannes. *Collected Compositions*, ed. Fredericus Feldmann. Rome: American Institute of Musicology, 1960.

Wert, Giaches de. *Collected Works*, 11 vols., ed. Carol MacClintok. Rome: American Institute of Musicology, 1969.

PATTERNS IN
SOUND AND TIME

Introduction to Patterns in Sound and Time

How are the temporal and spatial expressions of language related?

As you read this introduction, you are privately "performing" the printed page. You are transforming the spatial entity in front of you into a temporal one. As you make this transformation, you are governing your speed, or tempo, in accordance with how well you understand the words, the subject matter, or perhaps the habitual pace you use for reading everything. If you are like most readers, you are silently speaking the words, giving emphasis to those you intuitively deem important. What you will remember will not be the ordering of the words themselves but the ideas you realize as you assimilate this material with the relevant experiences of your past.

Events of the past and future can converge and be perceived concurrently with the present. As the writer writes, he or she is aware that what is written may be read by someone in the future. However, the moment the writer puts words on paper—that is, into a spatial dimension—they become a part of his or her personal past. By reading what was written, the writer will also "perform" it and become aware of the fact that it is impossible to regard it in the same way while performing it as while writing it. Moreover, continued performances of what you have written will vary with each subsequent reading, because, in a very real sense, you are constantly becoming a slightly different person; new experiences modify your point of view.

All of the words your eyes are now scanning have been transformed from an aural vocabulary, which is temporal in nature, to a visual vocabulary, which is spatial. Since people began transforming aural expressions to visual expressions of language, certain conventions have evolved to enhance visual intelligibility. The most obvious of these conventions are concerned with the uniformity of such spatial qualities as the size and spacing of letters in printed language. For example, the letters used in the printing of this page are generally of only two sizes, and the spaces they occupy and the spaces between them are relatively uniform. As a result, your eyes move without impedence in a regular flow. The relative lengths of words do not contribute as much to the evenness of eye movement as does the consistency of the spacing between the words. Because the spaces between words are relatively uniform and the letters are of the same size and style, no particular word stands in relief and is consequently emphasized. Reading Figure 9-1 will illustrate what occurs when the size, style, and spacing of letters departs from the conventional.

9-1

EMpʰAsiS l)IN   rHEtoRiC , a paR tiCuLA r
          stRes S   Of uTtEr AnCe OR   FOR cE

OF vOiCEgIveN   tO   ThE wOrDs
OR   pArtS   of   A dISCoUrsE
   WHosE   sIgNiFICaTION   tHe   sPeAkER...

Source: *Webster's Universal Unabridged Dictionary*

Because of the irregularity in the size, style, and spacing of the letters in Figure 9-1, our eyes have difficulty tracking what appears to be a random pattern. The result is a halting, confused performance; a shifting, misleading pattern of visual emphasis hinders our ability to organize and interpret printed words immediately and effectively. However, as you may have noticed, repeated readings can eventually defeat the effects of the impediment caused by randomness, rendering your performance more intelligible with each reading. If this entire book were printed in such a random manner, however, you would soon be defeated.

How do we humans show ourselves to be pattern makers?

As was shown in Unit One, we humans are pattern makers. We subconsciously organize complex arrays into patterns. Conversely, we tend also to construct extremely complex arrays from the simplest of patterns. From a simple dot (·) and dash (—), for example, Samuel Morse devised a patterned means of encoding a message in any language so that it can be transmitted over telegraph wires; and bricks of a single dimension can be organized in such a way as to construct gigantic edifices.

Making patterns is an interesting form of play for humans; a pleasant way to occupy idle time. Have you ever watched a child play with blocks—a truly universal toy? Perhaps you remember doing it yourself. Have you ever caught yourself doodling absent-mindedly while talking on the telephone or listening to a lecture? Isn't it almost impossible to be near sand without making patterns or building "castles," or near a new snowfall without making "angels" or building a snowman?

If we are not making spatial patterns, we find ourselves molding temporal ones. We pattern our time with calendars and clocks that are made to serve us with precision and regularity. We eat, sleep, work, play, and do most everything in conformity with temporal patterns that have become habits. We enjoy vacations because they allow us to break the established time patterns and create new ones. We make long-range temporal patterns for our lives—careers, family, personal goals—and then tend to be disappointed and frustrated if we are unable to keep in step with the timetable we have established for our future.

What about the patterns formed by our movements? Do we not repeat them in recognizably similar ways? Are we not recognized by our relatives and friends as much by the patterns of our movements—by the way we walk, gesture, play, and perform tasks—as by our features and other aspects of ourselves? Indeed we are. We might observe that the success of a mimic may depend more on his or her ability to imitate the physical bearing and mannerisms than the voice quality and articulation of the person being imitated.

The intent and consequence of a particular movement can be conveyed by a moving image but only suggested or implied by a static image. The painter or sculptor must deal with movement as an illusion. An action painting cannot move; it must convey the illusion of motion. The intent and consequences of an action in a motion picture are conveyed by a succession of frames. The illusion that constitutes motion in a painting, however, is not present in a single frame of a motion picture. Nonetheless, paintings and motion pictures both deal in illusions. The painter is able, for example, to create the illusion of a three-dimensional subject on a two-dimensional surface by the use of the vanishing point. The illusion of the third dimension is achieved in a motion picture through motion.

What patterns exist in your surroundings?

Stop your "performance," that is, your reading of this page, for a minute and observe the various patterns in your surroundings. . . . Did you notice any patterns that were not repeated? Did you see any varied repetitions of a particular pattern? Did you see any exact repetitions of a pattern? Did some pattern seem more interesting than the others? What was more interesting about them?

If, for example, you are sitting in a classroom, library reading room, lounge, or similar room, you probably have noticed that almost all the physical patterns—those that are a part of the room and its furnishings—are utilitarian; they are primarily functional and limited to a special use. The repeated patterns of chairs, tables, ceiling and floor tiles, doors, windows, books, counters, lighting and heating fixtures, and signs, for example, express those items in terms of their purpose and use. These items attract our attention only if they are arranged in some special manner, such as the chairs arranged in a V pattern, the windows and doors set on a slant, or some items painted an unusual color. Our attention would most certainly be drawn to anything that cannot be used because it is broken.

How do these patterns relate to each other?

Having observed the various individual utilitarian patterns that make up much of what can be found in a room, think about how these patterns relate to each other. Do the patterns made by such fixed objects as windows, doors, tile, or lighting fixtures appear to consist of identical or related shapes? Do the patterns of the furnishings and decorative objects in the room appear to consist of identical or related shapes? Do these patterns relate in any way to the patterns of the fixed objects in the room? Do the patterns that appear quite different from the dominant pattern or related patterns of the room provide a welcomed contrast and complement the other patterns in the room? Or, do the differing patterns disturb and disrupt the effect of the dominant or related patterns? Finally, does the room serve its utilitarian purpose within the context of an aesthetically desirable, coherent whole? We might conclude after observing a room in this manner that the skill of a very capable designer is required to make a room's patterns express more than its utilitarian function.

How do the occupants of a room contribute to its patterns?

If the patterns you are observing in the room include the postures and movements of people, these patterns, also, are essentially utilitarian because they are associated primarily with particular tasks. In a library, many people display postures appropriate for reading. Typical utilitarian movements there include such activities as searching the stacks, reaching for books, searching through card catalogs, writing, turning pages, and sharpening pencils. Students in a classroom may be in postures for listening, writing, talking, gesticulating, singing, playing instruments, or another activity that requires a variety of utilitarian movements. Some of the postures and movements express attitudes in the sense that they reflect agreement, disagreement, concern, confusion, and other responses to what they are reading, hearing, seeing, or doing. Some of the movements may be random, unconscious movements, such as idle tapping or tracing patterns with fingers, doodling, head scratching, running fingers through hair, or the unconscious adjusting of garments.

How are utility and beauty related?

The common definition of *utilitarian* as found in Webster's *New World Dictionary*, "stressing the importance of utility over beauty or other considerations," provides a rather short-sighted "either–or" relationship of the utilitarian and the beautiful. Such a definition diminishes the potential for a clear and workable concept of both utility and beauty. Utility and beauty should not be regarded as mutually exclusive concepts; they are, more properly, complementary concepts. We should wonder, instead, whether it is possible for something to be eminently useful and be without beauty, or for something to be eminently beautiful and serve no useful purpose. Something that is utilitarian and without beauty exemplifies poor design; it is not a matter of utility being more "important" than beauty. And something that is beautiful and serves no useful purpose is not truly possible, because the effect of the beauty of an artwork, for example, on the mind and spirit of humankind is "purpose" of the highest form. We would do better to regard **utilitarian** as relating to *the utility or functional aspect of something in contradistinction to its beauty or any other aspect*.

In observing the surroundings in a library reading room or classroom, we are certain to realize that most of the patterns we see, hear, and otherwise receive through our senses owe their existence to some utilitarian function. Fortunately, our total environment is more varied and provides patterns and opportunities for pattern making that are not utilitarian in nature or intent. Our involvement with such activities as the arts, games, and general recreation, for example, satisfies a side of human nature that affords us great pleasure because it provides us with the stimulus of personal discovery.

What might we expect from random patterns stirred up from paper fragments randomly cut from a sheet of paper?

Consider for a moment what can be done with something as simple as a sheet of black paper. Limited entirely to the sheet of paper itself (Figure 9-2a), how could we alter it without marking on it or adding to it? Certainly it could be folded or crumpled to produce interesting three-dimensional patterns. Or, it could be cut or torn randomly or purposefully into whatever shapes best suit our fancy. Let's imagine that we cut the black paper into the nine randomly shaped pieces shown in Figure 9-2b.

After cutting the black paper into the randomly shaped pieces, we might drop them on a white paper and stir them about, pausing at random images such as the one shown in Figure 9-2c. Theoretically, we could continue stirring the fragments, stopping periodically to notice the changing images—rather like a homemade kaleidoscope. Though we might be able to caption or assign expressive values to the random patterns, we would not expect the patterns to fall into a comprehensible sequence. Our only expectation could be that we would never see the identical image again. We also could not expect to see a progression of recognizable events. We certainly would not expect to experience any emotional or aesthetic response to the random images produced. Everything that occurred would be purely unpredictable; but we could not rule out the possibility that some image of credible beauty might result by chance.

9-2

(a)

(b)

(c)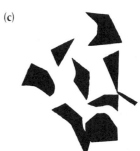

How does our recognition of the paper fragments' shapes lead us to produce more symmetrical patterns?

Our hypothetical paper fragments are related to each other because they are cut from the same piece of paper. Because of this, there is some inherent potential for rational design, for a sense of closure, that would not exist in a random collection of fragments of different sheets of paper. The more we stir the nine fragments, the greater becomes our feeling for a need to arrange them into more personal and significant patterns. We then begin to formulate our own micropuzzle by observing the individual pieces. Our paper fragments have two types of edges: some are basically pointed (convex); others are indented (concave). If we turn some of the pointed edges toward some of the indented edges, a pattern emerges to which we may respond aesthetically if not emotionally (Figure 9-3a).

Each person who looks at this pattern will respond differently to it. One person may feel that the points seem to be pushing the indented edges; another may feel that the indentations are on the verge of consuming the points. To some, this may simply appear to be another random image to which they have no response at all. However, if we were to arrange the fragments as in Figure 9.3b, there would be little doubt that someone had purposely made the pattern. It probably could not have occurred by accident. The pattern is quite symmetrical: two fragments are placed in each of the four corners of the enclosed space with one remaining fragment in the center. This kind of symmetry could have endless variations. The pattern in Figure 9-3c illustrates a less balanced symmetry.

These symmetrical patterns, of course, could be continued ad infinitum; we would need simply to rely on our inate sense of proportion to balance them. When the patterns would look right, we would stop adjusting the fragments. We could, with a speck of imagination, further humanize the images by regarding them as abstractions of some concrete or psychological condition. For example, Figure 9-3a could be considered a dancing puppet; 9-3b could be the desertion of the flock, or conversely, four individuals urging four others to join a central leader. Figure 9-3c could represent a conflict, a family of six lined up to greet three visitors, or even three candidates for political office being interviewed by reporters from six different newspapers. The possibilities for captions are endless. As we well know, if we are making similar random or symmetrical patterns, there are no hidden "messages" in any of them; there are only patterns that may or may not stimulate our imaginations.

9-3

(a)   (b)   (c)

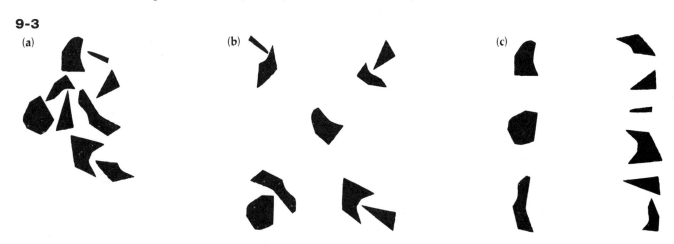

How might stylized caricatures be made from these paper fragments?

Let us now consider some deliberately made patterns. Examine the images in Figure 9-4 and make a guess as to what the patterns were intended to represent. Try doing this in a class or with a group of friends to see how much agreement there is in their judgments. Try viewing

9-4

(a)   (b)   (c)

(d)   (e)   (f)   (g)

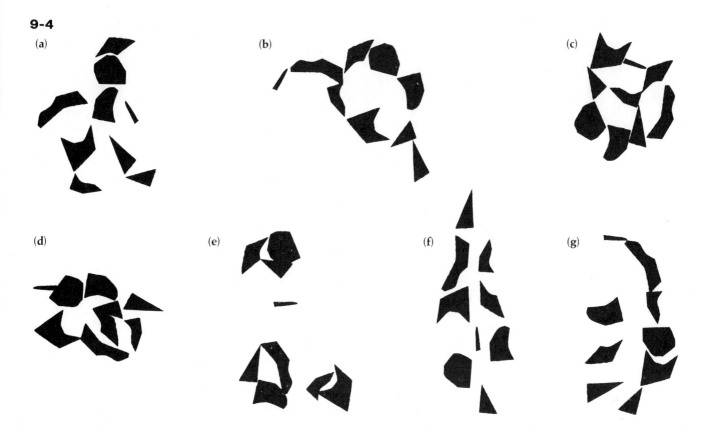

the patterns from differing angles. Does this alter anyone's judgment of what a pattern represents?

These are primarily static images. As a collection of images, they do not suggest a dramatic context within which the images can be understood. We could possibly construct a story that would incorporate each image as a character; however, this would be an imposition and not something generated by the images themselves. Because, as previously mentioned, we have used only the nine randomly cut fragments for all of the images, they all bear the same stamp: they are stylized. And, being stylized images of concrete objects, they have become caricatures because they are distortions of the familiar things they represent.

How might we introduce temporality into our pattern making?

Could we also have utilized our paper fragments to make images that would, by their design alone, enable them to be made to function within the dimension of time and be understood within a dramatic context in a manner similar to music? The first possibility that pops into mind is a motion picture. That would entail making frame-by-frame photographs, with the fragments in different relative positions in each frame. Our little caricature of the human form (Figure 9-4a), for example, could be shown to walk, run, fall down, and so on, if we were to photograph the fragments in a sequence that suggested the desired activity.

We could introduce visual temporality, also, by presenting a sequence of images implying animation on a single printed page and allowing the viewer's eyes and mind to establish a time period for the completion of the motion implied by the sequence. The sequence in Figure 9-5, for example, shows a familiar "stick-man" caricature of the human form doing the long jump.

The time period used by anyone in viewing the animated sequence in Figure 9-5 is open-ended. A motion picture, on the other hand, is viewed within a prescribed period of time;

9-5

Drawing by John F. Sherman

after it is finished, there is nothing more of it to see. When our eyes peruse the sequence in Figure 9-5, they may pause or review portions of the sequence.

How does subjective time differ from objective time?

The open-ended time frame of the animated sequence and the closed time frame of the motion picture represent the difference between subjective time and objective time, respectively. **Subjective time** is time measured in terms of our span of interest in a given pursuit concentrating on a given activity, or the time needed to complete a given task. Time spent watching children at play, enjoying a flower garden, having a tooth filled, viewing a painting, studying for a test, and thousands of other pleasures, obligations, and discomforts is measured in terms of its quality. **Objective time**, on the other hand, is time that can be measured in precise, quantitative increments (such as microseconds, seconds, minutes, or hours). The time it takes to show a movie, for the earth to complete a revolution, to play a recording of a musicwork, and so on, is objective time. What takes place in subjective time may be equally pleasurable, responsible, or discomforting; the difference is in how time is measured.

How does this imaginative image making relate to the making of music?

Up to now we have been occupied with an "open-ended," visual–spatial, image-making process. This brief exploration of the possibilities inherent in applying our imagination to a few fragments of paper is intended to suggest that we can apply our imaginations to fragments of sound in a similar manner. We cannot "tear up" or "cut up" a sound in the same sense that we can tear or cut paper. We can, however, come close to this idea by reducing a sound to its component parts. The component frequencies of an individual tone or the component tones of a collection of tones can be separated and reassembled to form a variety of patterns. The first of these is one of the many procedures used in the making of electronic music. The second is a procedure composers have used for centuries; the pitch content of the natural diatonic system and its transpositions have been separated and reassembled in countless ways to form music for hundreds of years.

If we are to separate and reassemble sounds to make music, we must first understand the complex patterns of sound that make up "tones," the behavior of sound, and the many identifiable pitch patterns available in the natural and transposed diatonic systems.

10 Acoustical Properties of Sound

How is acoustics related to music?

Originally, **acoustics** was defined as the science of hearing. In relatively recent years, however, the study of acoustics has broadened to include the production, physical properties, and behavior of the waveforms we perceive as sound as well as the responding characteristics of the enclosures within which waveforms are produced and heard. **Waveform** is simply the technical term that denotes the relatively simple or complex set of frequencies (the number of vibrations per second expressed in hertz*) that make up a sound.

Acoustics, as related to music, embraces a number of considerations, many of which are fields of study in their own right. Among them are (1) the physiology of hearing, (2) the waveform producing and amplifying characteristics of mechano-acoustical and electro-acoustical instruments, (3) the physical properties of waveforms produced on these instruments, (4) the behavioral characteristics of the pressure changes produced by these waveforms during transmission, (5) the responding characteristics of the enclosures in which the waveforms are produced, transmitted, and heard, and (6) the psychological effects of the ensuing sounds on the hearer.

What is sound?

Sound is a perceived manifestation. It exists as the result of our perceiving pressure changes in the atmosphere, the invisible mixture of gases within which we have our breathing–feeling–hearing existence.

*After Heinrich Rudolph Hertz, 1857–1894, German physicist; abbreviation, Hz.

How are atmospheric pressure changes made to occur?

When an object is made to vibrate—let us say at an audible frequency—each vibration results in the object's being displaced in one direction, returning to its original position, being displaced again in the opposite direction, and then returning again to its original position. See Figure 10-1. At the moment of displacement, the molecules of air immediately in the path of the object are also displaced. Because of the elasticity of air, these molecules follow the displacement pattern made by the vibrating object. As each molecule of air is displaced by the pressure applied to it by the vibrating object, it in turn applies pressure to the next molecule, which then applies it to the next one, and so on and so on. The molecules of air do nothing but move back and forth in a pattern determined by the vibrating object. This pattern of movement back and forth alternately creates **compression** (molecules of air are forced closer together) and **rarefaction** (molecules of air are drawn farther apart). The chain reaction of molecules bumping into one another and drawing back has the effect of transmitting these pressure changes from the vibrating object outward in all directions.

10-1

One Cycle of Vibration of a Tuning Fork

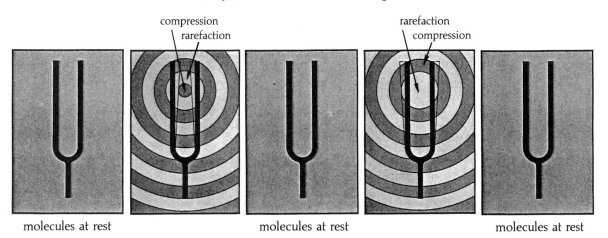

compression
rarefaction

rarefaction
compression

molecules at rest   molecules at rest   molecules at rest

Illustration by John F. Sherman

How are waveforms transmitted?

In dealing with our capacity to perceive atmospheric pressure changes as sound, we must understand some terms and habits of usage in light of the illusions they represent. For example, the commonly expressed notion that sound travels through air or another medium is oversimplified and misleading, although it is a convenient colloquialism. Though some people take exception to the use of the word *sound* for anything other than a perceived phenomenon, it is convenient to use *sound* rather than the technically accurate term, *waveform*, when expressing generalities. However, this is not the primary problem with the notion that sound travels. The problem is with the term *travel* or any similar term that implies that sound (or more properly, a waveform) physically moves through air or any other medium.

That a waveform emitted from a given source at one point in a room, for example, will be heard and perceived as sound by someone at another point in the room is a very reasonable expectation. However, if the waveform does not actually travel or is not actually transmitted in the same sense that an object may travel or be moved from one place to another, how does it, so to speak, get from one place to another? A waveform is not a physical object; and, strictly speaking, it does not move and is not transmitted in the same sense that an object could be transmitted. What we think of as traveling or movement is a series of pressure changes that give the illusion of movement. This may be likened to the illusion of movement created by the blinking lights on a theater marquee or an animated billboard.

The illusion of movement created by these pressure changes might also be likened to the children's game of "pass it on." One child taps, makes a face at, or does something to the next child and says, "pass it on." The process is repeated until the tap, or whatever, is received by the last child in the group. No one moves out of position, but whatever was initiated by the first child finally reaches the last one.

Finally, the transmission of a waveform might be compared to the "bucket brigades" used to fight fires in localities where the only source of water is a nearby well or stream. Lines of people, extending from the well or stream to the fire, pass buckets of water along the line to the fire. The people, like molecules of air, remain stationary except for the back and forth movement of passing the buckets. The buckets, in the same manner as the waveforms, are passed from the water's source to the intended destination.

When do atmospheric pressure changes become sound?

The molecules of air (or whatever medium is involved) do nothing but "pass on" complex pressure changes. Providing we are within hearing distance, the pressure changes that have survived the dissipating effects of friction ultimately reach the molecules of air immediately next to our eardrums. The pressure changes effect a corresponding displacement of the eardrums, causing them to vibrate in the same pattern. The vibrating eardrums transform the pressure changes into mechanical energy, causing the liquid in the inner ears to vibrate, which in turn causes the nerve endings within the inner ear to be electrically stimulated. Finally, the electrical impulses from the sensitized nerves reach the brain. At this point it can be said that the pressure changes have been perceived and have become sound.

Because we cannot close our ears to atmospheric pressure changes, is hearing automatic and uncontrolled?

To hear is to perceive; to perceive is to be selective. The chain reaction we call the hearing process (described in the previous paragraph) never stops, even though our attention may not be drawn to a particular sound. Our brain may choose to ignore most of the mass of information being transmitted to us, though the reception and processing of all available aural information continues. Obviously, therefore, we do not hear a good deal of what we could, because it does not interest us at the time. Usually, however, whether we are awake or asleep, we are conditioned to respond to certain sounds even though they may not be very loud. A siren heard while driving, a bell ending a class period, footsteps when we believe we are alone, for example, attract our attention rather quickly when they intrude on our activities. A new mother remains sensitive to the sounds of a baby's movements and cry during the night.

What are mechano-acoustical and electro-acoustical instruments?

Mechano-acoustical instruments (henceforth referred to as **mechanical instruments**) are those upon which the sound-producing waveforms are produced mechanically by such means as vibrating strings, reeds, air streams, lips, rods, membranes, or circular plates. These waveforms are amplified by the instrument's own resonance or by the resonating chamber or column of air formed by the shape of the instrument. A triangle, cymbal, or similar instrument would amplify whatever waveform it makes by means of its own resonance when it is struck and thus made to vibrate. Along with the amplification produced by the vibration of the materials of which it is made, a stringed instrument also has an air chamber (formed by its belly, back, and sides), which serves to amplify the waveforms made by the vibrating strings. The resonance of the material of which a woodwind or brass instrument is made, along with the resonant column of air within the instrument, serves to amplify the waveforms produced.

An **electro-acoustical instrument** (henceforth called either an *electric* or *electronic* instrument) is an instrument upon which waveforms are produced mechanically and amplified electrically. An electric guitar is such an instrument. Another kind of electrically amplified instrument is one that uses a contact microphone. Any instrument upon which waveforms are produced electronically and amplified electrically is an *electronic* instrument. Synthesizers and computers are electronic instruments.

Upon what do we base our terminology?

An individual sound produced by a musical instrument, the voice included, may be referred to in a number of ways depending on the particular aspect of the sound being considered and the frame of reference (musical or acoustical). Musically, when we refer to the quality of a violin tone, we in all probability use *tone* or *timbre* as the descriptor; acoustically, we describe a tone as a *waveform*. If we are concerned with the shape of the violin tone, acoustically we refer to its *envelope*. When we refer to the particular highness or lowness of a tone played on the violin, we use the perceptual term *pitch* if the reference is musical, the term *frequency* if the reference is to acoustics. We should note that all musical references to sound (itself a perceptual term) are perceptual in nature, whereas acoustical references are scientific in nature.

What are the limitations of musical terminology?

Much of the terminology we encounter with regard to the nature of sound came into common use before electronic tools were developed. Due to recent technological advances, however, we can now examine sound with a degree of refinement comparable to that with which a biologist examines tissue under an electronic microscope. Early interest in acoustics by musicians using mechanical tools of limited capacity and accuracy brought about the development of terms and concepts that were equally limited. With the development and dissemination of new knowledge, many of these older terms and concepts have become more "picturesque" (for example, *rounded tone, centered tone*, and so on) than descriptive of the perceptual and physical realities of the production and transmission of sound-producing waveforms.

Also, and not because our interest in the various components of sound is a rather recently acquired concern, musicians have not developed much purely musical terminology (perceptual terminology) for describing the relationships and behavior characteristics of the components of sound. This is understandable because most of the components of the unique complex of sound we call the "tone" of an instrument or voice combine to form an aural impression that we perceive as a single entity. Our sense of hearing, lacking the capacity to perceive such components individually, obviously has no need for perceptual terms to describe what the hearing sense cannot perceive. The musician's terminology for such components, therefore, is oriented to the needs of acoustics, mathematics, and the related sciences.

How is a waveform represented graphically?

Though we cannot hear the individual components of an instrumental or vocal tone, we can see them. With a cathode-ray tube (oscilloscope), the components of a tone can be transformed into a visual pattern. See Figure 10-2. It has been known for centuries that a tone is composed of a complex fusion of frequencies above a fundamental pitch, but a tone has not been visually represented until recently, except in hand drawings. In spite of the graphic clarity of these visual representations, they are only representations and nothing more; they are not graphic demonstrations of the atmospheric pressure changes that result in sound. A typical still picture of such a graphic representation is shown in Figure 10-2. Though useful in making visual comparisons, a still photograph is an expedient representation of an in-motion representation of sound demonstrated by an oscilloscope. Oscilloscope images of a tone would differ

10-2   Oscilloscopic Photograph of the Sound "Ah"

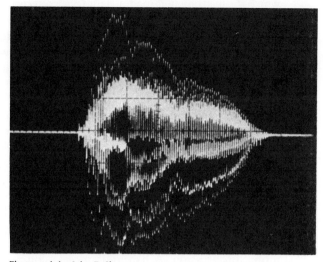

Photograph by John F. Sherman

constantly in response to the slight changes of nuance that occur constantly as the tone is sounding.

In what way is perception the faculty of perceiving combinations and patterns?

If the individual frequencies making up a tone do not impress our hearing system as separate, discrete pitches, we might wonder why so many individual frequencies are present in a tone and what purpose they serve. In considering this question, let us first look at the nature of perception; that is, the various levels and kinds of awareness made possible through our senses.

If it were not for the selective limitations of our senses, sensory discrimination as we know it would be impossible. Regardless of how acute our senses may be, they can function only within certain limits. Imagine, if you can, what it would be like if we could see absolutely every particle of every atom of everything there is to see. Though at times we might consider it an interesting novelty to be able to see all of the particles that make up the physical objects of our environment, the result would be disastrous: we would be incapable of distinguishing the familiar forms we are presently able to see and distinguish.

In like manner, if we could hear all of the component frequencies of even the simplest music, we would not be able to distinguish the patterns we regard as music. Therefore, if by being able to hear every particle of sound and to see every particle of physical objects we would distinguish nothing, it would seem that perception must depend on something beyond just hearing, seeing, and our other senses. **Perception** is the faculty that permits us to recognize combinations and patterns through our senses. The human capacity to perceive combinations and patterns is essential to the existence of the arts.

What is the harmonic series?

The tone of an instrument or voice, as we have said, is made up of a complex fusion of frequencies above a fundamental pitch. These weaker, individually inaudible frequencies are perfectly blended and serve to complement the primary or fundamental pitch, giving the tone its distinct timbre. Other factors that contribute to the identifiable tone of an instrument are (1) the onset transients (the attack harmonics), (2) the amplitude characteristics (attack height, sustaining levels, decay rate), and (3) the final decay (release). Another factor, which has the overall effect of varying the shape (the *envelope*) of an instrument's tone in different parts of its range, is the instrument's **formant** (the effect of the frequency response of the materials out of which the instrument is made). This factor affects the resonant response of the instrument to the various pitches produced by it.

The fact that a distinct timbre results from the fusion of a particular pattern of frequencies above a fundamental pitch is somewhat analogous to the phenomenon of a perceptibly distinct new color resulting from the mixing of two or more colors. We do not see the various colors that were combined to make up the mixture; we see only the results, a new color. Though we cannot hear the individual components of a tone or see the components of a color, our perception of distinct tone qualities and color shades is generally discriminating enough to enable us to distinguish relatively subtle changes.

The pattern of frequencies that, along with a fundamental pitch, forms a tone is *not* a random array of frequencies. The order of the frequencies is determined by a natural physical phenomenon known as the **harmonic series** (or **overtone series**).* The harmonic series is demonstrated in terms of musical notation in Figure 10-3. Bear in mind as you use this figure that the relationship between a notated pitch and the actual frequency it represents is approximate.

Expressed in mathematical or physical terms, the harmonic series is known as a **harmonic progression**. A harmonic progression is simply a series of fractions, the denominators of which have a common difference; for example, $\frac{1}{2}, \frac{1}{4}, \frac{1}{6}, \frac{1}{8}, \frac{1}{10}, \ldots$, or $\frac{1}{3}, \frac{1}{6}, \frac{1}{9}, \frac{1}{12}, \ldots$. The denominators of the harmonic progression that produces the harmonic series in music differ by one; that is, $\frac{1}{1}, \frac{1}{2}, \frac{1}{3}, \frac{1}{4}, \frac{1}{5}, \frac{1}{6}$, and so on. Expressed as fractions, each term (that is, each fraction) of the series expresses the relationship of the wavelength of that term to the wavelength of the fundamental pitch. For example, if the wavelength of a fundamental pitch were four feet, the wavelength of the fourth term would be $\frac{1}{4} \times 4$ ft = 1 ft. The harmonic series expressed as a harmonic progression, however, is of limited interest to the musician. The most apparent application of the harmonic progression to music is that the first several terms (fractions) express the divisions in the length of a string that produce harmonics on stringed instruments. Considering $\frac{1}{1}$ or simply 1 as the first **harmonic** (the fundamental pitch of an open string), $\frac{1}{2}$ the length of the string (touching the string in the middle) produces the second harmonic; $\frac{1}{3}$ the length produces the third harmonic; $\frac{1}{4}$, the fourth harmonic; $\frac{1}{5}$, the fifth harmonic, and so on to the point at which the physical properties of the string will no longer respond.

Though most musicians are not actively concerned about the length of a pressure wave, they *are* concerned about the fundamental pitch, (the perceivable consequence of a pressure wave) and about the distribution of the frequencies that make up the remainder of the complex waveform we perceive as a tone. The denominators of the terms of the harmonic progression make up what is known as an **arithmetic progression**. An arithmetic progression is a series of numbers that have a common difference, such as 2, 5, 8, 11, 14, 17, . . . , 1, 5, 9, 13, 17, 21, . . . , or 1, 6, 11, 16, 21, 26, ... The arithmetic progression can be used to determine the frequency of the harmonics, which, along with the fundamental pitch (the first harmonic), are the primary determinants of the timbre of a tone. We need only multiply the frequency of the fundamental pitch by the number of the harmonic to determine the frequency of the harmonic.

Perhaps the greatest marvel of the harmonic series has yet to be mentioned. Within the arithmetic progression are found what are called **geometric progressions**. A geometric progression is a series of numbers, the terms of which form a common ratio. For example, in the series 2, 6, 18, 54, 162, 486, . . . , the common ratio is three. If we look at the arithmetic progression Figure 10-3, we see such geometric progressions as 1, 2, 4, 8, 16, 32, 64, . . . , 3, 6, 12, 24, 48, . . . , and 5, 10, 20, 40. In each geometric progression shown, the common ratio is two. The marvel of the geometric progression as found here is that each term (each harmonic) forms an octave relationship with each adjacent member of the progression. Our perceptual awareness of the octave as the repetition of a pitch at a different pitch level provides us with the most fundamental principle of pitch organization known in music. Any kind of music based on discrete pitch relationships is subject to these octave relationships.

---

*The first overtone of the overtone series is the second harmonic of the harmonic series. *Overtone series* is not a useful term.

10-3

THE HARMONIC SERIES

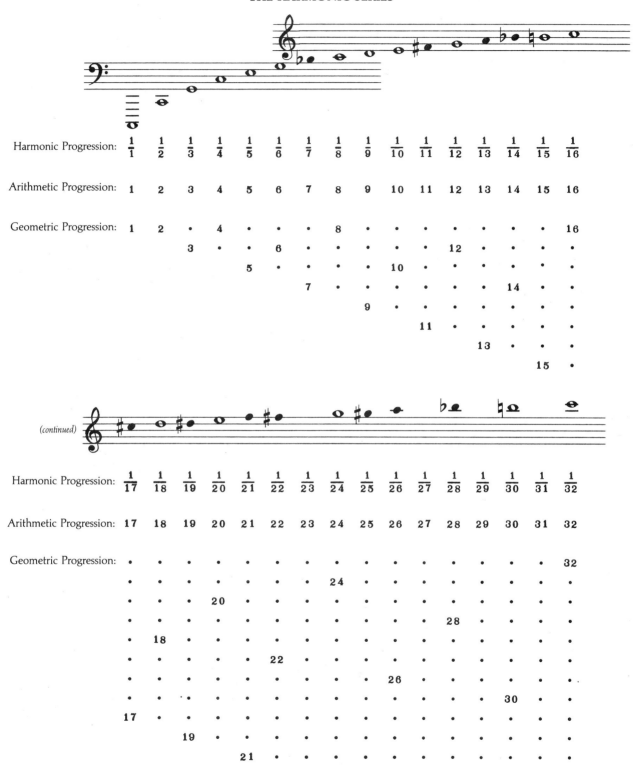

continued

10-3, *continued*

(continued)

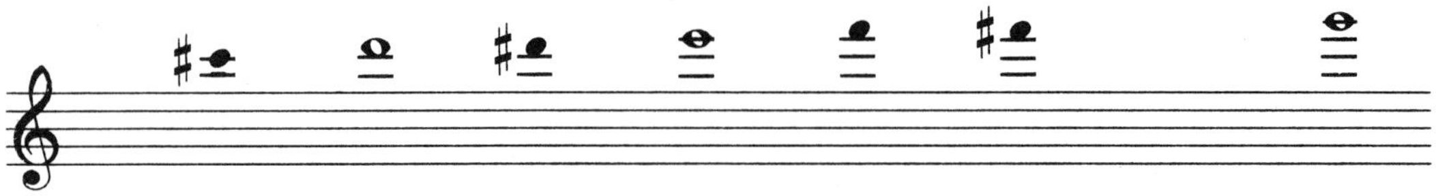

Harmonic Progression:	$\frac{1}{33}$	$\frac{1}{34}$	$\frac{1}{35}$	$\frac{1}{36}$	$\frac{1}{37}$	$\frac{1}{38}$	$\frac{1}{39}$	$\frac{1}{40}$	$\frac{1}{41}$	$\frac{1}{42}$	$\frac{1}{43}$	$\frac{1}{44}$	$\frac{1}{45}$	$\frac{1}{46}$	$\frac{1}{47}$	$\frac{1}{48}$
Arithmetic Progression:	33	34	35	36	37	38	39	40	41	42	43	44	45	46	47	48
Geometric Progression:	•	•	•	•	•	•	•	•	•	•	•	•	•	•	•	•
	•	•	•	•	•	•	•	•	•	•	•	•	•	•	•	48
	•	•	•	•	•	•	•	40	•	•	•	•	•	•	•	•
	•	•	•	•	•	•	•	•	•	•	•	•	•	•	•	•
	•	•	•	36	•	•	•	•	•	•	•	•	•	•	•	•
	•	•	•	•	•	•	•	•	•	•	•	44	•	•	•	•
	•	•	•	•	•	•	•	•	•	•	•	•	•	•	•	•
	•	•	•	•	•	•	•	•	•	•	•	•	•	•	•	•
	•	34	•	•	•	•	•	•	•	•	•	•	•	•	•	•
	•	•	•	36	•	•	•	•	•	•	•	•	•	•	•	•
	•	•	•	•	•	•	•	•	•	42	•	•	•	•	•	•
	•	•	•	•	•	•	•	•	•	•	•	•	•	•	•	•

(continued)

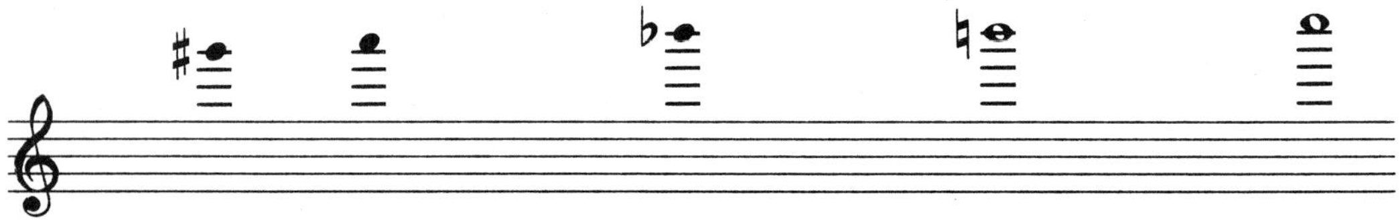

Harmonic Progression:	$\frac{1}{49}$	$\frac{1}{50}$	$\frac{1}{51}$	$\frac{1}{52}$	$\frac{1}{53}$	$\frac{1}{54}$	$\frac{1}{55}$	$\frac{1}{56}$	$\frac{1}{57}$	$\frac{1}{58}$	$\frac{1}{59}$	$\frac{1}{60}$	$\frac{1}{61}$	$\frac{1}{62}$	$\frac{1}{63}$	$\frac{1}{64}$
Arithmetic Progression:	49	50	51	52	53	54	55	56	57	58	59	60	61	62	63	64
Geometric Progression:	•	•	•	•	•	•	•	•	•	•	•	•	•	•	•	64
	•	•	•	•	•	•	•	•	•	•	•	•	•	•	•	•
	•	•	•	•	•	•	•	•	•	•	•	•	•	•	•	•
	•	•	•	•	•	•	•	56	•	•	•	•	•	•	•	•
	•	•	•	•	•	•	•	•	•	•	•	•	•	•	•	•
	•	•	•	•	•	•	•	•	•	•	•	•	•	•	•	•
	•	•	•	52	•	•	•	•	•	•	•	•	•	•	•	•
	•	•	•	•	•	•	•	•	•	•	•	60	•	•	•	•
	•	•	•	•	•	•	•	•	•	•	•	•	•	•	•	•
	•	•	•	•	•	•	•	•	•	•	•	•	•	•	•	•
	•	•	•	•	•	•	•	•	•	•	•	•	•	•	•	•
	•	50	•	•	•	•	•	•	•	•	•	•	•	•	•	•

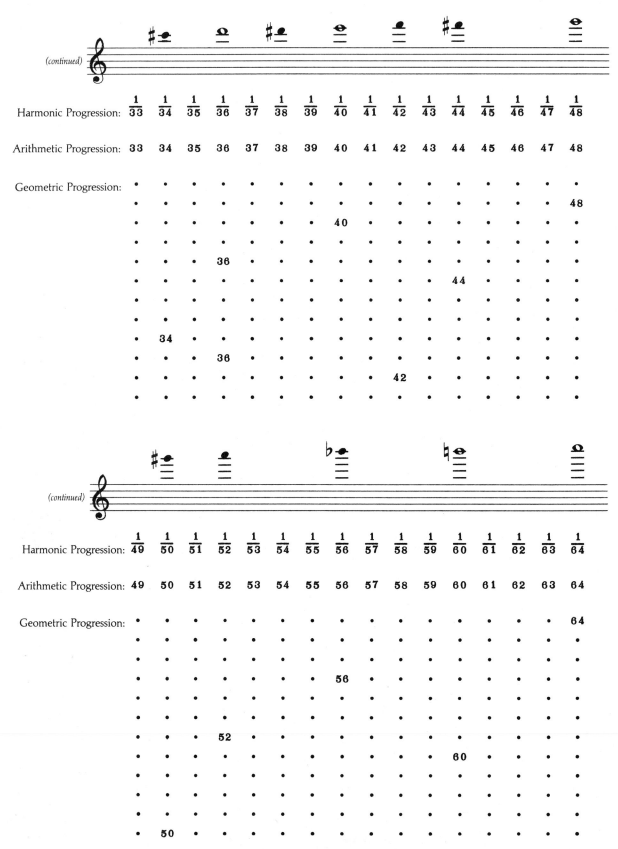

What should the harmonic series mean to us musically?

To be understood properly, the harmonic series must be recognized as a series of ever-decreasing frequency ratios beginning with a 2:1 ratio (the octave) and extending to extremely small ratios such as 64:63 (an interval considerably smaller than a half step) and beyond. In Figure 10-3, the whole notes represent pitches that come the "closest" to the actual frequencies of the series. The solid notes represent pitches that barely approximate the frequencies. After the twenty-fifth harmonic, the gradations of the series are too small to be approximated by the half-step increments of conventionally notated pitch. The harmonic series presented in Figure 10-3 represents a set of frequency relationships above the notated pitch C_1. The same set of relationships can be projected above any pitch in any octave. The number of effective harmonics available becomes more limited the higher the fundamental pitch, however.   **W61–63**

Our observations concerning the relationship of the harmonic series to music yields these conclusions:

1. The primary value of the series to music, in accordance with its function as a natural law, is what it contributes to the quality of a tone through the distribution and amplitude of the harmonics it provides above the fundamental pitch of a tone.

2. The harmonic series, as an expression of a natural law, plays an indispensable role in the functioning of mechanical instruments.

3. The relationship of the harmonic series to the actual pitches and the structural relationship of pitches in music is more coincidental than real, because the octave is the only frequency relationship of the series that does not require a tuning adjustment.

The inherent incompatibility of the natural harmonic series to any of the prevailing concepts of tuning in music is, from a purely musical point of view, one of the great strengths of the series.

We often describe the natural harmonics of a fundamental pitch as "pure." This is in contradistinction to the harmonics produced by an electronic instrument—such as the Hammond organ—in which the harmonics are "tuned." The description of the harmonics of the harmonic series as "pure" does not imply that the particular tone of which they are a part is also a "pure" tone. The harmonics are "pure" because of the purity of the mathematical ratios involved and the fact that the harmonics occur as a natural phenomenon. A **pure tone** has no harmonics above the first harmonic. A sound produced by a tuning fork or the sinusoidal signals of an audio oscillator is a pure tone.

Tuning: Temperament and intonation

Tuning refers to the nature of pitch relationships in music. **Temperament** is an objective term that refers to a standardized format for assigning audio frequencies to the twelve pitch classes used in Western music. **Intonation** is a subjective term that refers to the individual and collective practices of musicians in making pitch adjustments during the performance of music. The temperament used in tuning should be regarded as a "standard of measurement"; good intonation should be regarded as an "aesthetic ideal."

Tempered tuning systems have evolved as the result of compromising deviations from the pitch content of the acoustically pure frequencies generated by the harmonic series. **Pythagorean tuning**, the oldest known system, is derived directly from the harmonic series. **Just intonation** is a system of tuning derived by projecting a series of Pythagorean fifths (the ratio 3:2 in the harmonic series) from the pitch class C. The Pythagorean and just intonation systems have little or no direct application to tuning in music today. The harmonic series and the acoustically "pure" systems of tuning derived from it are regarded by some as having some limited application to and responsibility for the natural diatonic system. However, any assumed relationship between the harmonic series and the natural diatonic system can best be explained as coincidental. Though some relationship exists, it cannot be said that the diatonic system is "generated by" the harmonic series. In notating the pitch content of the harmonic series we are making approximations that help to explain the relationships within the series; any notational similarities with the diatonic system are coincidental and should not be construed to mean anything beyond the physical makeup of sound.

Meantone tuning and equal temperament are the two tempered systems that have evolved from the acoustically "pure" systems. The first appeared around the year 1500 and the second shortly after. **Meantone tuning** is a compromise system that enabled a keyboard player to play music with signatures up to three sharps and two flats or two sharps and three flats. **Equal temperament**, also a compromise, is the system presently used as the objective standard for tuning fixed-pitched instruments such as keyboard instruments. In equal-tempered tuning, the octave is divided into 1200 "cents," with each half step being equal to 100 cents. All mechanical instruments are made to be capable of producing pitch relationships in accordance with the standards of the equal-tempered system. Thus, as a compromise system, all pitch relationships are equally "out of tune" but acceptably so.

Perhaps the primary value of equal temperament as a standard of tuning is that it provides a common point of departure for performers in the exercise of aesthetically "good" intonation. Consistent with the nature of perception as discussed earlier in this chapter, an aesthetic sense of pitch relationships and patterns does not demand conformance to equal temperament. An aesthetic sense of "good" intonation requires the molding of pitch collections into perceptibly meaningful entities which necessarily depart from the non-discriminatory factors inherent in any standard of tuning. Good intonation, an aesthetic ideal, requires whatever distortions of the objective tuning standard are necessary to bring about a musically expressive, coherent performance of a musicwork.

Having just described the objective—implied accuracy—of equal temperament as a standard of tuning, we must state also that it is seldom if ever actually realized. Equal temperament is a standard that is subject to the effects of other acoustical phenomenon as well as to the highly subjective manner in which it is applied. Obviously, piano tuners and instrumentalists tune in accordance with what sounds good to them. Also, as L. Euler observed more than two hundred years ago, "the ear generally hears what it wants to hear." This, of course, means that listeners may also make adjustments in the intonation of music to satisfy their own aesthetic expectations about pitch relationships. For example, play the melodic shape shown in Figure 10-4 on the piano and observe whether you want to hear the second E_4 as being higher in pitch than the first one. The first E_4, drawn as it is toward the D sharp, functions in the design of this melodic shape, psychologically, to give us the aural impression that it is lower in pitch than the second E. The position of the second E in the melodic shape and the rhythmic configuration that focuses on it as the point toward which all else is directed give the second E a brighter, more expansive quality. This heightens the difference we seem to hear between the two pitches, even when they are played on an instrument that does not present a real physical difference in the frequency of a given pitch.

10-4

How can we experience the actual sound of harmonics?

Perhaps the most immediate way to experience the sound of at least some of the natural harmonics of the harmonic series as they would appear in an isolated state would be to ask a brass player (horn, trumpet, trombone, tuba) to play the lowest possible open pitch and then ascend, pitch by pitch, through the instrument's range without using the valves or slide and without skipping any pitches. You will notice that the trumpet cannot sound the first two harmonics of the series and that the trombone and horn may not sound the first harmonic. Though the actual number of harmonics that can be played on these instruments is determined by the ability of the performer, each instrument differs in the number of harmonics a player can reasonably expect to produce on it. The horn will typically yield the greatest number of harmonics, the trombone probably the next-greatest number, and the trumpet the least.

Because of their construction, brass instruments will not sound pitches outside of the harmonic series when played without valves (in the case of the horn, trumpet, and tuba) or varying the slide positions (in the case of the trombone). Each of these harmonics, when sounded on the instrument, is a new tone that generates a new harmonic series of its own. The pitch of each new tone, however, conforms to the frequency of the harmonic it represents within the harmonic series generated by the fundamental pitch of the particular length of tubing being used. All brass instruments are capable of producing the pitches of equal-tempered tuning by the use of valves and tuning slides. The valves and differing slide positions serve to add tubing, thereby increasing the length of the instrument. With each added length of tubing, the instrument provides a new fundamental having its own harmonic series. From these additional harmonic series the player is able to select usable pitches.

Brass instruments may appear to be rather complicated instruments, but essentially they are curved pieces of metal tubing with a mouthpiece at one end and a flared bell at the other end. The "complicated" aspect of a valved instrument's appearance is associated with the valve assembly and tuning slides. The most critical aspects of a brass instrument's design, however, are the characteristics of its "bore," the size and amount of flare in its "bell," and the metal of which it is made. These are the factors that contribute the most to the specific quality of each instrument's tone.

What is resonance and what is a resonator?

Resonance is the result of the reinforcement of vibrations by reflection or by the forced or sympathetic vibration of another body serving as a **resonator**. The first instance describes the kind of resonance encountered in a large enclosure having hard, reflecting interior surfaces. This kind of resonance is generally called **reverberation**. The second instance describes the resonance achieved by the design characteristics of musical instruments.

Stringed and wind instruments are **coupled systems**, in that the vibrating strings, lips, or reeds are directly *coupled* (joined) to the body of the instrument, causing the forced vibration of the body and air column of the instrument. It is axiomatic that the materials of which the instrument is made, the shape of the instrument, and the size of the enclosed column of air must be designed to maximize the desired evenness and degree of resonance. A poorly formed instrument can offer little more than an uneven quality of sound and insufficient resonance in relation to the amount of energy expended by the player. The difference between a well-made and a poorly made instrument is basically the difference between an efficient and an inefficient resonator.

How can we demonstrate the effect of a resonator?

For a simple and immediate demonstration of how a resonator affects the quality and amplitude (loudness) of a vibrating body (lips, reeds, strings, rods, membranes), do the following. Stretch a rubber band across your fingers and snap it so as to cause it to vibrate. You should hear a brief, faint sound that is relatively high in pitch. Now stretch the rubber band over the opening of a paper cup and snap it again. The empty cup should act as a resonator, permitting the sound of the vibrating rubber band to be heard more easily and with a clearer, enhanced quality. As a further demonstration of how the size, shape, and resonant frequency of the material of which a resonator is made affects the quality of the sound, repeat the experiment using other empty containers—plastic cups, tin cans, wooden boxes, cardboard boxes. The disturbance of the air caused by the vibrating rubber band in each case produces some sound, but that is not what causes the enclosed air of the container to resonate. The contact of the rubber band with the edge of the container provides for a coupled system causing the forced vibration of the sides and bottom of the container. The larger, vibrating surfaces of the containers produce the resonance.

How can we demonstrate the efficiency of forced vibration?

If we strike a tuning fork and hold the tines of the fork near one of our ears, the resulting effect will be a weak but reasonable sustained tone. However, if, after striking the fork, we touch the shank of the fork to various objects—such as a wooden tabletop, a chair, a wall, the floor, a pillow, and other objects made of hard and soft materials—we will hear equally varied sounds. From some objects we will hear a louder, pleasant-sounding but shorter-lived tone. From other objects, the resulting sounds will be louder but somewhat distorted. From still others, we may hear the sound only slightly, or there may be no sound at all.

The tines of a tuning fork are small and they encounter very little resistance from the molecules of air that surround them. Consequently, the tines do not provide much of a disturbance in the air. By coupling the tuning fork to an object that is capable of vibrating at the frequency of the tuning fork, the object is forced to vibrate at the same frequency. Touching the shank of the tuning fork to some objects may, on the other hand, result in a dampening effect because the material is too soft and may serve only to absorb the vibrations of the tuning fork. Other objects may be hard enough but have resonant frequencies that are incompatible with the frequency of the tuning fork. Some materials may be too hard and dense to respond to the low energy of a vibrating tuning fork. Except in cases in which the resonant frequency of an object is compatible with the frequency of the tuning fork, the potential energy of the vibrating tuning fork is dissipated without producing any vibration. Without the forced vibration of a responsive object there is no resonance.

How does forced vibration produce resonance in instruments?

A vibrating violin string when dissociated from the violin produces a very weak sound. The string is too thin to set up much of a disturbance in the air; hence, most of the energy used in making the string vibrate is wasted. However, the same string placed on the violin is coupled to the belly of the instrument by means of the bridge, and the belly is coupled to the back by means of the sound post. When made to vibrate, the string forces the larger surfaces of the belly and back, as well as the enclosed air, to vibrate and produce the desired resonant tones.

In like manner, a brass player may buzz his or her lips into the open air to produce a weak, ineffectual sound. When the player's lips are coupled to the mouthpiece of the instrument, the lip buzz forces the air column within the instrument as well as the material of the instrument to vibrate and thus produce the desired resonance. The increase in audibility—from the initial, weak buzzing of the player's lips to the full, resonant tone that emerges from the instrument—is due to the efficiency of the resonator.

<table>
<tr><td>

**MINI
PROJECT
5**

</td><td>

A musician's understanding of the "stuff" of which music is made and the conditions under which music is performed and heard are important to his or her development of the craft of making music. Toward this end, therefore, research and write a paper on the first of these three topics plus one of the remaining two topics.

</td></tr>
</table>

1. The acoustical properties and functions of the instrument you play or of the voice. Your study should include:

   a. the mode(s) of inducing vibration,

   b. information on the harmonic content, envelope, formant, and profile of the tone,

   c. the manner of achieving resonance, and

   d. the pitch range and tessitura.

2. The behavior of sound within an enclosure such as a small recital hall or church building or out-of-doors

3. The functional properties of a tape recorder, a synthesizer, *or* a computer as an instrument for making music

11 Scale Patterns in the Diatonic System

What is a diatonic scale?

Among the established and perhaps most familiar of the sonic patterns we associate with the diatonic system is the diatonic scale. Though our familiarity is limited mostly to what have come to be known as major and minor scales, a **diatonic scale** is simply any segment of three or more pitches of the natural diatonic system (or one of its transpositions). Some randomly selected scales are shown in Figure 11-1.

11-1

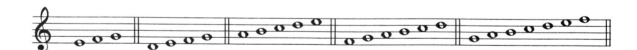

As with many relatively simple things in life, the various definitions, concepts, and general understandings about scales that have developed over the years are rather contradictory. Many of the potential problems in learning about scales will be avoided if we are careful to distinguish what a **scale** is—an objective set of pitch relationships having definition but no meaning—from the many subjective notions about its real or imagined uses in the construction and performance of music. An octave segment of the natural diatonic system—for example, D_4 to D_5—considered as objective material and defined simply in terms of its pitch and interval content, has no musical meaning until it is used and can be regarded within a musical context, regardless of how complex or limited the context is. If the D_4 to D_5 segment of the natural diatonic system is used by an instrumentalist in an exercise designed to improve intonation and evenness of tone, then that particular limited use is its meaning. Use of the same segment as the pitch content of a melodic line by a Renaissance composer or by an early-twentieth-century composer would imply something much beyond a mere scale.

How are modal scales, modes, and modality related?

In presenting, for twentieth-century purposes and historical understanding, what may be referred to now as "modal" scales, we should not confuse the scale with what, during the medieval and Renaissance periods, were called *modes* and were used in the practice of "modality." During the medieval and Renaissance periods, for example, "mode" represented both a scale and the particular connotations associated with its use. This dual application of the term cannot be made now, because *mode* denotes but one of several diverse uses of a modal scale. The term **modal scale** refers to its historical beginnings as well as its present limited definition as an identifiable set of pitches and interval relationships. For this reason, we continue to use the identifying names of the "church" (or "ecclesiastical") modes.

A **mode**, as a compendium of pitches having aesthetic and ethical connotations, functions within the formalizing principles of medieval and Renaissance modality. As an aesthetic and ethical expression, most of the subtleties of the historical modes and the principles of modality are lost to us, except, perhaps, among those who diligently cultivate the perception of modal music beyond the consideration of it as an auditory phenomenon from a previous age. A genuine feel for the cultural significance of the modes in terms of their subtle religious and ethical overtones, however, is not at all possible.

The modal scales presented in Figure 11-2, except for the Locrian scale, correspond to the modes customarily used during the medieval and Renaissance periods and bear place names from ancient Greece. Though their names are Greek, these modal scales provide the pitch relationships of the "church" modes, which are different from the ancient Greek modes. The technical differences need not be pursued here because the ancient Greek modes remain unrelated to the extant music of the Western cultures and to the purpose of this book.

11-2

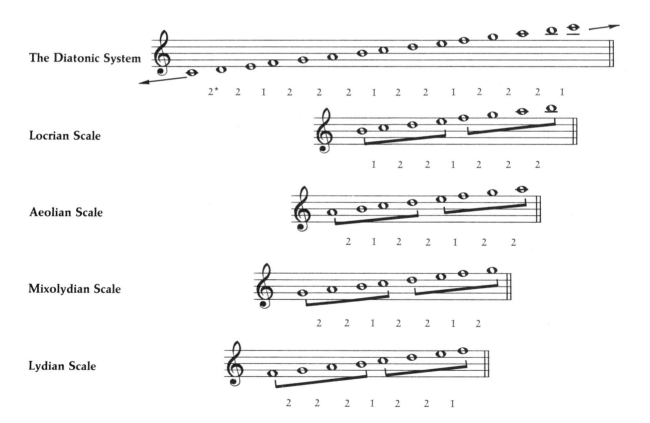

*Intervals expressed in cardinal nomenclature.

continued

11-2, *continued*

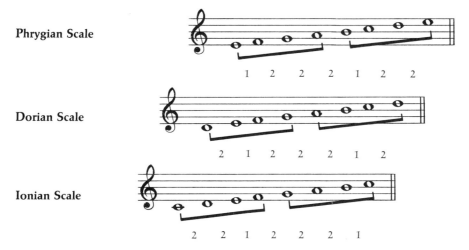

How are the modal scales transposed?

Each of the modal scales in Figure 11-2 can be transposed to other pitch levels either by using signatures or by using the appropriate sharps or flats within the body of the scale. Each modal scale, being an octave segment of the natural diatonic system, remains in the same relative position in a transposed system. In the natural diatonic system, the modal scale on the pitch class E (pc E) is called a **Phrygian scale**. If the system is transposed by means of a signature of one sharp (Figure 11-3), the pc B is then in the same relative position in the transposed system as the

11-3

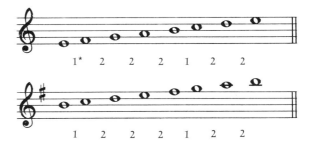

*Intervals expressed in cardinal nomenclature.

pc E was in the natural system. The Phrygian scale is then formed on the pc B. With a signature of two flats (Figure 11-4), the pc D is in the same relative position as the pc E was in the natural

11-4

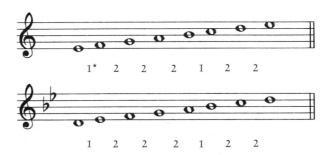

*Intervals expressed in cardinal nomenclature.

system. The Phrygian scale is then formed on the pc D. Realizing that a modal scale maintains the same relative position in a transposed diatonic system, all modal scales are transposable to any pitch level.

What are tetrachords, and how can they be used in the notation of scales?

A **tetrachord** is simply a four-member segment of the natural diatonic system. As scale structures associated with a particular form of pitch organization, they, too, have their origins in the music of ancient Greece. For example, the two four-member diatonic scales descending from the pc E and the pc A (Figure 11-5) were combined (Figure 11-6) to form an extended

11-5

Ancient Greek Diatonic Tetrachords

*Intervals expressed in cardinal nomenclature.

11-6

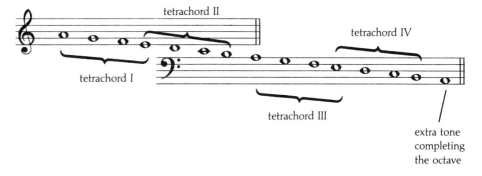

The Greek Greater Perfect System

Note: Each pair of outer tetrachords is joined conjunctly. The pairs of conjunct tetrachords are joined disjunctly.

scale system called the **greater perfect system**. Another descending tetrachord on the pc D and including a B flat was combined with the tetrachords on pc A and pc E to form an extended scale system called the **lesser perfect system** (Figure 11-7). This system is particularly interesting because of the occurrence of both B natural and B flat.

11-7

The Greek Lesser Perfect System

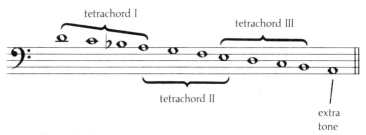

Note: All tetrachords are joined conjunctly.

There are four tetrachords within the natural diatonic system that differ in their intervallic relationships. Because the first four pitches of the Ionian, Dorian, Phrygian, and Lydian scales form the four tetrachords, it has become a practical matter to give the tetrachords the same names. The modal scales (Figure 11-2) are each divided into two tetrachords. In two of the scales (the Lydian and Locrian), the two tetrachords are joined disjunctly by the cardinal interval 1; the remaining scales (Ionian, Dorian, Phrygian, Mixolydian, and Aeolian) contain two tetrachords that are joined disjunctly by the cardinal interval 2. It may be seen, therefore, that the transposition and general notation of modal scales is greatly facilitated by the use of tetrachords. First, however, we must deal with the notation of tetrachords.

In learning to notate any of the four types of tetrachords on any pitch name, it is best to use the intervallic formulas as expressed in cardinal terminology (see Figure 11-8): Ionian 2 2 1, Dorian 2 1 2, Phrygian 1 2 2, and Lydian 2 2 2. The formulas should be used in the manner

W64—68

11-8

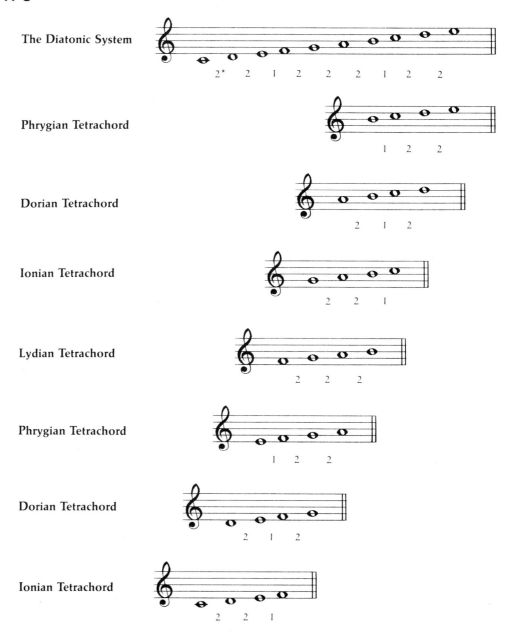

*Intervals expressed in cardinal nomenclature.

shown in Figure 11-9. An Ionian tetrachord constructed on an E flat, for example, would be as follows: E flat is 3; add 2, which makes 5 or F; add 2, which makes 7 or G; add 1, which makes 8 or A flat. As shown in Figure 11-2, the Ionian scale is made up of two Ionian tetrachords joined disjunctly by the interval 2 (i2). By remembering which types of tetrachords are joined disjunctly by which interval (i1 or i2), we can construct any of the modal scales (and of course our major and minor scales) beginning on any notated pitch.   **W69—71**

11-9

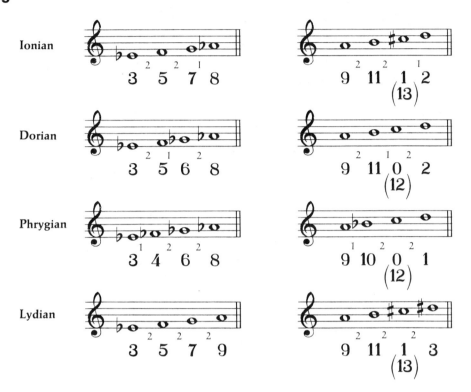

What are hexachords?

The term *hexachord* originated with the scale materials of the medieval theory of Guido of Arezzo during the early eleventh century. Today, **hexachord** refers to any six-member segment of the natural diatonic system or one of its transpositions (Figure 11-10). The

W72—76

11-10

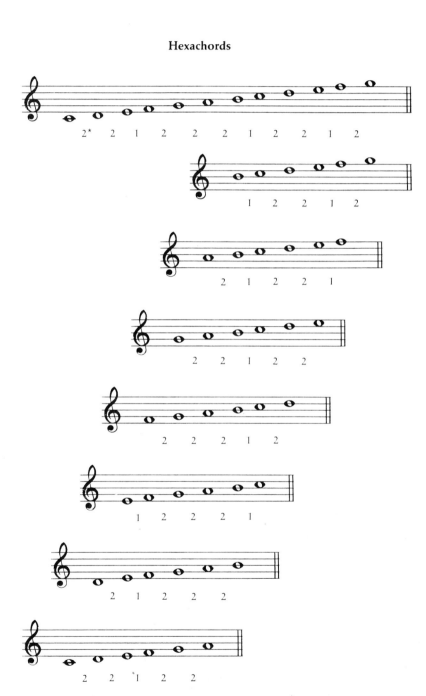

Hexachords

*Intervals expressed in cardinal nomenclature.

hexachords of Guido's theory specifically refer to the hexachords: C D E F G A, G A B C D E, and F G A B♭ C D, which are combined to form the system shown in Figure 11-11. Guido's hexachordal system is interesting for several reasons. First, each of the three hexachords contain the same intervallic relationships (2 2 1 2 2 in cardinal nomenclature). Second, the names of the scale degrees of the hexachords are the same (ut re mi fa sol la). Third, each of the three is identified by a different name: the hexachord on C is called *naturale* ("natural"), the one on G is called *durum* ("hard") because of the B natural, and the one on F is called *molle* ("soft") because of the B flat. All but the first (lowest) hexachord have their beginning pitch in common with a pitch in one or two of the other hexachords. The scale-degree names of the common pitches form the full names of the beginning pitches of each hexachord. For example, the full name of the hexachord on G is *G sol re ut*, and the one on C is *C sol fa ut*. These common pitches (Figure 11-11) are points of crossing over (mutation) from one hexachord to another. The system is purported to have helped the singer remain tonally oriented.

11-11

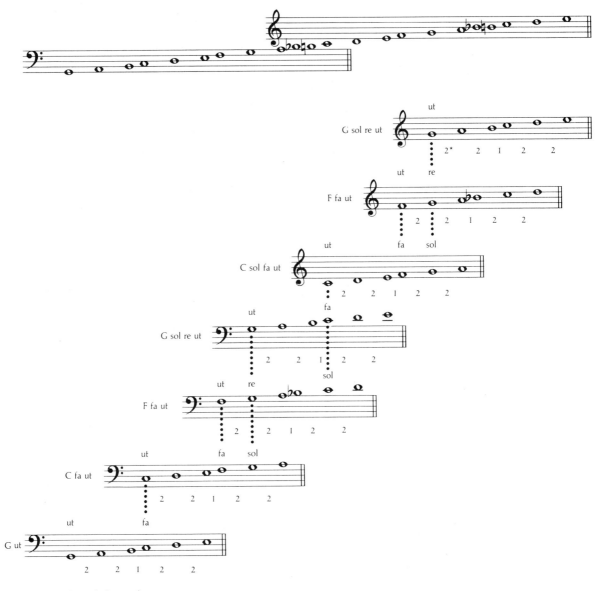

Guido's Hexachords

*Intervals expressed in cardinal nomenclature.

How are major and minor scales related to modal scales?

Except for the particular tonal organizations (structural hierarchies) with which they can be associated, the major scale, as an objective set of pitch relationships, is the same as the Ionian scale, and the minor scale is identical to the Aeolian scale. The change in terminology from modal designations to major and minor can be considered commensurate with the change from modality to the conception of tonality. It should be noted at this point that there is but one major scale and one minor scale in the natural diatonic system, and also only one major and one minor scale in each transposition of the diatonic system (Figure 11-12).

11-12

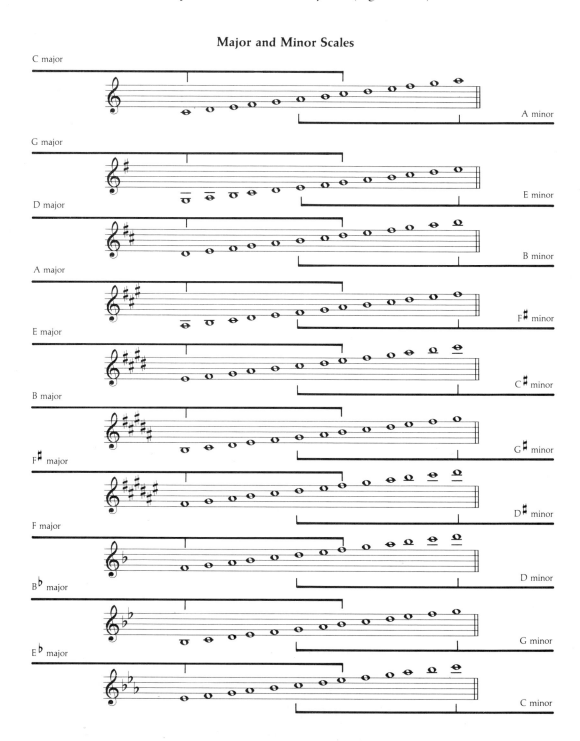

Major and Minor Scales

11-12, *continued*

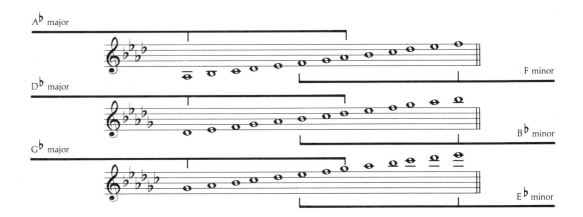

What are the remaining diatonic scale patterns?

After considering all of the diatonic scale patterns for which we have retained usable names from pre-twentieth-century theory, we have only the major, the minor, and the seven modal scales. Using modal scale names for tetrachords is a recently applied convenience with no genuine historical significance. Until we arrive at the study of the dodecaphonic system and pitch-class set nomenclature, we will simply designate the unnamed scale patterns as three-member, five-member, and six-member (hexachord) scales.   **W77–82**

UNIT PROJECT 2

Creating Expressive Diatonic Melody
from Limiting Resources

Introduction

After regarding our own behavior and the behavior of others, it is appropriate to conclude that before we speak, assume a posture, or initiate an action, we are prompted by an attitude or an expressive intent. It is appropriate to conclude also that this, as a process, is a complex, ongoing chain of expressive promptings and actions that continues throughout our waking hours. Each cycle of the process occurs within a time frame we would normally perceive as instantaneous. Reason would tell us, however, that speaking, posturing, or acting without intent or purpose would be irrational and that, no matter how closely an act followed intent, intent must come first.

If we are to make music, it is obvious that we must be prompted by an expressive intent throughout the process of making it. Whatever the expressive prompting of the music we make might be, the results constitute a personal attempt to create something to which others can respond.

In dealing with expression in music as a practical, professional matter, it is unusual for the musician to participate at all levels of music-making; whereas most musicians have experience as performers and listeners, few have had the opportunity to function in the composer's role. It is beneficial for you to experience the role of the composer during your formative years. This and all other creative projects presented throughout the text serve to provide important insights into how the composer, as a role model, thinks and functions. There is no other way to achieve this purpose than by assuming the role and performing the functions. Having some first-hand knowledge, however limited, can go a long way toward rounding out your understanding of the total process of making music.

Description

Using the pitch materials available in (a) the Dorian scale, (b) the Phrygian scale, (c) the Lydian scale, (d) the Mixolydian scale, (e) the Greek lesser perfect system, *or* (f) the hexachordal system of Guido, complete one of the following projects:

OPTION 1. Compose and perform a one- to two-minute musicwork for your instrument and one other instrument available in your class. Pianists should select two single-line instruments or a single-line instrument plus a pitched percussion instrument such as a marimba. Your chief objective should be to produce an expressive musical entity from the limiting pitch resources of the selected scale materials.

OPTION 2. Compose and perform a one- to two-minute musicwork for your voice and a single-line instrument available in your class. The text should be something about which you feel responsive and believe you can express musically. Your chief objective is the same as stated for option 1.

Notes

In this second attempt to produce an expressive musical product to which a listener may respond, your primary consideration should be addressed solely at achieving your expressive intent. This does not mean that you are free to abandon your pitch materials or that you should attempt something beyond your performance capabilities. It simply means that you should not do anything that does not contribute to your primary objective.

In this first attempt at dealing with two melodic lines, remember that they should be related but not the same. Though your expressive intent will govern the texture created by the two melodic lines, the two melodies should complement each other. It is neither necessary nor desirable to have the two melodic lines sounding together more than eighty percent of the time.

As a practical approach to getting into your composition, you might find it helpful to obtain assistance from the sound of your own instrument or voice. If you find it difficult at this stage of your development to **auralize*** (to realize, mentally, the timbre and pitch of your instrument or voice), use your instrument or voice to help you. For example, you will want to know which area of your range and tessitura, as well as that of the second instrument, is best suited to your expressive intent. Also, you must determine whether you can use the natural form of the selected modal scale (or other form of pitch material) or if you must use one of the transpositions. You can make this determination by a little experimental improvising, using a "sonic shape" (a melodic shape in this case) you believe is suited to your expressive purpose.

In music **shape**, or **sonic shape**, denotes the salient physical characteristics of any pattern of sound, from the smallest intelligible configuration to an entire musicwork, the differences being those of complexity and scope. Though this concept of shape may seem liberal beyond any practical use, it is, in fact, rather singular in its intent. In the process of describing the shape of visual objects, we might use such terms as *round, oval, square, curved, oblong,* and *triangular*. None of these terms provides exact dimensions of an object, but each denotes a quality that excludes all or most other qualities of shape. Because intelligibility is a condition required of all sonic shapes, to call something a "sonic shape" is to say that it has a discernible form.

In dealing with shapes in music, we are concerned with the idea of shape as a qualitative, aesthetic control in the construction of a musicwork. The perception and retention of a musical shape (or shapes) is essential to the listener's musical comprehension.

In chapter 9 we discussed and demonstrated the potential for producing shapes by cutting or tearing them from a sheet of paper and then arranging them into meaningful visual patterns. Though we obviously cannot cut or tear up a modal scale or any other organized collection of pitches as we can do with paper, we can extract melodic shapes, each related to the others, and arrange them in whatever intelligible order best satisfies our expressive intent. Improvising and relating, to one another, the possible melodic shapes extracted from the prescribed available pitch materials allows us to choose the pitch materials and melodic shapes that work best for us. The composition, then, will be the result of particular choices and refinements we have made along the way. If this process is used, improvisation is a *means* to an end, not the *end* of your means.

It might be said that this second project in composition, however simple it might appear to be on the surface, serves to allow you to make a personal assessment of your ability to express your feelings and temperament musically. During your lifetime you have cultivated attitudes and expressions, which you project as signals to those around you in almost everything you do. These signals should be embodied in the music you make. Within the limits of your present experience and capabilities, try to make your music a projection of yourself rather than of something drawn from your musical memory.

*Term is attributed to Morris Knight, Jr.

12 Chord Patterns in the Diatonic System

What is a chord?

A **chord**, or **chordal construct**, is three or more simultaneously sounding pitches that act as an entity to serve a singular musical purpose. There are a number of chord types. The first types we will consider are those classified as "tertian" triads.

What is a "tertian" triad?

Tertian, meaning "every other one," refers to chords that are notated using "every other degree" of the staff. A **tertian triad** is a chord having three pitch-name members, the *root*, the *third*, and the *fifth* (Figure 12-1a).

12-1

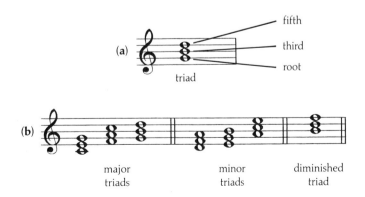

What tertian triads exist in the natural diatonic system?

Within the natural diatonic system there are three types of tertian triads (henceforth referred to as *triads*): (1) the *major* triad, (2) the *minor* triad, and (3) the *diminished* triad. As shown in Figure 12-1b, there are three major triads (constructed on C, F, and G), three minor triads (constructed on D, E, and A), and one diminished triad constructed on B. The notation of the three types of triads is facilitated by the use of cardinal nomenclature. In effect, the notation of a triad is simply an extension of the procedures used in notating intervals.

Figure 12-2 shows the three types of triads in the natural diatonic system. It also shows the two approaches to using intervallic relationships that are useful in learning to notate the triads in the natural and transposed diatonic systems. What can be said of the major triad constructed on the pitch-name C shown in Figures 12-2a and d can also be said of the major triads constructed on the pitch-names F and G. Also, what can be said of the minor triad constructed on the pitch-name D shown in Figures 12-2b and e can also be said of the minor triads constructed on the pitch-names E and A. The one diminished triad of the natural diatonic system is shown in parts c and f of the figure.

12-2

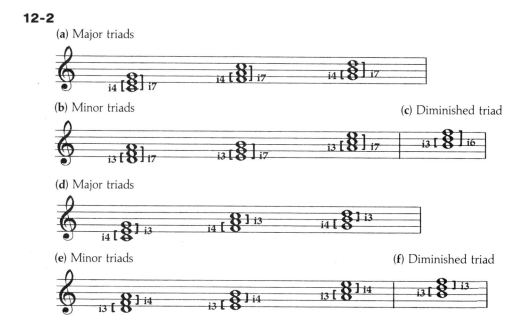

(a) Major triads

(b) Minor triads   (c) Diminished triad

(d) Major triads

(e) Minor triads   (f) Diminished triad

How can we notate triads from the root only?

The major triad is constructed by notating an i4 [+ 3 (M3)] and an i7 (P5) above the notated pitch upon which the triad is to be constructed (Figure 12-3a). To construct a major triad on the notated root D flat (see Figure 12-3b), we begin with p1 (pc D flat) and add i4 [+ 3 (M3)] to produce p5 (pc F) to complete step 1. Beginning with p1 (pc D flat) again, we add i7 (P5) to produce p8 (pc A flat) to complete step 2 in the process of notating the D-flat major triad.

Referring to Figure 12-3, the minor triad is constructed by notating an i3 [− 3 (m3)] and an i7 (P5) above the notated pitch upon which the triad is to be constructed. If a minor triad is to be constructed on the notated root E flat, we begin with p3 (pc E flat) and add i3 [− 3 (m3)] to produce p6 (pc G flat) to complete step 1. Beginning again with p3 (pc E flat), we add i7 (P5) to produce p10 (pc B flat) to complete step 2 in the process of notating the E-flat minor triad. The same procedure may be used to construct a diminished triad on the notated root D: p2 (pc D) plus i3 [− 3 (m3)] produces p5 (pc F); p2 (pc D) plus i6 [5° (d5)] produces p8 (pc A flat) to complete the notation of the D diminished triad.

12-3

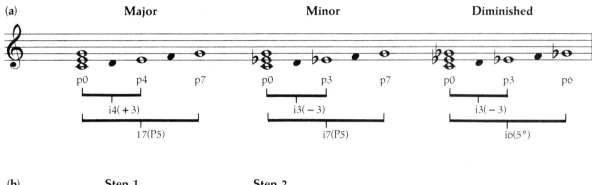

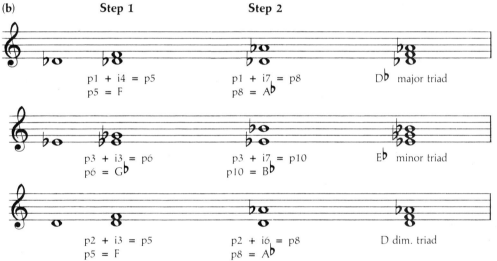

How do we notate triads by consecutive thirds?

Refer to Figure 12-4. Rather than notate a 3rd and 5th above a given root as in Figure 12-3, we construct the triad by notating two consecutive thirds. This procedure is similar to the one used in notating tetrachords in chapter 2 (adding successive notated pitches by an interval formula such as 2, 2, 1). The interval formulas for the triads of the natural diatonic system are i4 and i3 for the major triad, i3 and i4 for the minor triad, and i3 and i3 for the diminished triad

(Figure 12-4a). The interval formulas can be simplified to read: (4,3), (3,4), and (3,3). In notating the A-flat major triad, we begin with p8 (pc A flat) and add i4 (+3) to produce p12, which reduces to p0 (pc C) to complete step 1. In step 2 we begin with p0 (pc C) and add i3 (−3) to produce p3 (pc E flat), which completes the A-flat major triad. To construct the F minor triad, we begin with p5 (pc F) and add i3 (−3) to produce p8 (pc A flat) to complete step 1. In step 2 we begin with p8 (pc A flat) and add i4 (+3) to produce p12, which reduces to p0 (pc C) to complete the triad. To construct the diminished triad on C sharp, we begin with p1 (pc C sharp) and add i3 (−3) to produce p4 (pc E) in step 1. In step 2 we begin with p4 (pc E) and add i3 (−3) to produce p7 (pc G) to complete the diminished triad. **W83—88**

12-4

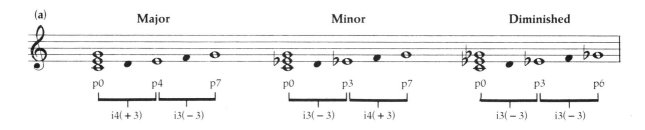

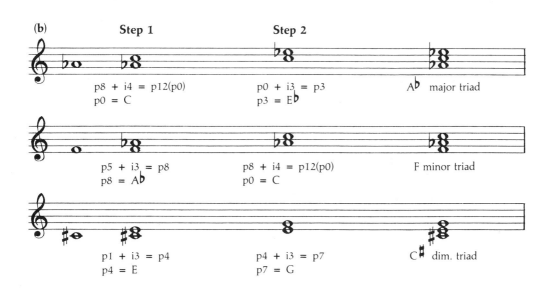

What is a seventh chord?

A **seventh (7th) chord** is a four-member tertian chord formed by adding a fourth member, which is regarded as either an interval of a 7th above the root of a triad or as an interval of a 3rd above the fifth of a triad. Within the natural diatonic system there are four types of 7th chords (Figure 12-5). Regardless of how we choose to learn the notation of seventh chords, the nomenclature for designating seventh chords is the same. The **major seventh chord** is made up of a major triad with an i11 [+7 (M7)] above the root of the triad. Because both the triad and seventh are "major," the nomenclature M⁷ is sufficient. The major triad with an i10 [−7 (m7)] above the root forms a **major-minor seventh chord**, which is identified as Mm⁷. A minor triad with an i10 [−7 (m7)] above the root forms a **minor seventh chord**, which is identified by the nomenclature m⁷. The **diminished-minor seventh chord** is the last of the seventh chords in the diatonic system. Identified by the nomenclature dm⁷, it is formed by adding an i10 [−7 (m7)] above the root of a diminished triad.

12-5

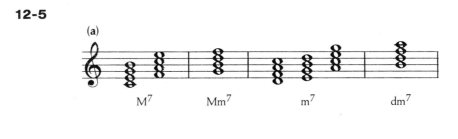

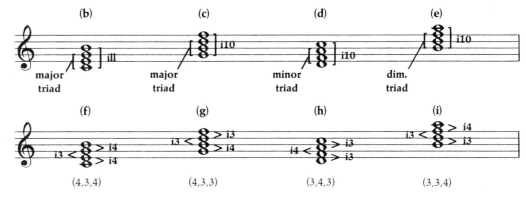

(4,3,4)   (4,3,3)   (3,4,3)   (3,3,4)

Using the successive-thirds approach to notating seventh chords, the interval formula for the major seventh chord is (4,3,4); the formula for the major-minor seventh chord is (4,3,3); the formula for the minor seventh chord is (3,4,3); the formula for the diminished-minor seventh chord is (3,3,4). **W89—91**

What is a harmonic inversion?

The **harmonic inversion** of any simultaneously sounding collection of two or more pitches when notated within the span of an octave, is a musical application of a cyclic permutation. A **cyclic permutation** is achieved by placing the first element of two or more elements to the end of the series and then repeating the process as many times as there are elements. For example, a cyclic permutation of a b c would yield: a b c, b c a, and c a b.

The harmonic inversion of the harmonic interval, i4 [+ 3 (M3)] (see Figure 12-6) is i8 [− 6 (m6)]. Inverting the major triad harmonically—that is, *permuting* it—yields: the root position F A C, the first inversion A C F, and the second inversion C F A. **W92—93**

12-6

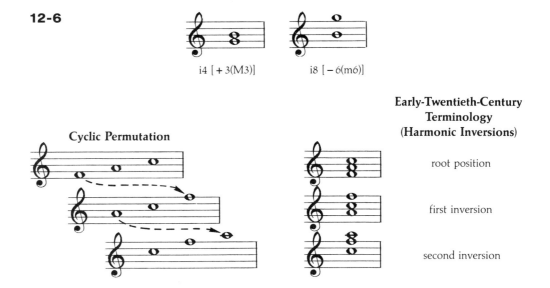

i4 [+ 3(M3)]   i8 [− 6(m6)]

Cyclic Permutation

Early-Twentieth-Century Terminology (Harmonic Inversions)

root position

first inversion

second inversion

The process for producing the harmonic inversion of a seventh chord is the same as it is for a triad. Because the seventh chord has four members, however, there is one more inversion than with the triad (Figure 12-7). The root position of the D-minor seventh chord is D F A C, the first inversion is F A C D, the second inversion is A C D F, and the third inversion is C D F A.

W94

12-7

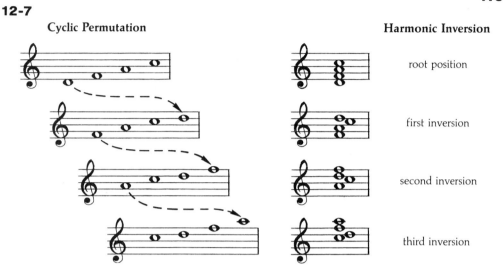

How are inversions determined in the open notation of chords?

The **open notation**, or **open position**, of a triad or seventh chord is a notation in which the pitches of the chord exceed the span of an octave. As we see in Figures 12-6 and 12-7, in the first inversion of triads and seventh chords, the 3rd of the chord is the lowest notated pitch. In the second inversion of triads and seventh chords, the 5th of the chord is the lowest notated pitch. In the third inversion of the seventh chord, the lowest notated pitch is the 7th of the chord. The importance of this observation is that, when triads and seventh chords are notated so as to exceed the span of an octave, the lowest notated pitch determines the inversion (Figure 12-8).   **W95—96**

12-8

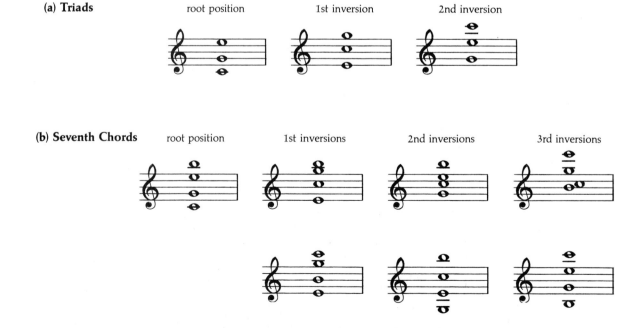

What is a quartal triad?

The term *quartal* triad may seem a contradiction, because we have associated the term *triad* with the tertian triad for so long. However, the newer materials of the twentieth century have forced the expansion of the concept of triad to include any collection of three notated pitches. A **quartal triad** is a three-member chord notated with an interval of a fourth (an i5 or i6) and an interval of a seventh (an i10 or i11) above a given notated pitch (Figure 12-9). A quartal triad can be constructed on each notated pitch of the natural or transposed diatonic system. Just as *tertian* refers to the idea of constructing chords in thirds, *quartal* refers to the idea of constructing chords in fourths. Therefore, quartal triads may be notated by using the interval formula shown below each notated chord in Figure 12-9: (5,6), (5,5), and (6,5). Though quartal triads have been possible since the diatonic system came to be used, they were not treated as identifiable chordal structures until the early part of the twentieth century.   **W97**

12-9

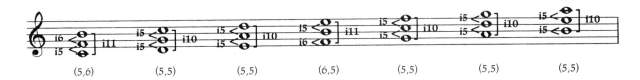

(5,6)   (5,5)   (5,5)   (6,5)   (5,5)   (5,5)   (5,5)

Quartal triads may be permuted in the same manner as tertian triads; however, such permutations are not referred to as *inversions*. The permutation of a quartal triad is shown in Figure 12-10a. Figure 12-10b shows notations of permutations that exceed the span of an octave. It is interesting to note that the permutations in Figure 12-10 are the six possible permutations found in a linear permutation, a fact that is also true of the six permutations of tertian triads shown in Figure 12-6 and 12-7. A **linear permutation** provides all of the possible orderings of a given number of items. For example, the linear permutation of a b c yields: a b c, b c a, c a b, a c b, b a c, and c b a. The number of permutations in a linear permutation may be figured in the following manner: three items, $1 \times 2 \times 3 = 6$; four items, $1 \times 2 \times 3 \times 4 = 24$. It is interesting to note also that quartal triads do not bear such descriptors as *major* or *minor*. The identification of quartal triads involves the use of a nomenclature to be introduced in another chapter.   **W98**

12-10

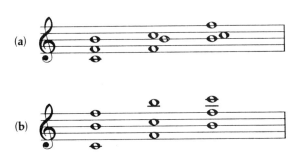

UNIT PROJECT 3

Creating Expressive Colors with Chordal Constructs

Introduction

The potential for musical expression in the color of chordal constructs and their relationships to each other is truly unlimited. Until the early twentieth century, however, the coloristic application of chordal constructs was accomplished within the limiting context of harmonic grammar. Using the coloristic qualities of chords for their own sake as a functional aspect of musical organization is primarily a twentieth-century formalizing principle.

Similar to the manipulation of colors in painting, the manipulation of colors to form interesting expressive relationships in music is an appropriate way of being introduced to the creative application of chordal constructs. The freedom to concentrate on achieving a particular expressive intent without having to deal with the burden of a sophisticated harmonic language allows us to become familiar with the subtleties of color that exist between the linear permutations (inversions and voicings) of particular types of triads.

Description

Produce a thirty- to ninety-second musicwork for one of the following: (1) three single-line instruments available in the class, (2) a marimba or similar mallet instrument with which three mallets are used, *or* (3) three voices with a common text. The music produced should be cast entirely in a homophonic texture using one of three sets of materials and procedures:

1. Use alternating major and minor triads in root position and first inversion as desired and voiced in closed and open position as needed. The music need not be confined to one version of the diatonic system; it is desirable that you select triads from any diatonic system for their individual colors and coloristic relationships to each other. See Figure 12-11.

12-11

* Sounds as notated

2. Use quartal triads (all three types) in any of the permutations or voicings needed. The music need not be confined to one version of the diatonic system; select quartal triads from any diatonic system for their individual colors and coloristic relationships to each other. See Figure 12-12.

12-12

* Sounds as notated

3. Use major triads in root position and first inversion in closed or open position as needed along with quartal triads in any permutation and voicing needed. The music need not be confined to one version of the diatonic system; select major triads and quartal triads from any diatonic systems. See Figure 12-13.

12-13

* Sounds as notated

Notes

If you have never experimented with chordal relationships of the kind suggested here, perhaps your initial approach should be to sit at a piano and "play around" with various permutations of major, minor, and quartal triads and with various triadic relationships. Start with one triad and follow it with one of a different inversion and voicing. Repeat this process (starting on the same triad), moving to a different triad each time. This "what if?" process (what if I follow this version of triad X with that version of triad Y) is necessary for building familiarity with the resources available to you. Continue the process with three, four, and more chordal constructs, all the while concentrating on your perception of the expressive quality of each set of relationships.

Once you have a feel for the expressive qualities of the triadic types and relationships, relate and translate these qualities to the instrumental or vocal timbres to be used. At the same time, concentrate on narrowing the available resources to those that will contribute to the expressive intent that has been forming in your mind in your experimenting. At this point, you should be ready to begin your composition.

Obviously, other factors will contribute to the music you are making—factors such as a leading melodic voice, rhythmic shapes, dynamics, articulations, and timbre. However, the colors and coloristic relationships of triads are to be the primary shaping forces of the music you produce for this project.

Finally, produce a score and set of parts for the performing instrumentalists (singers will use a vocal score). The score should be notated in sounding pitch. Performance parts for transposing instruments must, of course, be properly transposed.

Your project must be performed and evaluated. Your instructor will decide if the music is to be conducted. You should recognize, however, that the movements you make in the act of conducting help you cultivate your capacity to feel and convey the expressive quality of the musicwork. Of course, you can accomplish this in an out-of-class rehearsal prior to the performance.

13 | Pattern Making in the Temporal Domain

What is time?

Because of the particular ways people speak about it, "time" is typically regarded as though it were a commodity having substance. Time is thought of as a scarce resource that can be used wisely or wasted, as something that can be borrowed and returned, as something that can be extended or shortened, and as something that is gone forever after it has been used. Time, of course, is not a commodity; nor is it a raw material out of which something can be made. **Time** is a domain, the realm within which all things exist and function.

Whether it is referred to as a domain, a realm, a frame, a dimension, a medium, or whatever, time cannot, simply in and of itself, be perceived. Time is not a material. It has neither shape nor measurable dimensions; it *is* a dimension. Time has nothing about it that can stimulate our senses; in short, time is not directly perceivable as time. Time is perceivable only in terms of the events that occur within it. Our perception of any object or occurrence that forms a part of a continuum of events gives definition to time.

What is our primary concern about time in music?

In chapter 11 our primary concern was with the scale patterns within the natural diatonic system and their usefulness in the making of music. Our primary concern in this chapter will be with the formation of durational patterns and patterned occurrences of tones and other sonorous events. Obviously, we could not produce melodic patterns from the materials of the diatonic system without shaping them temporally. Nor could temporal patterns be present in a musicwork without the context of patterned pitch relationships. To deal with the events in music as they relate to each other in time, we must understand how temporal relationships are expressed in modern conventional notation.

What are the basic tenets of temporal notation?

The temporal values expressed in modern conventional notation are represented by a fundamental system of proportions based on a simple two-to-one ratio. This ratio functions within a wide range of tempos and it can be modified to achieve complex temporal divisions.

The system makes use of two different but functionally related kinds of notational symbols: (1) the **measure signature** (called the "meter" signature in older music), which provides the note-value content of the measure, and (2) symbols that represent the possible note-value combinations and divisions of sounds and silences within the measure.

The term *measure signature* is by no means universally used today. The lag time in the popular acceptance of new terminology among musicians is understandably long. A change of any sort must be initiated by someone, and if a change becomes widely accepted it generally is only after a long period of time. We must press on, however, to new terms and understandings when it is no longer possible to adapt existing nomenclature to new musical relationships.

The concept of measure signature is necessary. The term *meter signature* is inappropriate when signature changes within a movement of a musicwork require us to accept varying metric units. In what must now be considered a hasty and implausible reaction to the first application of changing signatures, "release from the 'tyranny' of the barline" was the common reason given for the changes; and the term *mixed meter* was the common and paradoxical nomenclature applied to the practice. Considering the function of meter, in any sense of the word, reason dictates that, except for metric modulation, there can be but one metric unit in a movement of a musicwork regardless of the number of signature changes. Inherent in the concept of measure signature is the understanding that the metric unit is simply an underlying, unifying note value that is *related to* but not directly *expressed by* the measure signatures used. For example, in a series of changing measure signatures such as those used in the melodic excerpt from Stravinsky's *L'histoire du Soldat* (Figure 13-1), it is appropriate, indeed necessary, to regard the sixteenth-note value as the underlying metric unit because it is the largest note value that can serve as a common denominator for all of the measures—$\frac{3}{8}$, $\frac{2}{4}$, $\frac{3}{8}$, $\frac{2}{4}$, $\frac{3}{16}$, and $\frac{2}{4}$.

13-1

L'histoire du Soldat, Marche triomphale du Diable

Igor Stravinsky

In the notation of temporal values, measure signatures can express simple beat units, compound beat units, or a combination of simple and compound beat units (Figure 13-2). Divisions within the beat unit, the metric unit, or the measure can be simple divisions based on a ratio of 2:1; complex divisions based on ratios of 3:1, 5:1, 6:1, 7:1, and others that are usable; or combinations of simple and complex divisions.

13-2

THE NOTATION OF TEMPORAL VALUES

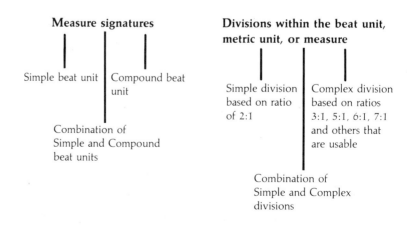

Measure signatures

Simple beat unit | Compound beat unit

Combination of Simple and Compound beat units

Divisions within the beat unit, metric unit, or measure

Simple division based on ratio of 2:1 | Complex division based on ratios 3:1, 5:1, 6:1, 7:1 and others that are usable

Combination of Simple and Complex divisions

The simple beat units of the measure signatures in Figure 13-3 are divisible by two, the result in each case being two notes (or rests) of the next-smaller value equaling the beat unit. The

13-3

MEASURE SIGNATURES: SIMPLE BEAT DIVISIONS													
Beats per Measure												Metric Unit	Beat Unit
1	2	3	4	5	6	7	8	9	10	11	12		
$\frac{1}{16}$	$\frac{2}{16}$	$\frac{3}{16}$	$\frac{4}{16}$	$\frac{5}{16}$	$\frac{6}{16}$	$\frac{7}{16}$	$\frac{8}{16}$	$\frac{9}{16}$	$\frac{10}{16}$	$\frac{11}{16}$	$\frac{12}{16}$	♬	♬
$\frac{1}{8}$	$\frac{2}{8}$	$\frac{3}{8}$	$\frac{4}{8}$	$\frac{5}{8}$	$\frac{6}{8}$	$\frac{7}{8}$	$\frac{8}{8}$	$\frac{9}{8}$	$\frac{10}{8}$	$\frac{11}{8}$	$\frac{12}{8}$	♪	♪
$\frac{1}{4}$	$\frac{2}{4}$	$\frac{3}{4}$	$\frac{4}{4}$	$\frac{5}{4}$	$\frac{6}{4}$	$\frac{7}{4}$	$\frac{8}{4}$	$\frac{9}{4}$	$\frac{10}{4}$	$\frac{11}{4}$	$\frac{12}{4}$	♩	♩
$\frac{1}{2}$	$\frac{2}{2}$	$\frac{3}{2}$	$\frac{4}{2}$									𝅗𝅥	𝅗𝅥
	¢											𝅗𝅥	𝅗𝅥
			$\frac{2}{4}$									♩	♪
			C									♩	♩
$\frac{2}{4}$	$\frac{4}{4}$											♩	𝅗𝅥
$\frac{2}{8}$	$\frac{4}{8}$											♪	♩

compound beat units of the measure signatures in Figure 13-4 are dotted note values, which are divisible by three. In each case, three notes (or rests) of the next-smaller value equal the beat

13-4

MEASURE SIGNATURES: COMPOUND BEAT DIVISIONS					
Beats per Measure				Metric Unit	Beat Unit
1	2	3	4		
$\frac{3}{16}$	$\frac{6}{16}$	$\frac{9}{16}$	$\frac{12}{16}$	♬	♪.
$\frac{3}{8}$	$\frac{6}{8}$	$\frac{9}{8}$	$\frac{12}{8}$	♪	♩.
$\frac{3}{4}$	$\frac{6}{4}$	$\frac{9}{4}$	$\frac{12}{4}$	♩	𝅗𝅥.

unit. The measure signatures shown in Figure 13-5 result from combining simple and compound beat units.

13-5

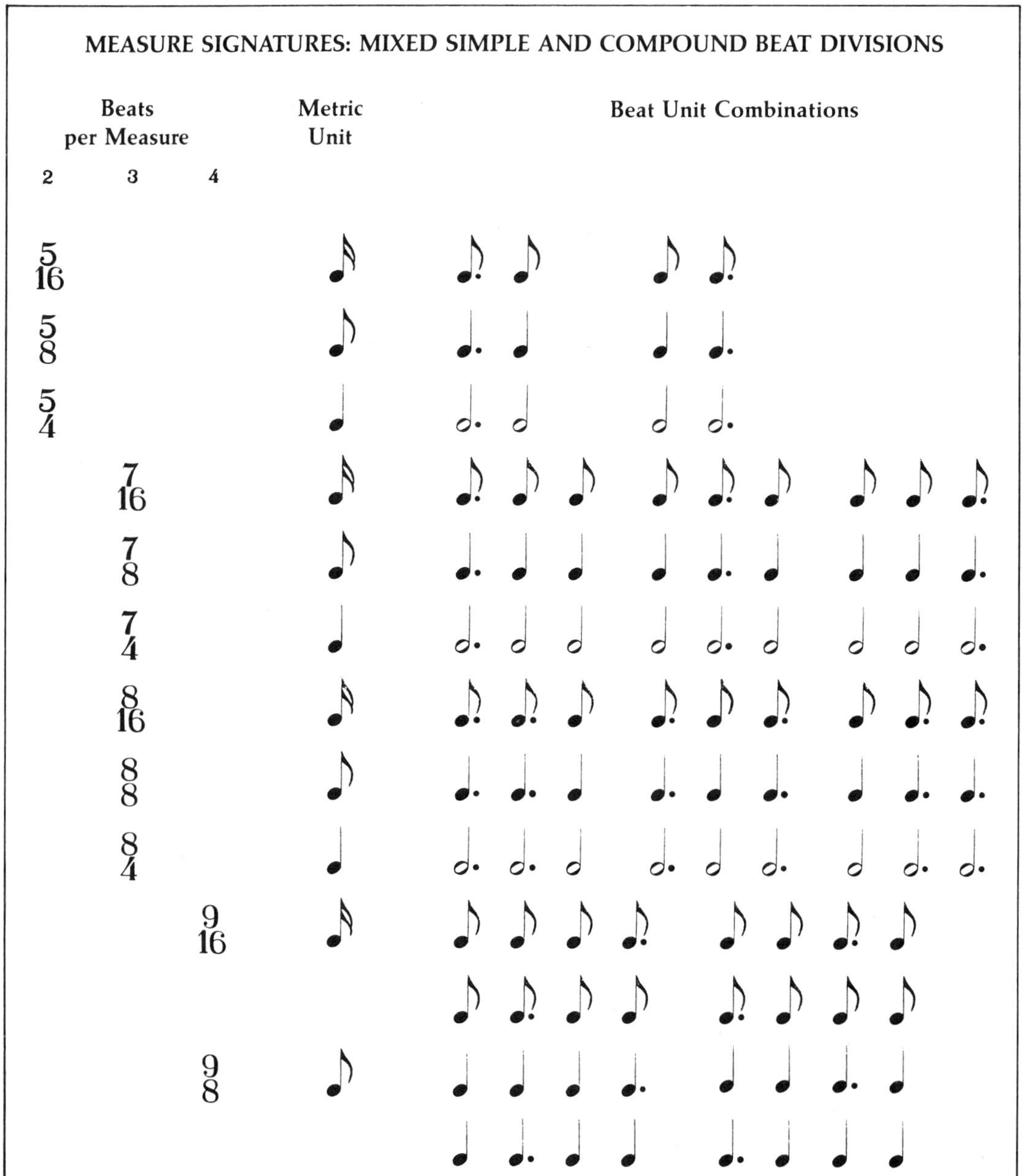

How do we distinguish measure signatures from meter signatures?

If, as in the melodic line from Benjamin Britten's *Les Illuminations* shown in Figure 13-6, the signatures used in a musicwork are $\frac{2}{4}$, $\frac{3}{4}$, and $\frac{5}{4}$, the metric unit is the quarter-note value.

13-6

Les Illuminations, Op. 18, V. *Marine*

Benjamin Britten

Though three different signatures are used, they can be considered meter signatures just as well as measure signatures. If, on the other hand, the signatures in a musicwork are $\frac{3}{8}$, $\frac{3}{4}$, $\frac{4}{4}$, and $\frac{3}{2}$, as they are in the flute line from Stravinsky's Octet for Wind Instruments shown in Figure 13-7, the metric unit is the eighth-note value. In this case, the signatures must be considered *measure* signatures, because the eighth note is the largest value that can serve as the common denomina-

13-7

from Octet for Wind Instruments (1952 version), Variation E

Igor Stravinsky

tor. If, as in the Stravinsky example in Figure 13-8, the signatures used are $\frac{3}{16}$, $\frac{2}{8}$, $\frac{3}{8}$, $\frac{2}{4}$, and $\frac{3}{4}$, the metric unit is the sixteenth-note value, which makes these signatures measure signatures. Because the term *measure signature* can serve every purpose, including those for which *meter signature* is used, it is both convenient and appropriate to use *measure signature* for all occasions.

13-8

from Octet for Wind Instruments (1952 version), Sinfonia

Igor Stravinsky

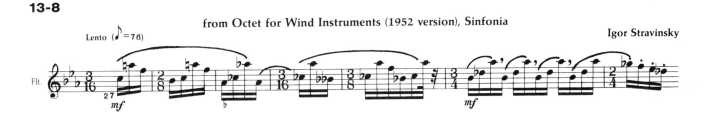

How are meter signatures related to tempo?

We should not assume that after the concepts of measure, metric unit, and beat unit became established, one, uniformly conventional interpretation of the relationship of meter to tempo prevailed. A comparison of two differing practices illustrates this point.

The Renaissance pavane (a slow, dignified, generally solemn dance) may, for the sake of comparison, be said to resemble in character and tempo Baroque slow movements and the slow movements of some eighteenth- and early-nineteenth-century sonatas and symphonic works. Most typically, the Renaissance pavane is notated in a slow, duple or triple meter having meter signatures that translate to a present-day $\frac{2}{2}$ or $\frac{3}{2}$ with slow half notes as beat units. In contrast to this, we typically find that Baroque slow movements and the slow movements of eighteenth- and early-nineteenth-century musicworks have varying meter signatures such as $\frac{4}{16}$, $\frac{4}{8}$, $\frac{3}{8}$, $\frac{6}{8}$, and $\frac{2}{4}$, all of which have beat units in note values as small as a sixteenth or eighth note (Figure 13-9).

13-9

To complete this comparison, the Baroque gigue (a quick dance) or giga (a much quicker dance than the gigue) may be said to resemble the Beethoven scherzo. The gigue and giga are generally notated in a fast $\frac{6}{8}$, which indicates a beat unit with a dotted-quarter-note value. The Beethoven scherzo, notated in $\frac{3}{4}$, has a beat unit of a dotted-half-note value (Figure 13-10). Other examples could further illustrate an interesting dichotomy between meter signatures and tempo. The purpose here, however, is simply to show that neither meter signature nor tempo is the consequence of the other. **W99—101**

13-10

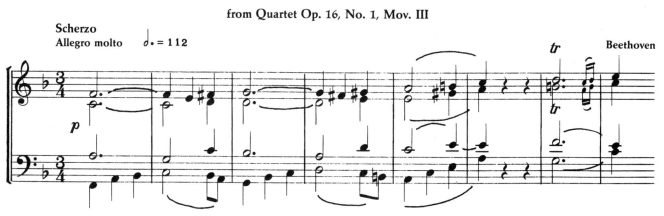

What are metric and nonmetric divisions in modern conventional notation?

In modern conventional notation, if the divisions in the notation of measures, beat units, or beat-unit divisions are in agreement with the basic metric unit and its normal 2:1 divisions, they are considered **metric divisions**. If the divisions are not in agreement at any level of consideration, they are considered **nonmetric divisions**. For example, the simple division of a half-note value into two quarter-note values is a metric division, as are further divisions of the quarter-note value into successively smaller note values (Figure 13-11a). The division of the half-note value into three quarter-note values is a nonmetric division, and it is identified

13-11

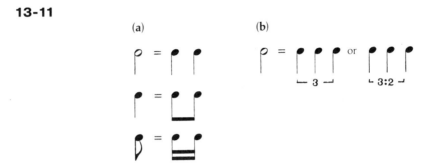

in notation by a 3 or 3:2 placed above or below the appropriate notes with a bracket (Figure 13-11b). Similar nonmetric divisions and the manner of notating them are shown in Figure 13-12.

13-12

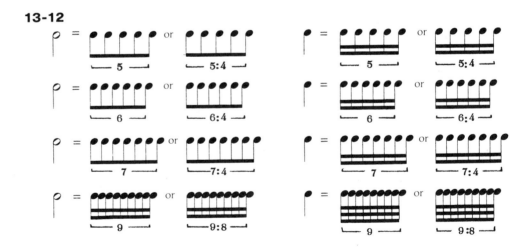

The division of a dotted-quarter-note value, a compound beat unit, is three eighth-note values; this is a metric division (Figure 13-13a). Successive divisions of a compound beat unit, unless otherwise indicated, would be simple 2:1 metric divisions (Figure 13-13a). The division of the dotted quarter-note value into four eighth-note values exemplifies a nonmetric division; it is identified in notation by a 4 or 4:3 placed above or below the appropriate notes with a bracket (Figure 13-13b).   **W102—103**

13-13

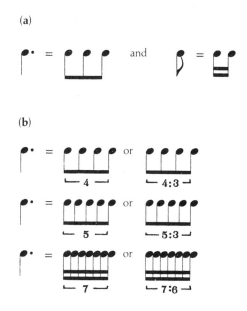

(a)

(b)

Are there limits in organizing the contents of a measure?

Limitations in organizing the contents of a measure are more a matter of imagination, aesthetic judgment, and formal relevance than of the technical capacity of composers or the availability of notational symbols. It is possible, within the context of measured music, to produce any organization of durational values a composer might desire. This is accomplished most simply by using combinations and multiples of twos and threes of particular note values. The technical framework for expressing such durational relationships consists of the metric and nonmetric divisions made possible by conventional notation and the available measure signatures. Perhaps the one limitation that overrides the composer's desires and the abundant symbols available in measured notation is the mental and technical capacity of the performer in the realization of music. It is much easier to specify a performance task than to achieve it. A portion of the alto flute line taken from Stravinsky's *Le sacre du printemps* illustrates a variety of combinations of metric and nonmetric divisions of the metric unit; see Figure 13-14.

13-14

Le sacre du Printemps, Introduction

Igor Stravinsky

Though measure signatures retain some conceptual vestiges of the "beat" and "metric" unit meanings characteristic of meter signatures, to many present-day composers, measure signatures serve a function having more to do with the organizing, note-value content of a measure, a concept more related to structure in music. The measure may serve a formalizing function similar to that of the familiar "phrase structuring" of music—that is, a kind of micro structure that imitates the function of phrase structure in eighteenth- and nineteenth-century music. In some twentieth-century music, this micro structure has replaced phrase structure entirely; and structures of a measure or less in size can serve a structural function similar to that of a phrase. For example, the excerpt from a musicwork by Anton Webern in Figure 13-15 contains brief melodic configurations that provide the same degree of "sensory closure" provided by the phrase structures commonly found in the music of previous and many present-day composers.

13-15

from Konzert, Op. 24, Mov. I

Anton Webern

What is metric modulation?

Metric modulation is the use of metric and nonmetric divisions of a note value to establish a new temporal relationship between measures or sections of a musicwork for the purpose of changing the tempo or the basic metric unit. In Figure 13-16a, for example, the dotted-quarter-note value of the first measure is shown, by the indicator over the barline, to be equal to the quarter-note value in the second measure. In Figure 13-16b, however, the absence of an instruction indicates that the eighth-note has the same duration in both measures. Explained another way, the beat units in (a) have the same duration, but the eighth-note values differ in duration. In (b), the beat units of the two measures differ, but the eighth-note values

13-16

are the same. The second of these two procedures is the more prominent convention when dealing with changing measure signatures. The first procedure, though less common, is intended both as a means of alternating simple and compound beat units and as a means of achieving abrupt and specifically calculated changes in temporal relationships. Examples of metric modulation from String Quartet No. 2 by Elliott Carter, one of the more practiced of composers using the technique, and from Leon Kirchner's Music for Orchestra are shown in Figure 13-17.

13-17

(a)

from String Quartet No. 2, 2nd corr. (1962)

Elliott Carter

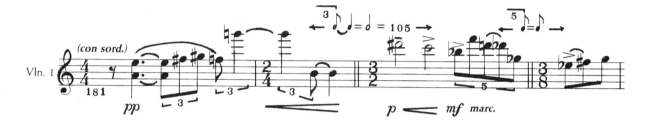

(b)

from Music for Orchestra (1969)

Leon Kirchner

What is the cyclic permutation of a durational pattern?

A **cyclic permutation** is the moving of the first item of a series to the end of the series and repeating the process until all combinations are revealed. The idea can be illustrated with the use of numerals: 1 2 3 4, 2 3 4 1, 3 4 1 2, and then 4 1 2 3. Cyclic permutations of durational patterns is one way the pitch content of music can be organized into intelligible musical structures. For example, consider the simple melodic line in Figure 13-18. Except for the final whole note, the line is made up of permutations of the original half-note–quarter-note–quarter-note pattern.

13-18

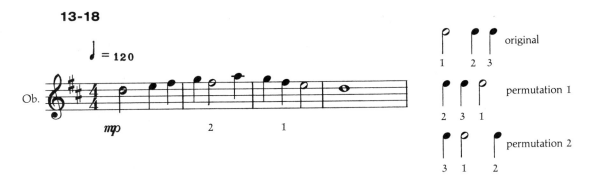

If we examine the temporal pattern in the last half of the ninth and the tenth and eleventh measures of a familiar bugle call (Figure 13-19), we see the pattern shown in Figure

13-19

13-20a. Permuting this pattern (Figure 13-20b), we find that permutation 4 has the durational pattern of measure twelve of the bugle call.

13-20

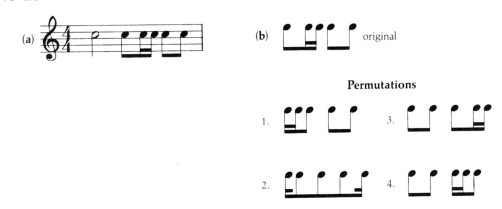

Figure 13-21 shows the cyclic permutations of ten simple durational patterns. They are presented without measure signatures because they need not coincide with measures. The

13-21

second of these occurs as part of a measure in Figure 13-22a; and the eighth one spans more than a measure in Figure 13-22b.

13-22

It is possible, as shown in Figure 13-22, to produce a melodic line having durational patterns produced by a series of permutations. To say "possible," however, is not to say "desirable" or "interesting"; it is just "possible." Whether or not such a melodic line proves to be more than just "possible" involves other factors as well. The unfolding of any line sets up tonal expectations that must be compatible, but not necessarily coincidental, with the expected temporal goals. Just as the choice of words, voice inflection, and rhythmic flow of speech are combined to create comprehensible language, pitch patterns, durational patterns, and appropriate tonal and rhythmic inflections must all work together to form intelligible music. Intelligible music cannot happen unless pitch patterns and durational patterns unfold intuitively and form the kinds of sonic structures we can realize intelligibly in performance. It is quite possible to use elements of a cyclic permutation that are conceived intuitively during the course of music making. The original pattern of item 6 of Figure 13-21 along with its first permuted pattern is a durational pattern that would very likely come about intuitively during the formation of a simple melody such as the one in Figure 13-23.

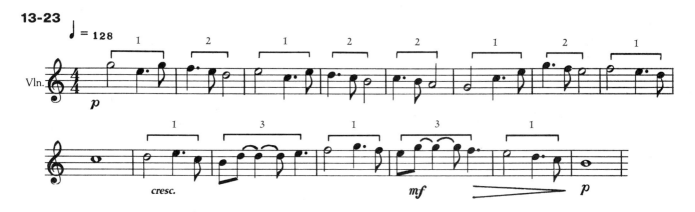

Obviously, we cannot work from preconceived patterns and then hope that the results will, by some magic, become embued with some degree of musical sense. We must begin with a "feel" for musical sense, a feel that is generated by an expressive intent. If this aspect of the process is substantial, we will have less trouble in giving the music substance and form by means of pitch and durational patterns. Whether or not these patterns are permuted or just partially the result of permutation depends on whether permutation appears intuitively as the best means of achieving the desired result. **W104**

14 Enharmonic Notation of Intervals

What is the enharmonic notation of an interval?

In considering the enharmonic notation of intervals, we must first recognize that every possible relationship between any two pitches can be notated so as to fit within either the natural diatonic system or one of its transpositions. However, when more than two pitches are sounding (either consecutively or simultaneously) it is not always possible to notate all of them so as to form diatonic relationships. In such situations the notated relationships may necessitate the **enharmonic notation** of intervals. In the natural diatonic system there is one built-in enharmonic notation of a given pitch relationship: the relationship between pc5 and pc11. This relationship can be notated as either a 4^+ (A4) or a 5° (d5). For each of the other diatonic intervals, there is an enharmonic notation (Figure 14-1).

Perhaps the most common enharmonic notation of a pitch relationship is the result of raising the seventh scale degree in the minor mode of a given key to create what is called the **harmonic minor scale**. The minor scales shown in Figure 11-12 are **natural minor scales**. The harmonic minor scale is essentially a theoretical construct resulting from an alteration of the natural minor scale. The **melodic minor scale**—the result of raising both the 6th and 7th degrees in the minor mode of a given key—also is a theoretical construct not contained in the diatonic system. The harmonic and melodic minor scales and the intervallic relationships between the altered scale degrees and the remaining scale degrees are shown in Figure 14-2.

W105—106

14-1

INTERVAL CLASS	ORDINAL NOMENCLATURE			CARDINAL NOMENCLATURE
	Diminished Intervals	Diatonic Intervals	Augmented Intervals	
	2°	Prime		
ic1		−2	P+	i1
ic2	3°	+2		i2
ic3		−3	2+	i3
ic4	4°	+3		i4
ic5		P4	3+	i5
ic6	5°	4+		i6
ic5	6°	P5		i7
ic4		−6	5+	i8
ic3	7°	+6		i9
ic2		−7	6+	i10
ic1	8°	+7		i11
		P8	7+	i12(0)

14-2

(a) Harmonic Minor Scale

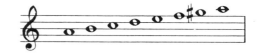

Intervals formed above and below G♯

−2 −3 4° 5° −6 7° 2+ +3 4+ 5+ +6 +7
        *   *   *   *

*enharmonic notation of interval

continued

14-2, *continued*

(b) Melodic Minor Scale

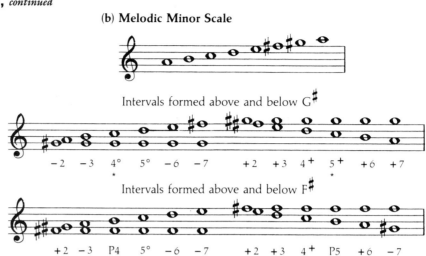

Intervals formed above and below G♯

| −2 | −3 | 4° | 5° | −6 | −7 | +2 | +3 | 4⁺ | 5⁺ | +6 | +7 |

Intervals formed above and below F♯

| +2 | −3 | P4 | 5° | −6 | −7 | +2 | +3 | 4⁺ | P5 | +6 | −7 |

What are hybrid scale patterns?

Numerous possibilities exist for combining three-, four-, five-, and six-member scales by joining them **conjunctly** (using the last notated pitch of one scale segment as the first notated pitch of another) or **disjunctly** (using cardinal interval 1 or 2 between the last notated pitch of one scale segment and the first notated pitch of another). A few possible combinations are shown in Figure 14-3. We can form many similar and extremely useful hybrid scales which, for the most part, can be notated diatonically but do not fit into any form of the diatonic system.

Hybrid scales can be purposely devised, as they were for Figure 14-3, or they can result "naturally" during the compositional process. Most hybrid scale materials show some form of

14-3

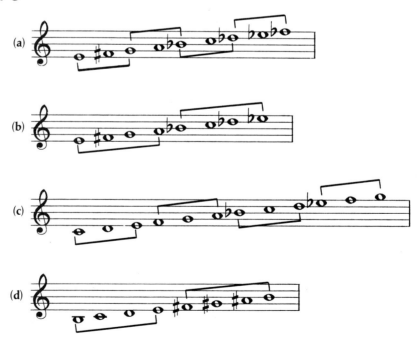

14-3, *continued*

internal organization. This is the case with the oboe line in measures 51–59 of the first movement of Bruckner's Symphony No. 7 (Figure 14-4a). Figure 14-4b and c present two different views of this hybrid scale's internal organization. In (b), the scale is organized as three-member scale patterns (2, 1 and 1, 2) joined disjunctly by an i2. In (c), the scale is organized as a series of conjunctly joined Dorian and Phrygian tetrachords. It is impossible to know the intended organization or even to know if any organization was intended. This example simply demonstrates the existence of some type of organization.

14-4

How does the internal organization of scale materials relate to the organization of melody?

The procedures and formalizing principles used in the design of melody from any set of pitch materials are extremely varied and a matter of personal choice. Nonetheless, we can categorize some of the procedures and formalizing principles at this stage of our study.

First of all, we must note that how we use a set of pitch materials to produce a melody is totally subject to our expressive intent. Though there will be a basic textural relationship between the scale material and melody, melodic organization is independent of the internal organization of the scale materials. The structural tones of the melody shown in Figure 14-4 are notated as B, D, G, B flat, F, A flat, E flat, G flat, and D flat. There is no apparent relationship between the organization of the melody and the particular organizations of the scale materials in Figure 14-4b and c.

Using scale materials deduced from a melodic configuration in the author's *Quintet for Winds*, we can arrive at several differing outcomes. Refer to Figure 14-5. The pitch materials (part a of the figure) are organized in two differing ways. The melody from the *Quintet* is shown in part b; the melodies in parts c and d were produced for comparison purposes only. Tonal goals provided the principle organization for each of these melodies, but the tonal goals—as identified—are quite different in each melody. In melody b the tonal goals are notated as F sharp, G sharp, D sharp, and C sharp; in melody c they are notated as E and A; in melody d they are notated as F, D flat, G flat, E flat, A flat, G flat, F, and E flat. The notated A in melody b and the notated C sharp in melody c are climactic points but not structural in nature. The notated E sharp is not an ornamental tone in (b), whereas it is an ornamental tone in (c). The notated E and B double-flat are ornamental tones in (d).

14-5

Quintet for Winds

Sherman

When forming melody from hybrid scales, it is possible to create a variety of tonal impressions with one scale by using the notated pitches of triads as structural tones. This is simply one of the common organizing principles used in the formation of melody from the resources of diatonic-scale materials. In Figure 14-6a, an eight-member hybrid scale is produced by joining an Ionian and Dorian tetrachord disjunctly by an i1. The pitch content of the scale in Figure 14-6b provides the D-flat major, D major, and B major triads. The melodies in (c), (d), and (e) of the same figure illustrate the use of each major triad as structural tones. The melody in (f) illustrates the use of two structural triads as a means of achieving a form of harmonic shape.

14-6

Generally, hybrid scales can be notated diatonically; however, on occasion it may be necessary to use chromatic or enharmonic notation of intervals between and within scale segments in order to avoid double sharps and double flats (Figure 14-7).

14-7

(a) Awkward Use of Double Flat   Chromatic Notation:

(b) Awkward Use of Double Sharp   Enharmonic Notation:

What tertian chords are not found in the diatonic system?

The augmented triad, diminished seventh chord, and diminished-major seventh chord are chords that commonly result from alterations in the diatonic system. The two approaches we have used to notate the triads and seventh chords of the natural diatonic system can be used to notate tertian chords having adjacent pitches that form diatonic relationships. The augmented triad constructed on the pitch-name D is shown in Figure 14-8a. We begin with p2 (D) and add i4 (+ 3) to produce p6 (F sharp). Beginning again with p2 (D), we add i8 (5 $^+$) to produce p10, which is A sharp. Using the consecutive-thirds approach, we merely need to use the formula (4, 4) (see Figure 14-8b). The augmented triad does not have a **sounding root**; that is, it does not have a root that can be perceived aurally. In terms of sound, there are but four augmented triads.

14-8

The augmented triads shown in Figure 14-9 represent three different notations of the same sounding chord.

14-9

The diminished seventh chord in Figure 14-10a is composed of a diminished triad constructed on the pitch-name B with a 7° interval above the root. The same diminished seventh chord is shown constructed in consecutive − 3 (m3) intervals in Figure 14-10b. The diminished seventh chord is also without a sounding root; its actual root is determined by how it is notated.

14-10

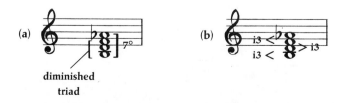

diminished
triad

There are only three sounding diminished seventh chords, and each can be notated in four different ways (Figure 14-11). The diminished-major seventh chord (Figure 14-12a) consists of

14-11

a diminished triad with an i11 (+7) added above the root. In Figure 14-12b the diminished-major seventh chord is shown constructed with consecutive thirds using the formula (3, 3, 5). Because this same collection of pitches can be notated differently (Figure 14-12c), it is possible to recognize the collection as a major triad with a −9 (m9) interval above the root.

14-12

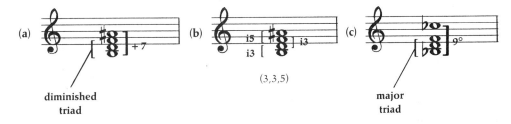

UNIT PROJECT 4

Introduction

All of the materials and procedures needed to complete this project are available in Unit Two. The project options offer sufficient choices to permit you to deal creatively with materials and procedures that interest you. When coupled with the timbre of instruments and voices, the wide range of colors made possible by the scalar and chordal materials and the colorful relationships that can be produced with them provide expressive tone colors ranging from delicate to bold and from ordinary to exotic. Whatever you do with the specific choices and limitations of this project, do not lose sight of the primary objective: to fashion a colorful musical expression by combining patterns in sound and time.

Description

After considering the three project options, select the one that is best suited to you and produce a musicwork of one and one-half to two minutes' duration. Select the tonal materials and the temporal and procedural considerations from what is permitted by the guidelines. The title of your musicwork should suggest some real or imagined colorful event, thing, condition, or expression; it should suggest what gave impetus to and narrowed your ideas and helped you define your expressive intent.

OPTION 1. Use two single-line instruments, a voice and one single-line instrument, *or* two voices. You may have both melodic lines share a single hybrid scale *or* you may assign each line its own hybrid scale. In either case, the scale (or scales) should be of your own making and should be constructed so as to contain:

1. two major triads common to both scales if two scales are used,

2. two minor triads common to both scales if two scales are used, *or*

3. two quartal triads common to both scales if two scales are used.

In each case, the two triads should be treated as melodic structural tones and serve as tonal goals. Except for some momentary overlapping, the two melodic lines should *not* use the same structural chord at the same time. See Figure 14-13.

14-13

OPTION 2. Use two trios *or* two quartets **antiphonally** (generally, two groups singing or playing alternately). The two trios or quartets should be made up of (1) a group from one family of instruments and a group from another family of instruments, (2) a group from one family of instruments and a group of mixed voices, *or* (3) a group of female voices and a group of male voices. The voices may be doubled to achieve good balance of sound. Use one of the following as your source of sound materials:

1. all major triads, with each one diatonically unrelated to its adjacent triads;

2. all minor triads, with each one diatonically unrelated to its adjacent triads;

3. all quartal triads, with each one diatonically unrelated to its adjacent triads;

4. alternating major and quartal triads that are diatonically unrelated to their adjacent triads;

5. only one kind of seventh chord, with each chord diatonically unrelated to its adjacent chords; *or*

6. two types of seventh chords used alternately, with each one diatonically unrelated to its adjacent chords.

The texture of the composition should be completely homophonic, and open and closed voicing of chords should be used judiciously. If quartets are used, each tertian triad should have a doubled root or third. All tertian triads should be used in either root position or first inversion. You may, but need not, be concerned with providing a discernible melodic line. Your primary concerns should be texture and color. A text should be used with voices. See Figure 14-14.

14-14

Fanfare (for a solemn celebration)

OPTION 3. Use a solo voice *or* a solo single-line instrument. Accompany the solo line with (1) four single-line instruments, (2) a marimba or similar instrument using four mallets, (3) a piano, *or* (4) a small organ or celesta. Fashion the accompaniment of block, arpeggiated, *or* broken chords (*or* a mixture of them) of the kind and conditions specified in option 2. The solo line and the accompaniment should be rhythmically independent of each other. See Figure 14-15.

14-15

Serenade

Guidelines

1. Use at least two different measure signatures within the texture of the musicwork.

2. Use cyclic permutation of rhythmic shapes if desired.

3. Produce legible performance parts (for instrumentalists) and vocal scores (for singers). A conductor's score in sounding pitch must be made if more than two performers are used.

4. Perform your work publically as a class concert if possible. Next-best is to perform the work in a class concert for other theory classes or for music appreciation classes. If possible, conduct your own work.

Notes

Probably the best way of "getting into" your project is to sit at a piano and experiment with the various sound materials presented in the three project options. Before you can use the sound materials, you must know how they sound alone and in relation to other sound materials. While you are experimenting, let your expressive intent emerge. Continue the process until you have established something with which to begin. The number of alternatives provided by the options is enormous. With such a broad spectrum of color options at your disposal, you must do a great deal of "sorting out" as you explore the expressive potential of each option and learn which colors and relationships best fit your temperament and your expressive needs.

It is wise to abandon something that does not seem to work for you. On the other hand, resist the temptation to be dissatisfied with everything you start; it is good to be critical but not to the point that you challenge out of existence every idea that enters your mind. As you become familiar with new materials and procedures, allow them time for gestation—give a new idea time to germinate before you pass judgment. Get something started, think about it, sleep on it. Very often, more is accomplished when we permit problems to "solve themselves" overnight than when we try to force solutions.

As you progress from project to project, you are expected to apply what you have already learned; at this point, this includes the mechanics of notation and setting up a score, and the proper notation of pitch, intervals, chords, and so on. Attending to these things will make your music easy to read and demonstrate your growth as a musician. Though this textbook and the workbook can help you attain a reasonably high degree of skill in applying the principles of music, they cannot provide the periodic review and reinforcement that all students need. Develop the habit of periodic reviewing.

U N I T

THREE

MUSICAL ABSTRACTION

15 Introduction to Musical Abstraction

What is musical abstraction?

Among the many definitions of the word *abstract* are some that express the concept of presenting something of some magnitude and scope in a manner that distills its essential aspects. An abstract may be simply a brief presentation that summarizes an author's biography or a scientific treatise. An abstract may also be a transformation of the essence of something into another medium such as an artwork. Thus, in considering music as an abstraction of human experience, we are saying that composers produce musicworks that are imbued with certain essential qualities of life drawn from the human experience. Consequently, humans respond emotionally to the many, varied aspects of life that make up their experiences when those aspects are evoked by the sensuous stimulation of music.

How do we respond to musical abstraction?

Our capacity to deal in abstractions with ease and certainty is not something we stumble upon unwittingly. Nor does it come to us at a certain time in life by a sudden revelation or some physiological change that marks a particular stage of maturity. We deal with abstraction from the moment we are born; we cultivate it, we compound it, we use it constantly. The realm of abstraction is the only realm within which we can traffic in ideas.

Our individual experiences constitute the complex accumulation of our reactions to events and conditions outside of ourselves. Each reaction is affected by our responses to previous and expected experiences. Each individual's experience is unique; but yet, people who have faced the same or similar events and live under the same or similar conditions have a common base for understanding abstractions. Therefore, although our emotional responses to the events and conditions of life are different from those of others, they remain within a general, universal realm of comprehension. A musicwork, as an abstraction of human experience, elicits varied responses but remains within the embrace of a common understanding. Our responses to music (or to any artwork) can be characterized as nonspecific but reasonably predictable.

In producing a musicwork, it might be said that the composer abstracts the pertinent aspects of his or her cumulative experience into a unique, dramatic unfoldment, an abstract musical scenario to which the listener can react. Because it abstracts, or distills, the infinitely complex set of events and conditions that make up the composer's experience, music is considered more capable of enriching our lives than are the ordinary events and conditions we encounter in the course of daily living.

How might the inexperienced composer approach the dilemma that lies between the conception of a musical gesture and the technical means of developing the gesture?

To answer this question, let us consider how children manipulate music in their play. We might assume that children at play do not think about the ways and means of doing things. A child's behavior and response to other children appears to be automatic. We might further assume, through similar observations, that a child's apparently spontaneous and unconscious capacity for extending and developing familiar melodic configurations while singing during play is also a form of behavior that is noncontemplative and unstudied.

The activities of a child are initially directed by instincts. A child is instinctively drawn to play, to verbal communication, to drawing pictures, to singing, and to a myriad of other activities which, on the surface, appear to require skill and planned or deliberate action. **Instinct**, as it relates to the arts, might be defined as a natural aptitude or talent. It is what gives us the initial capability to function in and respond to the arts.

How do we develop our instincts?

An instinct is not manifested directly in an articulated technique or identifiable cultural conventions; an instinct is essentially a capacity to do or comprehend something. An individual develops an articulated technique and an identifiable cultural convention through the various intellectual activities that effect *learning*. **Intuition**, for example, is instantaneous apprehension; it is an intellectual activity that allows us to learn and act without conscious reasoning. **Noesis** is the ability to perceive by means of the intellect alone. And **reason**, of course, enables us to think coherently and logically and draw inferences and conclusions from known or assumed facts.

How does a child use instinct and intuition in the "doing" that leads to knowing?

Though we use these and other forms of intellectual activity in the making of music and other forms of art, the creative and interpretive processes are essentially intuitive. Therefore, what appears as a dilemma with regard to the relationship of conception and craft is a dilemma only when we abandon our reliance on intuition. The child, spontaneously and unconsciously extending a melodic gesture, is functioning in accordance with normal, predictable behavior: the child's instincts provide the needed capacities to do; intuition and limited experience provide the form of intelligence and the learning that enable him or her to achieve the doing. By such behavior, the child tests and responds repeatedly to a myriad of cause and effect situations that serve to nurture and expand his or her basic and most useful form of knowing: expectations.

What is the relationship between technique and conception?

The impetus for making music must always be a conceptual notion of the desired expression. Technique, as such, must always be at the service of conception. Attempts to use a technical device as the impetus for making music generally fail to produce an expressively convincing product, most likely because such music is not based on experiential abstractions with which the listener can communicate.

The effectiveness with which musical ideas are presented and developed are, of course, a matter of communication. In communicating with a musicwork, we are dealing with it in terms of how our experiences enable us to feel about it. A musical idea, as such, must be developed; that is, it must be extended in a manner that "explains" it expressively. It must become something that can elicit an affective response from the listener. This type of communication process is the function of the arts.

What is the fundamental intent of music and the other arts?

If human communication processes were exclusively limited to stating and receiving ideas in pristine form, there would be no reason for music or any of the other arts to exist. Indeed, if communication were so limited and ideas so easily understood, what we think of as "the arts" would probably never have occurred to anyone. We recognize that music, as a relatively pure abstraction of human experience, must be concerned with and embody ideas. However, an idea must be expanded into an expressive entity (a musicwork) for it to become an artwork. The fundamental intent of music and the other arts is to provide the means by which ideas (abstractions) are made affectively lucid.

16 The Musical Gesture

What were our first encounters with gesture?

Perhaps the first and most useful fact of life we learned as infants is that our understanding of others and their understanding of us depends on our mutual understanding of *gestures*. We all began our understanding of verbal gestures when we recognized that certain vocal sounds were rewarded in some way. By the age of six months, we were receiving and assimilating an astonishing amount of sound information in the form of speech inflections. Along with this, we practiced forming the sounds of inflected speech; we were, obviously, more interested in expression and meaning than information. As we grew older, we became increasingly aware that vocal gestures reflect a speaker's emotional state and a speaker's meaning.

During the early months of our infancy, we also assimilated an astonishing amount of sound information not related to speech, and we were able to distinguish it from speech. With the same determination with which we learned the sounds of speech, we explored the sound-producing potential of every object within our reach. Our awareness of the effectiveness of nonspeech sounds—even those we made with our voices—provided us with further means of forming gestures that expressed our emotional states. Out of these pounding, rattling, gurgling, sighing, crying, and a host of other sound-producing experiences of our infancy developed our ability as older children to understand and use musical gesture as a means of expression.

What is a gesture?

When we hear the word *gesture*, we generally think of such body gestures as a shrug of the shoulders, a furrowed brow, a smile, a wave of the hand, and others. The more subtle body gestures—those that often accompany verbal exchange—form an area of study called "body language." Gesture, as a general concept, is much broader than body language.

A **gesture** is a verbal utterance, body movement, graphic portrayal, sound configuration, or anything else that embodies an understandable expression, intention, or state of mind.

Speech inflection, as a kind of verbal gesture, is important for conveying the meaning of verbal discourse. Our understanding of body gestures enables us to respond appreciatively to mime, dance, uncaptioned cartoons, and similar forms of visual expression. Graphic portrayals, also, use visual gestures to express ideas. Gestures are infinite in number, and new ones are constantly evolving in form and meaning. The form and meaning of gestures are established by cultural consensus, and they are our primary means of dealing with one another in terms of feelings and aesthetic orientations.

A gesture may be a single, indivisible entity in its form and meaning, or it may be a highly complex grouping of simple gestures. The single, indivisible gesture is sometimes a "building block" that is joined to other gestures to form a more complex gesture for expressing new and particular levels of meaning. In speech, a single word may be delivered in a number of ways, each conveying a particular meaning intended to produce a particular response. A single word expressed in print, such as the word *stop* on a stop sign, generally elicits the intended response. Expressed in speech, a single word carries with it a variety of voice inflections that serve to indicate the particular intended meaning of the word and thus the desired response. The "inflection" or attitude of the stop sign is expressed in its shape. When we consider the comparative complexity of an entire stage play as a gesture, we can see why a single interpretation, a single understanding, of a complex artwork is impossible. We might say, therefore, that the *object* of a gesture is to make a point about something; the *hope* is to be understood.

What is the nature of a musical gesture?

Musical gestures, for the most part, are expressive abstractions, the meanings of which are metaphorically associated with physical, psychological, spiritual, visual, emotional, and other forms of expression. Putting aside, for the moment, the notion that an entire musicwork (or any artwork) is itself a gesture, we will first discuss the simple, indivisible gesture that serves as the generating material of a musicwork.

Regardless of the function or expressive intent of a musicwork, it must be made of something. That "something" has two basic properties: (1) *a musically workable configuration* that gives shape to (2) *a discernible musical idea*. These two properties can be explained in a number of ways, but all of the explanations break down into the tangible and intangible, the physical and metaphysical, the sensory and nonsensory, and similar dualities. The first property describes the measurable qualities of a musicwork—the various physical dimensions and functional aspects of a musical shape. The second property, a discernible musical idea, describes the intangible qualities—meaning, feeling, aesthetics, spirituality, and similar aspects of music. The "something" of which a musicwork is made is what we call a basic **musical gesture**; it's what the musicwork is "about."

What are the measurable dimensions of a musical configuration?

A musical configuration has two measurable dimensions: a pitch pattern and a durational pattern. The pitch content of a configuration is presented either simultaneously or consecutively. For example, the opening gesture of Beethoven's Third Symphony (Figure 16-1a) consists of an E♭-major triad scored for full orchestra that occurs on the first beat of the first and second measures. In this configuration the pitch content is presented simultaneously. In the third measure and continuing, a contrasting gesture presents the pitch content of the E♭-major triad consecutively in an ordered series in the 'cellos (Figure 16-1b).

16-1

Symphony No. 3 in E-flat major, Op. 55, Mov. I

Allegro con brio   ♩· = 60   Beethoven

(a)   Orch.

(b)   Vcl.

The pitch content of this configuration is ordered so as to emphasize the notated E flat by duration and rhythmic placement. A simple change of duration and rhythmic placement in a pitch configuration can result in an entirely different musical idea, as shown in Figure 16-2.

16-2

Vln.

17 Physical and Expressive Qualities of a Musical Gesture

What is a musical shape?

Shape in music denotes the salient physical characteristics of a pattern of sound in a musicwork, from the smallest intelligible configuration to the entire musicwork. Though this concept may seem too general to be of any practical use, it is in fact rather singular in its intent. In describing the shape of visual objects, for example, we use such terms as round, oval, square, curved, oblong, triangular, thin, and pointed. Each of these, while not providing exact dimensions, can describe an object in terms of its general but most characteristic physical quality, which, in most cases, excludes all or most other generalized physical qualities.

In dealing with shapes in music, we are concerned with the idea of shape as a qualitative, aesthetic control in the construction of a musicwork. For the listener, the perception and retention of a musical shape (or shapes) is essential to musical comprehension. If we are unable to perceive musical shapes and distinguish them from each other, we are denied the aesthetically rewarding experience of being able to perceive and appreciate the evolution and juxtapositions of the contrasting shapes in the musicwork as it unfolds in time. As an initial step in becoming aware of shapes in music, examine the melodic shapes in Figure 17-1. Try to determine the most salient physical features of each shape. Then compare them in terms of their internal and overall similarities and differences.

17-1

(a) Gregorian chant XIII C, *Asperges me*

A - sper - ges me, Do - mi - ne hys so - po - et - mun - da - bor

(b) J. S. Bach, Cantata 139, Aria

(c) Joseph Haydn, Quartet No. 17, Op. 3, No. 5, Mov. IV

(d) Jean Sibelius, Symphony No. 2 in D major, Mov. III

(e) Anton Webern, Symphony Op. 21, Mov. I, meas. 16–23[a]

Using tracing paper as shown in Figure 17-2 (or by some equally effective means), draw the profile of at least a portion of the music you transcribed and performed as your Unit One project. Some interesting features should show up in sharp relief, features you may not have noticed before. Figure 17-2 shows a typical profile. Varying numbers of lines have been used to represent the varying sizes of intervals in the music. One glance reveals that the two melodic lines are remarkably similar. Depicted in this manner, we might say that the two melodic lines have the same shape but are not identical. This consistency is an important element in the makeup of the music. For the purpose of realizing how this particular consistency works with and contributes to the establishment of other consistencies in the music of Figure 17-2, we might consider:

1. that the two melodic lines almost invariably move in opposite directions,

2. that before a line makes a sizable leap in one direction, it usually moves stepwise in the opposite direction,

3. that if one line is active the other is generally less active, or even inactive,

4. that almost the entire musicwork—as demonstrated by the portion shown—is made up of a continuous line of diatonic half steps and whole steps, and that when a larger interval occurs, it seems to appear in sharp relief and at times might be considered an "event."

Because these factors are likely to be apparent in most of the music transcribed in the Unit One projects, we can conclude that they are typical, conventional practices of Renaissance composers.

17-2

Twelve cantiones duarum vocum

Orlandus Lassus

17-2, *continued*

What is an event in music?

An event of any type is simply a significant occurrence. In music an **event** is the occurrence of a sonic relationship or configuration that is significant in relation to its surroundings and significant with respect to the listener's comprehension of the music. Considering the complexity of even the simplest music, we must expect the significance of events in various musicworks to differ in importance. We must expect also that, within a musicwork, there is evidence of the ordering of events. This ordering is important to the general sense of continuity we expect in the overall shape of a musicwork.

How do a gesture's physical characteristics relate to its expressive characteristics?

One of the first musical abstractions most children come upon and generally remember for the rest of their lives is what we might refer to as a "mocking" gesture. Typically, it is sung with a text that has been improvised for the occasion. It can be represented by the configuration shown in Figure 17-3, but a variety of other, similar forms are also possible.

17-3

At this point in our discussion, we must ask some questions aimed at revealing the feature (or combination of features) that serves to establish the nature of this musical gesture:

1. Does the character of the gesture stem from the words or from the physical characteristics of the musical configuration?

2. Do the intervallic relationships establish the character?

3. Does the rhythmic configuration establish the character?

4. Does the musical configuration retain its "mocking" or "taunting" character if it is separated from its verbal association?

5. Does either the notated or the diagramed version of the configuration (Figure 17-4) suggest any characteristics of the original gesture?

17-4

Answers to these and similar questions, though certainly subjective and, at best, the product of informed conjecture, can direct us to some possible and even probable associations thought to exist between the physical and expressive characteristics of a musical gesture.

What assumptions can we make about the evolution of the "mocking" gesture?

As we search for reasonable answers to the questions just listed, a series of assumptions can help us sort out the possibilities and give some order to our thinking. First of all, let us assume that the various components of this gesture as it is presently constituted were not necessarily established at the same time. The establishment of the components could have been separated by an imperceptibly small increment of time or by decades. Accepting this assumption as reasonable, let us assume further that at some time in the distant past someone or a number of people in one place or in many places wanted to tease, taunt, mock, or otherwise tantalize someone else. That is, there was first the urge, the desire to initiate a mocking gesture, which was received and understood as such by someone, and which finally evolved to become the gesture we are presently discussing. We could not, of course, hazard a guess as to how many forms this gesture has had during its history.

Let us continue by assuming that teasing, taunting, and mocking were, first of all, expressed by various kinds of body gestures. We might, as part of this basic assumption, assume that such body gestures preceded the development of corresponding speech gestures.

Once a mocking gesture became a configuration of speech, we can assume that words—or whatever the vocal sounds were at the time—gave definition to the gesture, and that intonation and rhythmic inflection gave it meaning. Thus, if we look again at the "mocking" gesture (Figure 17-3), we can see that the words "Mary has a boyfriend" provide us with information about a girl named Mary. But this, in and of itself, does not constitute a mocking gesture or even a hint of one. What these words must have in order to become a mocking gesture is an expressive intent, a "meaning" that can be supplied only by the manner (the intonation and rhythmic inflection) in which the words are spoken or sung.

The repeated singing without words or playing of the configuration on an instrument can serve to convey some expression of mockery—anything from impish mockery to mockery of a meaner sort is possible. However, such singing or playing lacks definition of what it is about literally. The abstract quality of mockery, which is all we have left when the configuration is disassociated from the verbal connotations of the words "Mary has a boyfriend," is sustained in part by the implied need for redundancy built into the configuration itself—rather like a wheel that, once having turned, expresses a functional need by continuing to turn. When examined, the basic configuration of this gesture appears to be a tiny cell of one interval, the − 3, which possesses the impetus to repeat itself because of the notated pitch A; see Figure 17-5.

17-5

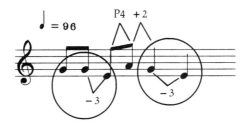

We might challenge the assertion that repeatedly playing the configuration in Figure 17-3 or singing it without words is sufficient to give it the character of mocking. The manner of playing or singing—that is, the intonation and rhythmic inflection—must still be of a quality that supports the expressive intent of a mocking gesture. To play or sing such a configuration with what might be called a "lovely" tone and with a rhythmic inflection that is "expansive" would certainly not achieve the desired effect of mocking. Therefore, in this brief odyssey in search of a touchstone that determines the character and expression of a gesture, we must conclude that what has been categorized roughly as *intonation* and *rhythmic inflection* is the most conclusive determinant of the abstract "meaning" of a musical gesture.

MINI PROJECT 6

Introduction

Much of what you will be doing in the study and practice of music will concern your affective (emotional) response to music you hear and other people's affective response to what you produce as a creative/performing musician. This book is intended to provoke your constant awareness of the expressive consequences of the music you produce and perform. Lack of competence in this aspect of musicianship, moreso than the lack of technical competence, is the ultimate barrier to a student's development of musicality. This mini project will provide you with an introduction to the multifarious, evolving nature of humankind's affective response to music.

Description

OPTION 1. Research and write a short paper on a singular aspect of the eighteenth-century treatise *Affectenlehre* by Frederick T. Wessel.

OPTION 2. Research and write a short paper contrasting what a composer from some previous century and a contemporary composer have written or reportedly said on the topic of musical expression.

OPTION 3. Research and write a short paper on any singular aspect of musical expression espoused in a book on aesthetics, musical criticism, or the psychology of music by any author.

OPTION 4. On the basis of your own insights, observations, and interests, write a short essay on some *singular* aspect of what you perceive as your generation's affective response to music. Contrast this with your own affective response, citing similarities and differences.

Notes

Although each topic is broad and could occupy your interest for a long time, you are to take seriously the words *singular* and *short* and the notion that this project is intended as an *introduction*. *Awareness* is the key word in understanding the intended purpose of the project. Awareness itself, functioning as an intellectual "leaven," can effect some rather profound changes in how and what we think during the process of making music.

To get the most out of this project, approach it with the expectation that you are writing the paper for the members of your class.

18 Transforming Melodic Configurations

What are the measurable dimensions of a melodic configuration?

We have established that how a melodic gesture is performed is the most relevant determinant of its character. However, it is easy to sustain and amplify the "meaning" of a gesture or to produce some new gesture by tranforming its configuration while retaining the integrity of its basic shape. A given melodic shape provides but a limited number of expressive possibilities unless we alter its configuration by changing the particularity of its pitch, intervallic, or rhythmic makeup.

The particular configuration that gives material definition to the shape of a melodic gesture has two measurable dimensions: its "pitch frame" and its "time frame." Discounting the dynamic, articulation, and other differences that evolve with repeated performance, the pitch content and the durations of the pitches are measurable "givens." Beyond the subjective considerations associated with performance, effectively sustaining and amplifying a melodic gesture involves changing one or both of these dimensions.

Why is "manipulated reiteration" necessary to the process of making music?

Consider again the gesture in Figure 17-3. Regardless of whether the configuration is sung in tune or rhythmically "perfect," its intent and the reaction of its "victim" will be the same. As a conventional musical abstraction, this configuration has what can be called a "closed meaning." Nonetheless, as soon as the configuration is heard or "invented"—that a child could "invent" this same configuration cannot be discounted—the child, in using it, begins the first task of music making by manipulating it to suit his or her own purpose. Such manipulations are as unconscious and instinctive as anything the child might do in other play activities.

To suit the characteristic conditions of mockery, the child will necessarily reiterate the gesture, effecting whatever modifications meet his or her fancy. For example, to get attention when being ignored, a child might add or repeat words. This quite naturally would result in the repetition of pitches, intervals, or melodic shapes, which, in turn, would effect a variety of rhythmic changes (see Figure 18-1). Or, in order to be heard better, to increase the dramatic

18-1

effect, or for some other reason, the child might change or rearrange the durations of pitches (Figure 18-2). The child, for any or no reason, might change the pitch level of some or all of the original configuration and might, in the process, effect changes that extend and give dramatic shape to his or her "musical" activity.

18-2

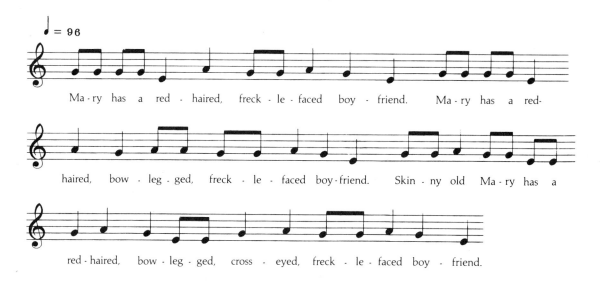

What are the three fundamental procedures in making music?

As the child repeats the playful mocking gesture, he or she rarely uses identical pitches and configurations. Such consistency is not important to the child. The elemental quality of the relationships remains constant; the gesture evolves, develops, and assumes dramatic shape, but its original idea or intent does not change. Through the instinctive process of sustaining the expressive intent of the gesture, the child is exercising one or all three of the fundamental procedures used to create music: *reiteration, rhythmic change,* and *projection*.

How do we maintain the integrity of a melodic shape while prolonging a gesture to amplify its meaning?

Though a musical gesture is defined primarily by the intonation and rhythmic inflection used in its performance and secondarily by its shape (its rhythmic and pitch configurations), it is not reasonable to assume that the character of a gesture can be sustained entirely simply by **reiteration**—that is, repetition. Without exception, it is technically unfeasible and aesthetically wanting to attempt to prolong the expressive intent of a musical gesture without using projection—reiteration on different pitch levels—as well as rhythmic change.

In any discussion of the real or imagined "rules" of composition, the one overriding rule is that the composer must not violate the premise of the work. The **premise**, in this usage, is what the musicwork demonstrates as being the underlying operant principle that governs the work's temporal and tonal ordering and its dramatic shaping. Knowing what kinds of changes will sustain and amplify the expressive intent of a particular musical gesture and what kinds of changes will modify or destroy it is the kind of knowledge that comes only through experience and the exercise of good judgment over unbridled whimsy.

The distinction between what sustains and what destroys would appear rather simple were it not for the fact that the same types of changes may either sustain or destroy the effective prolongation of a gesture. To judge which effect is occurring as we make music and to know how and when to maintain the integrity of a musical shape require a capacity for discrimination that is cultivated by experience in making music. Let us, therefore, continue by discussing the nature of rhythmic change and projection and then experiment with using them to sustain the expressive intent of a melodic gesture.

How do we sustain a melodic gesture by rhythmic change?

Figure 18-3a shows a reiteration of the basic shape in which a rhythmic change is effected within the time frame of the gesture. The rhythmic change in part b of the figure exceeds the time frame of the gesture. It should be noted that the rhythmic changes in these reiterations do not change the tonal goal of the gesture or emphasize different intervals.

18-3

How do we produce new melodic gestures by rhythmic change?

Notice, that if we simply change the rhythmic configuration of the original gesture (Figure 17-3) so as to emphasize a different interval—for example, the interval 5 (P4), as shown in Figure 18-4—the gesture also changes. The result in this case is that the pitch configuration

18-4

of the original gesture is maintained, but its rhythmic configuration suggests a more "heraldic" gesture. The new gesture lacks the mocking quality of the original gesture. The idiomatic characteristics of the horn further affect the quality of the expression of the new gesture. If, on the other hand, we should choose to emphasize the interval + 2 by effecting a rhythmic change (Figure 18-5), the gesture becomes rather light-hearted. Both of the new gestures, however, still resemble the original gesture in that they occupy the same pitch frame.

18-5

We could continue the process, making further rhythmic modifications, until we arrived at rhythmic configurations appropriate for every gesture we wished to make. Thus, the original gesture should be viewed "materially" as a specific pitch configuration, a specific set of intervallic relationships, and a specific rhythmic configuration, each subject to modification. Any new gesture we might make from these materials could be quite short (Figure 18-6a), or it could be lengthened by reiterations of a pitch or of the entire shape to produce a more complex gesture (Figure 18-6b).

18-6

What is a melodic projection?

A **melodic projection** is a reiteration of a basic melodic shape or some transformed version of it at a different pitch level or within a different frame of reference. A projection need not retain the rhythmic configuration of the original. There are three types of projections: transposed projections, tonal projections, and topological projections.

In a **transposed projection** (Figure 18-7), the basic melodic shape is presented on a different pitch level, and all intervals retain their discrete values. When we are using the diatonic

18-7

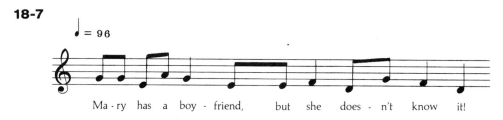

system, the transposed projection may be further distinguished as either within the same version (natural or transposed) of the diatonic system or in a different version of it (Figure 18-8).

18-8

In a **tonal projection**, the basic melodic shape is reiterated in such a way that the intervallic ordinal "types" remain the same but their discrete and interval class names are changed to conform to a different position within the same version of the diatonic system (if it is being used) Figure 18-9, or within different versions of the diatonic system (Figure 18-10). Transposed projections and tonal projections can be achieved in any tonal system.

18-9

18-10

In a **topological projection** (Figure 18-11), the basic melodic shape is retained but it is transformed so as to present a different pitch configuration. The topological projection is introduced here only for the purpose of explaining it as one type of projection. Topological

18-11

projections can be as simple as the one in Figure 18-11 and as complex as the one in Figure 18-12. Because they vary widely in complexity and because we need to deal specifically with the various means of forming them, we will discuss them in greater depth in chapter 20.

18-12

complex topological projection

What is the binary nature of a composer's options?

Though the following description would be grossly absurd as an actual compositional procedure, it does describe the nature of the choices we must make during the creative act of making music. Also, whereas each choice we make occurs within a complex of interdependent choices, the binary nature of choices is described here as a single series of independent decisions that would be woven into a complex musicwork as would a single thread in an ornately woven fabric.

Once we have presented a melodic shape, for example, we have the option of either repeating it or presenting a new shape. If we elect repetition (*reiteration*), we have the option of repeating all of the shape or just a part of it. If we elect to repeat all of the shape, we have the option of repeating it with the same configuration or with a different one. If we elect to repeat the shape with a different configuration, we have the option of repeating it within the same pitch frame or within a different pitch frame. If we elect to repeat the shape in a different pitch frame, we have the option of. . . . The chart in Figure 18-13 gives a general idea of the binary nature of options. Some of the terms in the chart will not be presented until later in this unit.

18-13

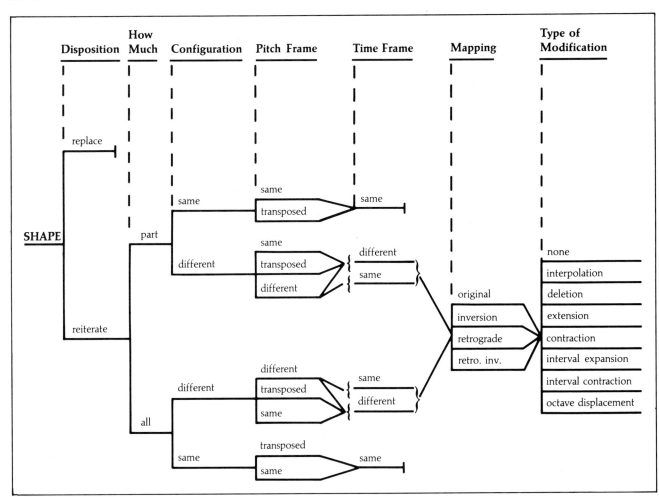

Might a child also use ostinato and musical dialogue instinctively?

Let us return for a moment to the instinctive musical activities of children. Having discussed the probability that a child will exercise rhythmic change and some form of projection as he or she reiterates the "mocking" gesture used as our model, we must assume further that a child will also engage in some activity such as swinging, jumping rope, skipping, or running while singing. The child's singing, therefore, will most likely be joined by a rhythmic **ostinato** (a persistently recurring pattern of sound) such as that suggested in Figure 18-14. The child would certainly adapt the rhythmic character of his or her singing to accommodate the skipping or similar activity.

18-14

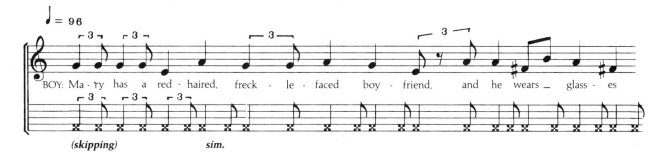

Upon hearing the mocking gesture in Figure 18-14 several times, Mary might be prompted to answer with a gesture of scorn to counter the taunting of the child—perhaps she would answer with something like what is shown in Figure 18-15. The combination of the child's taunting gesture, Mary's gesture in response, and some form of rhythmic ostinato illustrate yet another basic compositional process, counterpoint.

18-15

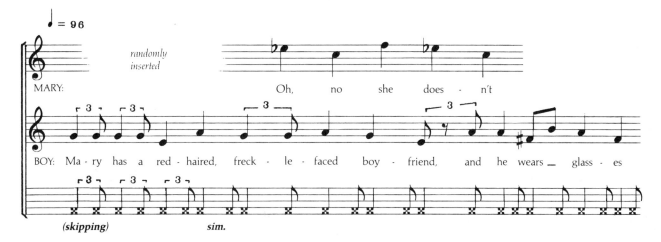

<table>
<tr><td>

**MINI
PROJECT
7**

</td><td>

Select a commonly known folk song or children's song whose opening melodic configuration contains no more than four distinct pitches. Treat it according to the following instructions:

</td></tr>
</table>

A. Using the configuration in its given form as a gesture, continue it, in character, by a single reiteration in each of the following ways:

1. Use the same pitches with a rhythmic change.

2. Use a transposed projection without rhythmic change.

3. Use a different transposed projection with rhythmic change.

4. Use a tonal projection without rhythmic change.

5. Use a different tonal projection with rhythmic change.

B. Using only the pitch material of the original configuration, produce a *new* gesture and continue it, in character, by a single reiteration in each of the following ways:

1. Use the same pitches with a rhythmic change.

2. Use a transposed projection without rhythmic change.

3. Use a different transposed projection with rhythmic change.

4. Use a tonal projection without rhythmic change.

5. Use a different tonal projection with rhythmic change.

C. Using the new gesture you produced for part B, continue the gesture and amplify it by using as many reiterations as necessary for achieving your desired transposed and tonal projections (with and without rhythmic change) to produce a melodic statement eight to twelve measures in length.

Notes

1. Base each item on an expressive intent.

2. Indicate the instrument used. If you choose to use the voice, supply a text.

3. Indicate the tempo.

4. Indicate the dynamic, articulation, and any other information relative to the expressive intent.

5. For part C, keep in mind the importance of sustaining and amplifying your expressive intent. It is of no value to use the available technical means if you use them without regard for your basic reason for making music.

Counterpoint: Musical Dialogue

The instinctive singing games of children: Are they antecedents of aesthetically directed acts of musical invention?

As we continue to explore the compositional processes we have observed in children's instinctive, unconscious music making, let us turn our attention now to Figure 19-1. This music, which could probably have become an **invention** (a short, two- or three-part contrapuntal composition based on a brief melodic shape) and which was given the title *Congenial Conversation* to stress the point of this chapter, is intended to illustrate something akin to the

19-1

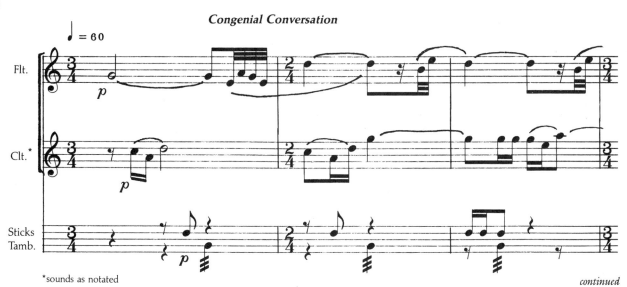

Congenial Conversation

*sounds as noted

continued

19-1, *continued*

instinctive, unconscious music of childhood. The playfulness shown in Figures 18-14 and 18-15 can be translated into an aesthetically directed act of musical invention by applying the compositional procedure called *counterpoint*.

How do we reshape a configuration to form a new gesture?

The gesture presented in the first measure and a half of Figure 19-1 is notable primarily for its rhythmic design. Sustained by a feeling of continuity throughout its rhythmic unfoldment and by several transposed projections of the basic melodic shape within the same diatonic system, the prolonged gesture makes a musical statement that is well described as "congenial conversation."

Figure 19-1 also demonstrates the rhythmic reshaping of the familiar pitch configuration presented in the gesture of Figure 17-3, a reshaping that gives material form to a new gesture. This, in turn, was fashioned into a musical statement intended to sustain the expressive quality of the new gesture, a quality somewhat removed from that of the original gesture. What is most important about the new gesture and the musical statement in Figure 19-1 is the realization that the dramatic character and aesthetic expression of a musicwork is more the product of the manner in which the work is formed and performed than anything that can be attributed to the material substance of it.

Maintaining the integrity of the material—in this case, not only the intervallic content but the actual intervallic succession of the original configuration—through projected reiterations (transposed projections) provides interest with consistency. Sustaining the gesture while effecting rhythmic changes, however, allows the entire "statement" of Figure 19-1 to take on a shape of its own by providing rhythmic direction and dramatic purpose. In the exercise of the compositional processes used, we must realize that there are no special formulas; there are no mechanical means by which we can either produce a gesture or sustain one. We must be *subjective* about the choices we make and *objective* about our control over these choices.

The flute and clarinet lines of the little invention *Congenial Conversation* have been joined by a rhythmic configuration that replaces the skipping or swinging ostinato of Figure 18-14. Whereas the ostinato is perfectly compatible with the redundancy of the original mocking gesture, we have now refined and expanded our purpose, and the gesture has been prolonged into a more complex and aesthetic musical statement. We would naturally expect the accompanying rhythmic configuration to reflect the same careful choices and controls used in fashioning the other parts. Also, having replaced the voices (those of the taunting child and Mary) with a flute and clarinet, it was appropriate to change the "skipping feet" to the percussion instruments available in a classroom: membrane drums, wood blocks, and triangles. (Empty plastic bottles, struck with the eraser ends of pencils, are good substitutes for membrane drums.)

In fashioning a percussion part (as shown in Figure 19-1), keep in mind that it must complement the gesture and contribute to the qualitative and quantitative characteristics of the total musicwork. Though the configuration formed by the sticks and tambourine appears to be quite different from what is in the upper two parts, the configuration bears a strong resemblance, rhythmically, to what the clarinet plays in the first measure. Had the choice been made to have the percussion participate in the conversation with the flute and clarinet rather than reiterate a related rhythmic figure as a subtle ostinato, more could have been done to have the percussion use some of the rhythmic configurations used by the other two instruments.

What is counterpoint?

As is readily apparent in Figure 19-1, we chose simply to allow the percussion to "comment" unobtrusively on the flute's dialogue with the clarinet; and, as it turned out, the "comment" quietly serves as an additional unifying factor. By changing the "skipping" ostinato to percussion "comments," we now have three instrumental lines participating in a kind of musical dialog called *counterpoint*.

Counterpoint (noun) is derived from the Latin *punctus contra punctum*, which translates literally to "point against point," meaning note against note or, more understandably, melody against melody. The term denotes: (1) a musicwork made up of two or more musical lines (melodies) sounding together, and (2) the art of producing music having two or more musical lines sounding together. Other terms that can be used interchangeably with *counterpoint*, in appropriate contexts, are (1) **contrapuntal** (adjective), a more literal derivation of *punctus contra punctum*, which, when combined with the word *music* (*contrapuntal music*), describes the kind of music produced by using counterpoint; (2) **polyphony** (noun), a term that has been used to classify the kinds of music that are contrapuntal in nature; and (3) **polyphonic** (adjective), a term that, when combined with the word *music* (*polyphonic music*), also denotes the kind of music produced by the use of counterpoint.

We could argue that all music—monophonic, homophonic, or polyphonic—is contrapuntal to some degree; that all music makes use of what might loosely be called the principles of counterpoint. In some **monophonic music** (music made up of a single melodic line) the melody is constructed so as to appear to combine the essential features of two melodic lines. This kind of writing was used most effectively in the unaccompanied suites and various other works of Bach. See Figure 19-2. Such implied two-part counterpoint has produced the term *contrapuntal melody*.

19-2

Sonata No. 3 for Unaccompanied Violin

Bach

Homophonic music is music with essentially one important melodic line (generally a solo voice or a solo instrument) supported by some form of keyboard or ensemble accompaniment. It may offer many moments in which various elements of the accompaniment assert themselves to create subtle contrapuntal relationships with the leading, solo line. See Figure 19-3.

19-3

Prelude, Op. 28, No. 4

Chopin

Thus we might conclude that all music, to some degree, contains evidence of contrapuntal relationships which may, in a limited sense, be called counterpoint. However, the primary distinction between contrapuntal music and other music is that contrapuntal music is made up of individual and relatively independent musical lines, each of which—theoretically, at least—is equal in importance. Whatever the degree of tonal and rhythmic "compatibility" or "incompatibility" we build into the relationship of the lines of a contrapuntal work, the lines must always and emphatically convey a sense of belonging together.

What is the nature and "tone" of musical conversation?

To continue our devlopment of the compositional processes, let us deal further with the dimension of counterpoint as first introduced by Mary's response in the childhood encounter conjectured in Figure 18-15. In Figure 18-14, we had only the taunting chant of a child, presented along with the "skipping" ostinato. The corresponding parts in Figure 19-1 would be the flute and percussion instruments. We could have approached the third part as we did the percussion part with either pitched or nonpitched instruments. However, because we wanted the additional voice to grow out of the material presented in the gesture, as did Mary's response, our task was no more difficult though more artistically intentioned. Whereas the counterpoint produced by the percussion part serves only to provide a relatively uninvolved "commentary" that demands little or no response from the flute part in Figure 19-1, a second pitched instrument (the clarinet), using material in common with the flute, produces a kind of counterpoint that enters the domain of "conversation."

For people to engage in conversation, each must understand what the other (others) is saying—this is required by definition. Also, we can assume that the "tone" of a conversation will be established by the disposition of the participants. For example, one party of a conversation might be contentious, another indignant, and a third party conciliatory. In such a conversation, all three parties may vie for attention; we could describe the "tone" of that conversation as argumentative. Other combinations of attitudes could produce conversations that could be described as elegant (if everyone is allowed to be heard in a display of refined manners) and one-sided (if one party dominates and the others are subdued).

The **expressive tone** (the composite of the abstract emotional qualities involved) of the conversations (counterpoint) in music can be likened to verbal conversations, in that the interaction of the parts may also appear argumentative, one-sided, elegant, imitative, cryptic, boisterous, and so on. However, if we are to have an effective interaction of parts throughout a musicwork, we must not only determine the expressive tone of the work but must also control it syntactically during its unfoldment.

The making (composing) of counterpoint may be likened to verbal conversation, also; it is produced effectively only when the interaction of parts is made to unfold all-of-one-piece in time rather than by adding part upon part. An intelligent verbal conversation could not take place if one party first recorded his or her statements, and then a second party superimposed his or her statements onto what was said by the first party, and this was followed by the superimpositions of all other parties until all were heard. Music composed in this manner is a kind of collage of independent parts (or voices) that "coexist" more than "converse" musically.

How is counterpoint used to achieve an expressive objective?

By retaining the shape and intervallic configuration (-3, P4, $+2$, -3) of the "mocking" gesture presented in Figure 17-3, we can form a variety of new gestures by using different rhythmic configurations. The new gestures can be prolonged (sustained) by reiterations that have been rhythmically changed and projected to various positions within the diatonic system or transpositions of it. When produced as a composite, interacting unfoldment of two or more lines supporting the expressive tone of the gesture, these prolongations have the effect of inducing the conversationlike effect of counterpoint such as in Figure 19-1. Observe that, in the examples in Figures 19-4 through 19-7, the counterpoint is used to achieve the expressive objectives indicated by the titles. For example, the counterpoint in Figure 19-4 has a quality we might characterize as quarrelsome because of the close pitch relationships and the rhythmic and dynamic crescendo. The louder, staccato of the first trumpet seems to intrude on the lyric quality first established by the second trumpet—metaphorically touching off a rather "quarrelsome" musical conversation.

19-4

The counterpoint in Figure 19-5, on the other hand, suggests the polite forms of conversation associated with refined, "elegant" manners. The voices are farther apart and display a give-and-take attitude that allows each voice to consider, figuratively, what the other voice is "saying" and then to respond while the other voice assumes the role of listener.

19-5

The oboe in Figure 19-6 is holding a rather one-sided conversation, figuratively, with the viola, which appears unable to interject more than a "word or two" in the nature of quiet agreement.

19-6

The two trumpets in Figure 19-7 are obviously in a follow-the-leader situation; they each "imitate" portions of what the other has done.

In each of the examples just discussed, the musical conversation, in effect, is carried on principally by the pitched instruments. The percussion instruments provide a kind of unobtrusive commentary similar to that used in Figure 19-1.

19-7

What is texture in music?

The term *texture* originally was associated with the appearance and feel of fabrics; it referred to the relative roughness of the feel, the relative thickness of the threads, the general characteristics of the weave, and so on. It came to be used to characterize similar kinds of sensory impressions in music; for example, sharp, angular shapes produce a **musical texture** quite different from that made with smooth, rounded, shapes. Contrapuntal music is texturally different from homophonic music. Music made of massive blocks of sound is texturally different from music made of light, subtle wisps of sound. As a most obvious and impressionable result of the physical characteristics and treatment of the materials making up a musicwork, texture is one aspect that determines the aura of sound.

The **aura** of a musicwork is an intangible though readily perceived quality that we might think of as its "personality." It is an expressive result that exceeds our intuitive assessment of the sum total of a musicwork's perceivable relationships.

Obviously, not all music is fashioned to provide a texture of perpetual "musical discourse"; that would be quite tedious for listeners as well as composers. The textural possibilities are extremely varied, even though any multiple-voiced texture would be regarded technically as counterpoint. A musicwork can be conceived as a simple melody within a simple harmonic/rhythmic setting or as several melodic lines and coloristic sonorities combined in a complex of intricately related rhythmic configurations. Regardless of how a musicwork is conceived, the aural effect must be one of a unified "fabric" of sound that unfolds spontaneously and provides an expression of inevitability and aesthetic purpose. Whatever compositional techniques the composer might use or the mechanics he or she might employ in committing a musicwork to some form of notation—or to tape in the case of electronic music—the fitness of each element and configuration in its relationship to the whole must be given utmost consideration.

MINI PROJECT 8

Using a pitch configuration of at least four distinct pitches and no more than seven notes, do the following:

1. Create a melodic gesture having a tempo, a rhythmic configuration, articulation, and dynamics that serve a particular expressive intent.

2. Using that melodic gesture, produce a two-part invention for piano that incorporates transposed and tonal projections and rhythmic change.

In producing the two-part invention, consider the following conditions:

1. The invention need not be longer than sixteen to twenty measures. Whatever the length, it should sound finished; it shouldn't just stop.

2. The pitch configuration should be basically diatonic in nature but it need not fit into the natural diatonic system or a transposition of it.

3. If the pitch configuration fits within the natural or a transposed diatonic system, the transposed and tonal projections need not be within the same diatonic system.

4. The intervallic, rhythmic, and textural relationships you establish between the two voices by manipulating the gesture should be the primary means of sustaining the character of the gesture.

5. In projecting the pitch configurations, take care that they follow in a musically logical manner and that your rhythmic design unites the projected configurations into a single, musical entity.

20 Auralization and the Creative-Process Spiral

What is auralization?*

We "hear" music mentally in very much the same way we form mental images. Just as *visualization* (to visualize) denotes "seeing" mentally, *auralization* (to auralize) denotes "hearing" mentally. Both terms denote the ability of our brains to abstract visual and aural sensations simultaneously.

What is the importance of auralization to musicians?

The ability to auralize is very important to musicians. With practice, auralization can allow us to audition, mentally, a certain amount of musical information without having to produce it physically. Auralization can give us a complete mental synthesis of our producing–hearing musical network; it is akin to the mental processes we know as imagination.

What is the value of concrete timbrel association in auralization?

Attempting to auralize music without making timbrel associations can be frustrating, because it is an attempt to call forth information that does not exist as a separate, perceivable entity. What we usually "hear" when we believe we are auralizing only pitch is an ambiguous, nondescript timbre that is a composite of our store of collected sounds. We tend to cultivate this utilitarian "inner voice" over the years and to use it for auralizing everything.

If, however, we make a concrete timbrel association at the outset, we can readily call forth musical patterns as if they were sung or played by a particular instrument. Though it might seem, on the surface, that auralizing both pitch and color is doing two mental jobs and thus doubling the work, the fact is that, by calling forth sound as we actually perceive and store it, we allow our minds to function the way they are programmed.

*Term attributed to Morris Knight, Jr.

As an exercise in auralization, try auralizing the musicwork you transcribed for your Unit One project. Auralize individual lines at first; then combine two lines, and continue until you are able to auralize the entire ensemble. Think of the instruments you used for your transcription. Conduct the "visualized" collection of instruments as you auralize the music.

Of what value is our tendency to vary the effects of spontaneity while auralizing?

A characteristic phenomenon we discover as our ability to auralize improves is the unconscious tendency to vary music as we auralize it. Spontaneous variations are most often directed toward an impulsive reaction to the character of the instrumental tone being auralized. Though the inclination to modify musical material as a "habit" is the very fountainhead of creative musicianship, it seems to imply conflict between those who are primarily composers and those who are primarily performers. This perception of conflict is without foundation when we realize that a balance between the spontaneous and the deliberate must exist in both categories of music making. The spontaneity of the person who invents music must be deliberate and expressed clearly in the notation for those who will perform it; the person who executes a musicwork with faithful exactitude must, finally, be quite spontaneous if the performance is to be convincing. To be able to blend deliberateness with spontaneity requires the utmost musical discipline.

What are the components of the creative-process spiral?

Making an artwork in any medium requires a monitoring system for keeping the maker informed and in control as the work evolves. This monitoring system provides the means for continuous feedback. The construction of a musicwork takes place in time, and the work emerges as a succession of intelligibly related sounds, which, when presented in performance, also take place in time. It is necessary, therefore, that each sound be evaluated in terms of its temporal as well as its physical relationship to the preceding sounds. A musicwork, then, is a series of sound relationships, each of which is subject to a string of interactions and reactions among the three primary components of the creative process: conceiving, making, and evaluating.

Study the illustration of the creative-process spiral in Figure 20-1. Each cycle of the monitoring system provides feedback for the creative process, involving the brain, mind, senses,

20-1   THE CREATIVE-PROCESS SPIRAL

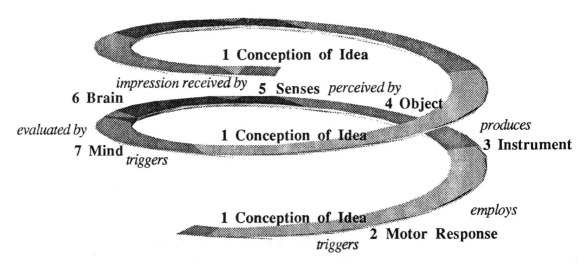

Reproduced through the courtesy of Morris Knight, Jr. Illustration by John F. Sherman.

and muscles. This represents the uniquely human combination of the visceral and intellectual; each gives impetus to the other, making the cycle appear to be automatic. Once initiated, the process can occur so rapidly as to seem instantaneous. With each completion of the cycle, the loop grows, forming a continuous spiral that ends only when the product is complete; conceiving + making + evaluating = deciding (that is, to keep, to change, or to discard) = conceiving + making + evaluating = deciding . . . on to the end.

What are the monitoring phases of the creative process?

The creative-process spiral (Figure 20-1) has essentially two separate phases: the inventing/making phase (steps 1–4), and the phase in which cognition and evaluation occur (steps 4–7). The first phase can be considered more creative; the second can be considered more analytical. The creative process in any human endeavor follows a course similar to this. Figure 20-2 contrasts the components of the creative-process spiral in the four major types of art.

20-2

				STEP			
	1. Idea	2. Motor Response	3. Instrument	4. Object	5. Cognition	6. Evaluation	7. Response
Aural Arts	sound configuration, etc.	fingers, voice	keyboard, voice, pencil or pen, paper, recorder, computer	music symbols, recorded sound, floppy disk	aural aided by visual; often delayed	in terms of interest and potential	repeat cycle, modify, or discard
Graphic Arts	shape, color, subject, etc.	hands, fingers	brush, canvas, knife, chisel, paint, etc.	image, object	visual; immediate	"	"
Literary Arts	theme, setting, situation	hands, fingers	pencil, pen, typewriter, word processor, paper	words	visual; reread	"	"
Kinetic Arts	gesture, humorous or tragic situation, etc.	body (all or part)	human body, stage, film, camera	movement, facial expression, mime, etc.	muscle feel; visual aided by aural	"	"

Reproduced through the courtesy of Morris Knight, Jr.

Comparing the activities of the creative musician with those of the graphic artist (Figure 20-2), we detect a problem of considerable magnitude with regard to what takes place between steps 4 and 5 in the process. A creative musician, employing his or her voice, for example, will (1) conceive a musical idea that (2) triggers a motor response utilizing (3) the voice to (4) realize a musical configuration that is simultaneously (5) sensed by the ears, sending (6) impulses to the brain and enabling (7) the mind to evaluate the idea. The first four steps of the process are roughly the same for the graphic artist and the creative musician. However, at the end of step 4, the graphic artist has produced a tangible image or object that remains; the creative musician is left with only the memory or notation of a voiced musical configuration. The creative musician knows that, if the cycles of the creative process are separated by even a short period of time, the original idea is apt to be forgotten or unconsciously altered. It is necessary, therefore, to notate the musical idea and all subsequent ideas as they occur.

What is the value of a secondary instrument?

To alleviate the difficulties of notating music having complexities beyond the capabilities of the voice, a creative musician must find a fixed-pitch instrument upon which tone can be produced easily. The most accessible and useful is usually a keyboard instrument such as a piano. The piano provides an easy-to-learn display of available pitches and permits the simultaneous sounding of two or more tones. A creative musician's task, once he or she learns to use the keyboard, is made somewhat easier; but the task remains complex because of the problems of audition.

What are the problems of audition?

A creative musician, having completed a graphic representation (a notated score) of the "object," must wait for a final cognition (audition) and evaluation. The "object" produced by a graphic artist is not a representation of itself; what the graphic artist produces *is* the object. It may be viewed and evaluated as it is. The creative musician has auralized the musical object and worked with it in some fashion at the piano. However, unless the music was intended for the piano and the musician happens to be a pianist, the music has not been auditioned.

As a perceivable art object, music is perceived only in terms of sound. Therefore, even though we may become extremely adept at translating representative visual symbols into sound objects mentally, the process remains auralization. Using the piano to audition a musical object intended for some other instrument (or group of instruments), can provide the pitch content of the music, but it can do so only in the guise of the piano's timbre and articulation capabilities. As a substitute for audition or as a partial realization of audition, the process remains an aid to auralization.

The need for continuous audition and the difficulty of obtaining it is perhaps the least understood and least appreciated facet of the musical art. In light of the creative musician's dependence on audition as the only valid basis for effecting and evaluating artistic growth, it is little wonder that the creatively active periods throughout history have been those when music was produced for performing groups that encouraged audition. This points up the paramount importance of giving each project you complete for this course time for audition and evaluation. The special knowledge of sound that is required for success in producing music can be acquired in no other way.

What are the problems of evaluation?

After audition comes evaluation. This should be the most natural and automatic part of the cycle. The mind, if allowed to function without the impediment of extraneous inhibitions, will trigger modifications and additions to the initial expression, and the cycle will begin again. Unfortunately, we can get caught up in a web of self-doubt at this point. Our initial attempts at making music may seem ridiculously feeble in relation to the world of recognized great music. We may even feel intimidated by the recognized masterpieces of the past and present. Also, we may be overawed by the fables of genius. The myths surrounding "the creative act" may lead us to infer that musical works result from divine inspiration and that if we just wait for inspiration to come, we will be able to write great music.

If all of these subconscious thoughts were not enough to inhibit the creative musician, the twentieth-century notion that success is based on wide public acceptance tends to make us doubt our judgment. Caught in this web of irrationality, we may seek an alternative that will save us from possible embarrassment. One typical alternative is to find a suitable model, one that contains the solutions to our problems. The trouble with this, however, is that we cannot quite stipulate what the musical problems are because we have not yet encountered them. Also, how do we go about selecting a model? What era? What musicwork? This momentary aberration is to be expected, because our era has a veritable "Persian market" of miscellanies.

Another, equally aberrant response that can occupy the mind of the creative musician and inhibit the creative process results in a premature and gross distortion of the desire to develop artistic independence. This alternative is chosen by the musician who mistrusts not only his or her judgment but also all current conventions and aesthetic criteria. For such a musician, relying on personal judgment is rejected for shot-in-the-dark speculations. This viewpoint is certain to create more problems than it solves and to frustrate valid expectations rather than to exploit them in a satisfying manner.

If the creative musician is to establish a workable aesthetic orientation and gain confidence in his or her capability of functioning in the art, he or she must concentrate exclusively on the problems and work to solve them rather than circumvent or ignore them. Creative problem solving is the creative musician's proper domain regardless of what else is happening on the periphery.

What about "originality"?

Another inhibiting factor that confronts every artist centers on originality: Why bother to make something if it is not going to be original? This question can be countered with another question: How can I tell if something is original before it is made? The fact of the matter is that every honest artwork is original—that is, if it is not a direct copy of another artwork—because every individual is an original. No two musical minds contain the same information; and no two nervous systems have the same rhythmic makeup. Being artistically honest (or original) really means being responsive to our own basic built-in feedback system. This is not a simple task.

The creative projects of this and later study units are designed to allow you to discover the working of your own creative-process spiral. Concentrate on the processes involved; they are important to your success. The topics discussed in this and other units are important in themselves, but their importance is best demonstrated in support of the intelligent use of your creative instincts.

21

Visual Mapping, Aural Tracking, and Modification of Melodic Configurations

What is visual mapping?

Visual mapping is the process we use when we recognize an object from various vantage points. For example, we recognize a classroom chair regardless of our angle of view. We simply accept the visual stimuli of lines, angles, curves, lengths, widths, and all other dimensional, textural, and color information and process the results through our memory banks. In what seems to be instantaneous cognition, we are assured that what we see is not only a classroom chair, it is the *same* chair we saw a moment ago or the day before from a different angle, and that it is the same (or one of the many like it) that has occupied the room since we entered the first time many weeks ago.

How is visual mapping affected by learned discrimination?

One of the basic problems children face in learning to recognize and reproduce the letters of the alphabet is learning to compensate for their natural capacity to recognize a shape in any of its mappings. Having used mapping to recognize people and objects from birth, a child, in learning letters, easily recognizes the four letters in Figure 21-1 as different mappings of the same shape and confuses them. What the child is being asked to do is to regard the four mappings as different *shapes*.

21-1

d b
q p

We must realize that without the ability to map objects visually and thus discriminate between the familiar and the unfamiliar, the visible world would be a rather frightening, kaleidoscopic jungle. Beyond our natural capacity to map and recognize visual stimuli, we must learn to discriminate between discrete positings of objects and symbols, especially when these positings project specialized information or represent specialized functions. We would not attach any significance to the random position of objects in a pile of trash just dumped from a truck. We would, however, attach significance to the arrangement of objects in a friend's home. Depending on the degree of order or disorder, we might regard the friend as overly organized, relatively organized, neat, a bit untidy, untidy, sloppy, or as a recent victim of a burglar.

What is the relationship between visual mapping and aural tracking?

Because we deal with the notation of music as well as music itself, we must learn to relate the **aural tracking** (discernment of the pitch and temporal ordering of a musical configuration from hearing it) of a melodic configuration to its visual mapping. Though tracking and mapping differ in how they function as ways of receiving sensory information, they serve the same basic purpose. Given a particular melodic configuration, we must learn to recognize and correlate the various possible positings of the configuration as expressed in sound and in notation. Because we deal primarily with notated music in the examples in this book and because the discussion related to these examples is directed at notated music, the term *mapping* will be used unless a specific situation requires reference to aural tracking. We would suppose that if we auralize the melodic configuration shown in a musical example, we are also mapping the configuration because there is no sound present to be aurally tracked.

What are the four mappings of a melodic configuration?

A melodic configuration can be posited so as to provide four different mappings of the configuration: the *original*, the *inversion*, the *retrograde*, and the *retrograde-inversion*. All of these mappings (or trackings) are generally thought of as differing views of the same thing, but that is only partially true. The following discussion will point out a definite correlation between an original melodic configuration and its retrograde. However, an inversion and a retrograde inversion present considerations that make them obviously different.

What is an inversion of a melodic configuration?

Two forms of inversion are possible. See Figure 21-2. The inversions in parts 1a and 2a are mirror inversions. In a **mirror inversion**, the order of discrete intervals is the same as in the original. The inversions in parts 1b and 2b are tonal inversions. In a **tonal inversion**, the order of intervals in terms of their ordinal types is the same as in the original, but the discrete ordinal name of at least one interval is different.

Whichever kind of inversion is used, it does not have to begin on the same pitch as the original mapping; it can begin on any pitch of the diatonic system (or whatever tonal system is used). We should realize that it is the set of intervallic relationships within the configuration—and even more fundamentally, its basic shape—that is being inverted, not the pitches themselves. There is nothing about a collection of pitches to invert except the intervallic relationships they produce. An inversion may also be cast in a different temporal configuration. Though a temporal configuration can be presented in retrograde, there is nothing about a temporal configuration that can be inverted.* There is, therefore, no particular reason to retain the original temporal configuration except as a preferred choice.

*This excludes the extended, nonphysical application of inversion used by serial composers such as Milton Babbitt.

21-2

In part 1a of Figure 21-3, after the original melodic configuration is stated, the line continues with a mirror inversion that begins on the notated pitch B$_5$ and is cast in a different temporal configuration. In (1b) the line continues with a tonal inversion. In part 2a of the figure, the brief initial configuration from Beethoven's *Leonore* Overture No. 1 is followed by a mirror inversion, is repeated as a tonal inversion, and is then repeated again as a mirror inversion. These repetitions use the rhythmic configuration of the original. The examples in parts 2b and 2c are from Brahms's Fourth Symphony. In (2b) we see a two-measure configuration followed by what sounds like a tonal inversion that uses the same rhythmic shape. It does, in fact, contain an expanded interval (E$_4$–A$\sharp_3$). In (2c) the tonal inversion is used as a relief variant in a series of repetitions. Part 2d presents a mirror inversion of an entire four-measure opening phrase of the third movement of Brahms's First Symphony. Figure 21-3 illustrates only a few of the many ways inversions can be used as a means of continuing a line. Other purposes for using inversions are also very common. The existence of an inversion can be extremely unobtrusive (as in parts 1a and 1b) or more literal rhythmically (as in parts 2a, 2b, 2c, and 2d).

W107

21-3

(1a) Ob.

(1b) Ob.

(2a)   from *Leonore Overture* No. 1

(2b)   from Symphony No. 4, Mov. I

(2c)   from Symphony No. 4, Mov. II

(2d)   from Symphony No. 1, Mov. III

What is a retrograde of a melodic configuration?

A **retrograde** of a melodic configuration is the reverse ordering of either its discrete interval or its ordinal types. Because a retrograde is a mapping of a pitch shape, we do not consider the reverse ordering of a temporal configuration alone as a retrograde. The various possible reverse mappings of the temporal configuration do, however, add to the total options available in producing a retrograde. The most obvious options are those of presenting the same pitch content in retrograde and of presenting a retrograde at a different pitch level. If the retrograde is presented at a different pitch level, we can then regard it as a retrograde of either the discrete intervals of the original configuration or of the ordinal interval types. In both cases, the retrograde would be a *projection*: the first one a transposed projection of a retrograde; the second one, a tonal projection of a retrograde. As further options, we can also include the temporal configuration in retrograde or in its original order, or we can change it to a slightly or even entirely different configuration.

Figure 21-4a illustrates a retrograde of both the pitch and temporal configuration of a melodic configuration. In Figure 21-4b, the pitch content of the melodic configuration is presented in retrograde, but the temporal configuration is retained. Part c of the figure, illustrates a tonal projection of a retrograde, in which the original temporal configuration is replaced by another.

21-4

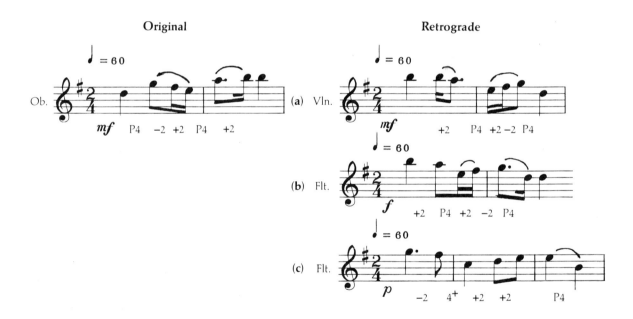

There are three possibilities with regard to pitch or intervallic content: (1) the retrograde of the original pitch content, (2) a transposed projection of a retrograde, and (3) a tonal projection of a retrograde. And there are three possibilities with regard to temporal content: (1) the original temporal configuration, (2) the retrograde of the original configuration, and (3) a different temporal configuration. This makes a total of nine possible combinations for producing a retrograde of a melodic shape. Figure 21-5 illustrates a tonal projection of a retrograde with the original temporal configuration in part 1a and a transposed projection of a retrograde with the different temporal configuration in part 1b. Part 2a of Figure 21-5 presents a retrograde with a varied rhythmic shape from Beethoven's *Leonore* Overture No. 3, and part 2b, a retrograde from Bach's *Invention* No. 4. Stravinsky's *Firebird* Suite provides examples of two retrogrades used to continue a line: the first one (part 2c) uses the same rhythmic shape; the second (part 2d) varies the rhythm.

21-5

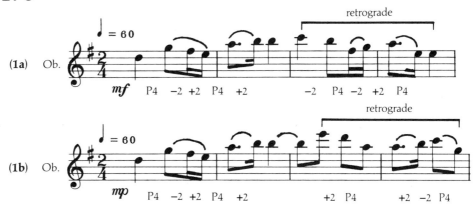

from *Leonore* **No. 3**

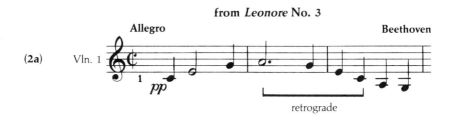

from *Invention* **No. 4**

from *The Firebird*

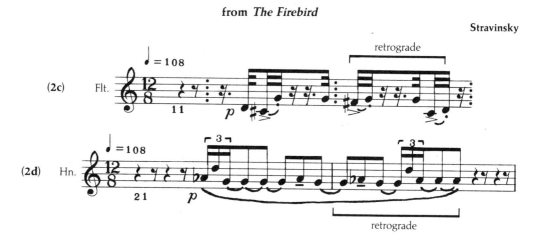

What is a retrograde inversion?

In a **retrograde inversion**, we are dealing with either the retrograde of a mirror inversion or the retrograde of a tonal inversion. In addition, all of the conditions applicable to the inversion of a melodic configuration apply to the retrograde inversion. Because we are relating a retrograde inversion to an original melodic configuration rather than to its inversion, only two options remain with respect to the pitch and intervallic content: (1) the retrograde inversion of a transposed projection, and (2) the retrograde inversion of a tonal projection. Both of these are illustrated in Figure 21-6, each using the original temporal configuration. The three options for temporal considerations are the same as for a retrograde. In part 1a of Figure

21-6

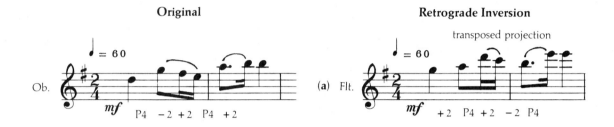

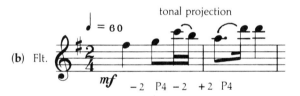

21-7, the line is continued by the use of the retrograde inversion of a transposed projection using a different temporal configuration. In (1b) the line is continued by the retrograde inversion of a tonal projection with a different temporal configuration. In part 2a of Figure 21-7 is a retrograde inversion of a transposed projection used in the continuation of the opening line of the Interlude from Benjamin Britten's *Les Illuminations*. This brings us to the point at which a detailed explanation of the manifold ways the mappings and projections thus far presented can be modified to form topological projections.   **W108—109**

21-7

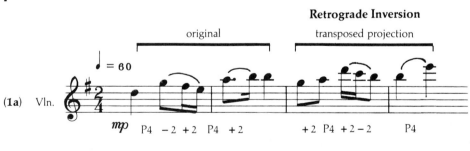

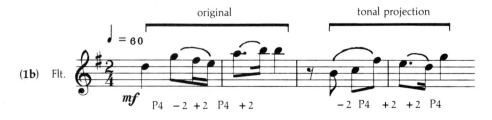

21-7, *continued*

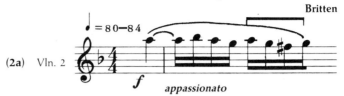

from *Les Illuminations*, Op. 18, VI. Interlude

Britten

(2a)   Vln. 2

f   *appassionato*

MINI PROJECT 9

A. Using the pitch configuration of the melodic gesture you produced for Mini Project 8,

 1. Produce two distinctly new melodic gestures using mirror inversion.

 2. Produce two distinctly new melodic gestures using tonal inversion.

 3. Produce two distinctly new melodic gestures using retrograde.

 4. Produce two distinctly new melodic gestures using retrograde inversion.

B. Using one of the new melodic gestures you have just produced:

 1. Continue the melodic gesture by a single reiteration using a mirror inversion with rhythmic change.

 2. Continue the melodic gesture by a single reiteration using a tonal inversion with rhythmic change.

 3. Continue the melodic gesture by a single reiteration using a retrograde with rhythmic change.

 4. Continue the melodic gesture by a single reiteration using a retrograde inversion with rhythmic change.

 In completing A and B, score each gesture for a specific instrument, supply tempo indications, and supply whatever dynamics and articulation marks are needed.

22 | Topological Projections of Melodic Configurations

What is a topological projection?

If we project an image onto a smooth surface at an angle that is not 90°, the projected image will be distorted; it will either be elongated or widened, or the distortion will be some combination of the two. The distortion will be a rather simple one, the degree depending on the difference in the angle. If, on the other hand, we project an image onto an uneven surface (a stone wall, for example) at an angle different from 90°, the resulting image will be internally distorted as well as elongated, widened, or some combination of the two. As long as we are able to recognize the image—identify what the original is—we can call the projected image a *topological projection* rather than a different image.

A **topological projection** of a melodic configuration is a modification of the configuration or any of its remaining three mappings without a change in its basic shape. A topological projection of a melodic configuration is a distortion—at times a rather massive distortion—that complicates but does not destroy a discerning listener's ability to associate it with its origin. A topological projection of a melodic configuration can be likened to the distorted image produced by a mirror in a carnival fun house; the distortion may be drastic, but the image is not beyond recognition. As with visual projections, topological projections in music may be very simple or very complex. The most common ways of modifying a melodic configuration to achieve a topological projection are *interpolation, deletion, extension, contraction, interval expansion, interval contraction, octave displacement, harmonic change, permutation*, and *rhythmic change*. These may, in some cases, be used in combination.

What is interpolation?

To modify a melodic configuration by **interpolation** is to place one or more pitches within the configuration. Figure 22-1 presents some examples of interpolation; the interpolated

22-1

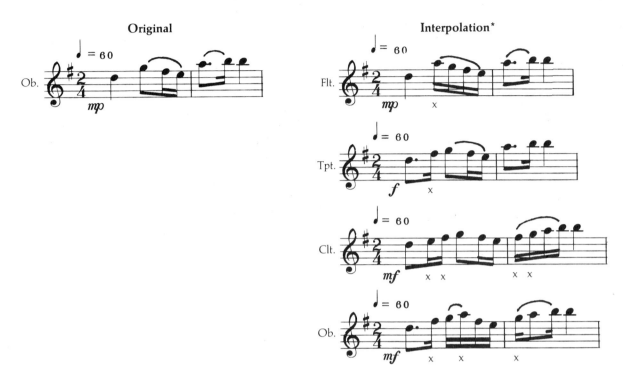

*x indicates interpolated pitches.

pitches are identified in each case. In part 1a of Figure 22-2, after presenting the original configuration, the line is continued with a repetition containing interpolated pitches. In (1b) the original is continued with a tonal projection with interpolated pitches. In (1c) the line is continued with a projected mirror inversion containing interpolated pitches. In part 2a of Figure 22-2 the opening three measures of the first movement of Haydn's Quartet No. 35 in F minor is followed by a repetition (measures 5–8) with interpolated pitches. In (2b), the dramatic opening line of the first movement of Brahms's First Symphony demonstrates an interpolated projection of either a tonal retrograde or a tonal inversion.

22-2

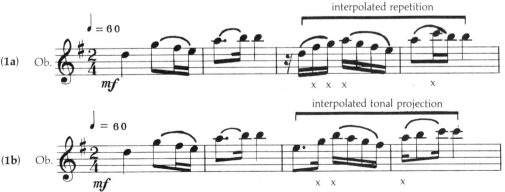

continued

22-2, *continued*

(1c)   Vln.

Note: x indicates interpolated pitches.

(2a)   Quartet No. 35 in F minor, Op. 20, No. 5, Mov. I

Haydn

(2b)   from Symphony No. 1, Mov. I

Brahms

Vln. 2

What is deletion?

A melodic configuration can be modified by removing one or more pitches from within the configuration. Some examples of **deletion** are shown in Figure 22-3. In part 1a of Figure 22-4, after the original configuration is sounded, the line continues with a tonal projection from which two pitches have been deleted. In (1b), the line continues with a projected tonal inversion with one pitch deleted. In (2a), the open-configuration of Bach's *Invention* No. 1 in C major is immediately followed by a transposed projection with deletions. In (2b) is a repetition of a phrase with deletions from the third movement of Brahms's Fourth Symphony.

22-3

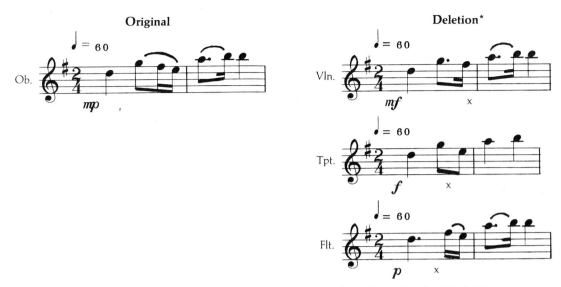

Original   Deletion*

*x indicates the location of a deleted pitch.

22-4

(1a)   Clt.

original   tonal projection
                           with deleted pitches

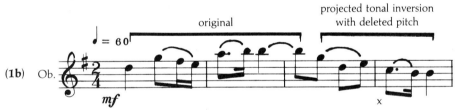

(1b)   Ob.

original   projected tonal inversion
                     with deleted pitch

Note: x indicates the location of a deleted pitch.

(2a)   **from *Invention* No. 1**

Bach

(2b)   **from Symphony No. 4, Mov. III**

Brahms

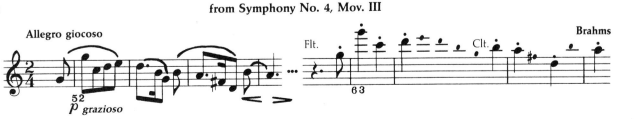

Note: Small noteheads indicate deleted pitches.

What is extension?

An **extension** of a melodic configuration adds one or more pitches to one end or both ends of the configuration (Figure 22-5). In Figure 22-6a, after presenting the original configuration, the line is continued with a tonal projection that is extended at both ends. Part b shows an extension at the end of a tonal projection of a four-measure phrase from the first movement of Mozart's Symphony No. 41 in C major. Extensions of this type are very common and are typically associated with some form of harmonic activity.

22-5

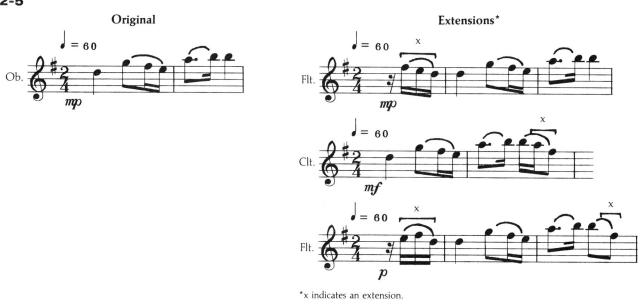

*x indicates an extension.

22-6

*x indicates an extension.

(b)

from Symphony No. 41 in C major, K. 551

Mozart

What is contraction?

To modify a melodic configuration by **contraction** is to shorten it by removing one or more pitches from one or both ends of it. Figure 22-7 gives two examples of contraction: the first pitch is removed in the first one; and the last pitch is removed in the second. In part 1a of

22-7

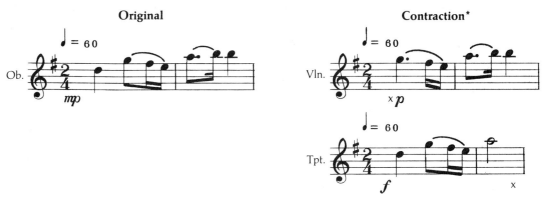

*x indicates location of eliminated pitch.

Figure 22-8, after the original configuration is presented, the line continues with a contracted version of a tonal projection. In (1b) the line continues with tonal projections of two retrograde inversions of the first measure, each of which is a contraction of the original. (What other mapping of a contraction can be found in part 1b?) In part 2a, from the second movement of Mozart's Quartet in D major for strings, K. 499, a four-measure phrase is contracted to two two-measure phrases: the first is a contracted transposed projection; the second, a contracted tonal projection. In (2b), a four-measure phrase from the third movement of Mozart's Quartet in D major, K. 575, is contracted to two two-measure phrases, both of which are transposed projections.

22-8

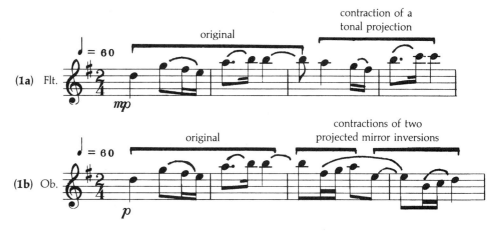

continued

22-8, *continued*

(2a)   from Quartet in D major, K. 499, Mov. II, Trio

Mozart

(2b)   from Quartet in D major, K. 575, Mov. III

Mozart

What is interval expansion?

Depending on the nature of the situation, any intervals of a melodic configuration can be expanded (made larger) to modify the configuration. Examples of **interval expansion** are shown in Figure 22-9; the expanded intervals are identified. In part 1a of Figure 22-10, the

22-9

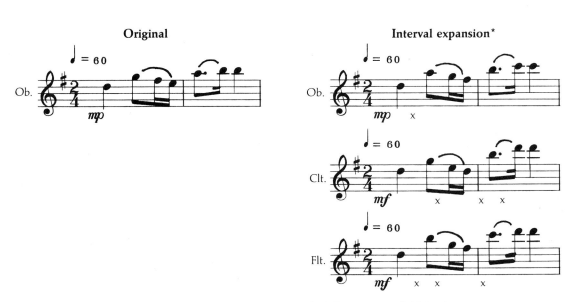

Original

Interval expansion*

*x indicates an expanded interval.

reiteration of the original configuration is presented as an inversion with expanded intervals as indicated. In (1b), the line is continued with a projected retrograde with expanded intervals as indicated. The excerpt from the second movement of Prokofieff's Symphony No. 5 in part 2a of Figure 22-10 shows a transposed projection with interval expansion at the end of the configuration. The excerpt from Hindemith's *Mathis der Maler* in (2b) shows an internal interval expansion that results in a partial repetition and a partial transposed projection.

22-10

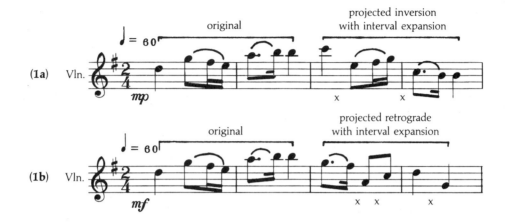

from Symphony No. 5, Mov. II

Prokofieff

from *Mathis der Maler*

Hindemith

Note: x indicates an expanded interval.

What is interval contraction?

Interval contraction (making an interval smaller) produces an effect opposite that of interval expansion; It is equally useful for modifying a melodic configuration. Examples of interval contraction are given in Figure 22-11. The reiteration that serves to extend the line in

22-11

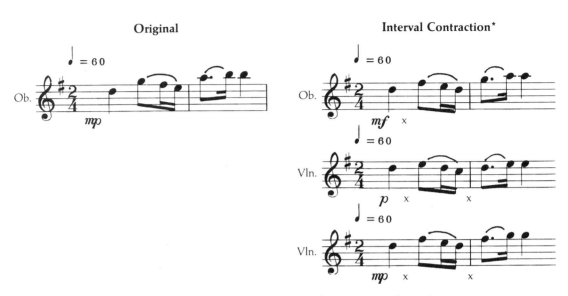

*x indicates a contracted interval.

part 1a of Figure 22-12 is a projected retrograde with two contracted intervals. In (1b), the line is continued with a projection containing two contracted intervals. In part 2a, the second measure of Debussy's Second Arabesque, in contrast with the first measure, contains interval contractions on beats one and three and interval expansions on beats two and four. The excerpt from Chopin's Mazurka, Op. 33, No. 4 (part 2b), illustrates a number of interval contractions as well as such devices as deletion and contraction.

22-12

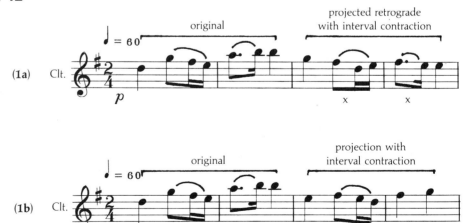

22-12, *continued*

Note: x indicates an interval contraction. z indicates an interval expansion.

What is octave displacement?

Of all of the common ways of modifying melodic configurations, only **octave displacement** (placing a pitch in a different octave) changes the basic shape visually. However, because the octave is recognized as a repetition of a pitch at a different level, the aural impression of the octave displacement is not always perceived as a genuine change of shape. Octave displacement is especially useful in such musicworks as concertos for instruments with extended pitch ranges. It permits greater utilization of an instrument's range and provides for the repetition of pitch classes within the same rhythmic configuration, a procedure that mollifies the effect of a literal repetition.

The octave displacements in the first two examples in Figure 22-13 serve as a means of moving from one area of an instrument's range to another. Example 3 uses octave displacement to utilize a major portion of the instrument's range and increase the intensity of the expression, an intensity that is suddenly relaxed by the relative displacement of the final pitch. The octave displacement of the last pitch in example 4 serves to soften the effect of the entire configuration. Example 5 outlines a tonal projection of a retrograde of a modified original; that is, B, E, F sharp, G. Example 6 can be regarded as preserving the visual impression of the basic shape of the original configuration though it is exaggerated slightly. The continuing portion of the line in

22-13

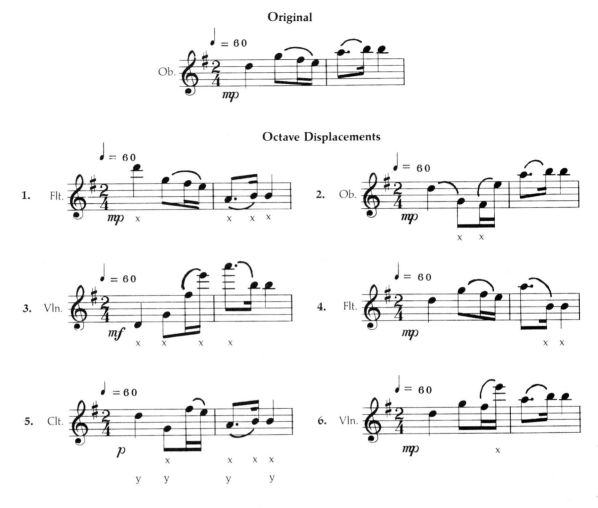

Note: x indicates an octave displacement. y outlines a tonal projection of a retrograde of a modified original; for example, B, E, F♯, G.

part 1a of Figure 22-14 is a tonal projection with octave displacements. In (1b), the continuing portion of the line is a tonal inversion with octave displacement. The excerpt from the third movement of Beethoven's Piano Concerto No. 4 in part 2a of the figure compares a portion of the piano solo with the opening melodic line in the violins. In (2b), a portion of a violin line from the second movement of Prokofieff's Symphony No. 5 is compared with the opening line of the same movement.

22-14

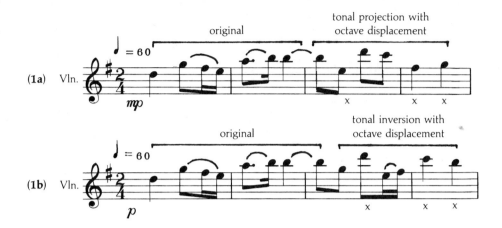

x indicates an octave displacement.

(2a)   **from Piano Concerto No. 4, in G major, Mov. III**

Vivace   Beethoven

(2b)   **from Symphony No. 5**

Prokofieff

What is harmonic change?

Harmonic change is a blanket term for the many minor changes in the intervallic makeup of configurations that either create or respond to changes in the harmonic color of a musicwork. Figure 22-15 shows examples of harmonic change using the melodic shape we have utilized in demonstrating the previously discussed devices. Along with each example, a suggested chordal background is given. It must be understood, however, that nothing specific should be inferred by these accompanying chordal backgrounds; a variety of such harmonic

22-15

accompaniments can be used in producing a musical texture. In Figure 22-16 we find a number of examples showing the continuation of the original configuration using harmonic change as the means of modification. The excerpt from *Les Illuminations* by Benjamin Britten in Figure

22-16

22-17a presents a repetition of both text and melodic shape which forms a C-sharp-minor triad then a D-flat-major triad. In part b of the figure, each of the four versions of the melodic shape from the Chopin Valse Op. 64 is different for harmonic reasons. The two versions of the melodic shape from the Chopin Valse Op. 69 in (c) differ for harmonic reasons, also.

22-17

(a)

from *Les Illuminations*

Britten

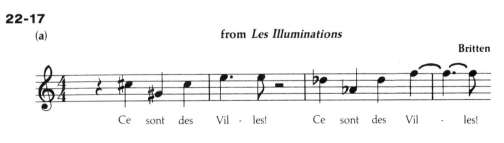

Ce   sont   des   Vil - les!   Ce   sont   des   Vil   -   les!

continued

22-17, *continued*

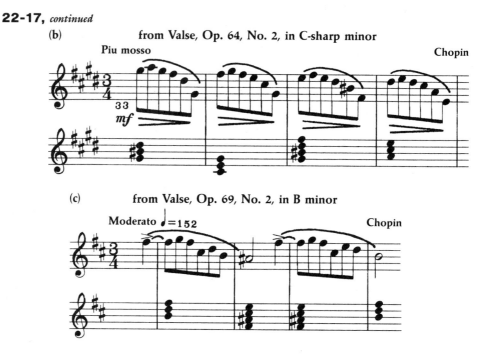

(b)   from Valse, Op. 64, No. 2, in C-sharp minor

Piu mosso   Chopin

(c)   from Valse, Op. 69, No. 2, in B minor

Moderato ♩=152   Chopin

What is rhythmic change?

Most shape-modifying procedures automatically change the rhythmic configuration of a melodic shape. **Rhythmic change**, to be considered a means of modification, must by itself be a change in the temporal makeup of a melodic configuration. By itself or in conjunction with other devices, rhythmic change is perhaps the most effective method of changing the expressive effect of a melodic shape. Rhythmic change can be accomplished within the framework of the same measure signature (Figure 22-18a) or a different signature (Figure 22-18b). A more extended rhythmic change is shown in Figure 22-18c. It must be realized that, without any changes in the pitch configuration of the original configuration used in these demonstrations, the configuration could be modified rhythmically many thousands of times.

22-18

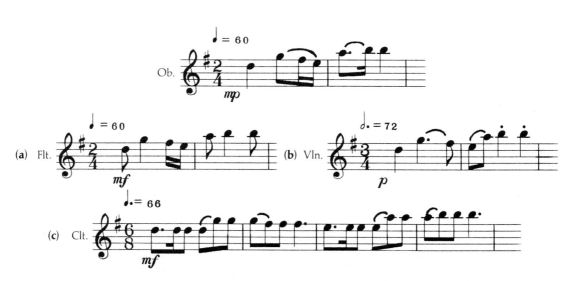

To depart from the practice of extending the melodic configuration used in demonstrating the various modifying procedures, it might be more profitable to demonstrate the changes in the expressive effect of rhythmic change on one of the principal melodic shapes in *Till Eulenspiegel*, Op. 28, by Richard Strauss. See Figure 22-19. The original configuration introduced by the violins in the opening statement is shown in (a), and a few of the various rhythmic transformations are shown in (1b) through (4b).

22-19

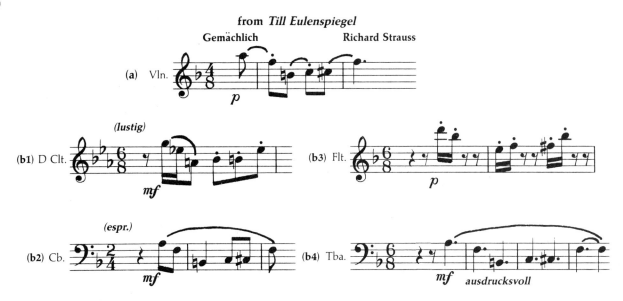

What is fragmentation?

Two other commonly used devices serve to transform rather than to modify the basic shape of the original pitch material while preserving other aspects of the original configuration. The first of these is fragmentation. Literally, a **fragmental melody** or portion of a melody is one that is produced from a fragment or fragments of another melody. **Fragmentation** denotes the practice of reiterating fragments of a basic configuration at various pitch levels for the purpose of extending a basic melodic shape or producing new melodic configurations. In Figure 22-20, the line is extended by using various fragments of the original configuration. The reiterated fragment is identified in each case. It should be noted that not all possible fragments are used.

22-20

Figure 22-21 shows examples of how fragmentation can be used to produce new melodic configurations. These could be used as the opening melodic gestures of the movements of a multimovement musicwork.

22-21

The continuation of an opening melodic statement of a musicwork by the application of fragmentation is rather common. The opening statement in the Allegro from the overture to Beethoven's *Leonore (Fidelio)*, No. 3, Op. 72, is interesting because fragmentation takes place on two levels. After the topological projection of the opening four measures (Figure 22-22a), there are two topological projections of the first two measures of the opening four-measure phrase. These form the first level of fragmentation; they are, in turn, followed by one-measure fragments of the first measure of the two-measure fragments. Brahms's Symphony No. 2, Op. 73, is a veritable "textbook" of melodic transformation. Figure 22-22b gives two examples of fragmentation, the first a fragmentary line produced from "a" of the original figure and the second a fragmentary continuation of a line from the fourth movement produced from "b" of the original shape. The beginning two measures of the line in part b of the figure show interpolation. Using a rhythmically changed repetition of the opening statement from Strauss's *Till Eulenspiegel*, two examples of fragmentation are given in Figure 22-22c. The first is a transposed set of fragments; the second is a group of tonal projections of the fragment.

22-22

Note: x indicates a pitch in the original shape.

What is pitch permutation?

Pitch permutation, used in this context, is the rearrangement, or internal "scrambling," of the pitch content of a melodic configuration. Though we are using the same melodic configuration we used to demonstrate the other devices, in general practice, configurations with fewer and more uniquely identifiable pitches would be used. This device can be applied to a reiteration of the same pitches, to a transposed projection, and to a mirror inversion. Though the basic shape of a configuration is not retained, the basic "aura" of sound is retained. It is the aura of sound that enables us to relate a permuted version to its original shape. Several permutations of the pitch content of a melodic configuration are shown in Figure 22-23. Because the configuration has six pitch members, a linear permutation would yield 720

22-23

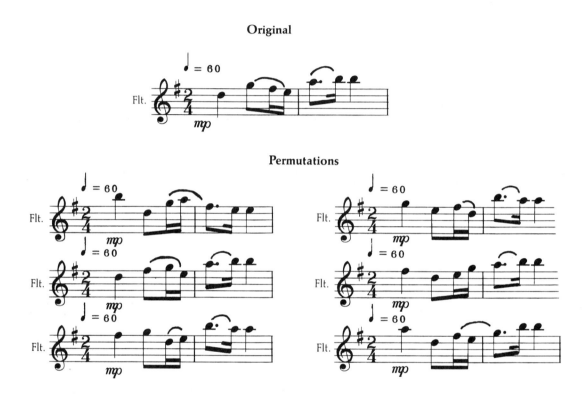

versions. In Figure 22-24, the line is continued by two and three permutations that are changed rhythmically as well. Pitch permutation, a practice confined primarily to scalewise and chordal

22-24

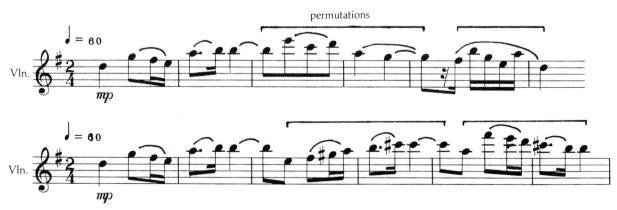

22-24, *continued*

pitch materials by pre-twentieth-century composers (such as in Bach's *Invention* No. 1; Figure 22-25a), was not a common means of modifying melodic shapes. An example from Stravinsky's *Capriccio* is shown in Figure 22-25b.

22-25

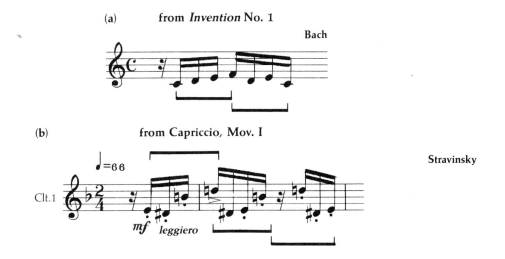

How do we use mapping and the common means of modifying melodic configurations when making music?

In describing the mapping and modifications of a melodic configuration, it is difficult not to make them appear to be devices that can be applied with equal effectiveness to all configurations at all times. A melodic line, we must be assured, cannot be made to unfold in an expressively lucid manner by mechanically applying some procedure or device. How, then, do we use the techniques that have been described and demonstrated?

Thus far we have introduced and described the most common ways a melodic configuration can be made to unfold naturally when used with normal and expressively purposeful musical intentions. In order to compare the effects of mapping and the various ways a configuration can be modified, the same melodic configuration has been used to demonstrate each procedure. Following each demonstration, examples from music literature have been presented to illustrate the concept. The examples are simply random, off-the-shelf selections;

they represent but a minuscule portion of what could serve as illustrations. It should be understood that the particular ways in which each modifying procedure was utilized represent but a few of the many ways the same kinds of modifications could be applied to the same melodic configurations. In some cases, dozens or even hundreds of different results could be obtained if desired. You should play and study the examples given, however, until you can think beyond the special cases they demonstrated and begin to sense the underlying principles.

How might we use more than one modifying device at a time?

Even though many of the modifications demonstrated thus far are in conjunction with different mappings of the original configuration, most of them demonstrate the use of only one kind of modification at a time. In general practice, it is both common and appropriate to use more than one modifying device in the prolongation of a melodic configuration. The original configuration in Figure 22-26 is extended by two reiterations, each of which makes use of more than one kind of modification. In part a we have the choice of considering the modification a contraction with interval expansion or an interval expansion with deletion applied to the retrograde of the original melodic configuration. We should realize, when we have such a choice, that the same or similar results can sometimes be realized by applying more than one modifying device at a time. In Figure 22-26b, we find a number of modifications (in the order of their use): interpolation, deletion, octave displacement, and extension. All of these are applied to a tonal projection of the original configuration.

22-26

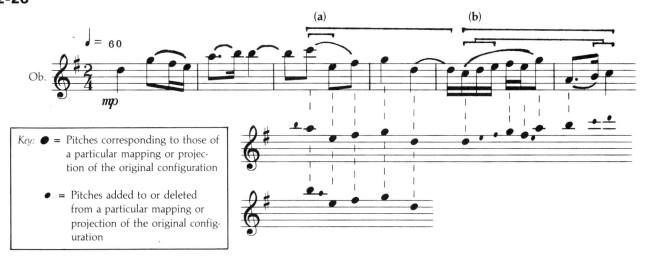

(a) Contraction plus interval expansion applied to a retrograde. (b) Interpolation, deletion, octave displacement, and extension applied to a tonal projection.

The point of our studying these and the other ways of modifying or transforming melodic configurations so thoroughly is to help you become extremely familiar with your options. This familiarity is a kind of knowledge that should function as an unconscious influence on our thinking during the process of making music. Even though it is difficult not to make conscious use of mapping and particular modifying devices during our first attempts at melodic unfoldment, we should seek the kind of intimacy with the concepts of mapping and modifying that will enable us to deal with them intuitively. This, of course, is one of the natural and desired goals of learning about all of the functional processes associated with producing and reproducing music.

The surest route to learning to read and understand the English language is through exercising its vocabulary and grammatical constructs by writing and speaking. The same is true for learning to read and understand music; we cannot expect to comprehend the intricacies and subtleties of melodic unfoldment in the music we perform if we are unaware of how the music is made to unfold the way it does.   **W110—122**

**MINI
PROJECT
10**

A. Using one of the new melodic gestures produced in part A of Mini Project 9 in chapter 21, produce ten distinctly new melodic gestures that demonstrate these means of modifying a pitch configuration:

1. interpolation
2. deletion
3. extension
4. contraction
5. interval expansion
6. interval contraction
7. octave displacement
8. harmonic change
9. rhythmic change
10. fragmentation

B. Using one of the new melodic gestures you produced in part A, continue the gesture by producing a single reiteration or projection to demonstrate each of these means of modifying a pitch configuration:

1. interpolation
2. deletion
3. extension
4. contraction
5. interval expansion
6. interval contraction
7. octave displacement
8. harmonic change
9. pitch permutation
10. fragmentation

In completing parts A and B, score each gesture for a specific instrument, supply tempo indications, and supply whatever dynamics and articulation indicators are needed.

23 Structural Syntax and Dramatic Context

What is the case for intelligible ordering?

In chapter 15 music is defined as an *abstraction of human experience* and, as such, an art that provides the means by which abstractions can be made *affectively lucid*. In support of this, we can find numerous words and phrases in this text and elsewhere—such as *technique, controls, process, craft, function, shape, configuration, characteristics,* and a host of others—that denote either the application or the effects of intelligible ordering.

Every musicwork is a unique synthesis of a complex array of aesthetic concepts and design principles. As such, it provides the unique circumstances within which the separate elements of the work can function, form intelligible relationships, and be understood. This fact rules out a uniform evaluation of familiar musical elements and their relationships without considering the conditions under which they are used in a musicwork. All musical elements and relationships, familiar and unfamiliar, must be evaluated in relation to the structural and dramatic principles that control the musicwork in which they appear. For example, the familiar pitch collections shown in Figure 23-1 would necessarily have to be evaluated one way in a work by Mozart and another way in a work by Stravinsky. These pitch collections can be defined by their pitch and intervallic contents, but they have no meaning outside of the structural syntax and dramatic context of a musicwork.

23-1

What is structural syntax?

Structural syntax refers to the intelligible ordering of the various sound elements used in a musicwork. The structural syntax of a musicwork—a formalizing condition similar to that produced in a spoken and written language by the function of words and grammatical constructs—is achieved by the application of conventions that are pertinent to the nature of the musical situation and appropriate to the composer's specific needs. It provides the sense of feeling we have that, as a musicwork is performed, the sounds we hear are where they are supposed to be at the time they are supposed to be there. It provides the cumulative formal justification for every component introduced into a musicwork; it is—from a formalizing standpoint—what makes a well-made musicwork sound inevitable. However, even though we may produce something that is rationalized as being structurally sound, this in itself is not enough. The structural syntax of a musicwork cannot be considered independently of its dramatic context; the syntax provides the means by which the dramatic aspects of a musicwork are realized and understood and, therefore, must serve that end.

What is dramatic context?

Dramatic context refers to the intelligible unfoldment of relationships within a musicwork that encourage an affective response from the listener. These relationships, based as they are on expectations generated and cultivated by experience, are subject to the whims of passing generations. This quality of the art is dependent on evolving conventions associated with feelings, likes and dislikes, and other affective conditions that render them relatively non-transferable from generation to generation. What may be accepted as an intelligible juxtaposition of dramatic elements or as a temporally well-paced dramatic unfoldment under one generation's conventions may be misunderstood, unacceptable, or not received at all at another time. We might opine that, after the dramatic impact of a well-constructed musicwork has lost its relevance, continued appreciation of the work is centered more on the beauty of its formal design and less on listeners' response to its dramatic qualities.

The dramatic qualities of a musicwork and the context within which they are understood cannot be achieved effectively if the structural syntax is faulty. The dramatic qualities must provide the impetus for whatever considerations are given to structure. A faulty dramatic sense, therefore, can mislead us in structuring a musicwork. If any of the various events or happenings in a musicwork violate the dramatic flow of the music, if the dramatic qualities appear confused and unintelligible, if certain dramatic elements sound out of context or are poorly timed, we can be reasonably certain that the dramatic faults are also apparent in the structural syntax of the work.

Initially, it is the dramatic aspect of a musicwork that brings the composer, performer, and listener together into an aesthetically productive relationship. The composer, performer, and listener function intuitively and empathetically within the framework of the common understandings and feelings of their common experiences. It is the special capacity of the composer to arrange the components of a musicwork so as to have it appear infused with an expressive, dramatic quality in the light of his or her own experience. The musicwork is presented through performance to the listener who, in accord with his or her own experience, has the special capacity to receive it and understand it.

Therefore, we must realize that, if the various components of a musicwork are to be presented with coherence, music cannot be regarded simply as a series of freely projected reiterations of a melodic shape having a variety of rhythmic changes. There is something more to musical design; something based on principles which govern the manner in which humankind receives and processes information. *What is this something?* What governs a composer's choices, and how do these choices form the intelligible complex called music? A satisfactory and understandable answer cannot be given in one piece or here and now. It is an answer that must grow and develop in our minds over a period of time; it is one of the kinds of musical understandings toward which *Concept and Design in Music* is directed.

What is the sound/time frame?

The sound/time frame provides the limits of the sonic and temporal relationships that occur in a musicwork. The sound/time frame is music's "realm of existence," consisting of the two dimensions within which we exercise control over our chosen materials. During the process of making music, we are concerned with the *what* and the *when* of the internal happenings of a musicwork and the nature of the relationships that ensue. Our control over all of the sonic relationships within a musicwork is accomplished by applying relevant principles of harmony. Sonic relationships have to do with *what* occurs in a musicwork; they occur as (1) consecutive, successive, cumulative (or in any other sense implying separate occurrences in time) and (2) as simultaneous occurrences. Our control over the temporal relationships within a musicwork is exercised by the·use of relevant principles of rhythm. Temporal relationships have to do with *when* something occurs. Though harmony and rhythm denote individual functions, it should be realized that neither can exist without the other in music. There can be no *what* without a *when* or a *when* without a *what*.

How do harmony and rhythm function in a musicwork?

Harmony is a perceptual term used to convey the sense of sonic intelligibility we perceive as a result of the physical ordering of sound in music. By virtue of its being a perceivable and intelligible member of the sound/time frame within which music exists, harmony connotes appropriateness in how the sonic materials (the *what*) of a musicwork are related. **Rhythm** is a perceptual term used to convey the sense of *temporal* intelligibility we perceive as a result of the physical ordering of sound in time. As another perceivable and intelligible member of the sound/time frame, rhythm connotes appropriateness in how the sonic materials of a musicwork are related in time (the *when*). Our perception of the what and the when in a musicwork presupposes some experience in dealing, aurally, with the particular harmonic and rhythmic conventions in the music being heard.

In connoting appropriateness in the physical ordering of sound in a musicwork, harmony and rhythm function as a synergistic, aesthetic expression of the *fitness* with which the various sonic materials are combined and temporally related. "Fitness," in this sense, is a personal judgment influenced by either subjective or objective comparisons with relationships existing within and outside the particular musicwork. All sonic relationships, we reiterate, are musically meaningless outside their existence in a musicwork; outside of a musicwork, sonic relationships have definition but no meaning.

Perceivable intelligible ordering in a musicwork is the natural consequence of choices made by the composer; these choices result in the development and realization of sonic expectancies. That a listener can perceive sonic expectancies implies the existence of mutual experiences and understandings within the complex composer–performer–listener relationship. These experiences and understandings are realized, compositionally, by composers' personalized applications of prevailing and evolving harmonic and rhythmic conventions.

UNIT PROJECT 5

Construct one movement (of three to five minutes' duration) of a three-, four-, or five-movement musicwork. The remaining movements of the musicwork are to be completed, one movement each, by other members of the group assigned to produce the project. The number of groups formed and the number of students in each group is dependent upon the size and makeup of the class. The musicworks should be scored to accommodate the instruments and voices available in the class and should be delimited by the following conditions:

1. The melodic gesture used to set the initial "tone" of each movement should be made of one of the four possible mappings (original, inversion, retrograde, retrograde inversion) of a pitch configuration agreed upon by members of the group producing the entire musicwork and approved by the instructor.

2. Each movement of the musicwork must project a musically dramatic theme (an abstract musical expression) that is generated by the expressive potential of the initial gesture and unfolds within a self-generating dramatic context.

3. The character of the melodic gesture of the movement should be prolonged, and the integrity of the melodic configuration should be sustained and made to evolve through reiterations effected by rhythmic change and projection. As a further means of achieving an evolving melodic configuration and heightening the dramatic character of the movement, use any mappings of the configuration that seem useful along with one to three of the techniques for modifying the configuration demonstrated in chapter 22—interpolation, deletion, extension, contraction, octave displacement, interval expansion, interval contraction, harmonic change, pitch permutation, and fragmentation. Do not attempt to use more than two of the techniques at one time; the bulk of the melodic development will consist of simple transposed and tonal projections and rhythmic change.

4. The texture of the movements can be contrapuntal or homophonic in nature. A texture that utilizes both contrapuntal and homophonic techiques provides more options and is generally more interesting.

5. Each student should prepare a conductor's score in sounding pitch and a set of parts (properly transposed for any transposing instruments being used). The score may be in pencil or ink; observe all of the requirements concerning alignment, spacing, ligatures, placement of dynamics and articulation markings, and general clarity of notation. The parts should be in ink and should be spaced for easy reading. Both the score and parts should be generously supplied with rehearsal numbers (every five measures at least). Extended periods of rest in an instrumental part should be broken up to accommodate rehearsal numbers. Full-measure rests need not be indicated in the score.

6. When completed, the entire musicwork should be carefully rehearsed and performed in public. This can be part of a weekly student recital, for another class, or for a student composition forum.

Notes

Before beginning any of the preliminary work for the project, chapters 18 through 23 should be studied carefully and the mini projects completed satisfactorily. As soon as the techniques of prolonging and transforming a melodic gesture are understood, the following precompositional planning steps can be completed:

1. Establish the student groups. Each group should contain some balance in the distribution of performers.

2. Select a pitch configuration. Before a group settles on a pitch configuration, each member should carry out some preliminary manipulations to determine whether a satisfactory melodic gesture can be produced from the pitch configuration being considered. Even though such a procedure may be thought of as a step-by-step process, it cannot work that way. To determine what needs to be done in the first stages, it is necessary to read *all* of these Notes in order to make choices that will serve what needs to be done at later stages.

3. Establish the general character. The general character of a group's musicwork is something that must be established primarily by the group collectively with help from the instructor. It is important that each member of the group has a clear understanding of what has been decided. Though each member of the group will complete a movement in accordance with his or her own manner of making music, it must be done within the framework of the overall character of the total musicwork. A decision to produce a work with an overall somber nature would preclude having a clownish or impish first movement.

4. Match students and movements. The decision as to which movement is to be completed by which student is best treated as a collective judgment by the group members in council with the instructor. It involves matching the students' desires and temperaments with the types of movements considered for the project.

Though some of the precompositional planning can be achieved quickly and without much fuss, some decisions will be difficult. These should be arrived at so as to satisfy as many of the group members' needs and desires as possible.

In establishing a melodic gesture for the musicwork, be concerned not only with the expressive quality of the gesture but also with what happens to the expressive quality as the result of a tonal projection, different mappings, and various kinds of modifications. It is possible for a melodic gesture to be so "precious" in its expression that nothing can be done with it. In short, a melodic gesture should not be accepted until everyone in the group has determined that it will work in whatever mapping each student intends to use. To select one mapping for the opening gesture of a movement and then use another throughout the musicwork would not make sense. The mapping of the opening gesture should be the predominant one used in the movement. Also, because no more than three techniques for melodic modifications may be used, the mapping selected should be one that works well with what the individual student wishes to do. After all of the trial manipulations of the pitch configurations are considered, the group should emerge with a melodic gesture that projects a clear and perceivable expression and that each member looks forward to using.

Though not all of the dramatic qualities of a movement of the project can be predetermined, the student assigned a given movement must have a well-developed notion of the dramatic context for presenting the melodic gesture. This dramatic context (objectively considered a texture) will, in itself, constitute a more complex musical gesture. It will determine the vertical intervallic relationships, the contrapuntal and homophonic textures, and the harmonic and rhythmic organization; in effect, it will determine much of what will occur in the movement. Whatever is done in the construction of this opening statement, the initial gesture, should be done for the purposes of projecting the expressive character of the movement and providing useful sound materials and workable relationships.

After reaching a relatively clear understanding of how the movement is to develop dramatically, this dramatic unfoldment should be the governing force for what is done in the process of producing the music. The materials and formal constructs used in the production of any artwork are at the service of the abstract expression of the artwork. Whether this is called beauty or something else, it is the primary function of any artwork and it cannot be subservient to any other function.

You are encouraged to produce your music on paper in the form of a full score, *not* in the form of a sketch. By doing it in score form, you will be constantly aware of what each instrument or voice is doing, how the individual lines unfold, how they work together, and how well each instrument or voice is being used. Auralize as much as possible during the writing, but also work at the piano for the purpose of auditioning the pitch relationships. Auralization will be most useful in the reconstruction of the instrumental and vocal timbres being used. Be advised that, in general, dissonances produced on the piano are comparatively more pungent than they will be when they are sung or played by other instruments, especially instruments with radically different timbres. In some cases, it is nearly impossible to produce anything but mild dissonances between certain timbrel relationships. Keep this in mind when working at the piano. As a last suggestion, it is a good policy to keep the preparation of performance parts abreast with the production of the score so that at any time the music can be read by the performing group. This form of audition will be most valuable.

24 Observations and Evaluations

What do we hope to achieve through an evaluation?

Our chief concern in evaluating the projects just completed should be the question of whether or not the individual musicworks are indeed "affectively lucid." Is the music aurally coherent? Do the means employed serve the intended expressive intent? Can those who hear the work communicate with it effectively? These and similar questions can and should be discussed by the class as each student work is evaluated. Valid criticism implies careful selection and application of evaluation criteria and an honest, forthright verbal exchange. Evaluation requires the same concern, practice, and cooperation as the making of the projects themselves. If the evaluation is poorly done, much of the value of the project is lost.

What is an evaluation?

In general terms, an **evaluation** is simply a judgment arrived at by comparing the action or thing being evaluated with a set of expectations. Our expectations, regardless of what they are or how appropriate they seem to others, provide the criteria we use as a standard for comparison. An evaluation or judgment, whether arrived at intuitively or with deliberation, must be regarded as purely subjective because it is formed within the mind of the person or group producing it.

What is the nature of comparisons?

Comparisons, per se, may be either subjective or objective. A **subjective comparison** is the process by which a person considers all things in relation to his or her thoughts, feelings, character, and personality. **Objective comparisons**, on the other hand, are those in which a person compares measurable sizes, weights, or other characteristics of known objects or conditions against measured and generally accepted standards. Objective comparisons are made by standard measuring devices that are accepted as final and not subject to question—even when known to be less than accurate. We are, for example, familiar with the *subjective* comparisons made between divers with respect to the execution, style, and difficulty of their dives as opposed to the *objective* comparisons made between swimmers by timing devices in a swim meet. The comparison of one diver to another is a matter of a consensus of several judges; the comparison of one swimmer to another is a matter of objective timing by a device capable of measuring time to within one one-hundredth of a second.

The criteria used as the standard for an objective comparison must be objective. Obviously, a comparison predicated on the concept of exact measurement cannot use unmeasured or unmeasurable criteria. The criteria used as the standard for subjective comparison can be either subjective or objective. If a comparison is based on a personal judgment or a consensus judgment, whether subjective or objective criteria are used undoubtedly alters the quality of the judgment but not the fact that a judgment was made. Therefore, in entering into a process that calls for an evaluation or judgment, we must acknowledge that the process is subjective. Thus, to speak of an evaluation as "subjective evaluation" is to be redundant; to speak of an evaluation as an "objective evaluation" is to utter a contradiction.

Demonstration of an Evaluation

Even though the circumstances of every evaluation are unique, we can "walk through" a step-by-step evaluation for the purpose of demonstration. The music in Figures 19-4 through 19-7 is intended to demonstrate the conversationlike qualities of counterpoint and to achieve several differing expressive qualities. Each of the examples is identified by an adjective describing a particular quality of dialogue: "Quarrelsome," "Elegant," "One-Sided," and "Imitative." The music for each figure was made from the same intervallic configuration used in the gesture in Figure 17-3, and each utilized the same fundamental means of sustaining the gesture: reiteration, rhythmic change, and transposed projections. Upon listening to the music in Figures 19-4 through 19-7, we readily perceive that the resulting expressions are quite different from that of the original gesture and much more complex. In spite of the differences, however, we recognize the relatedness resulting from the same pitch configuration being used for each example. Preparatory to evaluating the music of these four examples, let us make a few observations about the pitch, intervallic, and temporal makeup of the configuration of the original gesture (Figure 17-3).

The point of focus or emphasis in the configuration of the original gesture (Figure 24-1) is the pitch G_4. This is due to (1) the relatively strong position of G_4 within the temporal scheme of the configuration, (2) the number of onsets of G_4 compared to other pitches, and (3) the total sounding time allotted to G_4. Also, as shown in Figure 24-1, the -3 interval is emphasized, and the entire configuration is a movement down a -3 from G_4 to E_4. It is also

24-1

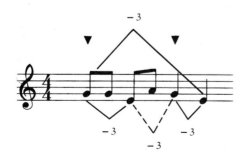

apparent in the figure that the rhythmic shape of the original configuration, when reiterated, takes on a definite sing-song quality; it would do so no matter what pitch combinations were used. The rhythmic shape is the dominant factor determining the character of the gesture in Figure 17-3.

Because transposed projections do not produce different intervallic relationships, we need to be concerned only with reiteration and rhythmic change when comparing the new gestures with the original in this part of the evaluation. In Figure 19-4, the opening line in the second trumpet retains some of the good-natured taunting of the original gesture (Figure 17-3). The remaining transformations of the gesture in both trumpet lines become increasingly agitated through the reiteration of pitches and rhythmic change. In Figure 19-5, the taunting has disappeared entirely except for possibly a slight hint in measures two and three of the violin part. In Figure 19-6, the taunting, because of the rhythmic change, has dissolved into a rather ho-hum, patient boredom in the viola part. The oboe part, however, has assumed a more expansive, gregarious, self-assured quality. In Figure 19-7, the taunting character remains but it has taken on a different though still good-natured quality. The taunting quality has become much more sophisticated through more rapid reiterations and the playful imitation within and between the two voices.

To follow through with our evaluation, it would be appropriate to examine the configurations of all the new gestures (Figures 19-4 through 19-7) by using the criteria demonstrated in Figure 17-3. However, let us examine just two of them here, those of Figures 19-5 and 19-7, and compare them with the original. Figures 24-2 and 24-3 show the results of this comparison. By comparison, we find that articles 1, 2, 4, and 5 of the description in Figure 24-3 indicate that the basic characteristics of the original gesture have been retained and emphasized. Only article 5 of the description in Figure 24-2 indicates a retained characteristic

24-2

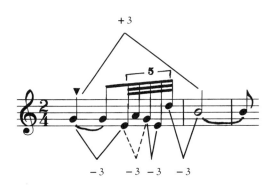

1. Strong temporal position of G_4 is not established.

2. 2 onsets of G_4, 2 onsets of E_4, 1 onset each of A_4, D_5, and B_4

3. Durations: $B_4 =$ ♩ ♪, $G_4 =$ ♩ ♫, $E_4 =$ ♪, $A_4 =$ ♪, $D_5 =$ ♪ (5:4)

4. Rhythmic shape:

5. 3 falling −3 intervals, 1 rising −3 interval weakened by the A_4, all of which are weakened by their temporal positions; 1 rising +3 interval in a strong temporal position

6. Some transposition

24-3

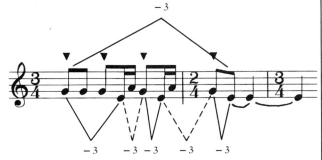

1. Strong temporal position of G_4 is established even more firmly than in the original gesture.

2. 5 onsets of G_4, 3 onsets of E_4, 2 onsets of A_4

3. Durations: $E_4 =$ ♩., $G_4 =$ ♩ ♪, $A_4 =$ ♪

4. Rhythmic shape:

5. 4 falling −3 intervals, 2 rising −3 intervals in strong temporal positions but weakened by the intervening A_4

6. Some reiteration

of the original gesture. If we listen to the two musical examples, we can conclude that: (1) as demonstrated in Figure 24-3, the aural impression of the music in Figure 19-7 is much like that of Figure 17-3; and (2) as demonstrated in Figure 24-2, the aural impression of the music in Figure 19-5 is very unlike that of Figure 17-3.

The results of our examination of the transformed configurations (Figures 24-2 and 24-3) support our aural impressions. We might conclude, therefore, that new gestures—or transformations of the original configurations, as we might call them—that retain more of the *physical* characteristics of the original gesture also retain more of its *expressive* character. We might also conclude that rhythmic change is probably the most effective means of changing the character of a melodic gesture. Of the six descriptions of characteristics listed in Figure 24-2, for example, the first, second, third, and fourth are the direct result of rhythmic change, and the fifth, though retaining much of the original character, was partially affected by rhythmic change.

Having considered some of the effects of reiteration and rhythmic change, let us now examine the music of Figures 19-1, 19-4, and 19-6 to compare the choices made with respect to projection. For easier comparison, the original pitch configuration is reduced to a composite pitch collection in Figure 24-4; for this comparison, we will simply call it the pitch collection.

24-4

(a) pitch configuration   (b) [4, 7, 9] pitch collection

If we reduce each transposed projection of the melodic configuration used in Figures 19-1, 19-4, and 19-6 to equivalent pitch collections and compare them, we have further support for the descriptive titles given to the music. Figure 24-5 shows the reductions of the projected melodic configurations in the three musical examples and indicates approximately where a projection takes place in each example.

24-5

PITCH COLLECTION ANALYSES

Figure 19-1:

24-5, *continued*
Figure 19-4:

Figure 19-6:

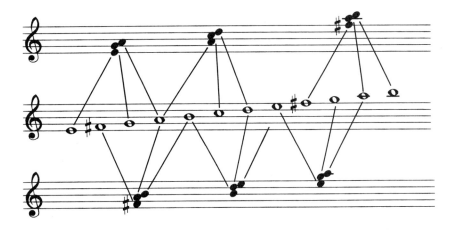

The first observation we can make about the melodic reductions (pitch collections) in Figure 24-5 is that all of the projections in Figures 19-1 and 19-6 will fit into the same transposition of the diatonic system (see Figure 24-6). In the reduction of Figure 19-1, we notice that the two voices begin with the two equivalent pitch collections sounding the interval of a P4 apart, and each voice roughly follows the same pattern of projection. The two voices

24-6

● represents the pitch content of melodic projections used in Figures 19-1 and 19-6.

○ represents a transposition of the diatonic system.

never occupy the same pitch range at the same time except for the one pitch shared by the first pitch collection of each voice (see Figure 24-7). Therefore, the pitch separation and acoustical compatibility support the expressive idea of "congeniality."

24-7

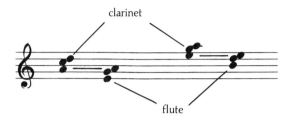

The reduction of Figure 19-6 (Figure 24-5) shows a series of projections in the oboe part that are nearly the same as those of the flute part in Figure 19-1. Though the viola part in Figure 19-6 is not projected at all, it remains separated from the oboe part except for the pitch E_4, which it sounds in common with the first, fifth, and seventh projections of the pitch collection in the oboe part. The pitch separation and acoustical compatibility, along with the contrast in tonal movement between the two parts, support the expressive idea of "one-sidedness."

The melodic reduction of Figure 19-4 (Figure 24-5), however, presents an entirely different situation. The pitch collections in the first trumpet sound the interval of a -2 below each of the pitch collections against which they sound in the second trumpet. Consequently, each of any pair of simultaneously sounding pitch collections is from a different transposition of the diatonic system. Also, each pitch member in each pitch collection of the series in the first trumpet is separated by the interval of a -2 from its counterpart in the series of pitch collections in the second trumpet. This presents the maximum possible conflict in pitch and acoustical considerations and, therefore, supports the expressive idea of "quarrelsomeness."

Some degree of compatibility exists between the two voices, however, because the first and second pitch collections of the first trumpet are the same as the third and fourth pitch collections of the second trumpet. Also, as shown in Figure 24-5, the fourth pitch collection of the first trumpet is the same as the first pitch collection of the second trumpet. We might conclude, at least in jest, that the two parties are presenting much the same argument in their quarreling!

What this kind of comparison shows is that a configuration can be placed in a variety of relationships with itself, consecutively and concurrently, by the simple process of projection. This can result in any number of pitch and acoustical relationships that can be designed to serve particular expressive intents. In effect, it is not the composer's choices of melodic configurations that determine the expressive tone of a musicwork so much as it is the combination of those choices with the choices about how the configurations will be modified and related within a musicwork.

What conclusions can we draw from these comparisons?

The preceding observations and evaluations were after-the-fact comparisons of what initially were intuitive manipulations intended to express the *tone* of the descriptive titles. These specific observations may never be made again; they were special to a particular situation. Because of this, it is impossible to draw analytical procedures from them that can be applied to any situation. Nevertheless, it is useful to make these kinds of observations in attempting to discover patterns that might explain what has been done. Though the aural impression we receive when we hear a musicwork will generally indicate the existence of faulty relationships or incongruent expressions, observations such as those demonstrated here can help us locate and identify such faults in a manner that suggests the means for correction.

U N I T

FOUR

THE NATURE OF CONVENTIONS

25

Introduction to Conventions

What are conventions?

One of the many stories that developed out of the early East/West encounters is about a group of Eastern dignitaries who were serenaded aboard ship by a United States Navy band. When asked which number they liked best, the group agreed that all of them were good. However, they acknowledged that the first number, the one played just before the national anthem, the one not listed on the program, was their favorite. The First Officer was too embarrassed to disclose that the band had just been tuning up at the time. Though undoubtedly apocryphal, the story indicates the real possibilities that exist for misunderstanding conventions. It also hints at the need to reconsider any notions we might have about music being a universal language.

On the other hand, a thorough knowledge and practice in the exercise of certain conventions make it possible, for example, for a current jazz performer to travel almost anywhere current jazz is being played and "sit in" with any group. However, a jazz performer's "bag" of conventions would be of little use in a Hindu orchestra, where an entirely different set of conventions would be at play.

Intelligibility, that which contributes to people's understanding and enjoyment of any activity, is based on recognition and application of conventions. A **convention** can be defined as any set of characteristics or preferences that are subscribed to or selected at the exclusion of all others. Music might be regarded as "games of sound." While music is surely much more than a game, this metaphor can help us see more clearly how conventions function.

How do games illustrate the function of conventions?

In the world of games, two prominent idioms are spectator games (football, baseball, basketball) and nonspectator games (cards, Monopoly, checkers). Each idiom has its own set of **idiomatic conventions**. In the spectator idiom, certain broad conventions entail the use of a relatively large playing field marked off in some fashion with restrictive lines and boundaries, colorful uniforms, and certain other less basic conventions as umpires, cheerleaders, and bands. Truly idiomatic spectator games are resplendent with all of these conventions plus others too numerous to mention. But can we imagine a spectator game without the conventional nourishment for the spectators? Ancient arenas offered grapes, we understand, and spectators in the modern stadium seem to prefer peanuts and hotdogs.

Nonspectator games have another set of idiomatic conventions—who, for example, would go to a card game wearing a uniform? Some of these conventions have probably already occurred to you, but we can mention a few. There are generally fewer participants than in spectator games, and the action is less physically demonstrative. The outcome is usually based on the average win of a number of shorter games. The manner of play is most often predicated on chance or on some form of intellectual rather than physical prowess, and often no distinct time limit is set.

We must recognize some of these truly idiomatic conventions before we make up a game or play one. But are there not factors that go beyond the idiomatic conventions and give the games greater interest? How about the conduct of play itself? In baseball, for instance, why are nine innings designated as a game, three strikes as an out, and four balls as a walk? And why all of the other features—some of them constantly being modified—that people have learned to expect? These features can be called **meta-idiomatic conventions**. They are just as important as the idiomatic conventions, for they set the limits for the kinds of events we expect in baseball as opposed to football or in cards as opposed to checkers. Meta-idiomatic conventions exist more in the realm of "idea," while idiomatic conventions relate to the physical realities of the game, but each set of conventions influences the other.

How do conventions relate to "style"?

If a recognizable set of conventions exists for a long enough period of time in the music of a composer or a group of composers, the music of the composer or group of composers is regarded as being in the same or a similar style. Style has to do with the kinds of choices that are made and the manner in which the choices are employed in the making or doing of something. The concept of style generally expressed is that of individual style. However, when the concept of style is extended to include groups of individuals in a region, country, and historical time period, for example, the concept refers to a compendium of similar individual styles. In any case, a consideration of what actually contributes to a composer's (or any other artist's) style must include recognition of his or her preference for certain materials and certain ways of using them. For the most part, **style** is the quality of an artwork that reveals who produced it and when and possibly where it was produced.

At times we use style as an instrument for comparison by using the general qualities of something that is well known as criteria. For example, we might say a particular musicwork is in the style of some composer or of the composers of some period of history.

Another concept of style is one in which a well-known characteristic of a particular kind of music is regarded as a style. We might say, for example, that a particular musicwork is in the "style" of a waltz or in the "style" of a march. This concept of style is referential: a relatively well known function, genre, composer, or group of composers is used to identify a musicwork in a generalized rather than specific manner. This is really not a substitute process, because referential comparison is, in many cases, our initial step in examining a musicwork. Essentially, this process is nothing more than the intuitive application of our experience as the initial stage in identifying a style.

How do we adapt to new conventions?

After repeated exposure, we unconsciously absorb a musical vocabulary and instantly recognize foreign elements in a musicwork. No doubt, we may have experienced this very thing during the performance of the Unit One projects when a part had been improperly transposed or a pitch miscopied or misplayed. Nothing is intrinsically "wrong" with sounds that are foreign to a musicwork; they are simply inconsistent with the conventions in use. The "wrong" sounds constitute events that are unrelated to the sonic framework built by the convention in use.

If given sufficient time to adapt, we could find any convention appealing, provided it is acoustically intelligible and the syntax (logical structure) is both comprehensible and consistently present. We need only to select and listen to several recordings of music at random from various cultures and times to realize that we can appreciate the aural impressions of diverse musical conventions even though we do not understand the music beyond the novelty of the sounds.

The fact that we recognize differences between diverse conventions suggests that aural recognition is an immediate response very similar to our ability to recognize immediately the voices of our friends on the telephone. The set of recognizable qualities that helps us distinguish one voice from another includes timbre, articulation, and inflection; each voice seems to leave us with an aural imprint that is reinforced each time we hear it.

26 Communication in Music

It is doubtful that any of us can think back to when and how we learned to distinguish music from other sounds. We might feel that we have *always* been able to distinguish music from other sounds. This would seem reasonable because of the ability of the unborn child to hear and react to sound.

Our ability to distinguish music from other sounds at an early age (possibly before birth) is all the more amazing when we consider the number of unique and varied sound combinations we accept as music and all of the ways music affects us. There is, nonetheless, a common ground of understanding that relates the affecting qualities of a musicwork to our responses to them. This common ground has its bases in the associations and experiences we share. The common ground gives a similarity of focus and meaning to our collective perceptions and is bound *to* and represented *by* an evolving set of musical conventions.

Because music is a nonverbal art, it is not surprising that the "what" and "how" of musical communication cannot be effectively explained with words. We can, however, discuss the general nature of communication and understand it as a process that is fundamental to all human experience. With this insight we can direct our thinking to make the process of communication in music work for us and enhance our appreciation of music.

In his book *Technology, Management, and Society*, Peter Drucker lists the fundamentals of communication:

1. Communication is perception.

2. Communication is expectation.

3. Communication is involvement.

4. Communication and information are totally different. But information presupposes functioning communications.*

As we discuss the process of communication and its function in the musical art, we will reflect and expand on these four fundamentals.

*Drucker, Peter, *Technology, Management, and Society* (New York: Harper and Row, 1970), pp. 4–5.

"COMMUNICATION IS PERCEPTION."

The basic concept of perception to be developed here concerns our capacity to receive the aural sensory stimuli we recognize as music and to understand them in relation to one another and to those from our previous experience. References to other arts, processes, and experiences will be made to the extent that they contribute to our understanding of the process of communication in music.

What are the physiological limits to the perception of pitch?

Human perception of audio frequencies is limited to frequencies from 16 Hz to about 20,000 Hz; we cannot perceive frequencies that exceed these physiological limits. The sounds of speech fall within the general frequency range of 90 Hz to 500 Hz. The general frequency range of musical pitch falls between 16.35 Hz (an octave below the lowest pitched C on the piano, C_1) and 16,744 Hz (C_{10}). Most music, however, does not exceed the pitch of C_8 (4,186 Hz), the highest pitch of the piano. Because the sounds of speech and music fall within a rather limited frequency range, any impairment that reduces the frequency range of our hearing generally affects only the *quality* of the sounds we hear.

What are the physiological limits to the perception of change?

Another physiological limitation to hearing concerns our capacity to perceive change. The lowest rate of change we can perceive is limited only by our memory. The upper limit of our perception of changing events cannot exceed the frequency of the threshold of sound, around 16 Hz. Any configuration of tones, for example, within which the tones change at a rate exceeding sixteen changes per second (16 Hz), is not perceived as a configuration of tones; instead, it is perceived as a timbre whose pitch has a fundamental frequency equal to the rate of change. For example, if a series of four tones were repeated at a rate of 22 times per second, we would no longer hear them as four different tones. We would, instead, hear one very low pitched timbre having a fundamental frequency of 22 Hz.

The dissolution of a configuration of tones into a single timbre when subjected to a rate of change exceeding 16 Hz is similar to what occurs when a Maxwell color disk (a disk on which two or more colors are presented in varying amounts) is rotated very quickly. The colors on the spinning disk cease to appear as individual colors; they appear to blend into one color that is different from those on the disk.

What are our limits in hearing multiple musical events?

Our capacity to "follow" and "comprehend" more than one musical event at a time while also comprehending their relationship to one another is subject to our physical and mental limitations. In dealing with these limitations, we must consider: (1) our aural attentiveness and concentration as we gather and process aural information, and (2) the demands made on us by the varying complexities of what we are hearing.

It is generally accepted, among musicians, that the average listener is capable of following and comprehending two to three separate but simultaneously sounding musical events such as melodies, accompaniment figures, or accentuated chordal effects. For a very experienced listener, the limit might be as many as five separate events. The greater the contrast among the events, the more likely that a listener can deal with more than three of them. The popular assumption is that the listener must focus attention entirely on all of the musical events at the same time. This is neither possible nor necessary, because effective listening requires only the "illusion" of focusing attention on more than one thing at a time.

What relationship is there between visual focusing and aural focusing?

Here, the word *focus* denotes the basic objectives of narrowing our attention to and sharply defining something. We know, for example, that our eyes can focus on only one point at a time. We also know that, while our eyes are focused on one point, we remain aware of most of what is going on within our field of vision. This awareness becomes increasingly less well defined toward the periphery of our vision. For our brain to register what is contained in our field of vision, our eyes must scan the field of focus, momentarily, on enough critical points for us to determine the shape, color, and relative position of whatever is contained in the field.

We tend to deal with aural information in much the same way that we deal with visual information: that is, we focus our attention on only one melody or other musical event at a time. For our brain to comprehend all of the musical events that are sounding at one time, we must sample information from each event. This sampling is a matter of focusing on what our intuition instantly considers to be most important to our relating and comprehending the separate events as a composite musicwork that we consciously perceive as whole and uninterrupted.

How do visual and aural information gathering differ?

We have likened focusing in hearing to focusing in seeing and have regarded them as similar. On the other hand, we gather information differently through hearing and seeing. In the first place, the information received by the ears is not gathered by scanning and piecing together at the pleasure of the listener (subjective time). Whereas the eyes receive different bits of information simultaneously, the ears receive bits of information in succession and in real time (objective time). Whichever ear is nearer the source of sound receives the information first. The slight difference in the time it takes for a sound wave to reach the other ear enables the listener to sense the location of the sound source (binaural hearing).

What is the effect of binaural hearing and location on the separation of timbres?

The capacity to perceive the quality of one instrument out of a group of simultaneously sounding instruments, though not at all dependent on the location of the sources of the separate timbres, is aided, nonetheless, by the factor of differing locations. The distinct timbres of a flute and clarinet playing the same melodic line in the same octaves, for example, can be perceived as two timbres as well as a composite sound if the two players are seated next to each other or even if the two timbres come from the same location such as from a loudspeaker. The separate timbres emanating from a single speaker are perceivable even if the listener is receiving the auditory information with only one ear.

How does location affect perception?

The factor of the separate and, by implication, the multiple locations of sound sources, though affecting only slightly our ability to separate timbres, introduces perceptual variances in what we hear that far exceed the simple notion of the separation of timbre. The spatial separation or multiple locations of sound sources results in aural experiences that require us to reassess our knowledge about the affective nature of what we can perceive and understand with regard to dynamics, consonance and dissonance, harmonic and rhythmic syntax, and the dramatic context of a musicwork.

"COMMUNICATION IS EXPECTATION."

Our expectations form a kind of knowledge that is the result of a given set of circumstances; we can be reasonably certain that what is expected to take place will indeed take place. For example, we can expect that a concert in the park will be called off if it rains. This is a consequence we can expect with relative certainty. However, if the concert can be moved into a shelter, we might expect the concert to be played even if it rains. An examination of our memory of recent experiences will help us realize that many of our experiences are fashioned according to the simple formula: *if* this, and this, and this . . . , *then* this.

How are our expectations both unique and similar?

Quite understandably, our expectations are the result of conditions and events that are far more complex than the concert in the park illustration. We might, in fact, assume that any set of circumstances that brings about an expectation in any of us is unique. **Uniqueness** is the quality of being different from all other things; it does not imply that a thing is dissimilar from all other things. Our expectations, though individually unique, can be similar to others' expectations when they result from similar circumstances. The expectations of a group of people hearing a particular musicwork, for example, will be similar if their individual experiences have been similar. This *common* ground of similar circumstances, personal experiences, and expectations is basic to the processes of communication. The *uncommon* ground of unique circumstances, personal experiences, and expectations is basic to the processes of personal decision making.

What are conventional expectations?

In a very basic sense, teaching grew out of the instinctive need of parents to pass on certain essential, conventional expectations to their children. Conventional expectations result when events either persist or are repeated. Considering the great extent to which our lives are affected by expectations, we might say that education is basically a process that alters and broadens our expectations.

How are expectations associated with the arts?

Many of our expectations, especially those associated with the arts, are concerned with such things as our expressiveness, personal likes and dislikes, and a number of other circumstances founded on personal abilities and preferences.

Our responses to the many conditions and events that make up our total life experience appear to translate into a great variety of expectations. Long after we have forgotten the experiences that created a particular expectation, that or a similar expectation can be generated by an aesthetic condition or artistic event that stimulates our senses. For example, long after forgetting the thrill of a movie battle scene during which the victory was heightened by the drone of bagpipes, we might sense an unaccountable thrill upon hearing bagpipes played during the halftime show at a football game.

By participating in the arts, we encounter new and varied experiences; the impressions from these experiences reinforce or alter our expectations or establish new ones. Through the repeated stimulus of unique but similar aesthetic conditions and artistic events, we are uniquely but similarly impressed in ways that arouse unique but similar expectations. Through this process, we establish the kinds of conventional *expectations* that are aroused and satisfied by conventional *stimuli* in the arts. Composers and performing artists, having shared life experiences similar to those of their public, know how to utilize their own versions of conventional stimuli to arouse and satisfy the personalized but essentially conventional expectations of the listener. Thus, a particular musicwork can be expected to arouse and satisfy similar expectations among the individuals who make up an audience.

How do our expectations function in music?

Hearing a musicwork gives rise to a constant array of expectations that we conceive, evaluate, and respond to in terms of our own experience. As we make each decision, it becomes a new expectation and is added to the total of our experience. The most immediate and pertinent of all the knowledge we use in responding to a musicwork emanates from the hearing itself. This simply means that, at any given moment as we listen to a musicwork, our understanding is based, for the most part, on what we have just heard. This ability to conceive, evaluate, and utilize aural information instantly is made possible through "aural tracking."

What is aural tracking?

Aural tracking is the process by which the mind receives, samples, compares, and draws useful conclusions from the information that constantly bombards our ears. For example, as we hear a musicwork, we receive more information than we can comprehend. In fact, we receive more information than what we need for comprehending what we hear. Each sampling of information is compared with an expectation generated by the previous sampling and with whatever else the mind holds as useful, related information. From this, the mind provides an appropriate assessment and projects a new expectation. This completes one cycle of aural tracking. However, as a rapidly recurring process, each cycle takes place within a time period too small for our conscious awareness. We think of such rapidly recurring processes as instantaneous. Sensory activities that occur below the threshold of consciousness can be likened to the rapid showing of the film frames of a movie or the bombardment of electrons on a television picture tube: they occur at a rate too rapid for us to see. The resulting effect is the illusion of smooth, uninterrupted action.

What is visual scanning?

Let us consider another kind of information gathering. Reading this book requires **visual scanning**; that is, the receiving, analyzing, and evaluating of visual information. Though your attention—your conscious awareness—is focused on understanding what you are reading, your mind is receiving and processing a great deal of visual information that is not the object of your attention. Subconsciously your brain is processing countless stimuli, comparisons, and expectations having to do with letters following letters to make words, words following words to make sentences, and sentences following sentences to make paragraphs. All along the way, you must make decisions about letters, words, sentences, and paragraphs based on what you have just read as well as the sum total of your accumulated knowledge and experience.

How do we evaluate new information?

We can regard our evaluation of new information gathered through aural tracking, visual scanning, and other sensory processes as overlaying a pattern of remembered knowledge with a pattern of newly acquired knowledge. We mentally evaluate the usefulness of the resulting similarities and differences. The results of this evaluation are stored to serve as new, redundant, similar, or replacement knowledge, or they are discarded as useless.

Are there limits to our comprehension of sensory information?

The amount of aural information in a musicwork is monumental. And while we are listening to music, we hear extraneous sounds, which we track aurally as well. Most likely, we will also be receiving information from our other senses at the same time. Though we are capable of receiving a great quantity of sensory information through aural tracking, there are limits to the kind and amount of sensory information we are able to accept, process, and utilize. Our personal limitations are the product of our basic capabilities modified by our experience and our ability to cope with distractions.

At what levels of mental activity do our expectations function?

By now, it should be quite clear that expectations exist on various levels of mental activity and that they are formed within differing time frames. We form and respond to some expectations subconsciously. We form and respond to other expectations at rates well within the scope of our capacity to deal with language and artistic relationships. Still other expectations evolve over an extended period of time, some of them taking as much as a lifetime to form. Our expectations function in relation to each other as do other mental functions. Our expectations are a kind of "multidenominational currency" that we spend continually in the marketplace of ideas and sensations.

"COMMUNICATION IS INVOLVEMENT."

Communicating requires the involvement of the person or persons to whom a communication is directed,* involvement implying that the recipient (the receiver) has been affected in some way. There are many possible ways of being affected. It can be acceptance or rejection of, like or dislike for, pleasure or displeasure with, or understanding or not understanding a sensory stimulus. Involvement, therefore, implies a response by the receiver—an aesthetic, emotional, psychological, intellectual, or physical response to a communication. Without some involvement by the person to whom sensory stimuli are directed, communication cannot occur. Consequently, it is not the function of an artwork, a creative artist, or a performing artist to communicate with the listening or viewing public. It is the listener and viewer who communicates with the artwork and the artist.

To what does a music listener respond?

What music is capable of awakening in a listener or what may be extracted from a musicwork should not be regarded as a "message" from the composer or the performer. A musicwork is a complex arrangement of sound relationships that set up the aural expectations to which the listener responds. The demands on the listener are the demands of the musicwork, not the demands of the composer. What there is of the composer in a musicwork does not extend beyond the effect of the composer's manner of making music. This effect is recognized as *style*.

*Drucker, *Technology, Management, and Society*, pp. 4–5.

How does the composer relate to the listener?

There is, of course, no such thing as a definable, structured musical language with a standard vocabulary and grammar for which we could produce a standard dictionary of sound definitions for use by composers, performers, and listeners. Nonetheless, a sensibility is exercised by composers, which enables them to set up appropriate aural expectations. Listeners respond to these expectations in terms of instinctive, relatively predictable emotions. The sound relationships produced by the composer appeal to listeners' aesthetic senses and empathetically to their emotions. For example, John Philip Sousa produced sound relationships in *The Stars and Stripes Forever* that are aesthetically appealing and emotionally exhilarating to listeners. Sousa's empathy for the feelings of others is demonstrated by the way he projected the conventional emotional state associated with flag and country through his rousing march.

What is meant by the "unidirectional" nature of a musicwork?

We cannot translate the "bidirectional" nature of conversation between two individuals into the relationship of a musicwork and an audience. In a conversation a series of unidirectional statements flows in two or more directions between two (or more) individuals to form the bidirectional (or omnidirectional) act we call conversation. Our response to a musicwork is not a response in kind; that is, we do not make a musical response. Regardless of the manner in which a listener responds to a musicwork, the response cannot be anything to which the musicwork can respond. Obviously, a musicwork is what it is and it will remain what it is unless the creative and performing artists change it. Being a unidirectional "utterance" produced by a creative artist and conveyed through the sensual realization of a performing artist, a musicwork cannot respond; it can only be repeated and reasserted. If change is to be effected between a musicwork and the listener, it must be effected by the listener.

"COMMUNICATION AND INFORMATION ARE DIFFERENT BUT INTERDEPENDENT."

Communication is associated with comprehension. Information is associated with the formal material and concepts a writer, for example, presents for our comprehension. The fundamental objective for the writer is to transmit information clearly and precisely to another person. There is also the fundamental intent to prove something to someone or persuade someone to do something. In such communication transactions, information is the important thing; a completed communication attests to the successful transmission and reception of information.

In the arts, however, communication implies success in achieving some kind of artistic understanding. Information, rather than being the *object* of a communication, is the *vehicle* for achieving the artistic understanding and expressiveness which is the intent of the communication. In the arts, information is used to bring about an aesthetic and emotional response from the listener or viewer. The particular information is of secondary importance. In a musicwork, the information is the "stuff" of which the aural stimuli are made. However, when we regard the relative importance of communication and information and consider their differences in the scientific, artistic, and other realms, it is obvious that one cannot exist without the other.

What are data, information, and meaning in music?

An artistic "utterance," an artwork of any sort, however simple or complex, contains data, information, and the potential for meaning. **Datum** (singular) is defined as a basic element of knowledge; datum is indivisible and is fundamental to the makeup of information. **Information** is any pure, unchangeable configuration of data having no meaning outside of itself. We would, for example, consider the frequency 440 Hz as a statistic datum; however, the configuration of frequencies (the data) that combine to make up the timbre (tone quality) of an oboe sounding an A-440 Hz would be considered information. As information, an A-440 Hz sounded on an oboe has no meaning outside of itself.

Whatever the intent of any form of utterance, the successful transmission of the information it contains is essential to communication. Communication between an individual and any of the phenomena of nature is totally dependent on *if, how,* and *when* the individual wishes to communicate with them.

Whether information is the object of a communication or the vehicle for the arousal of aesthetic awareness, if it is not received effectively, communication is diminished or not achieved at all. In music, once the transmission and reception of information are effectively achieved, the transmitted information (perceived as aural stimuli by the listener) functions as the generator of the aesthetic, psychological, and emotional expressions that constitute the substance of the communication.

What is the nature of meaning in music?

In the most general sense, **meaning** is what someone *implies* when transmitting information and what someone *infers* when encountering information. These two kinds of meaning can also be referred to as *intended* meaning and *perceived* meaning. Meaning in music is derived from the manner in which all of the pertinent information is inter-musically and extra-musically related and the manner in which the information is *conveyed to* and *received by* the listener. Meaning is private in the sense that, as a consequence of our perception and experience, it cannot be shared as a precise, measurable entity with another person. Meaning in music is also evanescent; once we transmit or receive information in the form of a musicwork, its meaning cannot be carried into the future without being affected by the intervening experiences. We can neither recall the precise meaning of a previous musical experience nor reconstruct a musical experience in order to relive it.

How is meaning represented in a musicwork?

The composer's meaning in a musicwork is represented by the manner in which he or she selects and manipulates the audio information of the work. Using the composer's meaning—to the extent that it is expressed by the conventions of musical notation—the performer's meaning is represented by the manner in which he or she interprets the composer's musical notation and presents the realization of the musicwork in a public performance. A listener's meaning is represented in terms of an evaluative response to the stimuli of the musicwork, which is subject to his or her experience and artistic values. Meaning neither resides in nor is a part of a musicwork. Meaning is that hidden quality, that momentarily gives purpose and artistic definition to the intent of the creative and recreative acts of composing and performing. It is what is inferred by the receptive act of listening. The relationships formed by these kinds of meaning are portrayed in Figure 26-1.

26-1

The Interrelatedness of "Meaning" in Music

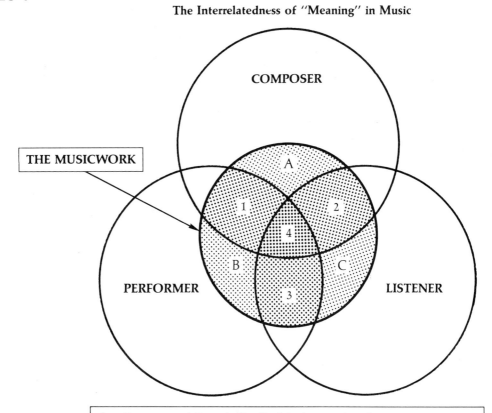

A — the composer's "meaning" as it relates to a musicwork

B — the performer's "meaning" as it relates to a musicwork

C — the listener's "meaning" as it relates to a musicwork

1 — abstraction of experiences common to the composer and performer

2 — abstraction of experiences common to the composer and listener

3 — abstraction of experiences common to the performer and listener

4 — abstraction of experiences common to the composer, performer, and listener

How is the definition of information distinguished from its implied and inferred meanings?

Information—which we have defined as any pure, unchangeable configuration of data having no meaning outside of itself—is measurable and may be transmitted to a recipient in a form acceptable to the senses. Information concerning the nature of anything that is not perceivable to the senses in its normal state can be changed to a form that is perceivable. Meaning, however, cannot be transmitted; it can only be implied or inferred. Being transmittable, information can be shared; meaning cannot be shared. Being unchangeable, information is a constant, at least for as long as it is known. Meaning, being the subjective intent or response to the objective and transmittable nature of information, is a momentary and affected product of our capacity to evaluate information. The transmission and reception of information is the *raison d'etre* of all forms of language.

In what way is music a language?

Music is regarded universally as a language. As a language, it transmits information that can excite the artistic sensibilities of the listener, But this idea of music as a language can be misleading. A language of any type, if it is to be understood, requires some common base of related experience between the communicator (the producer of a communication) and the one who communicates (the recipient of the communication).* Music, along with the other arts, may be regarded *universally as a language*. However, *none* of the arts should be regarded as a *universal language*, because the possibility of an artwork's being universally understood is remote. A musicwork, for example, is understood only to the degree that the experiences of the composer, performer, and listener are related and form a common base upon which to establish some mutual understanding. We cannot expect peoples of widely differing cultures to communicate in similar ways with the musicworks of all other cultures. In some cases, the differences may be sufficient to prevent any communication at all.

*Drucker, *Technology, Management, and Society*, pp. 4–5.

27 The Functional Idiom

What is the nature of musical conventions?

The arts, politics, manners, religious practices, and all other aspects of life are best understood when we consider them in terms of the conventions of particular cultures. A culture's conventions reflect its people's common interests, preferences, and ideas. Conventions are formed over long periods of time by the preferences of people as they make choices in their daily lives. As such, they provide the framework within which the people of the culture relate to each other.

Conventions, as they relate to music, can be grouped into three categories: idiomatic conventions, meta-idiomatic conventions, and idiosyncratic conventions. **Idiomatic conventions** provide the basic and, in many cases, unchanging conditions that affect the nature of the art. Some of them are self-imposed limitations, whereas others serve to control the physical limitations of natural laws. In either case, idiomatic conventions are accepted preferences and practices employed in the composition and performance of music. For example, the use of large numbers of brass instruments and drums in football halftime shows is a response to the behavior of sound out of doors, whereas the show-band itself is a convention concerned with the functional use of music.

Meta-idiomatic conventions include the accepted preferences and practices associated with the procedures and relationships employed in composing and performing music. Meta-idioms belong to the realm of idea; they serve to define music in terms of the principles by which the materials of music are fashioned into intelligible musicworks. These conventions are concerned with pitch relationships, temporal relationships, texture, and other formalizing "controls" in music. The structuring of tones into major and minor triads, for example, is a meta-idiomatic convention of eighteenth- and nineteenth-century composers.

Idiosyncratic conventions grow out of the way composers and performers do what they do; that is, out of habit or some personal characteristic. An idiosyncratic convention is one person's unique way of utilizing an idiomatic or meta-idiomatic convention. An eighteenth-century composer's manner of distributing the tones in a major triad would be an idiosyncratic convention.

Because our understanding of any kind of music is enhanced by our ability to recognize and apply the idioms and meta-idioms involved, it is important that we study the various conventions that define and shape them and that we become sensitive to the mannerisms of individual composers to the extent it is possible.

What were the first functional idioms in music?

It is doubtful that anything that is made, music included, comes to exist unless it serves some purpose or function. From its beginnings and wherever is has existed, music has been made to serve the religious rituals and social functions of cultures. In primitive societies, music accompanied religious rites, the hunt, various forms of work, the seasons, play, celebrations, and many other activities. In principle, nothing has changed today beyond the nature of the activities for which music is used. In Western cultures it was customary to differentiate between liturgical and secular vocal music. Prior to the thirteenth century, the music of the Western world was predominantly liturgical. Though we are less sensitive to the aesthetics of the liturgical and secular music of those times, we can, nonetheless, appreciate the differences of expression in their musicworks.

What were the secular functions of early instrumental music?

We cannot separate the emergence of the increasing numbers of musical instruments from the increasing interest in the secular functions of music that began in about the thirteenth century. Secular instrumental music, from its beginning, was primarily associated with dance; and dance, in past centuries, often expressed religious intents as well as purely secular ones. Throughout the ages, dance has been an important activity. The often-intense physical movement (leaping, turning, skipping) of early dance evolved into a number of stylized secular dance forms. The favored accompaniments were provided by instruments because of the kinds of things they could do. As the instruments developed technically, they could do an increasing number of things, all of which were regarded as uncharacteristic of the voice or impossible to do with the voice. The instruments' potential in the realization of technically complex music made them infinitely more compatible with rhythmic body movements. Not only did dance provide a purpose for inventing music, it also contributed to the shaping of music. Notice that rhythmical movement of muscles (dance, that is) contributed to the design and structure of music, not the other way around as is often presumed. Though the nature of dance has evolved considerably and will certainly continue to evolve, we must recognize the physiological limitations of muscular movement and the effects of gravity as two ever-present idiomatic limitations in music.

Does all music have a function?

It is fair to say that all music serves some function. We also can say that the function of a musicwork may change over the years. This is borne out by our use of early vocal music for making transcriptions in Unit One. In order to understand how function affects the nature of a musicwork, let us consider two examples of music that show sharp, idiomatic contrasts: a two-voiced Agnus Dei from the Ordinary of a Latin Mass by Josquin des Prez and one of the two-part *Inventions* of J. S. Bach.

The music of Josquin des Prez in Figure 27-1 was made to function as part of the liturgy of the Mass; that is, as a portion of the aural part of a larger experience. The music, the architecture and artworks of the church's physical setting, the vestments of the celebrant, and prescribed gestures all united to enhance a liturgical service. The dominance of any one element

27-1

Missa Pange lingua, Agnus Dei

Josquin des Prez

would be viewed as an intrusion not in keeping with the function of the liturgy. Therefore, nothing is overly dramatic; there are no frantic climaxes or highly intense moments. Even the relationship of music to text is balanced so that neither music nor text is obscured by the other. Motion in the music is balanced by lack of motion in the text; motion in the text is balanced by longer, clearer durations in the music. What we experience is an unarrested flow of sound with no sharp "edges" or overly significant events. In this complex, liturgical context, the voice, the music, and everything else is made to conform to the nature and function of the total liturgical service by not calling attention to itself.

The music in Figure 27-2a, however, illustrates a contrasting idiom. This music seeks to call attention to itself by offering the listener a dramatic aural shape. In Figure 27-2b, for example, the two lines begin two octaves apart, move "stalkingly" toward each other until they seemingly collide and produce a mild flurry of activity in the top line. This shape becomes an aural gesture that offers a kind of "play" to listen for and thereby builds our expectation with each of its varied repetitions. By further contrast, this music—much more than the music in Figure 27-1—offers the potential for expressive qualities that can heighten the aesthetic experience of the listener through the skill and sensitivity of the performer. The function of the Bach *Invention* was to provide instrumentally idiomatic music for people to play and enjoy in the home.

27-2

Invention No. 4

Bach

27-2, *continued*

(b)

What is the functional imperative?

The creative impetus is often contingent upon a functional context, which is another way of saying that "necessity is the mother of invention." Satisfying functional requirements should never be considered a routine, "formalized" job. Instead, it is one of the basic requirements for good design. Completely understanding the function of a creative endeavor frees the mind by eliminating unnecessary approaches. Metaphorically, if an artisan wishes to build a chair, he or she must first focus attention on the anatomy of the person who will use it, and then on how he or she wishes to seat the person. The artisan then designs the chair as imaginatively as possible—limited by such functional considerations as where and how the chair is to be used and how it might look in a visual ensemble with other furniture. Thinking of the function of the chair does not diminish the chair's potential beauty; it simply eliminates extraneous thoughts associated with functional requirements of different objects. Good design in music, as in any other art, is partially predicated on the understanding of its function.

MINI PROJECT 11

Considering the role of function in the design and character of music, complete the following:

1. List five distinctly different social functions of modern society that require the use of music.

2. Using the five social functions as headings, list or comment on the functional requirements or conditions that affect the nature of the music.

3. Select one of the social functions and write at least 30 seconds of music appropriate for that function. Utilize any of the musical materials made available in previous study units and the available performance resources of the class. A demonstration of your sensitivity to the musical needs of the particular social function is all that is expected of this project.

28 The Acoustical Idiom

The term **acoustics** (from the Greek *akoustikos*, "of hearing") had little explicit meaning for musicians prior to the invention of the phonograph, though an inate understanding was implicit in all musical undertakings. The making and playing of musical instruments, the development of tonal systems, and compositional design all demonstrated an aural awareness and sensitivity to acoustical necessities. In many cases, the recognition of acoustical problems brought about resolutions that gave rise to composing and performing conventions. An acoustical environment, for example, offers an immediate clue to the kind of music that is made for it.

How does environment influence music?

The two examples of music that were considered in chapter 27 illustrate a striking contrast in the acoustical idiom. The music in Figure 27-1 was made to be performed in a highly resonant church building, where the high reverberation rate would further enhance the relatively slower moving events. Indeed, in many cases, because of the prolonged reverberation, a listener would continue to hear the slow decay of one event during the onset of the following one. This, of course, sets up built-in complexities that were known and, in all probability, utilized by the composer in producing music to be performed in a particular church building.

The opening measures of the Josquin des Prez Agnus Dei as it might be heard in a highly reverberative church building is shown in Figure 28-1.

28-1

In contrast, the music in Figure 27-2 exemplifies musicworks expressly composed for small "chambers," rooms in private residences, drawing rooms possibly containing upholstered furniture, carpeting, books, draperies, and wall hangings, which would absorb the sound and further shorten the already brief decay time of the harpsichord tone. A much greater amount of rhythmic activity in a more complex texture, such as found in the Bach *Invention*, would become a necessary convention of music composed for this "drier," less reverberant room.

How do conventions change to solve environmental problems?

Solving environmental problems was especially important for those producing music for the large concert halls that emerged around the turn of the eighteenth century. The large numbers of human bodies not only absorbed sound but created sounds of their own. The problem demanded more than just compositional solutions; the vocal and instrumental idioms also had to change. In the case of vocal production for the opera houses, quality of tone became associated with voice projection. Conventions of singing came to resemble shouting instead of the modulated qualities favored before opera became the dominant idiom.

Conventions of instrumental preference and performance also began to favor the consequences of the acoustical idiom. The pianoforte virtually replaced the harpsichord because it was capable of the required dynamic power. String players began to use metal strings, and the instruments were modified structurally to produce more dynamic tones. Similar desires for more dynamic power and flexibility brought about changes in the design and manufacture of woodwind and brass instruments.

How has the audience become separated from the performer?

The trend that began with the large proscenium arch of the concert hall—increasing the distance between performers and the audience—continued with the acceptance of Edison's phonograph (patented in 1886). This trend demonstrated the **Helmholtz theory**: that the sensation of hearing can be enjoyed even when it is totally disconnected from visual, tactile, and even temporal associations. Edison's phonograph would probably have had a more immediate impact on the other musical idioms if it had not had two weaknesses: it had a maximum playing time of only two minutes, and the tone quality was very poor.

What was the effect of radio?

The electrical transmission of sound (1920), which advanced rapidly after the phonograph was introduced, was another revolution in the acoustical idiom that significantly affected the functional and instrumental idioms. Because of its fidelity and time limitations, the phonograph was restricted to short, loud pieces of music. Radio, which employed the use of a microphone that converted the sound-producing pressure waves into amplifiable electromagnetic waves, eliminated the time and fidelity problems. By transmitting the electromagnetic signals to home receivers, a totally new function was brought forth for musicians: composing and performing music for broadcasts that reached listeners over a wide geographic area. It was no longer necessary for people to travel to a large city to hear concerts by famous artists; they could "tune in" in the comfort of their own homes.

Musicians now had to learn new conventions of performing known as "mike technique." The need for great projection of sound required by the large concert hall was replaced by the need for well-modulated tone qualities. These new requirements affected vocal production especially. The soft, velvety tones of the "crooner" came to be preferred by the growing radio audience.

The role of music production in live radio broadcasts was short-lived, however, when electrical principles associated with radio were applied to recording. Because of concerns for expense and convenience, electrical transcriptions of music and assorted "sound effects" replaced radio-studio musicians. In order to gain sufficient fidelity for broadcast standards, transcriptions had to be cut at seventy-eight rpm. Giant transcription platters were used for radio broadcasts in order to get a sufficient amount of music on a disc. Marketable records for the home, however, demanded a more manageable size; these new records were limited to about four and a half minutes of material. For another twenty years, the time limitations of recordings brought about conventions that had an impact on the design of music as well as on the aesthetics of listening. The three-minute pop-song formula became accepted by millions of listeners.

What did the technological age bring to music?

Two world wars took place while these revolutions were occurring in the acoustical idiom of music. With each of the wars came further technological developments that would eventually have an impact on the acoustical idiom of music. One of these was the magnetic tape recorder (1940), which not only offered greater fidelity and an extension of recording time, it also allowed for the editing of sound after it had been recorded. By making many retakes and splicing in the best ones, it became possible to create nearly perfect recorded performances.

By 1948, the long-playing record (33 rpm) was introduced. This made it possible to record the edited taped version of performances on discs for mass consumption. By 1960, long-playing stereo records that were capable of storing and reproducing the full realism of sound were being marketed. Integrated electronic circuitry and miniaturization of components combined with computerized mass-production techniques to bring ultrasophisticated sound storage and reproducing units within the financial reach of a broad public.

What are the negative aspects of the electronic revolution?

Not everything that the electronic revolution has brought to the art of music has been good. In attempting to bring the electronic recording of musicworks to the point of perfection, the revolution has made us realize that the attained "perfection" is really a *distortion* of reality. Improving on "mother nature" in this manner may delight listeners, but it is partially detrimental to musicians-in-training.

Most of the music heard by budding composers and performers is recorded music. What is heard, from the standpoint of timbrel quality and projection and of instrumental and vocal balance in general is a distortion of reality. For example, a violin, viola, or 'cello concerto from the nineteenth or early twentieth century is recorded so as to allow the tone of the solo instrument to soar over the mighty orchestra—so much so, at times, that it overpowers the orchestra. Like the artful photograph, the "perfectly" recorded musicwork does a "clean-up" job that is an "improvement" on reality. As a consequence, the sounds we hear, remember, and auralize are primarily the sounds of recorded music. What the young composer produces for live performance and what the budding performer attempts to emulate as tone quality is largely based on a conception of sound produced on recordings. The harm of this is that the musician's cultivated sense of sound is actually a distortion of the acoustical properties of live sound.

Most young composers producing music for conventional instruments and voices believe they are producing musicworks for live performance. In reality, many of them are producing music that can succeed only if it is recorded. It isn't their expressive intent that is at fault; it is their distorted notions about the acoustical realities of live music performance. It is perfectly logical and proper to produce music to be realized in the recording medium; it is equally illogical and inappropriate to expect the same timbrel projection and balance to succeed in live performance. How often, for example, have we heard the fragile tone of the harmonica soar in a quiet, unforced manner over an entire orchestra during a scene in a Western movie? The harmonica would be *buried* by an orchestra in a live performance. How often has an accompanying orchestra had to practically "swallow" its sound in order to allow a solo guitarist to be heard in a musicwork by a composer whose sense of timbrel separation and balance was developed by listening to recorded music? The author recalls a live performance of a popular twentieth-century concerto for viola and orchestra during which the viola was not heard at all when the orchestra was playing. In a recorded version, the viola would enjoy a commanding presence.

Perhaps in the distant future all music will be available only in some recorded format. For the present and the foreseeable future, however, we must live and deal with both live and recorded music. To this end, therefore, you must cultivate an understanding of the acoustics of live performance commensurate with what is known about recorded music. Attend live concerts and rehearsals as a habit and as a means of developing a credible sense of timbre and balance. Without question, the cultivation of live sound is the number-one priority. What is produced for live performance cannot be "readjusted" in performance—recordings, by nature, are readjustments aimed at attaining optimal effect. Without question, the most "faithful" recordings provide the theoretical best-seat-in-the-house along with dynamic levels that can overstate or understate reality. When you are aware of the coloration effects of the best recorded music as opposed to live sound, recorded music can serve you very well as a viable and valuable source of learning a vast amount of musical literature and as a source of listening pleasure.

<table>
<tr><td>

**MINI
PROJECT
12**

</td><td>

Introduction

The purpose of this project is to compare the acoustical properties of a live performance and a recording. The ideal would be to compare a professional orchestra's live performance of a musicwork with its recording of it. This, of course, may not be possible unless you live in a large metropolitan area. Otherwise, the live performance can be a dress rehearsal or concert by your school's orchestra, band, or chorus and orchestra, a faculty quintet or quartet performance, or a solo recital. (If you wish to attend a dress rehearsal, be certain to ask permission.)

</td></tr>
</table>

Description

1. Select a musicwork currently in dress rehearsal or scheduled for performance by any of the organizations or individuals listed in the introduction.

2. Make a list of criteria that includes such items as:

    a. Overall balance

    b. Presence of soloistic passages

    c. Balance between soloist and accompaniment

    d. Timbrel separation (clarity of individual tone qualities)

    e. Masking (one instrument covering another)

    f. Dynamic presence

    g. Reverberant effects of the concert or recital hall

    h. Other relevant concerns

3. Prepare two copies of a rating scale that will permit easy rating of each of your criteria. A 1 to 5 scale is suggested.

4. Attend the selected concert or recital. Using one copy of your rating scale, evaluate the performance in terms of the criteria you have established. Keep in mind that this evaluation is not to address questions of musicality.

5. Listen to a recording of the same musicwork. (If your school records concerts and recitals and the recordings are of top quality, listen to the recording of the performance you attended.) Evaluate the recording using the same procedure you used for the live performance.

6. Compare the results.

29

The Instrumental Idiom: The Voice

What is the universal instrument?

How long humankind has made music with the voice is not known. We do know, however, that the voice has been a favored "instrument" throughout recorded history. Manufactured instruments have come into being, gained prominence, and fallen into disuse many, many times, but the voice continues on, even though its favored status falters occasionally. In spite of the highly technical and expressive performances possible on most contemporary instruments, the voice remains the most versatile and expressive musical instrument available; it is the one universal instrument.

Because of their particular tone qualities and pitch ranges, most instruments are limited in the kind and quality of expressions they can emit. The voice, as a category of instrument, is capable of producing a wide variety and quality of expressions. The voice can shape tones that no other instrument can imitate. The voice can make percussive and other nonverbal sounds; it can glide; it can be modulated and muted. The voice can combine musical tones with words. It can roar, whisper, sob, persuade; it can be sensuous, cold, humorous; it can do whatever enters the mind of the composer and performer to do, except for one thing: it cannot sustain a tone beyond the lung capacity of the singer.

What is the vocal apparatus?

The vocal apparatus (the functioning singing voice) is a sound-producing conglomerate that functions in a cooperative system with the ears and brain. By *sound-producing conglomerate* we mean the action of the lungs, serving as a bellows, which pressurizes the air, which activates the vocal cords located in the larynx. The initial rough, unrefined waveform produced by the vibrating vocal cords becomes a controlled, shaped tone when it resonates in the cavities of the head and chest. The tone is "enveloped" (shaped) in whatever way the singer wishes by the tongue and lips. The term **envelope** denotes:

1. how the tone is attacked (initiated),

2. how long it takes the tone to arrive at its desired loudness (amplitude),

3. whether or not the tone has any sustaining qualities (steady-state characteristics), and

4. whether its cessation (decay) is the result of natural attrition or of a purposeful stopping (release or dampening) of the tone. The cessation is usually achieved by some form of release, which may be further affected by dampening.

How has the voice influenced music throughout history?

Throughout the history of vocal and instrumental music, the voice has been the primary determiner of phrase structure for music as well as language. Obviously, the basis for this is the limit on how much can be spoken or sung in one breath. For centuries, most music was vocal music. It is understandable, therefore, that the mind-set that has evolved over the centuries favors musical structures that are compatible with the capabilities and limitations of vocal production. It would seem that we have become permanently conditioned, physically and mentally, to structuring our musical ideas into units that are controllable by the voice.

Another influence of the voice on instrumental music is the effect of the sounds of language upon the sounds of instruments that are native to a country or region and those that have been adopted and used for long periods of time. For example, the tone qualities (timbres) of instruments native to China are similar in tone quality to the sounds of speech in China. More subtle but no less true, the timbre of the French language is reflected in the timbres of woodwind instruments played in France, especially the double reeds. The sounds of woodwinds and brass instruments played by Germans, Americans, and Russians all reflect the general characteristics of the respective languages. The timbre of the spoken and sung language of a country or locality influences the timbre of the instruments used there.

This idea can be carried one step further in some observations regarding folk and popular music. Consider the various dialects or "accents" of American English spoken in the United States and the obvious exaggerations of these dialects or accents used in folk and popular music singing. The instruments and the tone qualities that have come to be used in accompaniments of vocal music favoring these dialects and accents are obviously influenced by the voice qualities of whatever singing style is used. Compare the timbre of the violin used in the accompaniment of a rousing "country" song with that of the violins used to accompany a suave, popular ballad. Then compare those with the timbre of violins used in Handel's *Messiah*. The tone quality used by the violinists in any one of the three examples would be totally unsuited to either of the other two.

The influence of language on music goes beyond its effect on tone quality. It is notable that the pace or tempo of the speech patterns of the various languages and the rhythmic patterns formed by the syllabic content of words has had an effect on the pace or tempo of instrumental music and its rhythmic makeup. This influence of language is partly responsible for the musical stereotypes of countries. For example, the rapid tempo and intricate articulations of the Spanish language are reflected in the tempo and rhythmic patterns of Spanish music. Slavic music has a different pace and rhythmic content. Inasmuch as all of the music we make or perform is a product of our physical and mental being as well as of our native language, it is easy to understand how our spoken or sung language has influenced all else that we do in music.

How are the conventional female voices classified?

The conventional voices used in the various types of art music are grouped according to two general categories: the overall pitch range, and the quality and agility of the voice as reflected in the temperament of the music generally sung by the voice type. The pitch range of a voice is further classified in terms of: (1) whether the tessitura (the most comfortable area of the total pitch range) of the voice is high, medium, or low, and (2) whether the voice is trained for solo singing or choral singing.

The quality of the voice is denoted by an adjective. A **soprano** voice (the highest-pitched female voice) is described as *lyric* soprano (light and flexible), *coloratura* soprano (brilliant and extremely agile), *dramatic* soprano (more emotional), or as the specialized *Wagnerian* soprano (large and forceful). Each of these describes the nature of the music to be sung and the quality of the voice needed to sing it.

The **mezzo-soprano** voice (slightly lower in pitch range and tessitura than the soprano voice) is generally a full, lyrical voice having a more mature quality. The **contralto** (alto) voice (the lowest-pitched, but nonetheless agile, female voice) has a mature, warm quality. These two solo voices are capable of spanning the full range of dramatic qualities from the extremely rich to the cold, and even mean, in temperament. In choral music, generally only two voice types are used, soprano and alto—mezzo-soprano and contralto being solo voice types.

How were boy soprano voices used?

Prior to the eighteenth century, it was the convention not to have female singers in church choirs. The high voices in church choirs, therefore, were boys' voices. Boy sopranos were customarily educated and trained as singers in choir schools. In some areas of Europe this convention continues—not out of any overriding social consideration but because of an aesthetic and artistic desire to retain the quality of the boy soprano voices when performing medieval and Renaissance liturgical music. The Vatican Choir, the Westminster Cathedral Choir in London, and the Vienna Boys Choir are a few of the better-known choirs that use boy sopranos.

How are conventional male voices classified?

The conventional male voices of today also are classified in terms of the overall pitch range (high, medium, and low) and the quality of the voice and temperament of the music produced for that voice. The **tenor** voice parallels the soprano voice in that it is the highest pitched of the conventional male voices and is also described according to quality and agility. There are lyric tenors, heroic tenors, and dramatic tenors. *Lyric* tenors are relatively light voices, suitable for singing music similar to what lyric sopranos sing. *Heroic* tenors combine agility with brilliant tone quality and are used primarily in heroic operatic roles. *Dramatic* tenors are simply tenors with full, vigorous voices whose tessituras generally favor the lower part of the pitch range.

The remaining male voices are the baritone and bass voices. The **baritone** voice roughly corresponds to the mezzo-soprano and contralto female voices and it fills a similar role in terms of the temperament of the music sung. The baritone voice is one of the most desirable from the standpoint of pitch range, clarity of sound, and timbre. Depending on its tessitura, the baritone voice is thought of as a low tenor or as a high bass voice. By convention, the baritone voice is a solo voice.

The **bass** voice, besides being the lowest-pitched male voice, is also distinguished by its qualities and type of music sung. The *deep* bass (known also as *basso profondo*) is the lowest in pitch. This is a powerful voice that may be extremely solemn in character. The singing or *lyric* bass (known also as *basso contante*) has a quality comparable to the lyric tenor and is used in a similar fashion. The *comic* bass (known in opera as the *basso buffo*) is used in comical situations and is generally an agile voice capable of exaggerated temperaments. In choral music, the male voices used are tenor and bass. The tenor voices, however, are often divided into first and second tenor.

What is the falsetto voice?

The **falsetto** ("false") voice is an "artificially" produced, high-pitched tone produced by tenors and baritones. The sound is "artificial" in the sense that the resources of the full and natural voice are suppressed, allowing only weaker, high pitches to sound. It was used to sing parts originally meant for boys during the medieval and Renaissance periods and was highly regarded then.

How do the conventions of choral singing differ from those of solo singing?

Perhaps the primary difference between solo singing and choral singing is the ultimate goal of each with respect to vocal production and quality. The solo voice is expected to *project*, to separate itself from other vocal or instrumental sounds. The choral voice is expected to *blend* with others of its kind to form a homogenous soprano, alto, tenor, or bass quality, which differs from the solo voice quality. With no disparagement intended, the choral voice has typically been considered an "untrained" voice. This is, of course, a half-truth. The choral voice may be untrained as a solo voice but it is not untrained as a choral voice. Training for choral singing is not necessarily less complicated or demanding than that for solo singing; it is simply different. Choral voice training is necessary, in fact. That a group of raw, uncultivated voices could be put together in a chorus and produce a desirable choral sound is unfathomable.

What is involved in setting a text to music?

What a composer does in setting a text to music to produce a vocal solo or choral work has varied over the centuries. Some things, however, are basic to the process. First, the composer will produce music that reflects his or her view of the expressive character of the text. Second, the composer treats the *sounds* of the words as sound material, the "stuff" of which the music is made. Each of these actions is accomplished within the context of the idiomatic and meta-idiomatic conventions in vogue at the time the music is made. Too often, the text of a vocal work is thought to serve no other purpose than to provide a literary function; that is, to tell a story. Although this function may be important, it is less important than the overall expression and sound of the text. Because of the musical importance of the sound of the language used, translation of a text into another language is musically and aesthetically undesirable.

What is the future of vocal music?

In the centuries to come, the musical instruments we know today may no longer be in use, except for the voice. The human voice will be used, and new and exciting things will be done with it. Even now, the voice is being exploited in several ways that we must regard as "probes" into future possibilities. Singers have learned to produce multiple sounds simultaneously, sounds that can be independently manipulated. Some composers have produced new sound materials by modifying vocal sounds with electronic devices to produce new sounds that bear little resemblance to their original sources. Other composers have achieved high levels of artistry by producing a singing voice through computer modifications of a normal speaking voice. By these means and others yet to be employed, we can be certain that composers and performers will produce new forms of vocal music that are beyond what is currently known or possible.

30 The Instrumental Idiom: Bowed and Plucked Stringed Instruments

How did the bowed stringed instruments evolve?

Of all the manufactured instruments in use today, the bowed stringed instruments—the violin, viola, violoncello (commonly called the 'cello), and the double bass (or contrabass)—have undergone the least amount of physical change since they came into being at the beginning of the seventeenth century. Rather than undergoing the constant evolutionary changes characteristic of the development of other instruments, once the string family of instruments was formed, it remained the same for about two hundred years.

At the beginning of the nineteenth century, the instruments of the string family were modified to produce the "bigger" tone necessary for use in larger orchestras and larger concert halls. Since then, they have remained the same. These changes involved: (1) lengthening, narrowing, and increasing the angle of the neck and fingerboard; (2) raising the bridge (a natural consequence of increasing the angle of the fingerboard); (3) inserting a stronger bass bar; and (4) going to solid-steel E and A strings, an aluminium-wound gut D string, and a silver- or copper-wound gut G string on the violin and making similar changes in the strings of the other stringed instruments. A new type of bow, the Tourte design, also came into use at that time. The original bow curved outward in a manner similar to the archer's bow. By the early eighteenth century, it had been replaced by a bow with a slight inward curve. That bow served as a transition to the Tourte design, which is still used today.

It was because of the basic simplicity of the instruments' design that they could be modified. Even though the dimensions, materials, and craftsmanship are critical in the making of a quality stringed instrument, the basic design principle is one of the simplest in use: strings are stretched over a resonating box. It is a very simple but wonderfully versatile concept. In fact, it is a machine with no moving parts. Except for the wear and tear on replaceable strings, there is nothing to wear out. Many of the first violins made, for example, are still in use—and being among the best sounding, they are valued at hundreds of thousands of dollars. The simplicity of the stringed instrument's design also contributes to its versatility; its limits are yet to be realized by players.

What has been the role of stringed instruments in the symphony orchestra?

As first conceived, an orchestra was a mass of stringed instruments. Later, a few wind instruments were added. In forming this mass of strings, the conventional practice was to model it after the string quartet, the one difference being that the 'cellos and double basses played the same bass line. It is reasonable to assume that the names *double bass* and *contrabass* both describe that instrument's use in the orchestra; the conventional practice was for the basses to double the bass line an octave below the 'cellos. The string section of the orchestra, therefore, was established as: violin I (or first violins), violin II (or second violins), violas, 'cellos, and double basses (contrabasses).

The strings formed the principal body of instruments of the orchestra and carried the responsible role in music making up to the early nineteenth century. During the first nearly two hundred years of the orchestra's evolution, the stringed instruments were the only versatile and dependable instruments except for the flutes. Because of the simplicity of their design and function, stringed instruments were able to do about anything composers called for. The remaining instruments were relatively crude by today's standards. It was, therefore, the convention to think of the orchestra as a body of strings, with a few wind instruments and timpani (kettle drums) available for added color and percussive accent.

What is the role of strings in the late twentieth century?

A number of factors have served to bring about changes in musical conventions during the twentieth century: (1) a loss of interest in prevailing conventions, (2) the invention of new instruments and the further refinement of existing ones, (3) the failure of many string players to develop the technical skills needed to meet the needs of new music, (4) declining cultural attachments caused by the mobility of society, and (5) the culture-forming dominance of the media as expressed through the recording, radio, and television industries. All of these factors have served to diminish the role of the bowed stringed instruments at the very peak of their development. In the hands of a few contemporary performing artists—those who have met the challenges of new music—the stringed instruments remain supreme among the manufactured solo-performance instruments. In the orchestra, however, this failure of players to meet the demands of new music has contributed to a decline in the use of strings. New musicworks are now appearing that call for only one string player per part, for example, and such musicworks require string players who are solo-quality players. In much twentieth-century orchestral music, strings are used in the same subservient roles that once fell to wind and percussion instruments.

What are the technical capabilities of stringed instruments?

The stringed instruments remain the most versatile of the manufactured instruments with respect to articulation and the capacity to sustain sound. The full range of bowings and other means of making sounds are possible over their full pitch ranges. Whatever we might wish to produce as the envelope of a particular sound, there is a bowing or other form of articulation that will achieve it.

There are two basic bowing strokes: up-bow (notated by ⌄) and down-bow (notated by ⊓), to which are applied a number of bowing techniques. All of the bowing techniques are intended to provide varying ways to produce: (1) a smooth transition in going from one tone to another, *legato* bowings, and (2) a separation of tones, *detached* or *nonlegato* bowings (Figure 30-1). Some forms of bowings combine the techniques of legato and nonlegato bowing to produce some very expressive music. Legato bowings include the playing of a number of tones

30-1

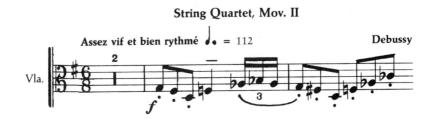

of a melody during the course of one stroke of the bow and the playing of one tone per stroke of the bow by the skillful and imperceptible change of direction of the bow as in (Figure 30-2).

30-2

From the imperceptible change of direction, every reasonable form of accent can be employed at the change of bow to mark the initiation of each tone while yet maintaining the technical definition if not the spirit of the legato bowing (see Figure 30-3).

30-3

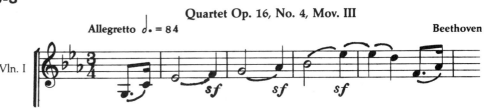

Bowings that separate tones from each other are achieved in a number of ways, each of which imparts a particular expressive quality. A percussive, accented tone is achieved by abruptly drawing and stopping the bow, keeping the bow on the string (Figure 30-4). Another

30-4

Symphony No. 8, Mov. II

Schubert

percussive effect is produced by making short strokes in the same direction—that is, all down strokes or all up strokes—removing the bow from the string between the strokes (Figure 30-5).

30-5

from *Petroushka*

Stravinsky

Several means can be used to produce short (*staccato*) or very short (*spiccato*) tones by bouncing the bow on the string. These range from single, controlled bouncing strokes or a number of controlled bounces in a single bowstroke (both shown in Figure 30-6) to throwing the upper

30-6

from **Symphony No. 6, Mov. III**

Tchaikovsky

part of the bow onto the string and letting it bounce the desired number of times as the bow is drawn (Figure 30-7). Another bowing effect, best regarded as unconventional, is produced by bowing or striking the string with the wood rather than the hair of the bow. For tapping or striking with the wood portion of the bow, the term *col legno battuto* is written in the music; for

30-7

from *Capriccio Espagnol*

Rimsky-Korsakov

drawing the wood of the bow on the string, the term *col legno tratto* is written in the music (Figure 30-8). Neither of these techniques is popular with string players. Some string players refuse to comply with the instructions, or use an old, valueless bow for the purpose. The risk of destroying a good bow is indeed a concern for players whose bows are worth many thousands of dollars.

30-8

from *Music for Strings, Percussion, and Celesta*, Mov. IV

Bartók

Another means of sounding a tone on a stringed instrument is to pluck the string or strum it in a manner characteristic of the guitar. In plucking a string (*pizzicato*) the player may, with varying degrees of force, pluck the string with the fleshy part of the fingertip or with the fingernail (Figure 30-9). This results in a variety of very soft, short, isolated tones to relatively loud, percussive tones, some of which may be sustained for a short time. The most percussive of the pizzicato sounds is achieved by having the string slap the fingerboard as the string is

30-9

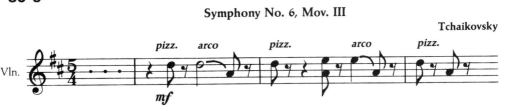

Symphony No. 6, Mov. III

Tchaikovsky

Symphony No. 2, Mov. II

Brahms

plucked. In some musicworks for solo stringed instruments, the pizzicato is indicated to be played with the left hand (Figure 30-10). For the most part, such musicworks are "exhibition" pieces designed to show off the versatility of both the instrument and the player. In strumming

30-10

from Sonata for Solo Violin

Vincent Persichetti

Note: + indicates left-hand pizzicato.

the instrument, either the fleshy part of the first finger, the thumb of the bowing hand, or the top side of the fingernail of the first finger of the bowing hand is used (Figure 30-11). Though pizzicato and strumming have been featured in some musicworks, their use is relatively limited compared to bowing techniques.

30-11

String Quartet, Mov. II

Debussy

The sounds of bowed stringed instruments can be varied by the conventional place-ment of the bow on the string. If the bow is drawn over the end portion of the fingerboard, the quality of sound produced is soft and less "edgy" because the upper harmonics that make up the tone are subdued. If the bow is drawn over the string immediately next to the bridge, a rather nasal, eerie sound is produced because the lower harmonics making up the tone are subdued. The typical or most prominent tone quality, the one having the full range of harmonics in the tone, is produced by drawing the bow across the area of the string midway between the end of the fingerboard and the bridge. Examples of music calling for bowing over the end of the finger-board (*sur la touche*) and next to the bridge (*sul ponticello*) are shown in Figure 30-12.

30-12

from *Petroushka*

Stravinsky

from Prelude to *The Afternoon of a Faun*

Debussy

The tone quality of bowed stringed instruments may also be altered by using a **mute**, a wooden or metal device that is attached to the top of the bridge. The mute reduces the resonance normally transmitted through the bridge to the body of the instrument. Muted tones are usually soft and silky in quality. The indication that a mute is to be used is usually *sordino* or *con sordino*, and *senza sordino* indicates that the mute is to be removed (Figure 30-13).

30-13

from Tristan und Isolde, Isolde's Liebestod

Wagner

Harmonics are tones produced by harmonic fingerings; that is, by touching a string lightly in predetermined places rather than by depressing the string against the fingerboard. This causes the string to vibrate on both sides of the point (the **node**) where the string is touched. As a result, the string can only vibrate in segments. See Figure 30-14. The fundamental

30-14

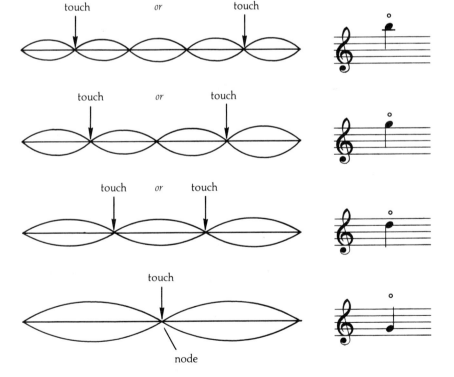

Natural Harmonics

G string

pitch of these harmonics is determined by the frequency of the vibrating segments of the string. Segments one-half the length of the string produce a pitch an octave above the pitch of the full length of the string; one-third the length produces a pitch an octave and a fifth above the fundamental pitch; one-fourth the length, a pitch two octaves above the fundamental; and one-fifth the length, a pitch two octaves and a major third (+3) above the fundamental. These harmonics are called **natural harmonics**.

Another group of harmonics is called **artificial harmonics** because they are produced by stopping the string at one point with one finger while touching it at another point with a different finger. On the violin this involves shortening the string by stopping it at a given point and then dividing that length into thirds, fourths, or fifths with another finger to produce the same relative results as the natural harmonics. Figure 30-15 shows how artificial harmonics are produced and notated.

30-15

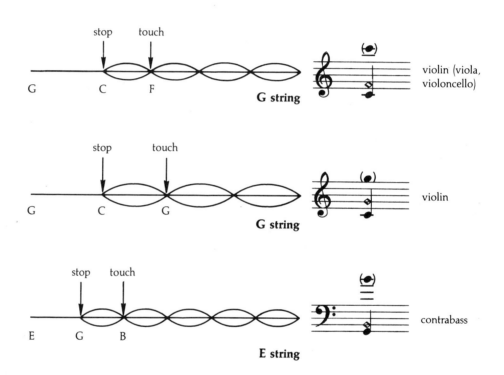

"Artificial" Harmonics

What are the plucked stringed instruments?

The plucked stringed instruments have their roots in antiquity. As an instrumental genre, they predate the bowed stringed instruments. Except for the modern harp, the plucked instruments have seldom entered the instrumentation of the symphony orchestra. This is due to the delicacy of their tone and their inability to sustain sound. The harp did not enter the orchestra until the beginning of the twentieth century, and its use has been limited. The guitar has enjoyed a resurgence during the second half of the twentieth century; its present mass popularity is as strong as it was during the Renaissance. The guitar may well have replaced the piano as the most popular recreational instrument.

How does the harp function?

The harp is a diatonically strung instrument having a total range of six and a half octaves from $C\flat_1$ to $G\sharp_7$. There are seven strings for each octave, representing seven diatonic pitch classes. It also has seven pedals, one for each of the diatonic pitch classes. The pedals activate stopping mechanisms, which shorten the length of the strings and thus raise the pitch. When the strings are at full length, the sounding pitch classes are C flat, D flat, E flat, F flat, G flat, A flat, and B flat. When the pedals are placed in the second of their three possible positions, all of the strings in each octave are raised a half step, to sound C, D, E, F, G, A, and B. Placing the pedals in the third position (completely depressed), raises the strings to sound C sharp, D sharp, E sharp, F sharp, G, sharp, A sharp, and B sharp. It is impossible to change the pitch of one string without effecting the same change in all strings of the same pitch class. Because of this peculiarity, enharmonic notations of pitch are common in harp music. We might find, for example, an F-minor triad notated as F, G sharp, C because of a previous or following notated A natural that is too close for an effective pedal change. Altered pitches within the context of the music must be carefully planned, and players must be given ample time to make the pedal changes.

In plucking the strings of the harp, the player uses the thumb and first three digits of each hand. When playing chords, the normal procedure is to "roll" (rapidly arpeggiate) them. Chords that are to be played as blocks—that is, with all tones sounding simultaneously—are bracketed. Music for harp is notated on two staves, the same as for piano music. Harp glissandi are very common; they are done by running the fleshy part of the thumb or fingers over a portion or all of the strings. Certain chords, the diminished seventh chord, for example, are treated as glissandi by using enharmonic tunings of the strings; a good example is C, D sharp, E flat, F sharp, G flat, A, B sharp. Octave harmonics are also common and are produced by touching the center of the string with the heel of the hand while plucking the string.

What constitutes the modern guitar?

It is really not possible to refer to *the* guitar as if to say there is but one instrument by that name. In fact, so many contemporary instruments (mostly electrified or electronic) are called guitars that there is no way of knowing how many there really are. Although the parentage of these instruments is unquestioned, there are many guitarists to whom an electrified or electronic instrument is something other than a guitar. For this reason, it has become the practice to call the **classical guitar** used in the long tradition of classical guitarists the **acoustical guitar**—although this is an unfortunate misapplication of the term *acoustic*.

The modern classical guitar obtained its present shape and level of development in the mid nineteenth century. After the Renaissance, the classical guitar was kept alive by performing artists, principally Spanish, who performed transcriptions of music by Bach and a number of Classical-period composers. The guitar has survived as a recital instrument and as an accompanying instrument in folk and popular music. Much of the credit for the development of performance techniques is attributed to the Spanish flamenco players. During the early part of the twentieth century, occasional jazz artists appeared to help keep interest in the instrument alive. The jazz players used metal strings and some used a pick rather than their fingers to pluck the strings. During the nineteen-fifties a massive swell in popularity began that made the guitar (in one form or another) perhaps the most widely used instrument in popular and recreational music. Partly because of this new popularity and because of such extraordinary classical guitarists as Andrés Segovia, interest in classical guitar grew rapidly and can now be said to be flourishing.

What are some technical aspects of the guitar?

The strings of the guitar are tuned to E_2, A_2, D_3, G_3, B_3, and E_4. Music for the classical guitar is notated an octave higher than it sounds and can be notated entirely in treble clef. It is still common, however, to find popular music for guitar printed in chord symbols or tabulature or both. From the sixteenth century to the eighteenth century, guitar music was notated in **tabulature**, a staff-like set of lines representing strings on which letters were placed to indicate finger stops.

The primary mode of producing sound in classical guitar technique is by plucking the strings with the fleshy part of the thumb and the first three digits of the right hand. Chords may be sounded by plucking or they may be arpeggiated (strummed) with the fleshy part of the thumb or fingers. Picking or strumming with the fingernails produces a louder, harsher tone quality. Classical guitar techniques allow for the sounding of multiple melodic lines in either contrapuntal or homophonic texture. Harmonics are produced the same as on bowed stringed instruments.

As a word of caution, producing music with any degree of sophistication for either the harp or guitar requires more than a casual acquaintance with the performing techniques. Any project utilizing either instrument should be produced under the guidance of a player. This, of course, is a wise policy when producing music for any instrument about which we have limited knowledge.

MINI PROJECT 13

Introduction

This project will exercise your consideration of problems associated with the instrumental idiom and further develop your ability to establish a musical gesture and carry out the unfoldment of a melodic line. Because the success of this project depends upon your ability to realize and utilize the special qualities attributed to a particular singing voice and a particular stringed instrument, precompositional considerations are crucial. In this situation, precompositional preparation includes learning what is and what is not *idiomatic* for the particular voice and instrument you are using. Your composition needs to be appropriate technically and effective expressively.

Description

Provide a musical setting of a lyric poem of no more than three or four lines. Select a poem that is appropriate for a particular singing voice. Provide an accompaniment using either a bowed stringed instrument or a plucked stringed instrument. Demonstrate your ability to establish a musical gesture and carry out an expressive unfoldment of the melodic lines generated by it.

How to Proceed

The first step is to determine who among the singers in the class will sing the song. Consider the type of voice selected when you are selecting the poetry to be set. After you've made these two decisions, decide which of the available stringed instruments will best serve to provide an accompaniment. The choices here might be rather limited.

After you have decided upon the voice, the poetry, and the instrument, study the voice and instrument to learn as much as possible about what is appropriate, technically and expressively, for them. Then establish an opening gesture having a melodic configuration that you can modify by reiteration, projection, and limited use of one or two other techniques. The opening gesture can simply be a mood-setting accompaniment figure, or it can be established by the voice itself.

If the harp or the guitar is the accompanying instrument, good idiomatic writing requires the use of both melodic and chordal structures or at least a two-part contrapuntal texture.

The projects should be performed in class and evaluated primarily in terms of the idiomatic use of the voice and the stringed instrument, the expressive treatment of the text, and the effectiveness of the melodic unfoldment.

31 The Instrumental Idiom: Woodwinds and Brass

How does the development of woodwinds and brass instruments contrast with the development of stringed instruments?

In contrast to how the modern stringed instruments came into existence, modern woodwind and brass instruments have taken a long time to reach their present states of development, and they continue to change gradually. Generally, each change in an existing instrument and each addition to a particular family of instruments is an attempt to correct some troublesome aspect of an instrument or to expand its capabilities. Some changes in brass instruments, however, are purely for visual effect.

Another contrast with stringed instruments is that woodwind and brass instruments are complicated mechanisms; some of them are extremely complicated. Also, the very best of any one kind of woodwind or brass instrument has idiosyncrasies that must be overcome by the player. For example, the flute, oboe, saxophone, and trumpet are among a large group of instruments that do not respond well to rapid articulation in the low ends of their pitch ranges. Other idiosyncrasies that contribute to the individual characteristics of woodwind and brass instruments have to do with: (1) unevenness of tone quality at various levels of the pitch range, (2) dynamics that become progressively softer or louder in going from the bottom to the top of the pitch range, and (3) certain pitches being "out of tune" with the standard frequencies they should be sounding. Though most of these idiosyncrasies are minimized in the highest-quality instruments, they cannot presently be eliminated.

Except for one instrument, the trombone, all woodwind and brass instruments are constructed so as to produce tones that have **discrete** (specific) **pitches**. Like the bowed stringed instruments, the trombone can produce a tone at any pitch within the instrument's total frequency range. This is because the trombone slide can be placed in any position—just as the string player can place his or her fingers anyplace on a string. It is interesting to note that the trombone, next to the stringed instruments, has the least number of moving parts: one slide and in some cases a valve. The simplicity of the instrument's construction is what makes it so flexible.

However, because of the distances the slide must move during performance, the trombone has other limitations.

In discussing the wind instruments of the orchestra, we will be concerned with how they work and how they complement each other. We will see that what is an extremely easy and conventional thing to do on one instrument may be utterly impossible on another. Though many new conventions have been established regarding the roles of woodwind and brass instruments in the orchestra, many old conventional uses are still employed. For example, even though the trumpet has developed into a prominent solo instrument in the orchestra and is capable of considerable delicacy of expression, it is still called upon to serve its longtime "heroic" role as a member of the brass choir.

How are woodwind instruments classified?

A number of characteristics distinguish the woodwinds from each other; for example, whether an instrument is made of wood or metal and whether it has a cylindrical or a conical bore. The characteristic that provides the general classification of woodwinds is the means of producing the vibrations that initiate the production of a tone. The woodwinds are generally classified as flutes, single reeds, and double reeds.

The flute tone is initiated by a vibrating stream of air produced by blowing across the mouth hole in the head joint of the instrument. The air stream strikes the plate at the far edge of the mouth hole and forms eddies—little swirls of vibrating air. Eddies formed in air are very much like the eddies seen in a stream of water when the flow of water is interrupted by an object protruding from the surface.

The vibrations that initiate the tone of the clarinets and saxophones are produced by blowing a stream of air through the opening between a single bamboo reed and the mouthpiece to which the reed is attached. The vibrations in the air column result from the reed vibrating against the opening of the mouthpiece as the air passes through.

The vibrations that initiate the tone of the oboes and bassoons are produced by blowing a stream of air between *two* slender bamboo reeds that are bound together. The vibrations in the air columns of these instruments result from the reeds vibrating as the air passes between them.

What are the characteristics and limitations of the flutes?

The instruments classified as flutes are the C piccolo, the C flute, the alto flute in G, and the bass flute in C. The C flute is the principal flute used in the symphony orchestras, symphonic bands, and the modern wind ensemble. The piccolo is quite frequently used in orchestras and might be considered standard in symphonic bands and wind ensembles.

The modern *Boehm-system** flute is the result of a long evolutionary process beginning with a simple bamboo, whistlelike instrument. The "end-blown," whistle flute reached its highest development in the sixteenth century in a family of instruments called **recorders**, interest in which was revived during the twentieth century. The first flutelike instruments and the recorders that followed were actually sophisticated whistles; there was little or no way for a player to exercise control over the tone of the instruments. The modern flute is called a **transverse flute** because the player blows *across* the hole in the side of the flute rather than through a mouthpiece at the end. The modern flute requires great skill to produce a tone but provides the player with complete control over the tone.

The basic flute tone is the simplest or purest of all instrumental tones; theoretically, the tone contains only the fundamental pitch and no other harmonics. In reality, however, a few

---

*Theobald Boehm (1794–1881), flutist and inventor of a modern fingering system for woodwinds that adapts the acoustical position of the holes to the natural spread of the fingers.

harmonics are produced by the player's *embouchure*—how the player shapes and places his or her mouth on the mouth-hole plate. These few harmonics enrich the tone to some degree. The various octaves within the instrument's three-octave range are produced by *overblowing* (blowing with enough increased force to cause the pitch to sound the next octave higher) and by special fingerings. Exaggerations of embouchure manipulations, overblowing, and specialized fingerings enable present-day flutists to sound several distinct pitches at the same time. This capability has brought about a new instrumental convention called **multiphonics**, a convention that has been used to great advantage in solo flute music produced during the second half of the twentieth century. Though multiphonics can and have been used in all woodwind music, they have proven most effective and aesthetically desirable in music for flute.

Basically, the flute tone is soft at the bottom of its pitch range and becomes increasingly loud at the top of the range. A skillful player can overcome this characteristic to a great degree but not entirely. Also, the flute does not respond well to rapid repetitions of pitch (rapid tonguing) at the low end of the pitch range. Except for these limitations, the flute is exceptionally responsive and agile.

The flute was one of the first woodwinds to be used in the orchestra. During the early years of the orchestra, it was the conventional practice for the flute to double the first and second violins at the same pitch level or an octave higher, especially in tutti passages. This practice simply provided an additional color to the basic string sound of the orchestra. As the orchestra developed, the flutes gradually assumed a more independent solo function. Though the flutes continued to double strings, they more often doubled the oboes and bassoons, and later the clarinets. In twentieth-century orchestral music, the flute emerged as a prominent solo instrument.

What are the single-reed woodwinds?

After a few centuries of metamorphosis, a single-reed instrument called the *chalumeau* came into being. This instrument, commonly regarded as the forerunner of the modern clarinet, was modified in the late seventeenth and early eighteenth centuries into what, in principle, would be called a clarinet. This instrument evolved further until the modern Boehm-system clarinet came into being early in the nineteenth century. Up to this point we have no problem with the classification called single-reed instruments. However, very shortly after the modern Boehm-system clarinet was introduced, Adolphe Sax (1814–1894) invented the instrument we call the saxophone. The saxophone is a single-reed instrument made of metal; however, it has a conical bore similar to the oboe's, rather than cylindrical like the clarinet. Because the saxophone combines features of both the single-reed and double-reed instruments, it is a hybrid. Nonetheless, it is classified as a single-reed instrument. Some people regard the saxophone as a member of the clarinet family, which seems to stretch a point of resemblance beyond reason.

What are the characteristics and limitations of the clarinets?

The clarinet family includes: the E-flat soprano clarinet, the standard B-flat and A clarinets, the E-flat alto clarinet, the basset horn (an obsolete alto clarinet), the B-flat bass clarinet, and the E-flat and B-flat contrabass clarinets. The standard B-flat and A clarinets are the conventional clarinets of the orchestra. The E-flat soprano and B-flat bass clarinets are relatively prominent in twentieth-century orchestral music. The remaining instruments of the clarinet family are seldom used in orchestral music. In marching bands and symphonic bands, the B-flat clarinet is the standard instrument. In these bands, the B-flat clarinet is used conventionally as a section of instruments—generally divided into first, second, and third clarinets. In the modern wind ensemble, all but the A clarinet are generally used. Depending on the size of the wind ensemble, they may be used singly or in groups of two or three. If used at all, the A clarinet would be used only in the most recent music for the modern wind ensemble.

The pitch ranges of the standard B-flat and A clarinets consist of four segments that differ in tone and flexibility: (1) the *chalumeau* register (named after its ancestor), (2) the throat tones, (3) the *clarino* register, and (4) the extreme high register. The chalumeau register (fingered E_3 to $F\sharp_4$) can be played as softly as a whisper or loudly and forcefully. This part of the range can be tongued as rapidly as the player is able. The throat tones, comprising only four tones (G_4 to $B\flat_4$) are among the most troublesome and awkward tones on the instrument. The clarino register (B_4 to C_6) has the clearest tone and provides for the greatest flexibility in tonguing and dynamics. It is the most used register for solo orchestral melodies. The extreme high register ($C\sharp_6$ to G_6 and possibly higher) is extremely bright, difficult to play softly, and difficult to tongue rapidly. All of these differences in tone quality and response to articulation can be smoothed over on a good instrument in the hands of a very good player. The distinctive tone of the clarinet is due in great part to its being the only instrument that does not produce even-numbered harmonics—that is, the second, fourth, sixth, eighth, and all subsequent even-numbered harmonics. Because of the taper of the mouthpiece and the flared bell, a few weak, even-numbered harmonics are present in the tone.

What are the characteristics and limitations of the saxophones?

The instruments of the saxophone family are the E-flat and B-flat soprano saxophones, the E-flat alto saxophone, the B-flat tenor saxophone, the E-flat baritone saxophone, and the B-flat bass saxophone. The E-flat alto and B-flat tenor are the standard instruments. The lowest four tones of the instrument are characteristically loud and relatively harsh; they are also difficult to articulate and somewhat awkward to finger rapidly. These tones are not used except for less demanding purposes. The remainder of the range has a good tone quality and is easily articulated.

Though the saxophone is nearly one hundred fifty years old, it has not been used in the symphony orchestra except in a very few instances. On the other hand, it has been used extensively in marching and symphonic bands and wind ensembles. In these musical organizations, a section of at least four saxophones is used; typically, more are used in the marching bands. The most prominent and demanding use of the saxophone to date has been its use as the reed section of the dance bands of the "big band era." A common explanation for this is that they were intended to have served the same function in the dance band as the strings were serving in the orchestra.

Over the last four or five decades the E-flat alto saxophone has gained serious attention as a solo recital instrument.* The kind of tone produced by the "concert" saxophonist is quite different from the tone produced by the jazz performer, the difference being primarily a matter of what sound is considered appropriate for each kind of music. The difference is due in large part to the different mouthpieces and embouchures used for the two kinds of music.

What are the double-reed woodwinds?

There are enough similarities among the double-reed instruments to place the oboes and the English horn in the same family with the bassoons. However, because the oboes and bassoons each formed a distinct family of several instruments at one time, the two groups continue to be considered different. In spite of the similarities between the oboes and the bassoons, they have some glowing differences. For example, their extremely different fingering systems would be enough to distinguish them. Also, there are considerable differences in the quality of sound and articulation.

---

*The rise of the E♭ alto saxophone as a solo recital instrument is largely due to the performance and commissioning efforts of Cecil Leeson.

What are the characteristics and limitations of the oboes?

The oboe family is presently made up of the oboe and the English horn. The *oboe d'amore* is in limited use; the *oboe de caccia* is no longer in use. The English horn (an alto oboe in F) is just a few inches longer than the oboe and differs slightly in appearance. The English horn reed is placed on a short, curved metal tube that is inserted in the reed end of the instrument. The bell of the English horn is bulb-shaped, whereas the bell of the oboe is flared.

As with the saxophone, the bottom four tones of the oboe are somewhat harsh and present difficulties in articulation. The bottom tones of the English horn, however, are very mellow and present very little difficulty in articulation. Both the oboe and English horn tend to become progressively softer toward the top of their pitch ranges. The tone of both instruments is rich in quality, the tone of the oboe often being compared to the sound of the human voice. Though the oboe was used very early in the development of the orchestra, the English horn did not come to be used until much later. The English horn, along with a number of other instruments, was not admitted to the "classical" orchestra and was not used in musicworks called "symphonies" until late in the nineteenth century. Even then and up to the present it has been used less frequently than the oboe. One possible reason for this is that the tone of the English horn, like that of the saxophone, is very distinctive and does not blend well with other woodwind instruments. The tone of the English horn seems to take over, to "color" the sound of the entire orchestra. This factor apparently did not strike the fancy of composers of the eighteenth century or of many composers since then. The English horn has always been considered a somewhat exotic solo instrument because of its tone.

What are the characteristics and limitations of the bassoons?

The instruments that presently make up the family of bassoons are the bassoon and the contrabassoon. A rather strange looking but beautiful instrument, the bassoon is an object of wonderment to most people. The manner in which the long tube doubles back on itself and extends above the player's head gives the instrument a unique appearance. The Boehm system used in the design of the other woodwinds has not been employed in the making of the bassoon. The fingering and key system of the modern bassoon used in the United States is modeled after the design of J. A. Heckel, a late-nineteenth-century bassoon maker, and is appropriately called the *Heckel system*. The French bassoon—produced by Buffet, a prominent French clarinet maker—has not been used much in the United States; it is mostly used in France, Italy, and Spain.

In spite of its complicated appearance—the result of its many keys, eight of which are manipulated by the player's left thumb—the bassoon is an amazingly agile instrument. Rapid articulation, a challenge in the lowest fifth of the oboe's range, is not difficult at all on the bassoon. The tone of the bassoon is basically softer than that of the other woodwinds and it is much less "reedy" or "nasal" than the tone of the oboe. Because of its mellowness, it blends well with most other instruments. However, because of this mellowness and capacity for blending, it is much more difficult for the player to project the sound so that solo orchestral melodies can be heard clearly.

How are brass instruments classified?

The proliferation and "cross-breeding" of brass instruments make classifying them difficult. The almost uncontrolled development of new brass instruments seems highly impractical, because the majority of these instruments do not have and, in all probability, will never have a solo literature and will not be used in any form of art music. The one exception is the group of recently developed "piccolo" trumpets; these are used mainly for performing seventeenth- and eighteenth-century musicworks whose pitch ranges and tessituras are too high for the standard B-flat and C trumpets. We can regard the many other instruments being produced as "props" for performing musical organizations and as being intended to appeal to the visual sense as much as to the aural. A brass instrument is basically a length of brass tubing. This tubing can be curled into various manageable and attractive shapes to produce visually appealing instruments for specific uses, in marching bands and various types of parade organizations. There is, therefore, a growing number and variety of shapes being used in the making of new brass instruments, most of which are hybrids that combine conventional characteristics of differing older instruments.

Some characteristics that serve as bases for classifying brass instruments are

1. the kind and shape of the mouthpiece

2. the amount of cylindrical and conical tubing

3. the diameter of the tubing

4. the length of the tubing in relation to its diameter

5. the number and kind of valves used (rotary or piston)

6. the shape, flare, and size of the bell

The possible variations and combinations of these characteristics are numerous. However, in order to have some useful basis for classification, we will group the instruments into the horns, the trumpets, and the tubas.

How are tone and pitch produced on a brass instrument?

The tone of a brass instrument is initiated by a "buzzing" sound the player produces by forcing a stream of air through pursed lips placed on the mouthpiece of the instrument. This procedure actually makes the player a part of the instrument. The buzzing sound produced by the player's lips serves the same function as a vibrating string or reed. The brass tubing serves as the resonating chamber for the vibrating column of air that produces the pitch and tone quality of the sound. By overblowing and making adjustments in the embouchure, a player is able to produce eight to twelve or more pitches of each harmonic series for each valve combination or slide position.

Except for the tuba, brass instruments do not respond well in the very low portions of their pitch ranges. They also tend to become increasingly louder toward the upper part of their pitch ranges. All brass instruments can be muted by placing mutes in the bells of the instruments. As with the stringed instruments, mutes serve to soften and alter the quality of the tone. Mutes for trumpets and trombones are the most successful and are produced in the greatest variety. In orchestral playing, a player does not use a mute unless it is called for by the composer.

How do "natural" and "valved" brass instruments function?

Valves for brass instruments were invented early in the nineteenth century, but players did not accept them readily. We might speculate that the players of **natural brass instruments** (instruments having no moving parts, such as the bugle), having invested a great portion of their lives perfecting the art of playing, were reluctant to abandon their instruments for new, unproven ones. Also, the concept of tone as produced on natural instruments, though not appreciated by us today, was most likely considered more desirable to the players of that time than the tone of the new valved instruments. In any event, the valved brass instruments did not become regular instruments of the orchestra until after the middle of the nineteenth century.

Before the introduction of valves, all of the natural brass instruments were narrow-bored instruments. The narrow bore enabled players to produce tones higher in the harmonic series where the pitches are closer together. The harmonic series based on different fundamental pitches were made possible by changing the *crooks*, (interchangeable, predetermined lengths of coiled tubing) used to tune the instrument to a given fundamental pitch. All of the pitch changes made within a harmonic series had to be made by adjusting the player's embouchure and the amount of air pressure.

On a **valved brass instrument**, the valves serve to vary the effective length of the instrument's tubing. For example, the second of the three valves of the conventional trumpet adds enough tubing to lower the pitch one half step. The first valve lowers the pitch two half steps, and the third valve lowers the pitch three half steps. These are used in the six possible combinations, with all three lowering the pitch by six half steps. The valves achieve the same effects as the changing of crooks.

What are the characteristics and limitations of the horns?

The horn typically in use today is the "double" horn, which is simply the F horn and B-flat horn combined in one instrument with a fourth valve used to move from one horn to the other. Because the function of the horns has, from the beginning, differed so much from the function of the other brass instruments, they have traditionally been separated from the other brass in the orchestral score.

How have the horns been used in the orchestra?

In the early classical orchestra, the horns were used in pairs; later in the nineteenth century, four horns were generally used. On rare occasions, six, eight, and even ten horns have been used. Since their inclusion in the early classical orchestra, horns have participated in the melodic material of symphonic musicworks. Quite often in the eighteenth-century orchestra, the horns were used to introduce certain kinds of melodic materials. It is interesting to note that much of the melodic material of that period even in music for keyboard instruments, has pitch configurations (horn fifths, for example) playable on the natural horn. In the nineteenth-century orchestra, the horns were among the most important of the melody instruments.

The horn player can affect the tone of the instrument by varying how much of the right hand he or she places inside the bell. It is standard conventional practice to insert the hand partially into the bell. This serves to dampen the tone just enough to take the brassy edge off the tone and produce the "normal" horn tone. On occasion, the composer asks to have the hand removed from the bell and to have the bell raised high; this produces a loud, "blaring" effect. Placing the hand deep into the bell, *stopping* the horn, produces a rather nasal, brassy sound that may be made to sound either soft or loud and rather nasty depending upon the occasion. A stopped horn will sound a half-step lower than the same notated pitch would sound normally. The player must, therefore, transpose music written for stopped horn a half-step higher.

What are the characteristics and limitations of the trumpets and trombones?

The trumpets and trombones are drawn together as a family of instruments primarily and initially because of the amount of cylindrical tubing used in them and the size of the bore (the diameter of the tubing). Since the middle of the twentieth century, the diameter of the bore of both instruments has been enlarged—a change that has made the tone less bright and somewhat "bigger." The change has also served to limit their upper pitch ranges somewhat—especially in the trumpet. As compensation for this limitation, a number of "piccolo" trumpets have been produced that can play the upper area of the trumpet's pitch range with relative ease.

The trombones, which are basically tenor and bass instruments, have been combined into one instrument with a thumb valve that enables the player to play either the B-flat tenor or F bass trombone. Enlarging the bore of the tenor trombone helped make the tenor and bass combination possible. The two instruments are still produced as separate instruments also. The seven positions of the trombone slide serve to add tubing to lower the pitch (in increments of half steps) as do the trumpet's seven valve combinations. It should be noted that the bass trombone has one less slide position than the tenor because of the increased length of the individual positions.

How have the trumpets and trombones been used?

During the early history of the orchestra (especially the late seventeenth and early eighteenth centuries, essentially the Baroque period) the natural *clarin* trumpet, a valveless instrument, was used to play extremely high pitched soloistic parts in musicworks for small orchestra. The clarin trumpet, pitched on F, was a rather long, narrow-bored instrument capable of sounding the third and fourth octaves of its harmonic series where the pitches are close enough to form a scale. These pitches are extremely high, higher than are presently practical or indeed possible on a modern C or B-flat trumpet.

In the early classical orchestra (the fifty or so years following the Baroque period), the trumpet was used primarily as an accentuating instrument combined with the timpani (kettle drums) to play rhythmic patterns. Such rhythmic patterns, generally found in **tutti** (full orchestra) passages, are usually louder and somewhat percussive in nature. This seemed to be the only useful role for the valveless trumpets during that period because the composers of the time did not care to use the high pitches of the clarin trumpets. They were producing a kind of music for which the high range of the trumpet was not suited.

Trombones have been used actively since the fifteenth century. Because the slide permitted all pitches in the total range of the instrument to be played, the trombone was used in the instrumental art music of the time. The instrument's tone quality was relatively soft and it blended well with the strings of that time. It is believed that the trombone, along with other instruments, was used to play along with and in support of the voices in the liturgical music of the Renaissance—that is, in what we call **a cappella** or unaccompanied music. A cappella music (literally, "music for chapel") was written without separate instrumental accompaniment. It is assumed by many that instruments were used to assist the singers.

The trombone has been used in the opera orchestra since the beginning of the seventeenth century. In spite of its use in the instrumental art music of the Renaissance and later in opera, the trombone was not a standard instrument of the symphony orchestra until about the mid nineteenth century. It was used before that only on rare occasions; the last movement of Beethoven's Fifth Symphony is considered the first of them. Solo music is more common for the trumpet than for the trombone, with both orchestral and piano accompaniment. A number of solo works originally for clarin trumpet are now played on piccolo trumpets. Most of the original solo materials for the C and B-flat trumpets and trombones are of recent vintage.

What are the characteristics and limitations of the tubas?

In one sense, the tuba classification is a catch-all for instruments that combine the horn's conical bore with the trumpet's shape and cupped mouthpiece. Though the tuba is a bass-pitched instrument, there are a number of instruments that are roughly classified as members of the tuba family: the euphonium, baritone horn, and sousaphone (bass-clef instruments) and the cornet, alto horn, flugelhorn, and other treble-clef instruments. The familiar sousaphone seen in marching bands looks like a giant French horn wrapped around the player's body. Tubas generally have four or five valves and come in three sizes: (1) the tenor tuba pitched on B flat, (2) the bass tuba pitched on E flat or F, and (3) the double-bass tuba pitched on B flat or C.

In general, the instruments of the tuba family are relatively agile, the cornets probably being the most agile. The tone quality of all the tubalike instruments is generally less brassy and less centered than that of the trumpets and trombones. The tuba is often more felt than heard in orchestral or brass ensemble music, because the broadness of the tone tends to permeate the total sound. Because of this, the tuba is difficult to record. This same quality is also a detriment to solo tuba music with orchestral accompaniment. The lack of focus in the tone makes it difficult to follow what the tuba is playing when heard in context with other instruments.

How have the instruments of the tuba family been used?

The F, E♭, CC, and BB♭ tubas are all considered orchestral tubas; the choice of instrument is the player's.* It is the lowest-sounding member of the entire orchestra, and its primary function is as the bass member of the brass choir; however, in tutti passages the tuba may double the double basses. On occasions the tuba is used in solo passages.

All of the currently used instruments of the tuba family are used in one or other of the contemporary bands or wind ensembles. Music for these organizations generally has separate parts written for cornets and trumpets. Euphonium and baritone horn parts are generally interchangeable. Though some bands use sousaphones in the performance of symphonic music, it is generally unacceptable artistically; financial expediency demands the practice in some school bands.

The tuba gained permanent acceptance in the orchestra during the nineteenth century. Even today, however, some orchestral scores do not use the instrument—the bass trombone is favored by some composers to do what the tuba would normally do in a musicwork. The cornet, also, has had limited use in the orchestra; when it does appear, it is generally used as a solo instrument and in situations in which a tone less brilliant than the trumpet's is desired. In orchestral scores from the nineteenth century, we can find an occasional euphonium or baritone horn part. Opera and music-drama composer Richard Wagner had a number of instruments made that were essentially tubas but used a hornlike mouthpiece. These very agile instruments were called **Wagnerian tubas**. They did not survive to become standard instruments in either the orchestra or bands.

*The double-bass tubas are conventionally designated as "double C" and "double B-flat" tubas.

32 The Instrumental Idiom: Percussion and Electronic Instruments

What are the percussion instruments?

Percussion instruments include a wide variety of instruments, ranging from extremely expensive, sophisticated instruments to literally anything we might choose to strike, scrape, or shake to make a desired sound. With such a plethora of available instruments, limitless in fact, we can best serve our purpose by classifying the conventional percussion instruments in terms of:

1. definite or indefinite pitch
2. the materials of which they are made
3. the manner in which the sound is induced

Many of the percussion instruments have been used for centuries, some of them predating all the wind and stringed instruments. It is reasonable to assume that percussion instruments were the first to be produced by humans and also that their function as musical instruments was secondary to other functions initially.

What are definite- and indefinite-pitched percussion instruments?

A **definite-pitched** percussion instrument is one that, when set in vibration, produces a discrete pitch. Such instruments produce **regular vibrations**; that is, their sounds are a product of a single fundamental frequency. An **indefinite-pitched** percussion instrument is one that, when set in vibration, produces **irregular vibrations**; their sounds are a product of a number of unrelated fundamental frequencies. Before the term was redefined to serve an aesthetic purpose, an indefinite-pitched percussion instrument was said to produce what was called *noise*. Indefinite-pitched instruments produce sounds that are perceived as high, relatively high, medium-range, relatively low, or low in pitch. Contrast the triangle with the bass drum, for example; both are indefinite-pitched instruments.

It cannot be assumed that all indefinite-pitched instruments are equally devoid of association with discrete pitch. Some of them possess qualities of sound that present the illusion of being definite-pitched when they are used with certain definite-pitched instruments. The probable explanation for this is that the frequencies of the definite-pitched instruments reinforce the same frequencies in the indefinite-pitched percussion instruments sufficiently to create the illusion.

What are the membrane instruments?

The membrane instruments are instruments that have an animal skin or plastic substitute stretched over the rim of a resonating enclosure (cylindrical, conical, barrel, kettle, and the like) or over an unenclosed cylinder or rim. The membrane instruments include an extremely large number and variety of drums, a few of which are definite-pitched. The most familiar of the definite-pitched drums are the timpani. The timpani have enjoyed a prominence in the orchestra which, within the "sociology" of instruments, has placed them above the once-lowly percussion. In an orchestral score, the timpani are listed next to but separate from the percussion. Most of the membrane instruments are indefinite-pitched. The most common of these are the snare drum, tenor drum, bass drum, tom-toms, and bongos. Another membrane instrument, a drum though generally not thought of as such, is the tambourine.

What instruments are made of rods or bars?

Instruments made of rods (metal) or bars (metal, wood, or synthetic materials) include definite-pitched and indefinite-pitched instruments. The definite-pitched instruments are the glockenspiel (orchestral bells), xylophone, marimba, and vibraphone. Instruments in this group provide sound by being struck by mallets with varying degrees of softness or hardness. Some contemporary scores call for setting the bars of the vibraphone and marimba in vibration by drawing a contrabass bow across the end of the bar. The tone produced by this method is very similar to that of the "musical" saw. Examples of indefinite-pitched instruments in this group are the triangle and claves.

What instruments are made of metal tubes?

Chimes or tubular bells are made of varying lengths of plated brass tubes that hang by cords from, but do not physically touch, a metal frame. The tubes are arranged in two tiers or ranks that correspond to the arrangement of the white and black keys of the piano. A sound-dampening device is operated by a pedal.

Though the chimes are a definite-pitched instrument, the method of inducing vibration in them results in an out-of-tune quality. Sound is produced by striking the top ends of the tubes with mallets made of rawhide, wood, metal, rubber, cord, or similar material. The initial "shock" of striking a tube results in a slightly lower initial pitch, a phenomenon that can be produced on the piano by sharply striking one of the lowest-pitched keys. This phenomenon plus the fluctuation in the amplitude of the harmonics of a vibrating tube contribute to the lack of focus in its pitch. Both of these characteristics are similar to those of church bells, and chimes sound much like church bells.

What instruments are made of metal plates?

The most familiar of the instruments made of metal plates are cymbals and bells. Cymbals come in a great variety and are played by striking them against one another, as in the case of hand (crash) cymbals, or by mounting them on a stand and striking them with snare-drum sticks, brushes, or mallets of varying degrees of softness and hardness. The tam-tam, similar in appearance to the cymbal is hung by a cord from its rim and generally struck with a soft beater. Cymbals and tam-tams are indefinite-pitched instruments capable of hushed and subtle sounds as well as loud, crashing sounds. The crotales are small, definite-pitched plates that are hung on a stand and cover a chromatic octave. Hand bells are enjoying a revival and are used in hand bell ensembles (bell choirs). Though they have not been used in the orchestra, some musicworks have been produced for hand bells in ensemble with chorus and brass. The cowbell, whose sound is anything but bell-like, is more akin to the cymbal. The cowbell is an indefinite-pitched instrument that comes in three sizes: small, medium and large.

What instruments are made of hollowed or grooved wood?

Temple blocks and wood blocks are the most common of the hollowed wooden instruments. Temple blocks come in five sizes and are struck with marimba mallets. Wood blocks come in three sizes; each is simply a wooden block with a slit hollowed-out in such a way that the block has a thick side and a thin side. The thin side provides a relatively high but indefinite pitch, whereas the thick side is relatively low in pitch.

What other percussion instruments are available?

Among the remaining hundreds of possible percussion instruments are a large number of instruments thought of as Latin American and African instruments. Some of these have become common in percussion ensembles, and a few have found their way into symphony orchestras and bands. Their popularity was originally gained through Latin American and other forms of popular music. Also available as percussion instruments are such common items as automobile brake drums; tuned, steel reinforcement rods of the kind used in concrete construction;* and various kinds of plastic, metal, and wood objects and containers. A useful reference for all manner of conventional and exotic percussion instruments is *Scoring for Percussion* by Reed and Leach.**

What is an electronic instrument?

Sound is the result of perceived pressure changes in our atmosphere (chapter 10). The waveforms produced by these pressure changes are the consequence of some form of oscillation. Basically, therefore, an **electronic instrument** is one in which the waveforms, ultimately perceived as sound, are induced by oscillating electronic circuits. This manner of sound production is in contrast to the mechanically induced oscillations of strings, air columns, reeds, lips, membranes, and so on, associated with conventional instruments. Electronic instruments should not be confused with conventional instruments that use electronic devices to amplify or modify mechanically induced waveforms. The electric guitar, electric bass, and the contact microphones used on flutes or violins exemplify such instruments. An electronic instrument of more recent vintage that should eventually replace most other devices is the computer. The

---

*First used by Robert Sutton.
**Reed, H. Owen, and Leach, Joel T., *Scoring for Percussion*, Englewood Cliffs, New Jersey: Prentice-Hall, Inc., 1969.

computer can be programmed to produce and store any waveform. The stored information can be used to activate a frequency generator (a synthesizer) or to produce audio signals by digital to analogue conversion.

How do the tone products of mechanical and electronic instruments compare?

Some inaccurate terminology has crept into discussions of the tone qualities of mechanical and electronic instruments. Such contrasts as *natural* versus *synthetic* and *real* versus *artificial* are very misleading. The concept that an electronic instrument is anything but natural and the sounds it produces are anything but real could translate into the argument that we ourselves are anything but natural and that our thoughts and actions are anything but real because we function mentally and physically as the result of a very sophisticated set of electronics. In truth, electronic functions are natural phenomena that we have only recently discovered and applied. Mechanically produced musical tones are no more natural than electronically produced musical tones. Both represent applications of natural laws—many of the *same* natural laws, in fact. We still lack the ability to deal with the electronic instrument as easily and effectively as we deal with mechanical instruments, but this ability is developing rapidly.

Mechanically produced waveforms are an end product of the resonant qualities of materials and enclosures, both of which are subject to the physical laws embraced by the harmonic series and the behavior of sound. An electronic instrument produces four basic waveforms: sine waves, square waves, triangle waves, and sawtooth waves. The **sine wave** is a single frequency (a pure tone). A **square wave** contains only the odd harmonics and has a determined drop in amplitude in the upper harmonics. The **triangle wave** also contains only the odd harmonics and differs from the square wave in that the drop in amplitude occurs sooner in the series and the drop-off is more significant. The **sawtooth wave** contains all of the harmonics, each with a determined amplitude. These basic waveforms are close "cousins" to the waveforms produced by mechanical instruments. The sine wave has its counterpart in the flute; the square and triangle waves have their counterparts in the clarinet; and the sawtooth wave has its counterpart in such instruments as the violin and oboe. These electronic waveforms do not sound much like those of the mechanical instruments because of the many other factors affecting the envelope of sounds produced by mechanical instruments. Each pitch of a mechanical instrument provides a variety of subtle timbres. Once an electronic waveform is realized, it is subject to the same natural laws that control mechanically induced waveforms. The kinds of waveforms produced by an electronic instrument (having all of the standard operational components) is limited only by the inventive capacity of the person producing them. In many respects this is also true of mechanical instruments.

In what ways have mechanical and electronic instruments been influenced by each other?

During the nearly forty years since electronic instruments were introduced, a mutual attraction has occurred between mechanical music and electronic music. This is probably best exemplified in the music produced for both mechanical and electronic instruments. Performance practices in voice, strings, woodwinds, brass, and percussion have taken on qualities characteristic of electronic instruments. And as electronically induced waveforms become more controllable (in the sense that we can generate electronically the idiosyncracies of mechanical instruments—that is, controlled imperfection) they can be made to resemble the waveforms of mechanical instruments. Compositions utilizing both mechanical and electronic instruments have helped to improve the compatibility of their sounds. As a final note concerning percussion, it is possible that the rise of electronic music has contributed to the recent rise in the use of percussion. In many respects, percussion instruments provided the initial nexus for linking mechanical and electronic instruments.

UNIT PROJECT 6

Producing a Public Service Commercial for Radio*

Introduction

Making and recording a public service commercial for radio is an ideal vehicle for setting up and solving a complex set of idiomatic problems within a thirty- or sixty-second time frame. Your initial reaction to a project of this nature may be skepticism because of the frivolous nature of most radio commercials. A public service commercial need not be frivolous, nor need it be overly serious; what it must be, however, is appropriate to the character of the public service message being "sold" to a listening public. Because the function and format of a public service commercial is essentially the same as that of a commercial that sells a product, the term *commercial* is appropriate. The basic task is to produce a convincing public service message that uses musical suasion to help capture and retain the attention of the listener. The goal—which should be your expressive intent—is to *sell* the message to the listener.

Public service announcements are heard at all times of the year in every community. They concern topics of interest to the campus, the local community, the state, and the nation. Some examples are fund drives for worthy causes; support for such community projects as clean streets and parks, proper care of pets, public events, and public celebrations; voter registration drives; support for such human services as blood banks, hospitals, and nursing homes; and support for the library.

Description

Depending on the nature and complexity of the message, produce a public service commercial of thirty- or sixty-seconds' duration utilizing any voices (singing or speaking) and instruments (mechanical or electronic) you choose. Record the project and deliver the tape to the campus or local radio station in accordance with the arrangements you have made with them before producing the commercial.

How to Proceed

Before you begin actual work on this project an individual or a class committee should meet with a representative (generally the program director) of the campus or a commercial radio station to establish a working agreement. Such a meeting should serve to establish that your class will achieve educational benefits and that the radio station and the community will also benefit by the project. The program director of the radio station can offer valuable assistance in helping to select the kinds of topics that will best serve the needs of the community at the time the commercials can be broadcast.** Your agreement with the station will express the station's right to evaluate and use only those commercials they deem of broadcast quality in both content and technique.

The following suggestions are things to consider as you seek solutions to the problems posed by the project within the circumstances of your situation. Though they are presented in what might seem to be a logical order, they can be considered in any order or they can be considered as a whole. As a matter of fact, what you do, how you do it, and when you do it are determined by the nature of the problem, the available resources and time, and your particular manner of approaching and completing a task.

1. Once the topic or topics are determined, you will very likely need to speculate on points of view or attitudes (verbal and musical) that might be used to approach and advance the cause or event you have selected as your topic.

---

*In the event this project is unfeasible, select one of the six alternative projects in Unit Project 7.

**Public service commercials celebrating the Bicentennial year produced by students at Ball State University were broadcast by radio stations throughout the state of Indiana.

2. After speculating on several points of view or on attitudes, you might speculate on what kind and how many voices will best serve your needs. This is an important consideration, perhaps the most vital of all.

3. If the length of the commercial has not been prescribed by the radio station, this must be considered. The length and nature of the text is critical in relation to the time to be filled. The preferred view is that less is best. Word images are more effective than explanations. Let the music provide the feelings and attitudes; in other words, let the music provide what, in other circumstances, would constitute explanations. For example, the majority of the time might be spent establishing an extremely pleasant, even loving attitude with music alone; toward the end, an equally pleasant and loving voice might simply say, "Give a kitten or puppy a home today. Visit your local animal shelter."

4. Using a stopwatch and a cassette recorder, practice timing and recording the voice(s) until the pace of delivery and the sense of the message come together comfortably within the time frame and convey the desired expressive intent. The pace of the voice will not necessarily dictate the pace of the music to be produced, but it should be related in some manner.

5. You have probably given much thought to the music. Now begins the actual work of selecting the instrumentation, establishing a tempo, and producing a score system with the required number of measures. (A sixty-second commercial accommodates 32 measures of music with a measure signature of 3/4 at a tempo of 96.) Using the information you gained in item number 4, type or write the text on the score system. Words can be placed appropriately by listening to the recorded cassette and using a metronome.

6. You will find that certain key words in the text may require some form of musical event or even silence. Do not conclude that there should be music throughout a commercial; the music should serve to set the mood and highlight the message. Use silence to complement the sound and to serve a formalizing function in the overall structure of the commercial. Apply all that you have learned about musical gesture, the mapping and modification of melodic configurations, idiomatic conventions, and all else. However, your initial expressive intent must remain paramount; draw from your knowledge to serve the needs of the musical problem at hand.

7. Rehearse and record the project. If stereo equipment is being used, the music can be recorded on one channel and the voice(s) on the other channel. You may need several takes to get the overall timing correct and the music and voice(s) synchronized and properly balanced. After you get a satisfactory recording, it can be mixed down to be recorded at whatever speed and format the radio station desires.

UNIT PROJECT 7

Alternative Projects

Introduction

If preparing a public service commercial is unfeasible, a number of other possibilities can be pursued. The main objective is to consider idiomatic conventions as you design something that serves a specific function. A list of suggestions that might be used or might suggest something else is provided here.

Description

Produce a musicwork of one- to three-minutes' duration to be used for one of the following functions:

OPTION 1. Music for unaccompanied choir (SATB) to be used as part of a worship service in a church or synagogue.

OPTION 2. Music for the drum corps of a marching band to be performed as part of the halftime show at a football game.

OPTION 3. Music to be used for a dance routine performed by a dance corps and pep band as part of the halftime show at a basketball game.

OPTION 4. Music to be composed and recorded for use with the floor exercise of a gymnastic competition. (This would need to conform to an exact and probably shorter time frame.)

OPTION 5. Music to be composed and recorded for use with the free-form exercise for a figure-skating competition. (This would be subject to the same restrictions as option 4.)

OPTION 6. Music for an unaccompanied instrument to be performed on a student recital.

How to Proceed

Each of the six projects requires some form of permission and, in some cases, a degree of control by the person for whom the music is produced. If, for example, music is to be composed for a religious or liturgical service, there would be requirements concerning the text, the length of the composition, and the level of difficulty. Music for a drum corps would require permission from the band's director and some coordination with the show theme. Music for gymnasts or figure skaters requires tempo and mood changes within specific time allotments. Music for a dance routine would require the permission of the band director, the choreographer of the dance group, and coordination with the show theme. If you produce something for an unaccompanied instrument for a recital, you will need the permission of the applied music teacher, the agreement of the student, and a great deal of understanding of what is idiomatic for the instrument.

Many of the problems inherent in this project are identical to those posed by Unit Project 6; for example, the need for absolute control of time, the need for a dramatic theme, and the need to record some of the projects. Preliminary or precomposition problems related to the functional idiom, instrumental idiom, and acoustical idiom must be carefully considered and mostly solved before you begin the actual composition. If you are to produce music for a church or synagogue, you should visit the building to get a feel for the resonance. The same problem (a more severe one to be sure) exists if you are producing music to be performed at a basketball halftime show. Acoustical problems *must* be addressed, because misjudgments will have adverse effects on the total outcome of your project.

Your understanding of the instrumental idiom as it relates to the instruments available in the class may be rather well developed at this stage. If, however, you are undertaking a project involving a percussion group or a pep band or any instrumental group different from that contained in your class, you must attend rehearsals of these groups and become more than just familiar with the instruments they contain. It is good to begin expanding beyond the class and to begin doing the things a responsible composer does to prepare himself or herself to produce music for a particular ensemble to perform for a particular function at a particular place. Music produced without consideration for the idiomatic conventions is destined to be nothing more than "shelf music." If music is produced for no particular individual or ensemble to perform for no particular function at no particular place, it probably will not be performed at all.

UNIT

FIVE

META-IDIOMATIC
CONVENTIONS:
MODALITY AND TONALITY

33 Introduction to the Principles of Design

How do principles function in the arts?

In functioning as creative artists, we do not develop our own principles of design or the principles that govern the materials we use or the results of our use of them. We can only discover principles, observe how they function and relate to each other, recognize the limits of our control over them, and learn how to work freely and effectively within them.

Implicit in the definition of *principle* here is that a **principle** is a law of nature. All things come into being, all things happen, all things relate to one another, all things function in accordance with the application of some one or more principles. All principles—whether or not they are known to anyone—already exist in nature. Any principles that remain unknown are those that govern what humankind has not done as yet or has not perceived as either being done or having been done by natural occurrence or by someone's intent.

Over the years, we have all become familiar with a number of the principles that govern our physical world. We know that it is sometimes possible to apply one principle that is known to affect the behavior of a physical body in such a way that it counteracts the effect of another principle on the same physical body. For example, the principle of aerodynamics, which permits a physical body to achieve flight, counteracts the effects of the principle we know as the law of gravity.

The principle of aerodynamics was not invented by anyone; it was discovered. A number of devices *have* been *invented*, however, which, along with applications of some other principles (such as propulsion), use the principle of aerodynamics to achieve flight. Of the many ways the principle of aerodynamics has been applied to achieve flight, those ways that have been widely adopted can be said to be *conventions*. Among the most prominent conventions are fixed-winged aircraft and the helicopter, which uses rotating airfoils. A **convention** is an invented or expressed realization of a principle; the convention itself is *not* the principle.

The principles underlying the conventions in the arts provide the predictability needed for consistency and reliability. They include:

1. principles governing the quality and behavior of the physical materials that are used
2. principles governing the physical makeup and delimiting functions characteristic of the tools that are used
3. principles governing the environment within which an artwork is exhibited and the technical means by which it is displayed or performed
4. principles governing the functions and capacities of the human sense organs
5. principles governing the functions of the intellect that determine our ability to perceive the sensory impressions of an artwork

Must we know a principle before we can use it?

Principles of design are extremely important to be sure, yet artists need not have great knowledge of a principle or consciously understand it in order to use it. A creative artist does not consciously select and use a particular set of principles in the process of making something. Rather, he or she is immediately concerned with making practical choices: choices that are subject to controlling principles but not dealt with directly in terms of them. The creative artist deals intuitively with the *effects* of principles—that is, in terms of such things as expectation, consequence, evidence, and behavior. These effects reflect subconscious or subliminal knowledge of principles. The observable phenomena that are brought together in even the simplest artwork are the result of choices by the creative artist, choices that bring into play a complex array of principles that can be dealt with only in terms of controllable results.

Having, in a sense, declared the creative artist virtually independent of and practicably incapable of dealing directly with principles in the practice of his or her art, why, we might ask, are we so concerned about principles? The seeming contradiction might better be understood if approached first by observing a few of the very common things we all do.

Just about everyone, at some time or other, has baked a cake; many people do it quite frequently. But how many people are actually cognizant of the principles that govern the chemical behavior of the ingredients as they are combined to produce the one thing called a cake? This kind of question could be asked and a negative response received with regard to nearly everything the average cook might make.

Each of us spends much of our day talking. But how many of us understand the prinicples that govern the production of speech sounds? Or, how many whistlers are there who can explain, in terms of principles, what takes place inside their mouths when they whistle a tune? The real truth of the matter is that we as a people are actually aware of and understand few—comparatively next to none—of the vast number of principles that govern much of what we do or make happen.

Why must we study principles?

But—and this is an enormously important *but*—some people are obliged, either by personal desire or the demands of their chosen vocations, to seek out, study, experiment with, and eventually come to know certain principles. For example, not all bakers of cakes need to know the principles by which a cake comes to be what it is; but there are some bakers who study these principles in order to develop tastier, more nutritious cakes that are easier and more economical to make. Such research and development programs can even lead to the production of new agricultural products.

There are also people who study the principles that govern the formation of speech sounds in order to understand and correct a variety of speech defects. The goal is to develop a more controlled awareness and application of these principles and their relationship to other principles that govern our physiological and psychological being.

As a last example, consider the developments in the field of medicine. For century upon century, humankind functioned almost entirely on the level of the observable medicinal effects of various plant roots, tree barks, and herbs. Today, however, humankind is indebted to the many individuals who concerned themselves with discovering and studying principles. Eventually, the nature and causes of many illnesses and deformities that have brought suffering to humankind have been discovered. Though present-day physicians continue to practice on the basis of their observations of their patients, the healing arts are constantly being advanced by the discovery and study of principles.

It is not considered sufficient in medicine, cookery, or any other human activity simply to hand down the same unaltered, knowledge generation after generation. It is human nature to seek to improve our understandings and applications of known principles. Thus the search for principles we do not know will continue.

Only a small percentage of the people involved in any science, art, or *whatever* are consistently concerned with discovering and studying principles and developing new applications of known principles. But even so, the general practitioners cannot function effectively or comprehend properly what constitutes the best knowledge available if they remain ignorant of principles in their field.

How does knowing a principle improve our understanding of music?

It is true that we need not understand a principle in order to use it, but we might question how effectively an unknown principle can be used and still remain unknown or not understood. Could we be so utterly lacking in observation as not to recognize the existence of a principle we are using? Could we be so lacking in insight as not to understand the observable effects of a principle? Could we be expected to develop and cultivate expertise in doing something based on a principle or set of principles about which we are totally ignorant? Hardly. But the question remains, how can we use a principle without being able to state it—how can we cultivate a knowledge of it in order to develop expertise?

First, we must realize that there is more than one way that we can come to recognize a principle—by observation and by noesis are two examples. Secondly, our recognition of a principle may be so coincidental to our use of it that we are unaware of our newfound knowledge. Thirdly, recognizing a principle by some means other than through using it does not guarantee our ability to use it. Also, there are many ways to demonstrate understanding of a principle; our understanding of a principle is not dependent on our ability to verbalize it. In our dealings with the arts, we must realize there is much we will come to know that we cannot verbalize or explain but which we will understand nonetheless. We must be careful, therefore, not to fall into the trap of believing that learning in music is directly correlated with verbalization; a number of roads lead to recognition and understanding of a principle. Sometimes our recognition and understanding of one principle enables us to recognize and understand another.

By far the most common manner of discovering a principle is by doing something— intentionally or by accident—that makes use of the principle. If the principle is discovered, it becomes known in terms of the evident results of what was done. From here on, we can conjecture that proof of recognition and understanding is further evidenced by our increased ability to use the principle in an inventive manner and to use it in conjunction with other principles. In the simplest terms, anyone who is able to make a principle work for him or her can be said to recognize and understand it.

A composer's choices are governed by principles that manifest themselves in terms of their individual and cumulative effects. Consequently, if our choices are carelessly made and bring conflicting principles into play, the conflict will result, quite probably, in confusion, aesthetic disorientation, and any number of other problems that can mar or even destroy our efforts. The more time and effort we give to serious contemplation of the nature and relatedness of the things that give substance and definition to what we do in making music, the more we should understand the principles and grow in our ability to use them. Without the questioning, wondering, reflecting, speculating, and curiosity and all of the other probing attitudes that drive us to seek personal improvement, our knowledge and application of principles cannot rise much above routine mimicry.

Units one through four have provided you with the kind of hands-on experience that brings you closer toward a functional knowledge of the principles necessary for producing and understanding music. The process has been cumulative; what you have learned and used in each unit has given you skills and understandings that you have applied in subsequent units. A few of the numerous functional and design principles you have dealt with thus far are those concerned with notation, transposition, scoring, pattern making, musical abstraction, and the modification and transformation of melodic configurations. In Unit Five we will continue our study of design principles. Our concern will be with the principles underlying the meta-idiomatic conventions dealing with the organization of pitch in music that utilizes the diatonic system.

34 Meta-idiomatic Conventions

What are meta-idiomatic conventions?

Whereas **idioms** foster conventions that reflect the physical conditions under which music is produced, meta-idioms foster conventions that go *beyond* the physical aspects of music. Meta-idioms relate to the psychological, aesthetic, emotional, organizational, and other non-physical aspects that define the musical art. For the most part we deal with meta-idiomatic conventions intuitively. However, we will consider those principles of design that have fostered widely used meta-idiomatic conventions.

Though the terms *idiom* and *meta-idiom* are relatively new to you, we have been dealing with both since the beginning of this course of study. Such things as pitch, the physical properties of instruments, and the harmonic series involve idiomatic conventions. The principles underlying the techniques of melodic modification and transformation are clearly meta-idiomatic in nature. In this unit we will deal with the meta-idioms concerned with modality and tonality, two exceedingly prominent principles of pitch organization that are based on the principle of "referentialism."

What is referentialism?

Referentialism is the result of any form of pitch ordering that singles out a given pitch as the pitch of reference for all pitch materials used in a musicwork. A **reference pitch** in music works in much the same way as the "vanishing point" in an eighteenth-century painting. Typically, the objects in an eighteenth-century painting are sized and placed so as to give the illusion of three-dimensional perspective, with the vanishing point being the point of reference; the size and location of objects in such a painting are understood by their relationship to the vanishing point. It is important for us to emphasize here that *the ordering of the pitches creates the referential pitch*; the referential pitch does *not* determine the order. The establishment of a referential pitch is a function of our expectations—a function that reflects a principle of cognition. We cannot assume that, because a certain ordering results in the pitch content of the natural diatonic system or a transposition of it, we can arbitrarily select a pitch reference. It is not the pitch *content* of a musicwork that establishes a referential pitch; the *ordering* of the pitches in the work establishes one pitch as the reference point for all pitches.

What is the nature of modality?

From the beginnings of the history of Western music until some point within the sixteenth century, referentialism was achieved by a number of conventions, all of which fall under the term *modality*. Though the particularity of the operant conventions of modality differed considerably over the centuries, their essential principles remained intact:

1. that the fundamental objective of modality be concerned with the aesthetic subtleties of the modes as they related to the religious and social expressions of the times,

2. that a referential pitch be discernable but *not* a forceful objective, and

3. that a referential pitch be arrived at for the most part by the cumulative results of linear design assisted by the relationships established between lines.

In studying modality, it is not possible for us to sense the aesthetic subtleties of the modes or to understand the religious and social expressions of times in which they were used. We can intellectualize about them, but that is not feeling. We *can* deal with the techniques involved in establishing a referential pitch, however.

Because of an aesthetic preference for independent melodic lines rather than mutually dependent lines, it was common for melodic lines to begin and conclude (**cadence**) at different times and on various degrees of the modal scales employed. The effect of one voice cadencing while the others continue on and melodic lines cadencing on different degrees of a modal scale is not conducive to the establishment of a strong reference pitch.

In considering the relatedness of melodies in linearly designed music, we cannot know for sure whether the effect of what we presently hear in the simultaneous sounding of pitches in modal music is the result of an acoustical principle or a learned bias. In any event, we presently accept the upper pitch or pitches of *harmonic* intervals (such as shown in Figure 34-1) as

34-1

supporting the making of the lower or lowest pitch the acoustical root. We will find, therefore, the fundamental reference pitch as the lower or lowest sounding pitch in the final cadence of a modal musicwork. This pitch is called a **final** in the terminology of modal music. A modal musicwork having more than one voice (melodic line), more often than not, begins with one voice. This beginning pitch may be the final or another pitch that supports the final—such as the pitch a fifth above the final. There also appears to have been an acknowledgment of (and a preference for) the acoustical properties of the tertian triad throughout that long period of multivoiced modal music, even though the triad was seldom a compositional objective or a source of compositional material.

The concept of referentialism is illustrated in the simple two-voiced musicwork by Orlandus Lassus in Figure 34-2. In accordance with the conventions of the time, the music is composed in the Dorian mode. As pointed out in chapter 10, *Dorian scale* is not synonymous with *Dorian mode*. The Dorian scale, like any modal scale, is simply an octave segment of the diatonic system. A mode embraces certain pitch relationships and compositional procedures

34-2

Twelve cantiones duarum vocum

Orlandus Lassus

34—2, *continued*

that have been variously expressed in conventions over several centuries. One convention that is important to our understanding of the Dorian mode as used in Renaissance music has to do with the notation of the **penultimate** (next to last) pitch commonly used in melodic phrases ending on the various degrees of the scale. As shown in Figure 34-3, the penultimate notated pitch in a phrase ending on A can be a B or a G sharp.

34-3

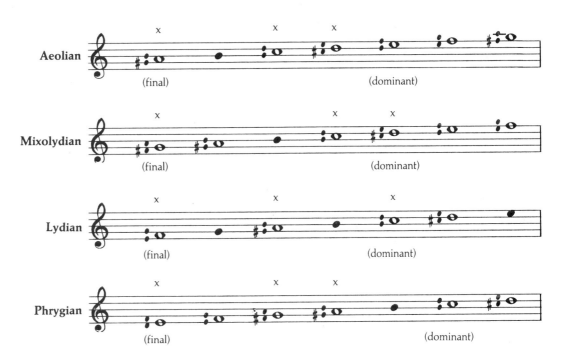

Note: x indicates the most common phrase endings and the penultimate pitches used in the stepwise approach.

34-3, *continued*

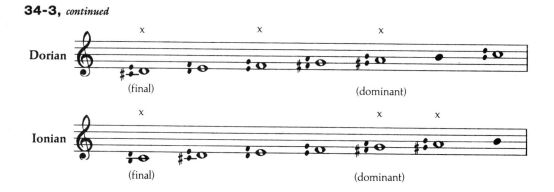

In Figure 34-3 we should note that there are no phrase endings on B in any mode within the natural diatonic system. This is because the fifth above B forms a diminished fifth, which makes it awkward if not impossible to establish B as a final. During the Renaissance there was some reluctance to using a diminished fifth (5°) or an augmented fourth (4⁺) as a harmonic interval. Within the context of a melody, therefore, it was common to use a B flat in places where a diminished fifth or augmented fourth would appear.

Examining Figure 34-2, one of the first observations we should make is the weakening effect of melodic imitation on the establishment of a referential pitch when the imitation is not at the unison or octave. Except for the second pitch, the *cantus* (the melody, generally in the upper voice) in Figure 34-2 is an exact imitation of the *altus* (alto) at the interval of a P5 (i7) higher, and it continues as such for the first seven measures. In effect, therefore, both D_4 and A_4 are felt, though weakly, as referential pitches. In the next two measures, both voices come to a close, one on A_3 and the other on A_4. In measures 11–18, we find the ordering of pitches in the cantus cadencing on G_4 and the altus cadencing on F_4. In measures 18–26 the cantus, as the leading voice, cadences on A_4. In measures 19–27 the altus, as the imitating voice, cadences on D_4. From this point to the end, the two voices cadence on the final, D_4.

By convention we are to accept D as the referential pitch of the music in Figure 34-2. We are also to recognize the importance of A; it is important enough to be labeled the **dominant**. The dominant, as we would expect from the name, is the dominant pitch in a mode. Even though A is the most prominent pitch in Figure 34-2, it is viewed as acoustically supportive in establishing D as the referential pitch. Because of the pitch interval of the imitation and the cadences on A, G, and F, we can observe the inner complexities of an application of the Dorian mode. It should be emphasized again that the degree to which a musicwork establishes a reference pitch is determined by the degree to which the pitch is needed for the tonal orientation of the listener. The reference pitch is not an aesthetic entity to be listened for or even thought about when listening to music; it is simply a function.

What is the nature of tonality?

Tonality is not a principle of tonal organization that came into being overnight. For a time in the sixteenth century there was a gradual gravitation toward what later became tonality. (In many respects, the process was similar to the gradual hint and final arrival of the "vanishing point" in early Renaissance painting.) Even after tonality was firmly established, vestiges of modality were present in music for some time. It is interesting to note also that certain principles of modality were called upon by some early-twentieth-century composers as either a respite from what was considered the overbearing force of tonality or as an avenue of approach to a new form of modality, referred to as *neomodality*.

Tonality differs from modality in that, regardless of what events take place within a musicwork, all the events set up expectations that are understood tonally in terms of a common reference pitch. As a further difference, we can describe modality as a loosely structured form of referentialism that lacks a common conventional grammar. Tonality, by contrast, is highly structured and has a highly developed grammar that incorporates a number of well-developed and differing conventional practices. Tonality provides for a method of ordering that results in a strong, basic structural relationship expressed as a basic movement from the **tonic** (or **key-tone**) pitch, to the *dominant* pitch, and back to the tonic. It is a structural relationship that is emphasized by the projection of triads on these tones. See Figure 34-4.

34-4

St. Antoni Chorale from Variations on a Theme by Haydn

Brahms

Perhaps the most interesting aspect of the change from modality to tonality is that all of the components required for tonality were already present in modality. The final and dominant in the Ionian mode, for example, as points of reference in modality became the tonic and dominant in the *major mode* in tonality. Similarly, the final and dominant in the Aeolian mode became the tonic and dominant in the *minor mode* in tonality. All that was required to effect the change from modality to tonality and the ensuing change of emphasis was a change in the point of view as to what aspects of formalism composers wished to use as the "centerpiece" of their controls. As the reference pitch was strengthened in tonality, other aspects that were the strong, formalizing controls in modality were liberalized and eventually ceased to be controlling forces in music. Philosophically, we can readily accept that there is good and bad music; but we cannot accept the notion that it is possible to have good music without a strong, underlying formalizing principle. The once-prevalent notions that *classicism* can be defined as "form at the expense of expression" and *romanticism* as "expression at the expense of form" are totally lacking in credibility. Intelligible music of any kind is formally strong. ·

35 Modal Music: Consonance and Dissonance

Much more important than referentialism to the modal composers were their conventions with regard to consonance and dissonance. To condense the practices of several centuries and to consider both the liturgical and secular idioms, we must generalize broadly indeed. In this chapter we will explore the modal conventions of consonance and dissonance.

What are the consonances and dissonances in modal music?

Consonance and dissonance in modal music cannot be understood and appreciated in an aesthetic sense because they require an obscure, subjective comparison. We would probably have difficulty agreeing on what is consonant and dissonant today. The terms are actually not relevant to much of our present-day music. We can, however, point out the relationships that were considered consonant and dissonant in modal music and the manner in which they were calculated. As shown in Figure 35-1, only the octave and P5 (i7) were considered perfect consonances. The − 3 (i3), + 3 (i4), − 6 (i8) and + 6 (i9) intervals were considered imperfect consonances. The P4 (i5), 4⁺ (i6), 5° (i6), − 2 (i1), + 2 (i2), − 7 (i10), and + 7 (i11) intervals

35-1

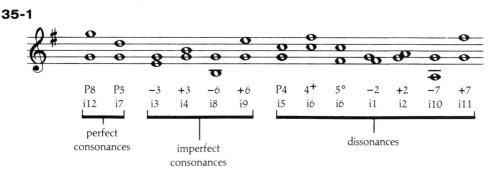

were considered dissonances. The conventions seen in modal music indicate where it was appropriate to use perfect consonances, imperfect consonances, and dissonances. In liturgical music using two voices sounding together at the beginning and end, only perfect consonances could be used (Figure 35-2). Otherwise, perfect and imperfect consonances were used anywhere. The conventional controls over the use of dissonance, on the other hand, were profuse and involved both metrical placement and particularized configurations that provided for the approach and resolution of dissonances.

35-2

Palestrina, *Missa Ut re mi fa sol la*

Palestrina, *Missa Gabriel Archangelus*

Lassus, Benedictus

Note: ✶ indicates a perfect consonance

How were consonances and dissonances calculated?

All consonances and dissonances in modal music were calculated as one-to-one relationships between the pitches of the upper voices and the lowest sounding pitch. Figure 35-3 shows several examples of three- and four-voice interval relationships in which all of the upper pitches are consonant with the lowest sounding pitch. In part c, the P5 and +6 intervals both

35-3

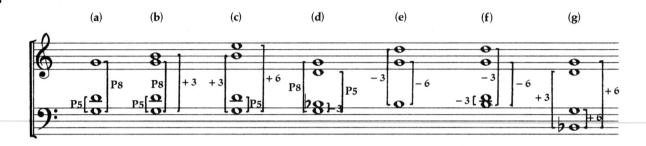

form a consonant relationship with the G; however, they form a +2 with each other. This set of pitch relationships, though considered consonant, required special treatment.

Because the study of modal music has centered primarily on liturgical music, the examples of dissonance in this chapter are drawn from that genre. Even here, there appears in our historical information what we might call aesthetic and theoretical "whitewashing" for the purpose of "purifying" the idiom; that is, expunging what is not common to the idiom. For the most part, what we know about Renaissance contrapuntal practice is a distillation of the music of Orlandus Lassus and Giovanni Palestrina. Therefore, what are generally presented as meta-idiomatic practices of sixteenth-century contrapuntal composers are actually the idiosyncratic practices of two of its better known practitioners. This situation is common, and unavoidable, in historical investigations of music.

The dissonances of Renaissance modality explained in the following discussion are notated primarily in ¢ and $\frac{4}{2}$ and occasionally in $\frac{3}{2}$.

What is a passing tone?

A **passing tone** is the most common of all forms of Renaissance dissonance. It is approached and left by stepwise movement of a voice in the same direction. It is described as either ascending or descending and either accented or unaccented; it was used in half-note, quarter-note, and eighth-note values.

The half-note passing tone occurs on the second or fourth beat of a measure in $\frac{4}{2}$ or ¢ and on the third beat in $\frac{3}{2}$. The examples shown in Figure 35-4a and b demonstrate the descending and ascending half-note passing tone in a number of characteristic situations in two-

35-4

continued

35-4, *continued*

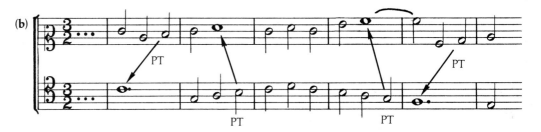

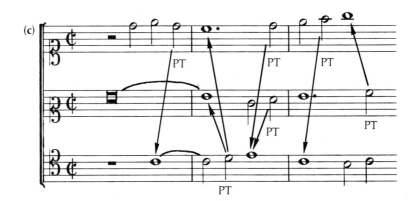

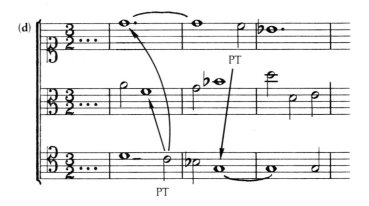

voice writing. The examples in Figure 35-4c and d demonstrate the descending and ascending half-note passing tone in three-voice writing. Observe that the notated pitches against which the passing tones occur are stationary during the approach and dissonant phases of the passing-tone configuration. (The parts of the configurations you are to observe are marked PT, and arrows indicate the dissonances.)   **W123**

The accented quarter-note passing tone occurs only in descending motion and only on the first half of the second or fourth beat of a measure in $\frac{4}{2}$ or ¢. The unaccented quarter-note passing tone occurs in both ascending and descending motion on the second half of each beat in $\frac{4}{2}$ or ¢ (Figure 35-5).   **W124—125**

35-5

Note: x indicates an accented passing tone, and + indicates an unaccented passing tone.

Eighth notes generally occur in pairs, occasionally in groups of three, and rarely in groups of four in Renaissance contrapuntal music. When they occur in a pair, either eighth note may be a descending or ascending passing tone (Figure 35-6a). In a group of three eighth notes, the first of the three will follow a dotted quarter note (Figure 35-6b). Any of the eighth notes in a group of three can be a descending passing tone. Ascending motion in eighth notes is less common; in fact, no ascending groups of three eighth notes have been found in Renaissance liturgical music. Only one example of four eighth notes has been found in the music of Palestrina. The configuration in Figure 35-6c permits only the third and fourth eighth notes to be passing tones.

35-6

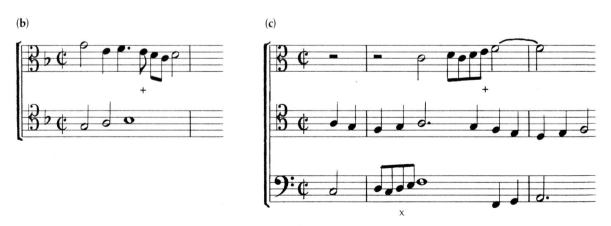

Note: x indicates an accented passing tone; + indicates an unaccented passing tone.

What is a neighboring tone?

Another very common form of dissonance, the **neighboring tone**, is approached stepwise and left stepwise in the opposite direction. In Renaissance music, the neighboring tone occurs only in quarter-note and eighth-note values. When approached from above, the dissonance is called a **lower neighbor**; when approached from below, the dissonance is called an **upper neighbor** (Figure 35-7). The lower neighbor is used more often.   **W126**

35-7

Note: x indicates a lower neighboring tone; + indicates an upper neighboring tone.

What is a suspension?

The **suspension** is a common dissonance, however it is not used as often as passing tones and neighboring tones. Its importance is due to its dramatic qualities more than to the frequency of its use. In Renaissance music the suspension is used in half-note values only. In $\frac{4}{2}$ or ¢ the suspension dissonance is prepared on beat two or four as a consonance, suspended on beat three or one as a dissonance, and resolved downward on beat four or two as a consonance. In $\frac{3}{2}$, the suspension dissonance is prepared on beat one, suspended on beat two, and resolved on beat three. The three types of suspensions are identified by the ordinal number of the dissonant interval and the ordinal number of the interval of resolution. Two of the suspensions occur when an upper voice creates a dissonance with the lower (lowest) sounding voice; they are identified as the 4–3 suspension and the 7–6 suspension. The third kind of suspension occurs when a lower (lowest) sounding voice creates a dissonance against an upper voice; it is identified as a 2–3 suspension. The essential elements of each form of suspension are shown in Figure 35-8.

35-8

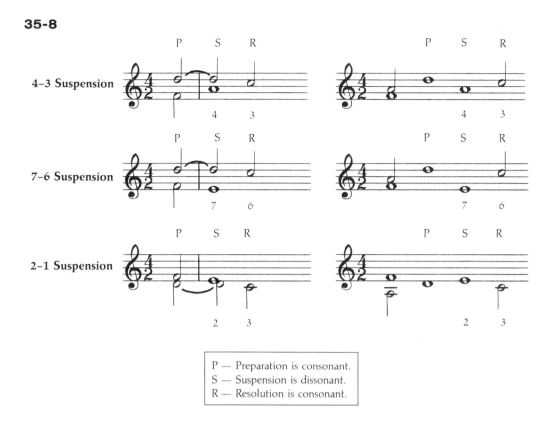

P — Preparation is consonant.
S — Suspension is dissonant.
R — Resolution is consonant.

The resolution of a suspension is ornamented in a number of ways in Renaissance music; see Figure 35-9. Observe that the resolution of the suspension does not occur any sooner because of the ornamentation.

35-9

Ornamental Resolutions

P — Preparation is consonant.
S — Suspension is dissonant.
R — Resolution is consonant.

A suspension configuration can also be varied by moving the notated pitch against which the suspension takes place to another notated pitch that is consonant with the resolution at the time of resolution; see Figure 35-10.

35-10

Note: x indicates a change of pitch that is consonant with the note of resolution.

Suspensions may occur in a series—called a *chain*—of suspensions, with three being the usual number. In such a chain, the resolution of the first suspension becomes the preparation of the second, and the resolution of the second suspension becomes the preparation of the third. The essential elements of a chain of suspensions utilizing one of each kind plus ornamentation are seen in Figure 35-11. Figure 35-12 shows a chain of suspensions in a three-voice musical texture.   **W127—128**

35-11

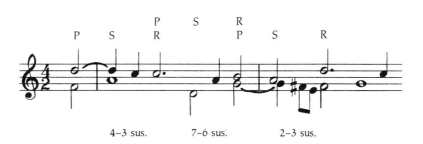

35-12

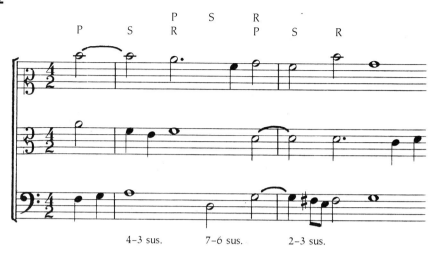

What is a portamento?

The **portamento (anticipation)** is a dissonance that occurs on the second half of a beat and is approached from above. It serves to anticipate the next notated pitch. The essential elements of the portamento are shown in Figure 35-13a. The use of portamento in a typical Renaissance texture is shown in Figure 35-13b.   **W129**

35-13

Note: x indicates the portamento.

What is a nota cambiata?

The **nota cambiata (escape tone)** is a dissonance that is approached by a consonance from above and left by a leap down a third to a consonance. The dissonance in a nota cambiata occurs on the second half of a beat. The essential elements of the nota cambiata are shown in Figure 35-14a. The nota cambiata in a three-voice texture is shown in Figure 35-14b.   **W130**

35-14

Note: C indicates consonance; D indicates dissonance.

What is a consonant fourth?

The **consonant fourth** is a dissonant preparation of a suspension within a texture of three or more voices. The rationale for the consonant fourth is that a third voice moves to the fifth above the lowest voice and creates the interval of a second or seventh with the suspended voice. Thus, at the point of the suspension there is a greater total dissonance. See Figure 35-15.   **W131**

35-15

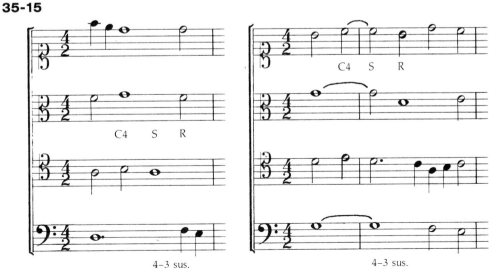

Note: C4 indicates the consonant fourth. S indicates the suspension. R indicates the resolution.

What is a $\frac{6}{5}$?

The $\frac{6}{5}$ is a consonance in a technical sense. It is treated in a special manner that requires the fifth to be prepared on the previous beat. Figure 35-16 shows the essential elements of the $\frac{6}{5}$ and its use in a four-voice texture.

35-16

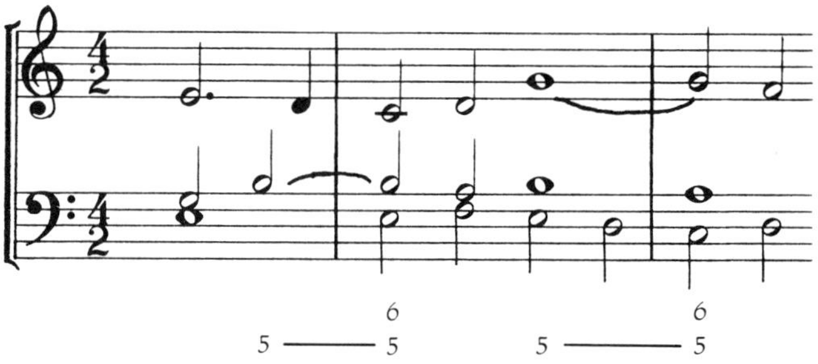

Note: 5——$\overset{6}{5}$ indicates the prepared 5th and the subsequent $\overset{6}{5}$. C D C indicates the dissonance and consonance of the nota cambiata.

What is a $\frac{6}{5}$—consonant fourth combination?

The $\frac{6}{5}$ **and consonant fourth combination** occurs most commonly in a final cadence. Figure 35-17 shows its essential elements and how it is used in a four-voice texture.

W132—137

35-17

36

Renaissance Liturgical Music: Text Setting and Rhythmic Subjugation of Meter

What conventions controlled the setting of a text during the Renaissance?

Renaissance conventions for assigning notated pitches to the syllables of a text were similar to those of Gregorian chant. A **syllabic setting**, in which one articulated pitch is assigned to each syllable (Figure 36-1), was one convention. It was used often with lengthy texts, occasionally in settings of portions of the Mass in a homophonic texture, and when an unadorned, short setting was desired. A **neumatic setting** was used with less lengthy texts and

36-1

from *Missa Vestiva i Colli,* Gloria

Palestrina

Cantus

qui tol - lis pec - ca - ta mun - di, Su - sci - pe

when a more elaborate musical setting was desired. In Gregorian chant **neumes** (special symbols) were used to notate groups of two, three, and four pitches; see Figure 36-2a. In modern conventional notation, such groupings of pitches are gathered together in ligatures; see Figure 36-2b. A neumatic setting of a text assigns several (usually two to five) pitches to each

36-2

(a)

(b)

syllable (Figure 36-3). A **melismatic setting** was often used for very short texts and when an elaborate musical setting was desired. In Gregorian chant, a **melisma** made up of two or

36-3

Benedictus

Lassus

Tenor

Be - - - ne - dic - tus _____ , qui

more neumes (perhaps six or more notes) was assigned to individual syllables. In a melismatic setting of a Renaissance Mass, six, seven, or more notes are assigned to individual syllables (Figure 36-4).

36-4

from motet *Alleluia Tulerunt*

Palestrina

(Al - le-) lu - - ja _____ ,

During the Renaissance it was also common—at least in the music of Palestrina and Lassus—*not* to change a syllable in a neumatic or melismatic passage containing quarter or eighth notes until *after* a white note (half-note or longer duration) sounded; see Figure 36-5. A

36-5

Exaltabo te (offertory)

Palestrina

ex - al - ta - bo te ____ , Do - - - mi - ne,

common exception to this convention was the setting of such words as *Ky-ri-e*, *Do-mi-ne*, *cym-bal-is*, and *Chri-ste* (and such word combinations as *et in*) using a dotted half note and a quarter note followed by a white note of some value (Figure 36-6). Generally, quarter and eighth notes

36-6

from *Missa Vestiva i Colli,* Kyrie and Gloria

Palestrina

were used as part of a neumatic or melismatic passage. A change of syllable could, however, begin on a pair or series of quarter notes (Figure 36-7). The one and only example of four

36-7

from motet *Laudate Dominum in tympanis*

Palestrina

consecutive eighth notes found in the music of Palestrina is from the Benedictus of his Mass *Ut re mi fa sol la*. The four eighth notes begin on a strong portion of the measure and are assigned to the first syllable of a word; see Figure 36-8.

36-8

Missa Ut re mi fa sol la, Benedictus

Palestrina

What were the conventions concerning rhythmic texture?

Renaissance composers produced some music that is obviously chordal in nature and metrical in its rhythmic makeup; see Figure 36-9, for example. The prevailing convention concerning the rhythmic texture of Renaissance music, however, emphasized linear and rhythmic independence. Most Renaissance music has a rhythmic texture that is dominated by such considerations as accents of duration, accents associated with pitch levels, and **agogic accents**

36-9

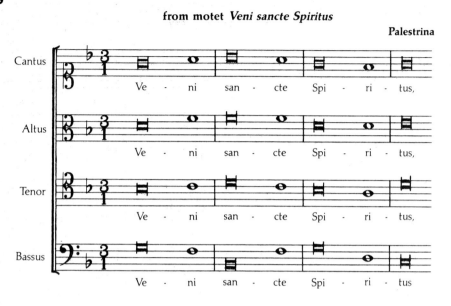

from motet *Veni sancte Spiritus*

Palestrina

(syncopation without dynamic stress). All of these serve to de-emphasize the aural impression of meter. This results in a kind of music that flows unobtrusively under the formalizing control of meter but with a minimum of metrical assertiveness (Figure 36-10). Paradoxically, the second great strength of Renaissance music is also the result of subjugating a basic formalizing and controlling mechanism, in this case meter.*

36-10

Missa Pange lingua, Agnus Dei

Josquin des Prez

continued

*The first great strength is the subjugation of *referentialism* by the weakness of *modality*.

36-10, *continued*

Figure 36-10 also illustrates the common use of **canonic imitation** in Renaissance liturgical music. Though rigorous, it provides one of the most independent kinds of rhythmic texture. The word *canon* (Latin, "rule, model, standard") denotes that this was a demanding convention of early polyphonic music. Musicworks called "canons" vary in the amount of canonic writing that is used and in the pitch intervals (any diatonic interval) and the temporal intervals (the number of measures or portion of a measure) at which voices enter the imitation. For example, in Figure 36-10, the second voice enters at the pitch interval of a P5 below and the temporal interval of two full measures. In less vigorous kinds of polyphonic music, voices generally enter one after another and imitation is not carried beyond the first few notes (Figure 36-11).

The rhythmic design of melodic lines in Renaissance liturgical music is subject to the same idiomatic conventions as all vocal music—for example, consideration for voice ranges, tessituras, and types; use of a conventional notation system; and recognition of the need for singers to breathe. However, some interesting meta-idiomatic conventions are peculiar to the

36-11

from *Missa Peccata mea*

Jachet of Mantua, ed. by Philip T. Jackson

works on which our knowledge is based. For example, a melodic line will begin on at least a half note if it is an *internal* phrase, whereas it will begin on at least a dotted half note if it is the *beginning* phrase of a musicwork. An internal melodic phrase will end on at least a half note, and a final phrase will end on at least a whole note. It is common for a melodic phrase to gather rhythmic momentum internally by the introduction of shorter note values (quarter notes and occasionally eighth notes) and then slow down toward the end of the phrase. The general rhythmic texture tends to de-emphasize meter.

How should we regard these Renaissance conventions?

If we accept the word *convention* to mean that which most people—composers in this case—do at a given time in history, it is implied that some people (composers) do not follow the conventions. It is also implied that a composer who generally practices a particular convention is not a slave to it and may subscribe to certain exceptions that could themselves be considered conventions if they were known. Along with this, we must acknowledge that some of these exceptions constitute the idiosyncratic conventions of individual composers.

Compared to what is generally known of eighteenth- and nineteenth-century music, our knowledge of Renaissance music is relatively skimpy. Our knowledge is confined to a few well-known liturgical and secular composers. We must be careful not to make assumptions about the entire period on the basis of the work of these few composers. Though there has been a great deal of research in Renaissance music, few of the findings are reported in textbooks on music theory or general music history.

Composers of the Renaissance were not particularly concerned with preserving their works for posterity, and the concept of protecting musicworks by copyright did not exist. We have no idea of how much music was composed, performed, and then lost or discarded.

We must realize also that, even though Renaissance music may appear tightly bound by conventions, a great deal of theoretical research and experimentation with **microtones** (intervalic relationships smaller than the half step) was going on at the time. Then too, how many composers were there such as Carlo Gesualdo? Was he the lone "bad boy" of music of his time, or were there others whose inventiveness separated them from the prevailing majority? Considering the various conventions that have prevailed over the years, some of Gesualdo's music contains practices that were not conventional until early in the twentieth century. The excerpt from *Moro lasso* in Figure 36-12 provides evidence of his "foresight."

36-12

from motet *Moro, lasso, al mio duolo*

Gesualdo

In dealing with the known or supposed conventions of any historical period, we should not seek to "purify" them by expunging everything considered to be an exception or deviation. Exceptions and deviations which contradict established conventions abound in any historical period as well as in the works of any composer. The exceptions and deviations should be regarded as the natural product of a composer's fancy, not as stylistic clutter.

MINI PROJECT 14

Introduction

Because the application of Renaissance music to introductory theory studies is limited, chapters 34 and 35 provide only a brief overview. They serve primarily as background for our study of tonic-dominant tonality. Mini project 14 provides for a brief creative experience that should relate to Renaissance liturgical style without mimicking it. Students for whom Renaissance style is academically and professionally important will very likely take a course in sixteenth-century counterpoint later in their studies.

Description

Select a relatively brief text from the Latin Mass or a Latin text from a short Renaissance motet. Following the general tenets of the Renaissance view of consonance and dissonance, the setting of texts, and the relationship of rhythm to meter, set the text to music for two or three voices. Notate the musicwork in score form, using either ¢ or $\frac{4}{2}$ as the meter signature (measure signature) and the appropriate C clefs for the soprano, alto, and tenor voices and the F clef for the bass voice. Rehearse and sing the musicwork in a recital or in class.

37 Tonic-Dominant Tonality: Key and Harmonic Structure

Early in the twentieth century, music theorist Heinrick Schenker discovered the basic principle of harmonic practice that defines the nature of harmonic structure in tonic-dominant tonality and the relationship of "harmonic grammar" to "harmonic structure." Before Schenker's discovery, theorists had considered only what we are considering here as harmonic grammar. The notion that a structural principle underlies all music utilizing tonality—if it had ever been known or felt—was not expressed in a well-developed theory until Schenker's work was published. Though his theories have been known for half a century or more and gained the respect of theorists through Felix Salzer's book *Structural Hearing*, they have yet to be presented in a form suitable for beginning students. In this book, the general principle of Schenker's theory serves as a stepping stone for dealing with tonic-dominant tonality in a creative learning situation.

What is the meaning of *key*?

When the concept of modality gave way to tonality, the terminology of modal music also gave way to a new terminology. The seven modal scales ceased being used, and the major and minor scales came into use. Whether we think of the major and minor scales as transformations of the modal scales or as replacements for them is a moot point. However, to establish some historical connection, we have observed that the modal scales can be grouped; see Figure 37-1.

The term *mode* has different meanings in relation to tonality than it has in relation to modality. In discussions of tonality, *mode* denotes "mood" in the sense of character or temperament, "form" in the sense of the makeup of the available resources, and "manner" in the sense of how the harmonic resources are used. We recognize, for example, that the quality of a musicwork cast in a minor mode is different from that of one in the major mode and that the coloristic resources of the minor mode are greater than those of the major mode.

37-1
MAJOR "MODE"

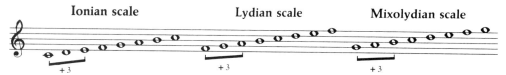

MINOR "MODE"

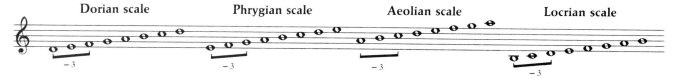

In tonality, the **tonic** is the basic reference pitch; it is the "key" tone. The term **key** as in "the *key* of D major," for example, denotes a principle of organization in which the tonic-dominant relationship is the means used to set up the tonic pitch as the referential pitch of a musicwork. It is essential that we realize that a movement of a musicwork, regardless of its complexity, is in one key, *not* in several keys. To think otherwise is to have a limited view of a rather grand and complicated meta-idiomatic convention.

What historical condition has contributed to the confusion about the nature of key?

Looking at the portion of Lassus's Benedictus in Figure 37-2, we find that the melodic line of the cantus (the upper voice part) begins on and establishes G as the reference pitch. G continues to be the reference pitch until the cantus cadences on D in the seventh measure. In the cadence, the D is emphasized by being preceded by a C sharp. Though this cadence is nothing more than a strengthened move to the dominant pitch, it represents a common practice that has been a source of confusion in the teaching of tonality for many years.

37-2

As illustrated by Figure 34-3, it was common during the Renaissance to precede a cadence point by a whole step from above or a half step from below. In so doing, a sharp was introduced in cases such as the one in Figure 37-2. Though it is not known when the term *modulation* came on the scene to confuse the concept of key, the following quotations from Gustave Soderlund's *Direct Approach to Counterpoint** indicate that the confusion has been with us for some time. On page four of Soderlund's book we find the following statement: "While modulation usually meant cadence, actual modulation was recognized." He is writing about Gregorian chant. The phrase "actual modulation" (as in change of mode) is an astounding assertion about something foreign to the thinking of a medieval composer. There may have been some confusion in medieval times about the centrality of the sun in the solar system, but it is extremely doubtful that there was any confusion about the centrality of the final in the modal system. Later in the same paragraph he writes: ". . . some chants will show that change of mode, or key, attained a great degree of subtlety." The assertion that Gregorian chant contained changes of mode or change of "key" is beyond comprehension. Then on page six, in referring to sixteenth-century polyphony he writes: "The terms *modulation* and *cadence* were synonymous in plainsong as well as in polyphony." In all of these statements, this last is the one breath of truth concerning cadence and modulation.

In modality, as well as in tonality, it is essential to provide a point of departure, a cadence ending on some pitch other than the final (or tonic) in order to establish a tonal shape of any sort. To consider this point of departure a change of mode or a change of key is contrary to the most basic principle of design. It is necessary (as in geometry) to have at least three points not on the same plane—that is, either final/alternate cadence/final or tonic/dominant/tonic—to establish a harmonic shape. The point being made here is not a denial of the existence of modulation as a process but the assertion that a modulation is *not* a change of mode or a change of key. Perhaps it is reasonable to assume that, writing during the 1940s when change of key was the prevailing explanation for the process of modulation, Soderlund would think in terms of change of mode. His use of *key* in a medieval context is an unfortunate reverse extrapolation.

For most of the twentieth century, Bach chorales have served as models for teaching the harmonic practices of the eighteenth century. Bach's chorale melodies are actually rhythmically simplified versions of Renaissance hymn tunes; their phrase structures are foreign to eighteenth-century melodic conventions. Bach harmonized the melodies in a rich, colorful manner with elements of eighteenth-century practice that are foreign to Renaissance melody. Though the chorales are undeniably beautiful and suited to their intended purpose, they give a distorted view of eighteenth-century harmonic practice.

How are harmonic relationships represented symbolically?

Each degree of the diatonic scale (major or minor) of a given key and any chord constructed on the scale degree is identified by a Roman numeral (Figure 37-3). The names given the scale degrees, while appearing arbitrary, describe their relationship to the tonic pitch.

37-3

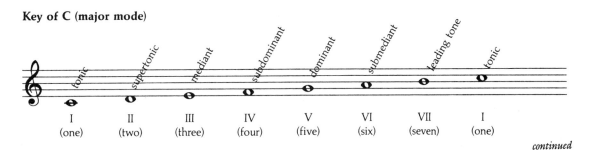

Key of C (major mode)

I	II	III	IV	V	VI	VII	I
(one)	(two)	(three)	(four)	(five)	(six)	(seven)	(one)

continued

*Soderlund, Gustave Fredric, *Direct Approach to Counterpoint in Sixteenth-Century Style* (New York: F. S. Crofts, 1947).

37-3, *continued*

Key of C (minor mode)

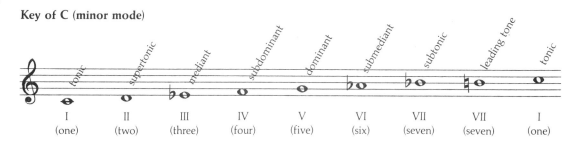

The **dominant** is a fifth above the tonic. Refer to Figure 37-4. The dominant is so named because in both modality and tonality the pitch (a fifth above the final in modality and the tonic in tonality) is next in prominence to the tonic; it is the dominant pitch in comparison to all the other pitches. The term **subdominant** simply means the fifth below the tonic or the "under dominant." The **mediant** is so named because it is midway between the tonic and the dominant. The **submediant** is midway between the subdominant and tonic. The **supertonic** is the notated pitch above the tonic. The **leading tone** is so named because of its affinity to the tonic. The seventh tone of the *minor* scale is a +2 (M2) below the tonic and as such is called the **subtonic**. When the seventh degree of the scale in the minor mode is raised to a half step below the tonic, it is called the *leading tone*.

37-4

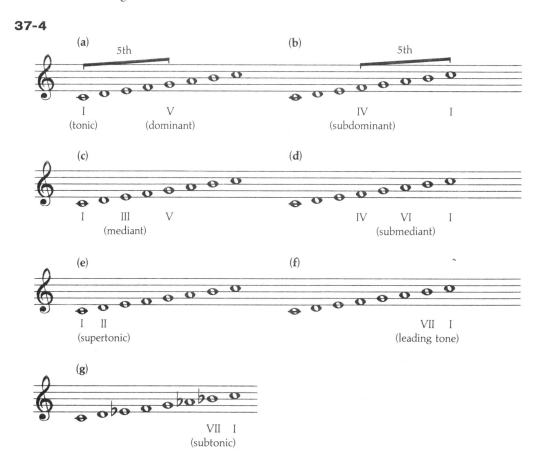

What is the nature of harmonic structure?

In considering what we might call the "anatomy" of a musicwork, the **harmonic structure** would be the "skeleton." Or if we related the structure of a musicwork to that of a building, we might think of structure as the framework. Structure is the aspect of a thing that gives it a shape and provides the frame upon which to attach the material of what we perceive the thing to be. In a musicwork, harmonic structure is provided by a framework of pitches that is the product of ordering. To be a meta-idiomatic convention, any particular scheme of ordering must have attained a certain degree of currency.

In his theoretical treatise *Der freie Satz* ("Free Composition"), Heinrich Schenker describes the three levels of harmonic shaping:

1. *background*—the fundamental harmonic structure of a movement expressed as I V I

2. *middle ground*—the harmonic structure described in terms of its various forms of prolongations

3. *foreground*—the smaller descriptive elements that provide the surface harmonic functions

This three-tiered classification of structural shaping is generally serviceable. However, there is a level of structure that might be thought of as *cellular* in that it demonstrates harmonic intelligibility in the smallest of melodic configurations. As a basic premise of tonic-dominant tonality, it must be assumed that intelligibility in any pitch configuration perceived as an entity, however small, owes its intelligibility to an implied I V I structure. Therefore the opening four-note melodic configuration in Brahms's Second Symphony (Figure 37-5a) is intelligible as a **motivic entity** (a complete, distinguishable gesture) due to its implied I V I structure. A similar but more elaborate melodic configuration opening the Opus 16 No. 1 Quartet of Beethoven, (Figure 37-5b) is intelligible as a motivic entity for the same reason.

37-5

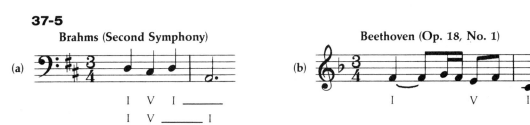

The point being made about the intelligibility of a pitch configuration perceived as an entity is that our expectations regarding a reference pitch are due to the ordering within a structural frame. Our expectations are not based on an implied need for the I V I structure to be fleshed-out in chords but rather on a cumulative ordering of pitches that has a built-in, predictably perceived harmonic shape of I V I. It is important at this juncture to point out that this concept of harmonic shape or structure differs from that of Salzer in *Structural Hearing*. Salzer purports that all harmonic shaping is in terms of triads, rather than individual pitches.

The problem with thinking of a harmonic shape as a chordal relationship is that chords add nothing to assist our understanding. The harmonic structure of a single melodic line is easier to perceive than the same structure presented within a chordal texture. Chords can strengthen a structure, but they can also provide coloristic ambiguity that weakens our perception of a structure. Both of these consequences of chordal use are natural, legitimate musical functions. However, interpretations of the chordal information sometimes lead to a considerable amount of confusion. The confusion is generally not in the musical impression received but in the words people use to describe the chordal information.

How may analyses of harmonizations lead to distorted understandings of harmonic structure?

Harmonization—itself not a compositional process—is the practice of imposing a chordal sequence on a melody to produce a more colorful, expressive result. The practice of chorale harmonization was common during the eighteenth century. Bach, for example, sometimes provided a half-dozen or more harmonizations of the same chorale melody. We might regard such a profusion of harmonizations as Bach's defense against the monotony of repeatedly playing the same chorales in the many church services for which he played. The erroneous belief that harmonic structure is established by chordal relationships rather than the pitch frame established by the ordering of pitch can lead to serious misunderstandings about harmonic structure.

As an analogy, let us consider what occurs in remodeling and redecorating a building. We know that a building's structural elements give it a basic shape and hold it together. We know also that there are many other elements of a building that perform *no* structural functions. Removing a structural element from a building can result in disaster. However, we can remove some walls and add others, move doors and windows, change the facade, remove or add decorative elements, change the heating and lighting systems, and make other changes that totally change the building's *appearance* without changing its basic *structure*. In like manner, we can change the appearance of a melodic configuration without changing its harmonic structure. And both harmonizing a chorale melody and remodeling a building can create incongruities between structure and appearance.

A recently published programmed-learning text* provides a few examples of incongruity between harmonization and harmonic structure. Unfortunately, the harmonizations in the examples portray some seriously flawed concepts of key and modulation. Let us examine three of the examples. See Figure 37-6. The chorale-melody fragment in (a) is clearly and entirely in B-flat major. The melody in (b) is clearly and entirely in G major. The melody in (c) is simply a prolongation of the tonic in A-flat major. B-flat major, G major, and A-flat major are the pitch frames within which the structures of the three fragments are to be found and understood.

37-6

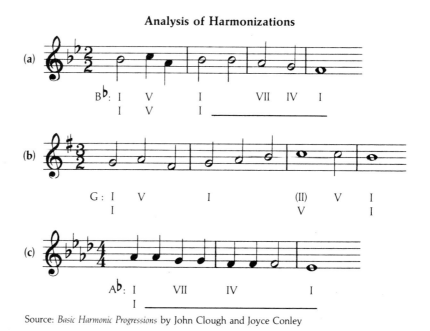

Source: *Basic Harmonic Progressions* by John Clough and Joyce Conley

---

*John Clough and Joyce Conley, *Basic Harmonic Progressions*. New York (W. W. Norton & Company, Inc., 1984), p. 303.

The harmonizations of these examples provided by Clough and Conley demonstrate incongruous relationships with the harmonic structures of the respective melodic configurations. As was said before, this kind of incongruity is musically legitimate. The problem here is not with the harmonizations, which we may consider good, bad, or indifferent; the problem is with how the authors describe the harmonizations: they characterize them in terms unrelated to the basic harmonic structures. The descriptors for the colorations of such harmonizations must be produced from within the context of the harmonic structure.

The harmonizations in Figure 37-7a and b are reasonable deviations from the basic harmonic structures of the given melodic shapes. Based on what is given in Figure 37-7c, the harmonization is a total distortion of a simple harmonic structure. Unlike the harmonizations in

37-7

Analysis of Harmonizations

(a) and (b), the harmonization in (c) is also musically ambiguous. In each example, below the analysis given by Clough and Conley, another analysis appears, one that is entirely within the framework of the harmonic structure of the given key. Harmonizations that are consonant with the basic harmonic structures of these melodic fragments appear in Figure 37-8.

37-8

Analysis of Harmonizations

How is harmonic structure related to phrase structure in music?

Phrase structure in music is similar to phrase structure in rhetoric (spoken and written language). That is,

1. both music and rhetoric are subject to the physiological limitations of breathing;

2. both music and rhetoric are subject to a hierarchical system in which the *parts* are understood in relation to the *whole*, in terms of both the mechanics of grammar and the levels of perceivable meaning;

3. both music and rhetoric are capable of insinuating and juxtaposing any abstract, expressive affectation desired by the creative and performing artists.

Phrase structure in both music and rhetoric has always been subject to the formalizing conventions of the language being used.

The formalizing structures of rhetorical languages have necessarily accommodated the physiological constraints associated with breathing. And, because rhetorical languages have been the *raison d'être* for *singing* over the entire history of music, the formalizing structures of music have necessarily developed with respect for both the physiological need to breathe and the formalizing structures of rhetoric. By the time instrumental music became a separate medium of performance, the basic structure of musical thought was firmly established. The equally important impact of the physiological constraints of dance did not change the fundamental structure of music; dance simply enhanced it by means of internal rhythmic variety and tempo. Though we presently have the technical capacity to produce all manner of sound structures under the name of music, the essential principles of what constitutes a musical structure remain unchanged.

In tonic-dominant tonality, the conventional understanding is that phrase structure is directly related to harmonic structure. Harmonic structure and phrase structure are related in that phrase structures are encapsulated units of harmonic sense. **Harmonic sense** is the product of the aggregate effect of the melodic design and the ordering of all other supportive pitch content. Because it is an abstract concept, we are better able to deal with harmonic sense intuitively than with objective definitions. It is impossible to explain phrase structure in music adequately in terms of definition and function. In our working vocabulary we use such terms as *motive (motif)*, *phrase*, *sentence*, *period*, and *statement*. *Motive* connotes "a significant generating idea" in all of the arts, but the others are essentially rhetorical terms. And, as musical terms, *sentence*, *period*, and *statement* are ambiguous and often used interchangeably. The definition and function of phrase structure is best understood in relation to the concept of cadence.

W138—143

What is cadence?

The two definitions of **cadence** in music both relate to our understanding of the function of phrase structure: (1) the sense of *pace* we feel as the result of the tempo and rhythmic flow of music, and (2) the sense of *relative conclusion* we feel as a result of the harmonic shaping of phrases. Although the first definition is generally used exclusively with respect to the overall pace of a musicwork, it is essential to our perception of harmonic shape. The second definition has been corrupted over the years by being reduced to simplistic chordal formulas. Such formulas are as meaningless to music as attributing the relative sense of conclusion in rhetoric to punctuation marks. Although the role of these ending chordal formulas should be considered within the total concept of cadence, the formulas themselves are *not* the cadence.

The harmonic sense of a phrase structure can only be *felt* in combination with the consequential effect of rhythmic flow. The sense of relative conclusion (or lack of it) we perceive in a phrase—either rhetorical or musical—is a product of cadence: the rhythmic flow (the *when*) of the constituent elements (the *what*). Cadence in music is not a *thing*; rather, it is the quality of a phrase structure that results when the harmonic syntax and rhythmic syntax of a phrase are brought together to realize a unified sense of purpose.

What is the cadential role of the concluding chordal formula of a phrase structure?

Cadence in music is characterized in part by the degree to which the listener's expectation of finality or continuation is aroused by the particularity and rhythmic ordering of its pitch content. The cadential "feel" of a phrase structure is unique in the way its pitch materials are related and ordered in time and in the way the phrase structure relates to the cadential "feel" of the preceeding and following phrase structures. We might regard each phrase structure as being part of an organic whole and liken the cadential feel of the structure to that which "quickens" an organism. With this comparison in mind, we might liken the concluding chordal formulas of phrase structures to the function of connecting or closing tissue of organisms. The concluding chordal formula of a cadence provides: (1) a final close for a terminal cadence, and (2) an internal closing or connecting function for implied continuation cadences.

What is a terminal cadence?

A **terminal cadence** is the resultant effect of a phrase structure that provides a sense of tonal and rhythmic finality. From a mechanical point of view, it provides the final resolution of the musicwork's tonal and rhythmic goals. Musically, it provides a final sense of aesthetic gratification, the final fulfillment of the dramatic flow of the music. Figure 37-9a shows the chordal formula of a terminal cadence. The root of the tonic triad provides both the highest and lowest sounding pitches of the final chord, and the penultimate chord is the dominant chord in root position. This closing chordal formula provides the strongest, most conclusive acoustical arrangement of the pitch materials. Figure 37-9b shows a less strong closing chordal formula. The formula is the same as in (a) except that the tonic pitch is not the highest sounding pitch.

37-9

(a) Quartet, Op. 18, No. 1, Mov. IV

(b) Quartet, Op. 18, No. 5, Mov. IV

Without the tonic as the highest sounding pitch, the concluding effect of the tonic is not as emphatic. The final tonic triad in Figure 37-10 is borrowed from the major mode. Because of the borrowed chord in such terminal cadences, more emphasis is placed on the quality of the chord than on the tonic itself. In some respects, the terminal expectations of such a cadence are enhanced by the closing major triad.

37-10

The Musical Offering, Ricercare

Bach

Another closing chordal formula uses the subdominant rather than the dominant triad as the penultimate chord. However, the melodic material of the top line provides a leading tone that leads forcefully to the tonic, suggesting the feeling of a dominant (Figure 37-11). This formula is commonly used for the concluding *Amen* of hymns and other religious and liturgical musicworks and for music that retains many of the harmonic characteristics of modality.

37-11

Symphony No. 1, Mov. IV

Brahms

C: IV   I

What is an implied continuation cadence?

An **implied continuation cadence** is the resultant effect of a phrase structure that concludes with the expectation of more music to follow. Except for those instances in which the final cadence of one movement of a musicwork serves as the connecting link to the opening of the next movement, implied continuation cadences are internal cadences. Internal cadences generally conclude on the tonic or dominant. However, depending on the duration and complexity of a musicwork, interior cadences may conclude on any scale degree. Two examples of interior cadences that conclude on the tonic from Beethoven's Quartet for Strings, Opus 18

No. 1, are shown in Figure 37-12. In (a) the concluding tonic is separated from the following phrase. In (b) the concluding tonic is also the beginning of the next phrase.

37-12

(a)

Quartet, Op. 18, No. 1, Mov. I

Beethoven

(b)

We might observe that the chordal formula of the implied continuation cadence in Figure 37-13a does not differ from that of the terminal cadence in (b) of the same figure. Also, we might observe that the implied continuation cadence is no less complete than the terminal cadence. This situation is comparable to the relationship of an internal sentence to the final sentence of a paragraph. The sentences may be grammatically complete in every respect, but the meaning of the paragraph will be far from complete in the internal sentence. In like manner, the terminal and implied continuation cadences are entirely different; because of their configurations, the expectations they arouse are different. The expectations generated by the internal cadence require continuation and those generated by the terminal cadence do not.

W144—145.

37-13

String Quartet in G major, Op. 18, No. 2

(a)   Beethoven

37-13, *continued*

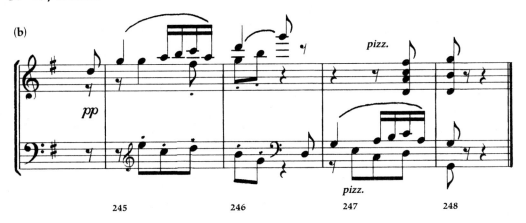

245   246   247   248

MINI PROJECT 15

Introduction

As explained in chapter 34, a referential pitch is a product of the expectations generated by pitch ordering. The pitch orderings themselves are a product of the particular meta-idiomatic convention being used. At this point in our study, the meta-idiomatic convention in use is tonic-dominant tonality. We should not regard the referential pitch generated by the harmonic shape I V I as an aesthetic goal, nor should we regard it as something we should consider and think about while we listen to music. A referential pitch regardless of how it is established, simply provides a point of focus that facilitates the listener's tonal orientation.

In order to exercise the harmonic principle that is fundamental to tonic-dominant tonality and to do it intuitively, we will deal with it first as it manifests itself through melody. There are two advantages to this approach: (1) the harmonic principle is best understood when it is not "colored" by the ambiguities of chordal structures, and (2) harmonic movement in melody is achieved through the establishment and ordered arrival at a tonal goal. For example, if we were to begin a phrase structure on the pitch class D and then provide a melodic ordering of pitches that terminates several measures later on the pitch class E (as in Figure 37-14a), we would have established a movement from tonic to dominant in the key of D major. Movement from the dominant back to the tonic is shown in Figure 37-14b. The harmonic structure of the

37-14

eight measures in Figure 37-14 is I V I. Using the same basic melodic material, the harmonic structure can be expanded to I II V I, as in Figure 37-15. Another example, using melodic

37-15

materials that are less triadic, is shown in Figure 37-16. In each of the melodies shown in Figures 37-14 through 37-16, the primary concern is the ordering of pitches to form intelligible melodies. The resulting tonal goals expressed as I V I, I II V I, and I V I provide the structural frames that serve to orient the listener. If these three melodies were cast in full musical textures, chordal and contrapuntal colorations would not alter their basic harmonic structures.

37-16

Description

Create a very short melodic shape (similar to those in the first full measures of Figure 37-14 and 37-16) and use it to design five melodic phrases with these harmonic structures:

1. I V I; four to six measures

2. I V I; six to ten measures

3. I II V I; ten to sixteen measures

4. I III V I; ten to sixteen measures; in a minor mode

5. I VI V I; ten to sixteen measures; in a minor mode

38 | The Concept of Chord, Prolongation, and the Illusion of Motion

When is a collection of pitches a chord?

For decades, musicians have had an extraordinary interest in chords. This continuing interest is perhaps due to the fact that relatively few elements in music can be named or labeled. Triads and seventh chords, unfortunately, have become the primary elements in which musicians look for order and stability in music. Some of the more simplistic analytical procedures in use make the finding of chords and all semblances of chords (regardless of how complete or obscure they may appear) the primary objective of analysis. This procedure seems to ignore an individual chord's function, relevance, and even the reality of its existence. However solid or obscure the "find," each is acknowledged as a chord "equal" to other chords. This lack of distinction between the concept of chord as a collection of pitches that forms a compositional entity and the concept of chord as an element of pitch organization leads to confusion. The essential problem here is not that of knowing what a chord *is* but, rather, when a chord exists.

What is harmonic prolongation?

Prolongation, as a general concept, is associated with all aspects and activities of life. With whatever we associate prolongation, the intent is to make something last for a given or indefinite period of time. **Harmonic prolongation** serves to sustain the presence of an element of the harmonic structure of a musicwork. The prolonged element may itself be part of the prolongation of yet another element.

What are structural chords and chords of prolongation?*

Chords that function as elements of harmonic organization need to be distinguished from those that are intended as sonorous, compositional entities. The concept of chord as an element of harmonic organization may be related coincidentally to the concept of chord as a compositional entity. As an element of harmonic organization, a chord should be regarded, first and foremost, as a theoretical extension or amplification of a harmonic element. For example, in the opening measures of the second movement of Beethoven's Symphony No. 1 in C major, we find a prolongation of the tonic. In the first six measures there is but one voice; in the next three measures there are but two voices (Figure 38-1). Physically, there are no chords; theoretically, however, this is a prolongation of the tonic (F), the key tone of the movement. Though it is most appropriate that we regard the tonic in this and similar situations as a point of focus represented by a particular pitch, the practice of regarding such focal points as chords even when a chord is not physically present is a common, and sometimes confusing, theoretical convention.

38-1

Symphony No. 1, Mov. II

Beethoven

Within the concept of chord as an element of harmonic organization in musicworks that utilize tonic-dominant tonality, two types of chordal structures are recognized:

1. **structural chords**, chords that serve as real or theoretical projections of harmonically important structural tones

2. **chords of prolongation**, chords that are the biproduct of melodic motion

Chords of prolongation can also be real or theoretical projections of tones; however, these real or theoretically projected tones would be intervening tones in whatever element of harmonic structure is being prolonged. Chords of prolongation are far more interesting than structural chords. Structural chords are triadic (major or minor) projections of structural tones; it is not their function to be interesting as such. Structural chords serve to provide harmonic shape and pitch orientation. Chords of prolongation may be of any type; and because of this, they supply the color, the tension, and the illusion of motion in music. A composer's manner of prolonging harmonic structures is one of the primary contributors to a stylistic identity. The movement of the tones that make up the chords of prolongation is identified within a system of nonharmonic and nonchord tones described by a nomenclature we used for identifying Renaissance dissonance plus a few terms that will be new to you.

How do nonharmonic tones differ from nonchord tones?

Among most musicians the terms *nonharmonic* and *nonchord* are used synonymously in describing dissonance in tonic-dominant tonality. There is nothing in theoretical writings or in texts to suggest that we should differentiate between the two terms. The phenomenon for which

*These terms were originated by Heinrich Schenker. Felic Salzer used them in his book *Structural Hearing*.

this terminology is used is treated in a simpler and more effective manner in Schenkerian analysis as "neighboring and passing chords." However, if we are to use *nonharmonic* and *nonchord* as descriptors of dissonant tones, the terms must be considered different functionally, because the terms *harmonic* and *chord* are conceptually different and describe differing levels of function in the hierarchy of tonic-dominant tonality. *Harmonic* is the adjective form of *harmony*. Harmony is organization; it is concerned with structural relationships and tonal expectations. Chords, as part of harmonic organization, may be regarded as real or theoretical projections that serve to prolong a harmonic element. Consequently, nonchord tones may very well be **harmonic tones**—that is, tones that form the triadic projection of a structural element. Likewise, harmonic tones can be considered nonchord tones when they sound against a chord of prolongation (Figure 38-2). Though nonharmonic and nonchord tones may at times appear identical in terms of their preparation and resolution, nonharmonic tones are not subject to the

38-2

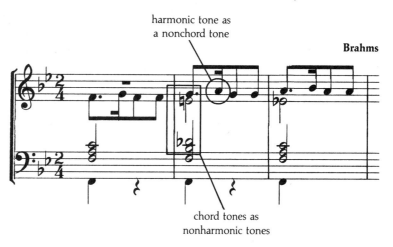

from Variations on a Theme of Haydn

controls to which nonchord tones generally are. The terms *neighboring* and *passing chords* better describe nonharmonic tones. If the nonharmonic tone is part of a chord that intervenes between two positions of a structural chord, the intervening chord is regarded as a **passing chord** (Figure 38-3a). If the nonharmonic tone is part of a chord that is approached stepwise or by leap in one direction and returns to the structural chord, the intervening chord is regarded as a **neighboring chord** (Figure 38-3b). A **neighboring/passing chord** is one that contains both neighboring and passing tones (Figure 38-3c).

38-3

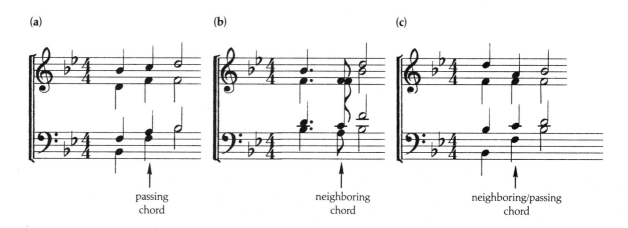

How did the concept of nonchord tones evolve?

The passing tone, neighboring tone, and other kinds of dissonances of the Renaissance were understood in relation to the lowest sounding pitch, except when the dissonant tone occurred as the lowest sounding pitch against a pitch (or pitches) in an upper voice (or voices). A nonharmonic tone that is subject to the same controls as the nonchord tones forms a dissonance with one or more members of the prevailing structural chord. For example, in the I V I structure in B-flat major, when the dominant triad (F major) is the prevailing structural element, the nonharmonic tones would be G, B flat, and E flat (Figure 38-4). Nonchord tones

38-4

would be those notated pitches that are dissonant with any pitch member of a chord of prolongation (Figure 38-5). Suspensions and retardations are dissonances against the lowest sounding pitches; these are entered into, resolved, and generally regarded in a manner substantially the same as the suspension was during the Renaissance. They are, however, rhythmically freer than those of the Renaissance; the same is true for all dissonances (nonchord and nonharmonic tones).   **W146–150**

38-5

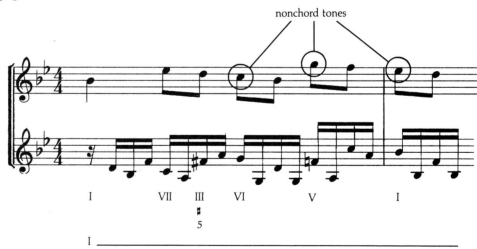

How do we distinguish between directed and nondirected motion?

What we think of as motion in music is purely an illusion. In dealing with this illusion, we might first assume that our primary concern is with the temporal aspects of the art. Though temporality is certainly a factor, the illusory feeling of motion in music, whether directed or nondirected, is primarily a function of harmony. The familiar term *harmonic rhythm* is used in recognition of the comparative pace at which harmonic elements of a musicwork unfold in time. The curious thing about time, however, is that not only do we perceive time in terms of the events that occur within it, we also perceive events in the ever-present present. Our concept of the pace of events is based on our evaluation (a subjective term) of an event and its recurrence or the occurrence of another event. The familiar saying "the past is prologue," used so often to describe the effect of history on the present and the future, expresses what we call *sonic expectancies* in a musicwork. The unfolding sonic events in a musicwork, as "prologue," set up our expectations for the continued recurrence (**nondirected motion**) of harmonic events or the continued occurrence (**directed motion**) of new harmonic events.

The term *nondirected motion* might be equated with the term *static harmony* except that *static harmony* is often used uncomplimentarily. *Nondirected motion* refers to a prolongation of a harmonic element that is not directed toward or not inclined toward another harmonic element. The *motion* portion of the term is in recognition of the illusion of movement established by the sonic events occurring within a fixed harmonic framework. For example, the first five measures of the Allegro following the Introduction to the first movement of Beethoven's First Symphony (Figure 38-6) illustrate nondirected motion within the framework of a

38-6

structural tonic. The first three measures of the Introduction itself (Figure 38-7), on the other hand, provide directed motion toward a prolongation of the dominant which, in the overall harmonic scheme of the movement, is simply a harmonic **anacrusis** to the structural tonic of the Allegro; in other words, a lengthy harmonic "upbeat" to the Allegro.

38-7

Nondirected motion provides a feeling of stability, in contrast to the feeling of instability produced by directed motion. For example, the opening statement of Brahms's

Second Symphony (Figure 38-8) is a prolongation of the tonic. It has a I II V I shape that is principally nondirected motion except for the brief moments of directed motion leading to the II and to the V. This opening statement "feels" stable harmonically. Contrast the stability of this

38-8

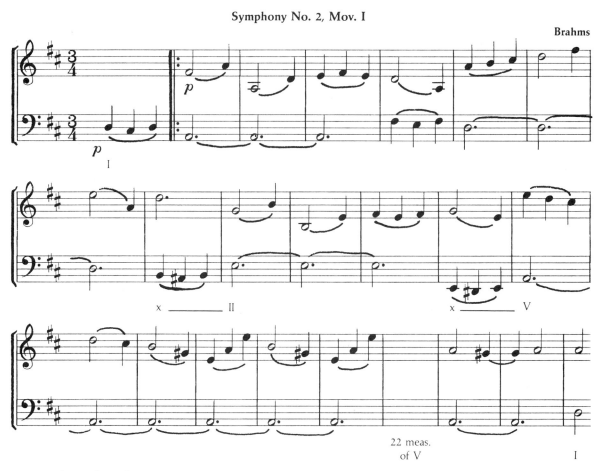

Symphony No. 2, Mov. I

Brahms

Note: x indicates directed motion.

example with the opening statement of Bruckner's Symphony No. 7 (Figure 38-9). It has nearly complete directed motion toward the dominant in measures 6–11, and directed motion continues through the prolongation of the dominant.

38-9

Symphony No. 7, Mov. I

Bruckner

38-9, *continued*

Note: x indicates directed motion.

Directed and nondirected motion are illusions that, on the larger scale, result from the total pitch content of a musicwork. On the lowest level of analysis (what Schenker calls "foreground"), we often find a melodic shape that suggests only nondirected motion supported by other voices that provide brief expressions of directed motion. Such is the case with the excerpt from Brahms's *Variations on a Theme of Haydn* (the *St. Anthony* Chorale) in Figure 38-10.

38-10

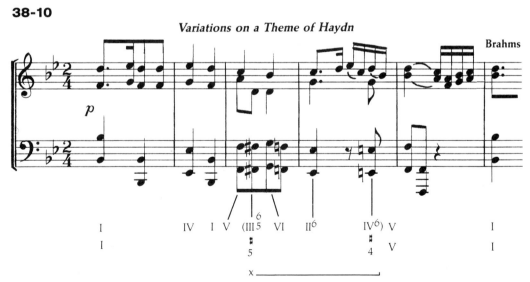

Note: x indicates directed motion.

How can we diagram directed and nondirected motion?

An elongated parallelogram can be used to represent directed motion; see Figure 38-11. An elongated rectangle can then represent nondirected motion; see Figure 38-12. The parallelogram and rectangle can be combined to show admixtures of the two forms of motion.

38-11

38-12

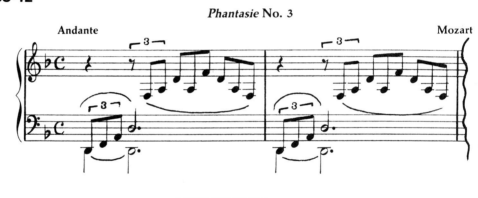

For example, the opening statement in the Allegro of the first movement of Beethoven's First Symphony can be diagrammed as in Figure 38-13. The overall prolongation of the tonic is represented as the dashed rectangular outer line. The solid admixture of rectangles and parallelograms represents the nondirected prolongations of the I II V and the brief use of directed motion leading to the II and V.

38-13

Symphony No. 1, Mov. I

Beethoven

A series of prolongations using nondirected motion may result in an overall prolongation that can appropriately be represented as directed motion; see Figure 38-14. Also, a series of prolongations using directed motion can result in an overall prolongation that is represented as nondirected motion; see Figure 38-15.   **W151—152**

38-14

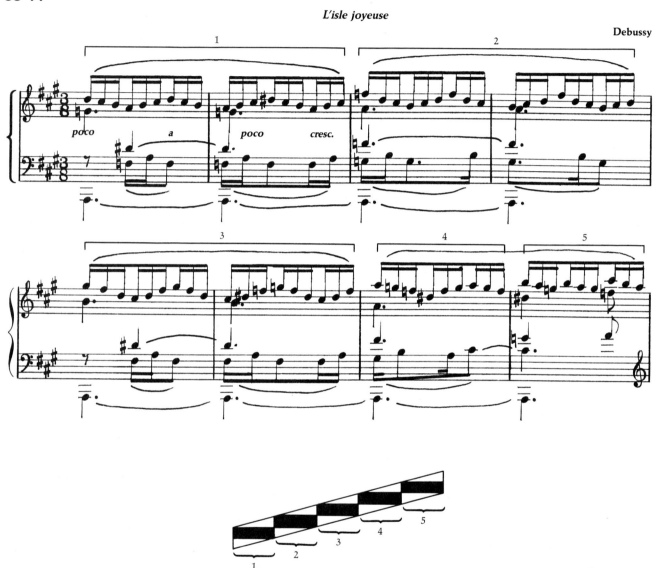

L'isle joyeuse

Debussy

38-15

Second Arabesque

Debussy

Introduction

**MINI
PROJECT
16**

Your objectives for this mini project should be (1) to develop an aural awareness of directed and nondirected motion, (2) to realize the possible expressive effects of each kind of motion, and (3) to develop skill in using directed and nondirected motion in the unfoldment of an accompanied melodic configuration.

Realize, first of all, that it is possible to treat a harmonically nondirected melody with a chordal setting that (whether directed or nondirected) creates tension by being at odds with the harmonic shape of the melody. The melodic content of the opening statement of Beethoven's String Quartet in F major (Figure 38-16) has a melodic line that is a series of four-measure

38-16

String Quartet in F major, Op. 59i

Beethoven

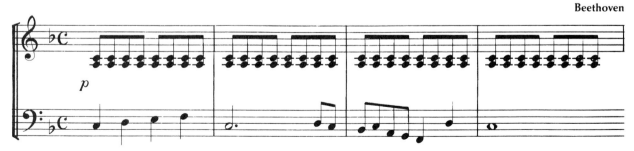

continued

38-16, *continued*

phrases, each of which is harmonically nondirected. Its chordal setting is static in its nondirectedness. Because the implied harmonic shape of the static chordal setting is ambiguous, if not somewhat at odds with the implied harmonic shape of the melodic line, the effect is an increasing tension that terminates in a much-desired release in measure nineteen. Aesthetically, we might say that the melody's natural harmonic shape is held captive by the chordal setting until it finally bursts free in measure nineteen.

If we look again at the directed motion in the opening of Bruckner's Seventh Symphony (Figure 38-9), we find compatibility in the directed motion of the melody and its chordal setting. Though the directed motion is easily perceived, the resulting expression in this portion of the musicwork is not tense. In the section that follows, however, the directed motion (assisted by dynamics) becomes relatively dramatic.

Description

AURAL ANALYSIS: Listen to the opening statements of musicworks of such composers as Bach, Mozart Beethoven, and Brahms (or any of their contemporaries) and try to determine the patterns of directed and nondirected motion. Be prepared for occasional differences in the type of motion existing between the principal melodic lines and the chordal textures that provide the settings.

VISUAL ANALYSIS: After making an aural analysis of the opening statements of selected musicworks, produce a visual analysis of the scores and compare the results with your aural analysis. In preparing your analyses, use the graphics suggested in this chapter or a simple horizontal line (_____) for nondirected motion and a slanted line (_____) for directed motion. These can be superimposed on manuscript paper or simply blank paper upon which barlines have been drawn.

CREATIVE PROBLEM: Using a brief melodic configuration of your own design, produce what would constitute the opening statements of two musicworks utilizing the performance resources of your entire class. Adhere to the following conditions:

1. One of the opening statements should be a principal melodic line placed in a simple but rhythmically and texturally interesting setting, all of which is mostly nondirected motion.

2. The other opening statement should follow the same procedures except that it should use mostly directed motion.

3. There should be just one principal melodic line, but it can be doubled (in unison or octaves), remain as a single line in one voice, or be treated antiphonally.

4. Produce the melodic line and its setting at the same time; that is, do not write a melody first and then try to add a chordal setting.

5. If voices are used, provide a suitable text.

6. Produce a score and set of parts.

7. Perform your project in class.

39 The Grammar of Harmonic Prolongation

What is "grammar" in tonic-dominant harmony?

Grammar in tonic-dominant harmony refers to the organized, syntactical relationships established by pitches, which, as nonstructural elements, serve as the roots of chords or as the reference pitches of melodic configurations. The function of such organized grammatical constructs is to provide the intelligible, individualized means of achieving directed and non-directed motion. In tonic-dominant tonality, harmonic grammar is a primary component of a composer's personalized harmonic conventions.

While it is true that any purely diatonic construct (such as a tertian chord or a melodic configuration) used in the context of tonic-dominant tonality can precede or follow any other such construct, a grammatical syntax gives reason and design to all harmonic relationships. The basic factors of the grammatical syntax of harmony are the intervallic relationships between diatonic constructs, the relative strength and weakness of such relationships, and whether such relationships are clearly perceived as progressions or retrogressions. This outline provides a structured breakdown of the relationships that function in the grammatical syntax of tonic-dominant tonality.

1. The possible intervallic relationships between diatonic constructs are

    a. up or down a fifth (or fourth)

    b. up or down a third (or sixth)

    c. up or down a second (or seventh)

2. The relative strengths of such intervallic relationships are perceived as

    a. strong (fifths and fourths)

    b. moderately strong (seconds and sevenths)

    c. weak (thirds and sixths)

3. Progression (movement toward the tonic) or retrogression (movement away from the tonic) is

a. clearly perceived when the intervallic relationship is a fifth or a fourth

b. generally though not always perceived clearly when the intervallic relationship is a second (or seventh) or a third (or sixth)

How are the syntactical relationships of harmonic grammar classified within a key?

Progression and retrogression, as harmonic relationships in tonic-dominant tonality, can be demonstrated systematically with a classification chart; see Figure 39-1.* The harmonic constructs are identified by the Roman numerals representing the scale degrees that serve as the roots of tertian chords or the reference pitches of melodic configurations. Reading from right to left, each classification is one of a succession of fifths above the tonic class. This succession is represented by the upper Roman numerals. The lower Roman numerals represent constructs that—in the case of the tonic, 1st, and 2nd classes—serve as substitutes for those represented by the upper Roman numerals. The tonic shown as 3rd-class represents a chord or melodic configuration containing a pitch alteration; a 3rd-class tonic would not be possible without a pitch alteration to the triad or its seventh. The movement of the tonic to any other harmonic construct is not considered here as either a progression or retrogression.

39-1

Classification Chart

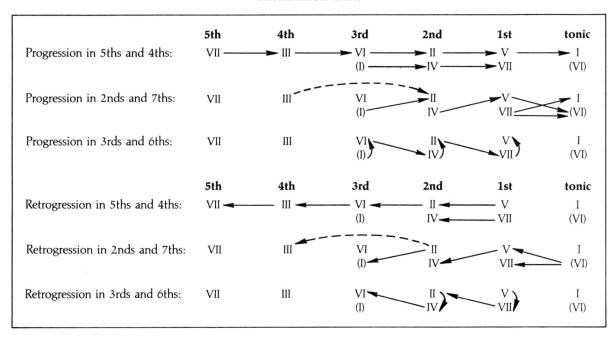

----

*The author first encountered this chart while at the Eastman School; he does not know who, other than Allen McHose, may have originated it.

How are pitch alterations and chord inversions indicated with the Roman-numeral designators?

Writers of theory texts have devised numerous ways of combining information about pitch alterations and chord inversions with the Roman numerals that identify the degrees of scales. Most early combinations joined information used in "figured bass" (Figure 39-2) to

39-2

upper- and lower-case Roman numerals. The upper- and lower-case Roman numerals indicated major and minor qualities of triads, respectively. In this early symbolism, the inversions and chords and pitch alterations were encoded in the "figured bass" form of information (Figure 39-3). This symbolism was serviceable for people who had the time to become practiced in reading figured bass. It is not a serviceable symbolism for those who need a simpler, more flexible, and more clearly accurate nomenclature or for those who lack the time necessary for learning it well.

39-3

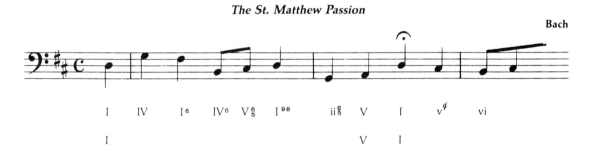

The system of symbols advocated here (Figure 39-4):

1. retains the upper-case Roman numerals for all scale degrees and regards the scale degrees as the primary references for the roots of chords and the reference pitches of melodic configurations,

2. separates information concerning pitch alterations from information relating to chord inversions and permits pitch alterations to be indicated when chord inversions are not relevant, and

3. identifies the altered pitches in terms of scale members (expressed in cardinal numbers) rather than as altered members of chords.

Figure 39-4 shows how pitch alterations (part a) and chord inversions (part b) are indicated in this system.

39-4

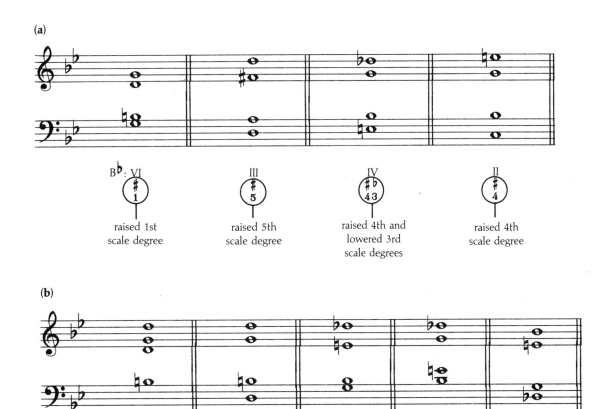

How do pitch alterations affect the classification of tertian chords and melodic configurations in tonic-dominant tonality?

In understanding the effects of pitch alterations on the classification of harmonic constructs within a given key, we must first realize that with or without pitch alterations the classification status of a harmonic construct does not change. Pitch alterations can: (1) enliven or strengthen the movement of a chordal or melodic construct from one classification to another and also result in an imitation of the dominant to tonic function, (2) result in a change of mode, or (3) create useful harmonic constructs that have no counterparts in the natural or transposed diatonic systems.

The various functional relationships expressed in the 1st-class–tonic-class constructs can be imitated in the 2nd-class–1st-class relationships. The V–I relationship, for example, can be imitated by introducing the raised fourth scale degree in the II of the II–V relationship (Figure 39-5). The same relationship is produced in the minor mode by raising both the fourth

39-5

5th	4th	3rd	2nd	1st	tonic
VII	III	VI	II	V ⟶	I
		(I)	IV	VII	(VI)
VII	III	VI	II ⟶	V	I
		(I)	IV	VII	(VI)

String Quartet, Op. 18, No. 1

Beethoven

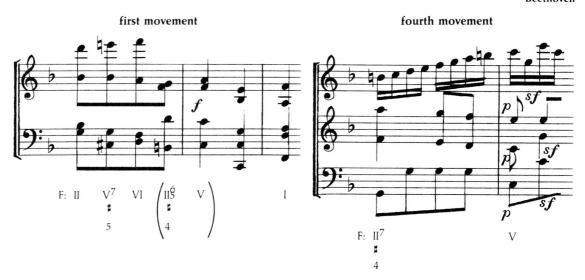

and sixth scale degrees in the II of the II–V relationship (Figure 39-6). Also in the minor mode, the V–I relationship can be imitated by the IV–VII relationship by introducing a raised sixth scale degree in the IV (Figure 39-7). And finally, the VII–I relationship can be imitated by the IV–V relationship by introducing the raised fourth scale degree in the IV (Figure 39-8).

39-6

5th	4th	3rd	2nd	1st	tonic
VII	III	VI	II	V ——→	I
		(I)	IV	VII	(VI)
VII	III	VI	II ——→	V	I
		(I)	IV	VII	(VI)

String Quartet, Op. 18, No. 4, Mov. I

Beethoven

39-7

5th	4th	3rd	2nd	1st	tonic
VII	III	VI	II	V ——→	I
		(I)	IV	VII	(VI)
VII	III	VI	II	V	I
		(I)	IV ——→	VII	(VI)

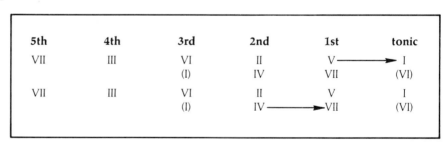

String Quartet, Op. 18, No. 4, Mov. I

Beethoven

39-8

5th	4th	3rd	2nd	1st	tonic
VII	III	VI	II	V	I
		(I)	IV	VII	(VI)
VII	III	VI	II	V	I
		(I)	IV	VII	(VI)

String Quartet, Op. 18, No. 1, Mov. I

Beethoven

F: V   IV   V
        #
        4

The relationships expressed in the 1st-class–tonic-class constructs can be imitated in the 3rd-class–2nd-class relationships. The V–I relationship can be imitated by introducing the raised first scale degree in the VI of the VI–II relationship (Figure 39-9). The V–I relationship can be imitated in the (I)–IV relationship by introducing a lowered seventh scale degree in the (I) (Figure 39-10). The VII–I relationship can be imitated in the (I)–II relationship by

39-9

5th	4th	3rd	2nd	1st	tonic
VII	III	VI	II	V ⟶	I
		(I)	IV	VII	(VI)
VII	III	VI ⟶	II	V	I
		(I)	IV	VII	(VI)

String Quartet, Op. 18, No. 1, Mov. I

Beethoven

F: VI
#
1

II
#
4

F: VI⁷
#
1

II
#
4

39-10

5th	4th	3rd	2nd	1st	tonic
VII	III	VI	II	V ⟶	I
		(I)	IV	VII	(VI)
VII	III	VI	II	V	I
		(I) ⟶	IV	VII	(VI)

Beethoven's Symphony No. 1, Mov. I, meas. 1

Adagio molto

I⁷
♭
7

IV

introducing the raised first scale degree in the (I) (Figure 39-11). The V–I relationship can be imitated by the III–VI relationship expressed in the 4th-class–3rd-class constructs by introducing a raised fifth scale degree in the III (Figure 39-12). The V–I relationship can be imitated by VII–III relationship expressed in the 5th-class–4th-class function by raising the second and fourth scale degrees of the VII (Figure 39-13).

The imitated functions shown in Figures 39-5 through 39-13 serve only to strengthen the transitory movements of harmonic constructs within a prolongation. In the process of moving from one major prolongation to another, however, the imitation of the 1st-class–tonic-class relationship may be viewed as a "borrowed" function. Such borrowed functions are often referred to as **secondary dominant–tonic relationships**. In such cases, the term *secondary dominant* refers to the construct that is imitating the dominant function.

39-11

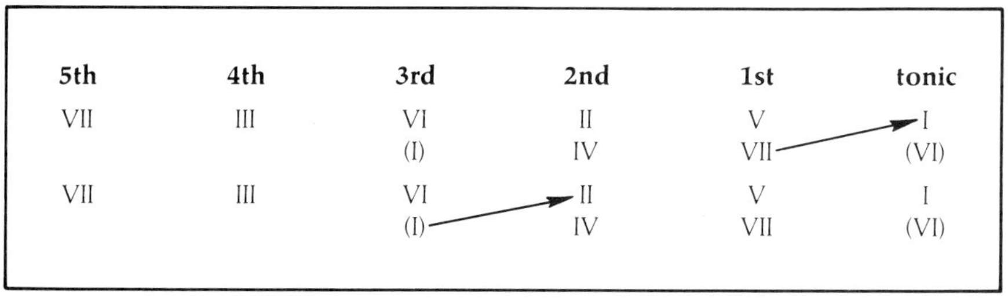
5th 4th 3rd 2nd 1st tonic
VII III VI II V I
(I) IV VII (VI)
VII III VI II V I
(I) IV VII (VI)

String Quartet, Op. 18, No. 1, Mov. I

Beethoven

cresc.
cresc.
cresc.
f
f
f
fp
fp
fp
I6 ♯ 1
I6/5 ♯ ♭ 1 7
II 6

39-12

5th	4th	3rd	2nd	1st	tonic
VII	III	VI	II	V ⟶	I
		(I)	IV	VII	(VI)
VII	III ⟶	VI	II	V	I
		(I)	IV	VII	(VI)

Die Forelle Quintet, Op. 114

Schubert

III   III ⁴₃ ♯₅   VI

39-13

5th	4th	3rd	2nd	1st	tonic
VII	III	VI	II	V ⟶	I
		(I)	IV	VII	(VI)
VII ⟶	III	VI	II	V	I
		(I)	IV	VII	(VI)

Symphony No. 2 in D major, Mov. I

Brahms

VII⁷
♯ ♯
2 4

III

What is a secondary dominant?

In answering this question, let us first consider again what a dominant is. In tonic-dominant tonality, the **dominant** is the fifth degree of the major or minor scale that provides the diatonic pitch material of the key. When a major triad, major/minor-seventh chord, or equivalent melodic configuration is constructed on the fifth scale degree of a key, the construct is referred to as the **dominant**. When dealing with harmonic relationships (as demonstrated in the classification charts in Figure 39-1), the dominant triad, dominant seventh chord, or any melodic configuration having the dominant as its reference pitch, the term *dominant* represents a function as well as the fifth scale degree. The dominant–tonic (V I) relationship is thus a functional relationship within the key. When the imitation of this functional relationship exists only as a colorful strengthening of harmonic relationships within prolongations or between structurally insignificant prolongations, the relationship can be noted, but it should not be elevated to the status of a borrowed function. However, when the imitated relationship is used in the movement from one major structural prolongation to another—as in the movement of a tonic prolongation to a prolongation of the dominant in a I V I structure—the V may be preceded by an altered II (that is, a II chord or melodic configuration with a raised fourth scale degree). If the altered construct on II is in root position and moves to a construct on V in root position—as occurs in the Beethoven String Quartet excerpt in Figure 39-14—the construct on II is properly regarded, secondarily, as a **secondary dominant**. The secondary aspect of this

39-14

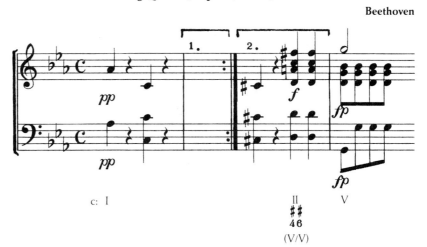

String Quartet, Op. 18, No. 4, Mov. I

Beethoven

relationship should not be overlooked. The construct on II in this case, remains and is identified as a II, but its secondary dominant function may be described parenthetically as (V/V) below or in close proximity to the II designation. Figure 39-15 gives three examples of secondary dominants. **W153—156**

39-15

(a)

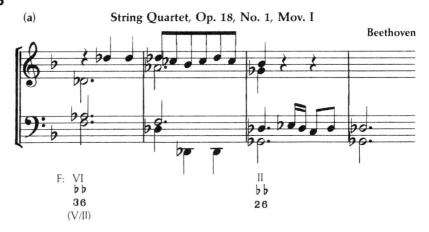

String Quartet, Op. 18, No. 1, Mov. I

Beethoven

(b)

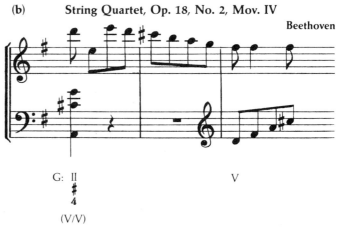

String Quartet, Op. 18, No. 2, Mov. IV

Beethoven

continued

39-15, *continued*

(c)   Symphony No. 2, Op. 73, in D, Mov. I

Brahms

D: III⁷
  ♯
  5

(V/VI)

MINI PROJECT 17

Introduction

This mini project will offer you some practice in recognizing and using some common nonstructural chordal and melodic constructs in the prolongation of a structural harmonic element. Your objectives in completing the project should be to develop your abilities to: (1) recognize prolonged harmonic structures aurally and visually, (2) provide appropriate descriptors (Roman numerals) for the chordal or melodic constructs used in prolongations, (3) distinguish between the transient imitations of the tonic-dominant relationship and the secondary dominant, and (4) use the syntactical relationships of harmonic grammar as a means of conveying a musical expression.

Description

AURAL ANALYSIS: Listen to the opening statements of some musicworks by Bach, Haydn, Mozart, Beethoven, Brahms, or any of their contemporaries and take note of the prolongations. Are the prolongations achieved by diatonic neighboring and passing chords or by altered neighboring and passing chords? Provide Roman-numeral descriptors for your findings.

VISUAL ANALYSIS: After you have aurally analyzed what you believe is the nature of the prolongations of the music, consult the music scores to determine the accuracy of your aural analysis.

CREATIVE PROBLEM: Using a brief melodic configuration of your own choosing, produce what would constitute the opening statements of two musicworks utilizing the performance resources of your entire class. Adhere to the following conditions:

1. Each opening statement should be a principal melodic line placed in a simple but rhythmically and texturally interesting setting.

2. The first opening statement should be cast in the major mode and should be a prolongation of the tonic that moves to the dominant via a secondary dominant. The prolongation of the tonic should contain at least two transient imitations of the dominant–tonic relationship or the leading-tone–tonic relationship.

3. The second opening statement should be cast in the minor mode and have a I III V I harmonic structure. The movement to III and V should each be preceded by a transient imitation of a dominant–tonic or dominant-seventh–tonic relationship.

40 Diatonic Constructs Borrowed from Parallel Major and Minor Modes

What is a parallel major or minor mode?

Parallel modes are modes that share the same tonic; that is, the minor mode whose tonic is the notated pitch F is parallel to the major mode whose tonic is the notated pitch F. One of the minor mode's borrowings from the major mode is so common that we may forget it is borrowed. Because of the basic need for a leading tone in tonic-dominant tonality, the V and VII in the minor mode must contain a raised seventh scale degree when they are used as 1st-class constructs. The first-class dominant and leading-tone chords and any melodic construct performing a similar function are basically borrowed from the parallel major mode.

How do the chordal constructs of the major and minor modes differ?

As shown in Figure 40-1, the triads and seventh chords constructed on the corresponding scale degrees of the major and minor modes are different. This provides a variety of colorful possibilities for enhancing the basic resources of either mode. From the earliest days of tonality, for example, it was a common practice to end a musicwork composed in a minor mode with a major triad borrowed from the parallel major. Except for the eighteenth- and early-nineteenth-century practice of casting an entire section of a musicwork in a parallel mode (Figure 40-2), the borrowing of individual constructs from a parallel mode was most often practiced in the late eighteenth century and the nineteenth century.

40-1

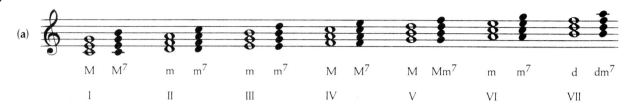

40-2

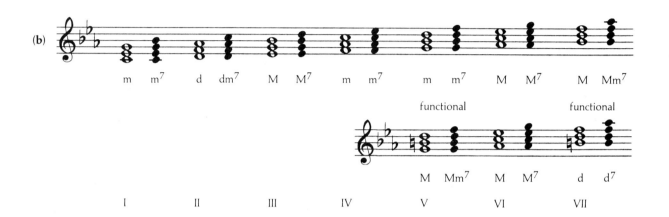

Symphony No. 2 *(London)* in D, Mov. II

Haydn

What diatonic chordal constructs are most effectively borrowed from the minor mode for use in the major mode?

The IV chord in the major mode may be replaced or followed by its counterpart from the minor mode (Figure 40-3). The VI chord in the minor mode is a major triad and it provides a colorful substitute for the VI of the major mode (Figure 40-4). The III chord in the minor

40-3

Requiem, Op. 45, Mov. I

Brahms

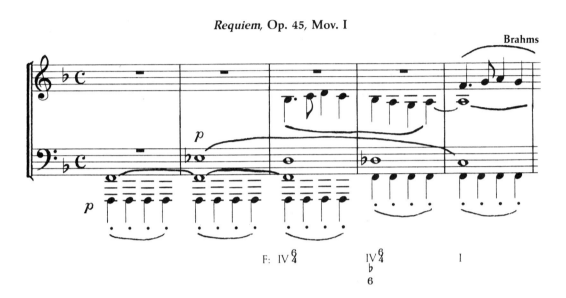

F: IV $\begin{smallmatrix} 6 \\ 4 \end{smallmatrix}$ IV $\begin{smallmatrix} 6 \\ 4 \end{smallmatrix}$ I
                     ♭
                     6

40-4

Symphony No. 3, Op. 90, Mov. II

Brahms

C: I   VI   I
        ♭♭
        36

mode, also a major triad, provides a colorful substitute for the III chord of the major mode (Figure 40-5). The major triad projected from the subtonic pitch of the minor mode is another of the major triads available for use in the major mode (Figure 40-6).

40-5

40-6

What diatonic chordal constructs are most effectively borrowed from the major mode for use in the minor mode?

Already mentioned was the common practice during the seventeenth and eighteenth centuries of ending a musicwork cast in a minor mode with a major triad as the tonic chord (Figure 40-7). This practice was a carry-over from the Renaissance.

40-7

As a result of the required raised seventh scale degree in the 1st-class V and VII chordal constructs, it was common to raise the sixth scale degree in the 2nd-class chordal constructs when the sixth scale degree progressed to the raised seventh scale degree melodically (Figure 40-8). Note that the major IV in Figure 40-8 is used for melodic reasons, whereas the minor II is used for color. When the raised sixth scale degree is encountered as a melodic construct, it is

40-8

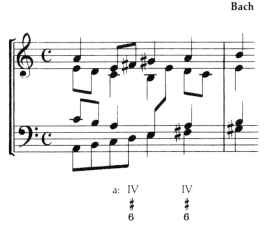

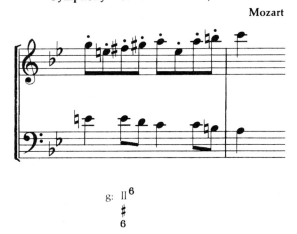

very seldom a member of either a II or a IV chord; it is most often part of a contrapuntal texture (Figure 40-9).

40-9

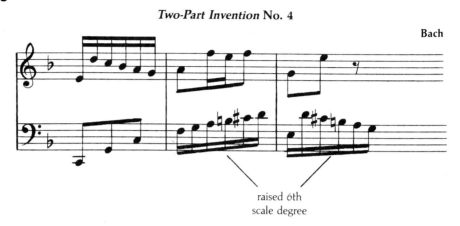

Two-Part Invention No. 4

Bach

raised 6th
scale degree

What are the resultant effects of borrowed chordal constructs?

First and foremost, the coloristic effect of borrowed chordal constructs is the overriding effect. The coloristic effect exists even when the borrowed construct is used for a different purpose. Though coloristic effects are perceived with varying degrees of subjectivity because of their comparative intensities and intrinsic values, the major VI and III chords borrowed from the minor mode are particularly bright and expansive.

Melodic chromaticism is also achieved by following a particular chordal construct by its counterpart from the opposite mode. An example of this is shown in the excerpt from the Brahms Requiem in Figure 40-3; the chordal construct on IV in the key of F major is followed by its counterpart in F minor.   **W157—158**

MINI PROJECT 18	**Introduction**

This mini project will give you some practice in achieving expressive goals by borrowing chordal constructs from the parallel mode. Your objectives in completing the project should be to develop the abilities to: (1) recognize borrowed constructs in a harmonic prolongation aurally and visually, (2) provide descriptors (appropriate Roman numerals and alterations) for borrowed constructs, (3) recognize a composer's idiosyncratic choices and uses of borrowed constructs, and (4) utilize borrowed constructs expressively in making music.

Description

AURAL ANALYSIS: Listen to portions of several musicworks produced from the time of Bach through the nineteenth century and attempt to recognize chordal and melodic constructs borrowed from the parallel mode.

VISUAL ANALYSIS: Listen to the same portions of music again while reading the score in order to (1) verify what you considered as borrowings from the parallel mode and (2) find borrowings that you did not recognize aurally. Select a portion from two or three of the musicworks where such borrowings occur and (on separate paper) provide the appropriate Roman numerals and alterations for them.

CREATIVE PROBLEM: Using a brief melodic configuration of your own making, produce two opening statements (one in a major mode and one in a minor mode) in which the harmonic texture and the unfolding melodic line contain chordal constructs borrowed from the parallel mode.

41 Harmonic and Coloristic Functions of Altered Chordal and Melodic Constructs

How do harmonic and coloristic functions differ?

At the outset we must acknowledge that everything in this world possesses color. Whether we are dealing with a visual art, sound art, or anything else that stimulates our senses, there is an aspect of our sensory impressions that we might categorize as color. As used here, *color* represents that aspect of a thing that is affectively perceived: a delicious flavor, a pungent odor, a neutral tint, a brilliant timbre. Each of these sensory impressions suggests that within the nature of the particular stimulus, a wide range of coloristic possibilities exists. In music, a coloristic possibility is an aspect of function that goes beyond the harmonic function of a chordal or melodic construct. The harmonic function, as previously explained, relates to structure and the grammar of prolongation.

Coloristic harmonic effects are purely subjective and, as such, reflect changing aesthetic values. Whether music evokes heroic, sentimental, delicate, angry, joyful, or other expressive feelings is due in great part to coloristic harmonic effects. A common coloristic harmonic relationship that generally elicits an expansively bright "sunny" response is demonstrated in the excerpts shown in Figure 41-1. In each excerpt a major triad is followed by another, the root of which forms a +3 (M3) or −3 (m3) relationship to the first triad. In part a, from Beethoven's Sixth Symphony (the *Pastoral* Symphony), a prolongation of a B-flat major triad moves to a prolongation of a D major triad. In part b, from Bruckner's Seventh Symphony, we find a sequence of pairs of major triads (G–B flat, F–A flat, and E flat–G flat).

41-1

What is an altered diatonic construct?

An **altered diatonic construct** is any diatonic tertian chord or melodic configuration whose pitch content differs from the pitch content of a given key. A common altered tertian triad is the Neapolitan triad. The **Neapolitan triad**, or **Neapolitan 6th chord** as it is often called, is a major triad constructed on the lowered second scale degree. It is generally found in first inversion in the minor mode (Figure 41-2a), but is also found occasionally in the major mode (Figure 41-2b). An example of an altered diatonic melodic configuration is shown in Figure 41-3.

41-2

41-3

The possible altered diatonic constructs within a given key and mode are too numerous and varied to present individually. As an example, however, all of the reasonable versions of a supertonic (II) triad in the key of F major are shown in Figure 41-4.

41-4

What is a nondiatonic chordal construct?

A **nondiatonic chordal construct** is any nondiatonic tertian chord or melodic configuration whose pitch content does not fit into the natural diatonic system or any transposed version of it. The most common nondiatonic chordal construct is the diminished seventh chord; see Figure 41-5a. A melodic configuration that is related to the diminished seventh chord in both pitch content and general impression is shown in Figure 41-5b. A well-known but

41-5

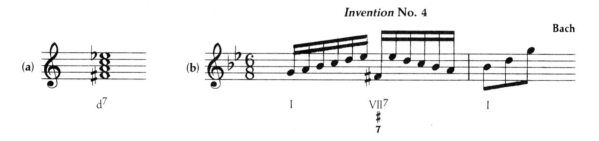

infrequently used nondiatonic tertian triad is the augmented triad (Figure 41-6). The augmented triad, quite often the result of chromatic movement, is considered relatively rare in music composed in tonic-dominant tonality.

41-6

What are chords of the augmented sixth?

Chords of the augmented sixth are a family of nondiatonic chords that are indigenous to the minor mode of a given key. These chords first appeared as second-class chords (chords constructed on II or IV) and later as first-class chords (chords constructed on V or VII). The second-class chords used are the II[7], IV, and IV[7] (Figure 41-7a). Second-class chords of the augmented sixth are formed by raising the fourth degree of the scale of the key (Figure 41-7b). The conventionally favored inversions of augmented sixth chords are shown in Figure 41-7c.

41-7

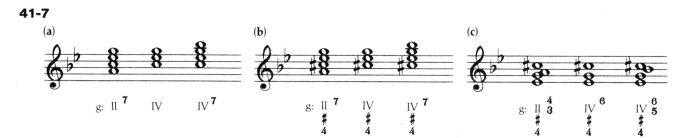

Chords of the augmented sixth are so named because, when used in their most favored inversion, an augmented sixth (6^+) interval appears between the lowest sounding chord member and one of the other chord members (Figure 41-8). Though the inversions shown in Figure 41-7c were favored by composers, augmented sixth chords were used occasionally in root position and all other inversions. Because the augmented sixth chords are highly active harmonic constructs, they occur as part of a directed motion. The second-class types, therefore,

41-8

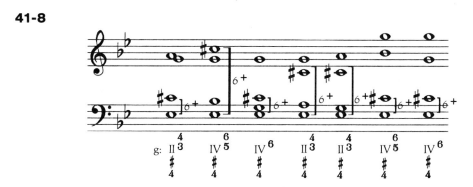

typically move to the dominant. Figure 41-9 shows the root position and all possible inversions of the second-class chords of the augmented sixth resolving to the dominant triad. Examples of the typical use of the second-class chords of the augmented sixth are shown in Figure 41-10.

41-9

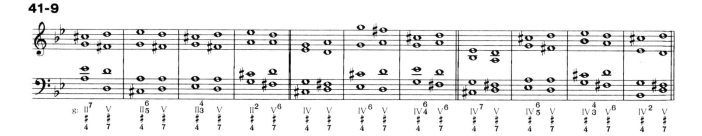

41-10

(a)   *Cariolanus* Overture, Op. 62

Beethoven

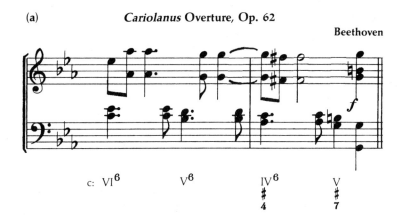

c: VI⁶   V⁶   IV⁶   V
                                 ♯   ♯
                                 4   7

(b)   **Symphony in C**

Schubert

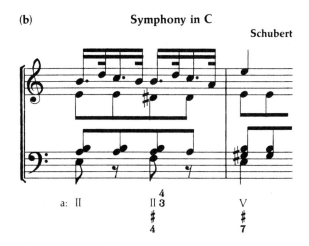

a: II   II 4   V
                    3   ♯
    ♯   7
    4

(c)   **Sonata, K. 457**

Mozart

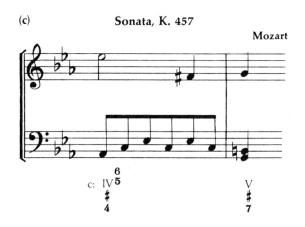

c: IV 6   V
       5   ♯
    ♯   7
    4

First-class chords of the augmented sixth are formed by lowering the second degree of the scale of the key in the V⁷, VII, and VII⁷ (Figure 41-11a) to produce the V⁷, VII, and VII⁷ (Figure 41-11b). The favored inversions of the first-class chords of the augmented sixth (Figure 41-11c) are the same as for the second-class chords. When used in the favored inversions, the interval of the augmented sixth (6^+) occurs between the lowest-sounding pitch (the lowered

41-11

second scale degree) and the raised seventh scale degree in an upper voice (Figure 41-12). First-class chords of the augmented sixth may be used in root position and in any inversion.

41-12

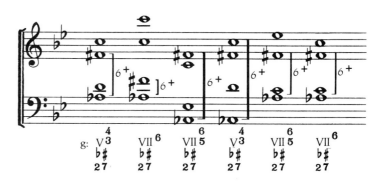

How are chords of the augmented sixth formed in the major mode?

Because chords of the augmented sixth originated in the minor mode of a given key, we might regard their application in a major mode as being borrowed from the minor mode. Second-class and first-class chords of the augmented sixth are the same in both modes. What differs, of course, is the appropriate pitch alterations. For example, in Figure 41-13, the chord of the augmented sixth constructed as a second-class harmonic construct on II in the key of G minor is shown as it is notated and identified in G major. The same chord of the augmented

41-13

sixth constructed as a first-class harmonic construct on V is shown in Figure 41-14 as notated and identified in both G minor and G major. Examples of chords of the augmented sixth used in the major mode are shown in Figure 41-15.

41-14

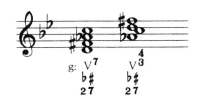 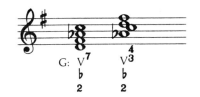

41-15

Symphony No. 1, Op. 21

Beethoven

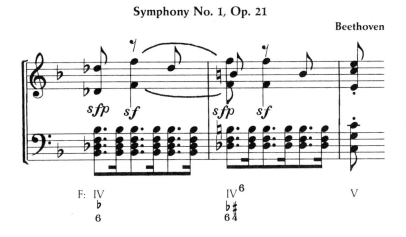

Adagio

Mozart

Quartet, Op. 168

Schubert

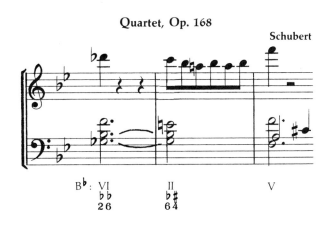

Are the conventional applications of the augmented sixth chords the only ones used?

From the mid eighteenth century to the beginning of the twentieth century, composers constructed chords of the augmented sixth on any notated pitch within a given key. This practice would seem to be a logical extension of the concept of "borrowed function." An example of this practice from the eighteenth century and one from later are shown in Figure 41-16a and b, respectively. Other applications, not shown here, include the use of augmented

41-16

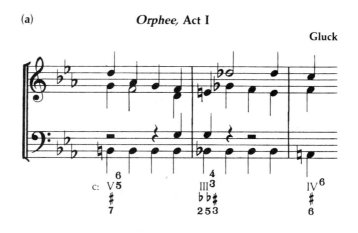

(a) *Orphee,* Act I

Gluck

(b) *Prelude, Op. 28, No. 22*

Chopin

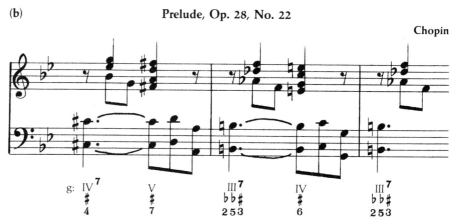

sixth chords in a series. On occasion, Beethoven would use all three types of augmented sixth chords of a given classification in a series in a manner similar to the pattern shown in Figure 41-17. Another practice of the late nineteenth century was to notate the sound of what would be a Mm[7] chord as an augmented sixth chord instead and to resolve it as such. These enharmonic exchanges worked both ways and resulted in some very colorful harmonic diversions.

W159—162

41-17

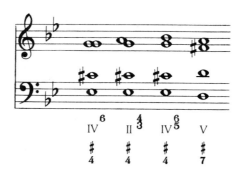

UNIT PROJECT 8

Introduction

The primary thrust of Unit Five is aimed at differentiating between (1) the concept of chord as a compositional entity and as a theoretical harmonic construct, (2) the concept of a theoretical harmonic construct as a structural element and as an element of harmonic prolongation, (3) the concept of a grammatical function and a borrowed or imitated grammatical function, and (4) the concept of a chordal construct serving a harmonic function and a coloristic function. These as musical concerns, along with a host of others, provide the kinds of differentiations in the use of sound materials that facilitate musical expression. These are differentiations that the composer and performer draw upon as they exercise their particular functions within the communication process. Also, when these differentiations are understood and effectively applied, they enable the listener to communicate effectively with a musicwork.

Your purpose in this project is to apply the understandings you have acquired in Unit Five, as well as those of the previous four units, to produce an expressive product that "works" musically. Whatever techniques and relationships you employ must serve your expressive intent.

Description

Produce a three- to five-minute musicwork within the framework of the tonic-dominant meta-idiom. You must determine the following:

1. The function for which the musicwork is being made

2. An instrumentation (instruments or voice) that is available in your class

3. An expressive intent that is suitable to the function of the musicwork

4. A melodic configuration that reflects your expressive intent and that will work within the framework of tonic-dominant tonality

5. The application of directed and nondirected motion

6. The application of chordal or melodic constructs borrowed from the pitch content of the parallel mode

7. The application of diatonic and nondiatonic constructs (harmonic and melodic) whose pitches are not members of the pitch content of the key and mode used

Notes

Though the first two conditions presented are precomposition considerations, the others are not necessarily to be considered in terms of a series. As you produce the opening gesture of your musicwork, you may find that several of the remaining conditions are present. It is not unlikely that you will read the conditions, consider them all, and then decide on how you will fashion an opening gesture that embodies the essence of your desired expressive intent.

Do not try to inject a little bit of everything presented in Unit Five into this project. The object is to produce music that is convincing in its intent, not to produce a kaleidoscopic glossary of harmonic devices.

U N I T

SIX

PITCH-CLASS SETS

42 Introduction to the Pitch-Class Set

What barriers must we overcome in using a language?

Because all knowledge is encoded in a language and requires a rhetorical language to discuss it and write about it, we cannot think about knowledge outside the framework of a language. **Language**, as considered here, embraces all of the means a person uses to encode knowledge that another person is to receive through the senses. Whether we are dealing with music, mathematics, nuclear physics, or any other area of thought (including rhetoric itself), the degree to which we are able to think and comprehend anything is limited by our ability to use the language within which the ideas are formed. Language is thus both the vehicle by which we acquire knowledge and the barrier that separates us from knowledge. There is not much we can do to increase our innate capacity to think in and comprehend a particular language, but there is much we can do to remove the barriers that prevent us from utilizing our individual capacities to the fullest.

It is generally accepted that most people do not realize their full intellectual capacities. This implies that, because we think in language, we are all capable of extending the level of our thinking and comprehension of a language and of extending a language itself. Our ability to think is limited by (1) our ability to understand and use language and by (2) the limitations of a given language. The first of these barriers can be pushed back, if not completely removed, by studying and creatively applying what is already known. The second barrier is more formidable; it is a product of the circumstances of environment and ignored opportunities. For example, most of what there is to know about the world is available only in the vocabulary of verbal languages. We are limited not only by what we can think and comprehend in our own language; we are also limited by what little we know of other peoples' languages. The languages of other people present a barrier to our knowing what and how they think.

Our basic means of communicating with the peoples of other cultures is through the process of translation. At best, translation works only—and even then in a limited manner—when the translator is equally competent in both languages and when there is some commonality in definition and structure between the languages. What is possible to think and express in one language is often not possible to think and express in another.

How should we react to changes in musical languages?

In our previous discussion of communication and how it works in the arts, we pointed out that *music is universally regarded as a language* but that it is *not a universal language*. Also, we discussed the difficulty of responding to the musical languages of other cultures except in terms of the novelty of the sounds produced. Before the twentieth century, changes in all of the verbal, scientific, artistic, and other languages were generally a matter of gradual evolution; change was sufficiently gradual to give the illusion of no change at all except in a long-term historical perspective. During the twentieth century, however, changes in the language of music and other areas of knowledge have occurred very rapidly. The differences within our own culture now are as profound as the differences found between cultures. Unfortunately we do not have the benefit of translators to help us deal with the profound changes that now occur so rapidly in the musical art within our culture and other cultures. Unless these changes in musical language are approached head-on and learned, they serve as a genuine barrier to our understanding and ability to deal intelligently with the music produced.

Which forms of musical language are most vital to the musician?

In dealing with music and the concept of language, essentially three distinct forms of language are involved. The primary language—the language of *sound*—is learned through familiarity and, in principle, it is accessible to all who can hear and have the patience and desire to learn. The other languages—those of *symbolism* and *terminology*—are peculiar to and vital to us as practitioners of the musical arts.

What problems accompany the changes in symbols, descriptors, and terminology in our evolving musical language?

The symbolism used in the notation of music can be deceiving because the same symbols can be used to notate distinctly different musical languages. This can be likened to the use of the same alphabet for symbolizing (with minor exceptions) the French and German languages. In some of the music produced during the twentieth century, we can see that a number of changes have occurred in the symbols and descriptors. Some of these changes are modifications of old symbols and descriptors; others are brand new forms. Regardless of whether the changes are effective, lasting, self-serving, ineffectual, or simply novel for the sake of novelty, we must familiarize ourselves with the new symbols and descriptors if we are to deal with the music for which they are used.

In many cases we are late to discover and respond to changes in the principles of musical design that have occurred when applications of long-standing principles have been stretched or extended. The terminology and descriptors we use to give rhetorical expression (verbal and written) to musical notation is slow to evolve or change as needed along with the evolving applications of familiar symbols and descriptors and the invention of new ones. Any terminology we use should serve to describe the symbols and descriptors themselves as well as the principles of musical design the terminology seeks to explain.

Unit Five introduced two of the three historical stages in the application of referentialism in music. The first two stages are referred to as modality and tonic-dominant tonality. The third stage, not yet discussed, is a multifaceted stage in which the music produced has been variously described as "neomodal," "pandiatonic," "extended tonality," and other terms that denote new applications of referentialism and suggest eventual avenues that music might take in its movement away from the diatonic system to some other system.

It would seem appropriate to assume that the music of any historical period contains aspects of declining, established, and developing principles in varying degrees of aesthetic balance. To be sure, no music is completely new in all respects. Even though music composed in the Western world during the nineteenth century differed in many aspects from the music of the eighteenth century, the music of both periods was fashioned according to the principle of tonic-dominant tonality. Music composed during the third stage of referentialism (roughly 1900–1960) is not subject to any such universal convention. Composers during that period of history seemed to be searching for a new organizing principle to exploit—each one probably with the hope that a new convention would result. All of this, of course, took place amid the decline and eventual disappearance of referentialism as a current convention of the art music composer.

How does the pitch-class set serve us?

Unit Six introduces the **pitch-class set (pc set)**. This new descriptive nomenclature serves to identify and compare many new musical relationships and design principles that have been achieved within the framework of an essentially unchanged musical notation. In some respects, this new nomenclature is a bridge between the referential music produced with the resources of the diatonic system during the third stage of referentialism and the nonreferential music produced with the resources of the dodecaphonic system. Though the pc set provides a nomenclature intended for nonreferential relationships and design principles, it can embrace all of the pitch combinations in the music of any previous historical period.

A New Nomenclature

What is a pitch-class set?

A **pitch-class set (pc set)**—the term and concept originated with Milton Babbitt—is any collection of two or more distinct pitch classes that, when arranged in an established conventional order, become an easily classified and identifiable entity. The pitch content of a pc set is expressed in terms of integer nomenclature.

What is integer nomenclature?

Integer nomenclature is simply the representation of each pitch class by an integer (a whole number) with the pitch class C represented by 0 (zero); see Figure 43-1. Integer nomenclature was presented in Unit One for the purpose of calculating intervals and naming them with cardinal numbers. The *cardinal nomenclature* used then as a convenience in calculating and identifying intervals is now indispensable to our understanding of pc-set nomenclature.

43-1

0	1	2	3	4	5	6	7	8	9	10	11

What are the advantages of integer nomenclature?

Recognizing the redundancy of the enharmonic equivalencies inherent in conventional notation and the alphabetical identification of pitch, there are only *twelve* distinct *pitch classes* to be named as the twelve *pitches* contained within the octave. This provides us with an advantageous one-to-one relationship between a pitch class and its name. The selection of the pitch class C to be identified as *0 (zero)* conforms to the previously established convention of considering the pc C as the primary reference in staff notation. The use of 0 as the first integer enables us to interpret the pc integers as intervallic relationships (expressed as cardinal intervals) above 0. For example, the integer *8* represents the pc 8 (G sharp or A flat) as well as the interval 8 (-6, m6).

In what way is pc-set nomenclature practical?

Pc sets have proven extremely useful in the development of analytical techniques for expanding our understanding of twentieth-century design concepts. But first among the many virtues of the pc set is the obvious practicality of having a nomenclature that can be universally applied and that serves as an accurate and uniform descriptor of what it is meant to identify.

For example, let us examine the two melodic shapes shown in Figure 43-2. If for no other purpose than to consider each of these melodic shapes as being made up of a particular collection of distinct pitches, they are gathered into a collection in Figure 43-3. In Figure 43-3a we find what we have known as an E-flat major triad. The collection of pitches in (b) is not anything for which we have a name—that is, a conventional name like the one in (a). The point here is that, prior to the conception of the pc set, we could name only a very limited number of pitch collections.

43-2

(a)   Tpt.

(b)   Tpt.

43-3

(a)   (b)

E-flat major
triad

?

The pc set provides a means for naming every collection of distinct pitch classes from two up to and including the one collection that contains all twelve pitch classes. This, of course, is a comprehensive, theoretical possibility; as a practical matter, we will seldom have to deal with collections of more than six distinct pitch classes, and rarely with collections of more than nine.

The limitations imposed by the conventional concepts of what constitutes a viable pitch collection and the nomenclature used to describe it in tonic-dominant tonality, for example, is finite. Neither the concept nor the terminology can be effectively expanded to serve any new purpose. The inclusiveness of the pc set, on the other hand, permits the renaming of every triad, every seventh chord, and all other chordal constructs as well as any scale structure associated with the music of any previous historical period. Another advantage of pc-set nomenclature is that, as a descriptive vocabulary, it is not derivatively dependent on any particular concept of music construction or analysis that uses discrete pitches. The pc set is essentially a neutral nomenclature applicable to a number of musical design concepts.

What is the established precedent for the ordering of pitches in pc sets?

Because of an established convention, the pitch collections in Figures 43-2a and 43-3a can be identified as E-flat major triads. We are able, therefore, to view or hear any of the possible permutations (inversions and voicings) in Figure 43-4 as an E-flat major triad. At the same time, however, we recognize that, as part of this convention, an ordering is in use with respect to the manner in which the pitches are arranged when notated for identification or spelled orally. We do not *spell* the E-flat major triad as "G, B flat, E flat" or as "B flat, G, E flat"; the conventional ordering is "E flat, G, B flat" in ascending order.

43-4

How do quality and content in tertian nomenclature differ from that in pc nomenclature?

Though the nomenclature *E-flat major triad* and *[3, 7, 10]* (the pc-set equivalent of the E-flat major triad) both appear to fulfill the same practical need for ordering, there are striking differences in what is demonstrated or meant by the manner in which these needs are fulfilled.

In using the term *major triad*, for example, we are recognizing a particular kind of triad whose sound differs from that of other types of triads. In identifying a particular pitch collection as a *pc set*, we recognize a set of distinct pitch classes and a specific set of intervallic relationships that differ from those of other pc sets. Though we recognize that pitch and intervallic relationships are what produce the particular sound of a major triad, these pitch and intervallic relationships are secondary to the basic intent and function of this kind of nomenclature. In like manner, we must surely realize that quality of sound is of paramount importance to anyone dealing with pc sets. As used here, **quality** refers to the unique aural impression that renders the sound of a particular collection of distinct pitches, whatever the identifying nomenclature, as different from all other pitch collections.

In what way is pc-set nomenclature more informative than tertian nomenclature?

The difference between these two nomenclatures can be clarified further by pointing out that the name *E-flat major triad* does not indicate or even suggest, except by empirical association, what pitches other than E♭ or what intervals it contains. The spelling of an E-flat major triad is a separate operation from the naming of it.

The pc set [3, 7, 10], on the other hand, does indicate the pitch classes and intervallic relationships contained in it: the pitch classes are directly identified by the integers, and the intervallic relationships are readily available. [3, 7, 10] represents the pitch classes E flat, G, and

B flat (Figure 43-5a). The intervallic differences, expressed in terms of cardinal nomenclature, may be determined by simple subtraction (Figure 43-5b). The intervallic difference between the first integer and each subsequent integer can also be determined by subtraction (Figure 43-5c).

43-5

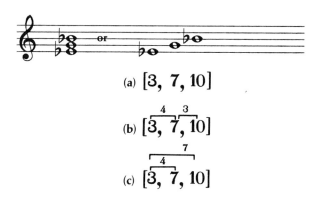

(a) [3, 7, 10]

(b) [3, 7, 10]

(c) [3, 7, 10]

Do we hear, auralize, and think music in terms of pitch, of intervals, or of both pitch and intervals?

Among the preliminary matters we must yet consider is a brief discussion of the various views musicians hold concerning the intervallic relationships contained in a collection of distinct pitch classes. First, we should not suppose, because we are dealing here with collections of distinct pitch classes and are discussing a nomenclature that is obviously pitch oriented, that all musicians hear, auralize, and think music only in terms of pitch. Whereas some musicians claim that they hear, auralize, and think only pitches, others say they do so only in terms of intervals. These differences probably express personal bias more than actual fact. It is more reasonable to assume that what a musician does in this regard is more of an intuitive act involving both pitch and intervals. All of this, of course, is purely speculative. The purpose of this discussion is to establish that some musicians, at least, are inclined toward regarding collections of distinct pitch classes—whether they are called triads, pc sets, or whatever—as collections of intervals as well as (or rather than) collections of distinct pitch classes.

What are the differing views on the interval content of triads and similar chord structures?

To further complicate matters, musicians do not think alike when considering the interval content of triads and similar collections. For example, there are two principal views of the discrete intervals that form the major triad. Some musicians hold the view that the major triad is formed by projecting the intervals +3(M3) and P5 above the fundamental pitch (Figure 43-6a). Others hold the view that a major triad is formed by superimposing a −3(m3) on a +3(M3) (Figure 43-6b). In considering the discrete intervallic *content* of a major triad, one view combines the intervals shown in (a) and (b) of Figure 43-6 to arrive at a +3, −3, and P5. Yet another view considers all of the possible intervallic relationships, six of them in all (Figure 43-6c).

43-6

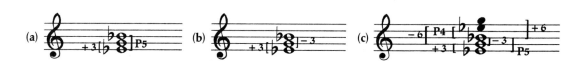

Those who express the intervallic content of a major triad in terms of interval class would regard a major triad as being made up of one each of the following interval classes: 3, 4, and 5; see Figure 43-7a. These interval classes are translated into the discrete intervals −3(m3), +3 (M3), and P4 in Figure 43-7b.

43-7

The differing views about the interval content of triads and similar collections represent the conventions that prevailed up through the early twentieth century. None is right or wrong; each view is plausible. Such differences in viewpoint simply illustrate the fact that we cannot and should not expect uniformity of thinking with regard to any aspect of any area of the arts—and the more people involved, the more varied and speculative will be the views. Actually, the phrase *uniformity of thought*, when applied to the arts, might better be taken as a synonym for *nonthinking*.

How should we respond to the question of new definitions of old terminology versus new terminology?

However varied and plausible, not all of the differing views on musical nomenclature can be taken as equally useful. With the establishment of new conventions comes new terminology for expressing new concepts about pitch materials and intervallic relationships and new ways of looking at these materials as elements of old musical conventions.

Because free inquiry is basic to scholarship in the musical arts, some musicians will always elect to redefine or expand the conventional terminology to apply it to new situations, and others will choose to establish new terminology for new situations. Although this dual approach is plausible as a generality, it cannot be accepted automatically as plausible in all cases. Each redefined or expanded meaning of a term and each new term must be examined with respect to its usefulness and the clarity of its meaning.

We should observe also that the analytical concepts and procedures that develop around particular musical conventions are not uniformly useful. Some initial explanations of new musical practices are short-sighted and later must be altered or abandoned. For example, Heinrich Schenker's concepts of key and modulation have replaced the previous, limited concepts of key and modulation. All too often, first explanations of musical phenomena—just as first impressions of people—are extremely difficult to change even when shown to be inadequate or faulty. There appears to be some sociological comfort in the binding qualities of common knowledge, even when it is found to be useless, misleading, or otherwise wanting.

Humans also have a basic reluctance to "backtrack" for the purpose of changing their views, terminology, concepts, and other aspects of things in which they have made a substantial investment. In the interest of improved scholarship, however, we must resist this reluctance to rid ourselves of useless or faulty concepts, processes, and nomenclature. This is *not* meant to imply that something new should be regarded as superior to something old. The merits and usefulness of any concept, process, or nomenclature must not be determined by when it was developed but rather on *how well it performs its intended function*.

The inevitable burden that accompanies change in our pursuit of knowledge is that we must acknowledge history and what historians have handed down to us. This requires that we must become and remain familiar with the nomenclature that history provides even if we do not use it or consider it useful.

What makes integer nomenclature particularly useful?

The pc set is a welcome addition to music. Pc-set nomenclature provides the musician with one of the most universally serviceable tools ever developed. Throughout the following chapters, all calculations and relationships represented as pc sets will be expressed in integer nomenclature. However, as an aid to relating integers to staff-notated pitch classes, staff notation also will be provided. Collections of distinct pitches—not pitch classes—will be notated only in staff notation. Probably the most basic value of integer nomenclature is that arithmetic functions can be performed with it. Whole numbers can be added, subtracted, and otherwise related; staff notation and the letter-names of notated pitches provide no such relationships. Integer nomenclature is not intended to replace staff notation; it is used only as a tool for performing manipulative and comparative operations on collections of distinct pitch classes.

The Discrete Set

What is a discrete set?

The term *pc set* is used in two applications, one of which is the topic of this chapter: the discrete set. A **discrete set** is a collection of distinct pitch classes that make up—or represent—the pitch-class content of a melodic shape, a simultaneously sounding collection, or any intelligible portion of a musicwork.

How do we form a discrete set?

Referring to Figure 44-1, we observe that the pitch content of the melodic shapes shown in (a) and (b) are gathered in (c) and (d). Bringing the pitches together in this way allows us to examine the pitch content as a simpler, easy-to-deal-with collection. This simpler collection can be expressed on the staff as either a vertical or a horizontal representation of the actual pitches in the music being examined. It matters little how it is done because this step of the process is eliminated as soon as a person becomes adept at perceiving a collection of discrete pitches as a discrete set arranged in ascending numerical order.

44-1

continued

44-1, *continued*

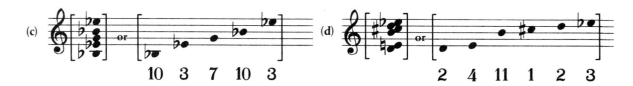

Using the pitch content of the two melodic shapes in Figure 44-1a and b—as simplified in (c) and (d) of the figure—the first step in reducing the collections to discrete sets* is to arrange the integers in ascending numerical order without numerical repetitions; see Figure 44-2a and b. By rearranging the integers of the discrete pitches in ascending numerical order, we place them in an order that better enables us to determine which cyclic permutation of the integers will produce what we call the "prime order" of the discrete set.**   **W163**

44-2

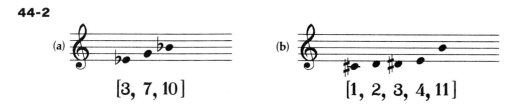

What is a prime-ordered set?

The **prime order** of a discrete set is the set that, by cyclic permutation, yields the smallest (smaller) numerical difference between the first and last integers. If two permutations yield the same smallest numerical difference between the first and last integers, the one with the smaller numerical difference between the first and second integers provides the prime order. If these are the same, use the permutation with the smaller numerical difference between the second and third integers, and so on. The process seldom extends beyond this point. The final result of this process yields a **prime-ordered set.*****

What is a permutation?

Various procedures can be used to determine the total number of ways the elements of a particular group of things can be arranged, ordered, or positioned—permuted—in accordance with specified conditions. A **permutation** is any one of the conditioned arrangements, orderings, or changes in the position of the elements of a group.

Perhaps the most common type of permutation is a **linear permutation**. There are six possible linear permutations of the elements, a, b, and c: a b c, a c b, b a c, b c a, c a b, and c b a.

Discrete set should be regarded as a shorter, more convenient form of the term *discrete pc set.*

**Prime order* is used here to represent what Forte calls the "normal order" of a pc set.

****Prime-ordered set* should be regarded as a shorter, more convenient form of the term *prime-ordered discrete pc set.*

Circular permutation and cyclic permutation yield more limited results. The **circular permutation** of the elements a, b, and c yields two possible arrangements: a b c and a c b. The **cyclic permutation** of the elements a, b, and c yields three arrangements: a b c, b c a, and c a b.

Though all of the linear permutations of a pitch collection are usable in music, our concern right now is limited to permuting the order of pitch classes in a discrete set in order to determine the prime order. Cyclic permutation is applicable to this purpose.

How is a cyclic permutation used to determine the prime order of a discrete set?

Figure 44-3 demonstrates the use of cyclic permutation to determine the prime order of the two discrete sets presented in ascending numerical order in Figure 44-2. As shown, cyclic permutation is a matter of moving the first integer of a series to the end of the series. As each integer is moved, we add 12 to it to facilitate the subtraction required for finding the numerical difference between the first and last integers of each permutation. This process is repeated until all of the possible permutations have been presented.

The prime-ordered set in Figure 44-3a is shown to be [3, 7, 10]; in part b it is shown to be [11, 1, 2, 3, 4]. Obviously, this can be a rather lengthy and tedious procedure. Therefore, as soon as you clearly understand the nature and objective of a cyclic permutation, use the procedure explained in the next two paragraphs.

If your primary objective in using cyclic permutation is to find the permutation with the smallest numerical difference between the first and last integers of a discrete set, you can determine this by simply finding the largest interval formed by any two adjacent integers. The numerical difference between any of the integers of a pc set are expressed in terms of the number of half steps—in cardinal nomenclature. The largest interval produced by any two adjacent pitches of a discrete set is the **complement** of the interval formed by the smallest numerical difference between the first and last integers of the appropriate permutation; that is, when its number is added to the number representing the smallest numerical difference between the first and last integers of the set, the sum is 12.

44-3

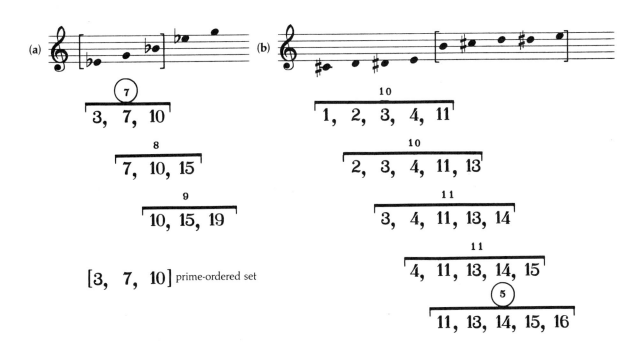

Refer to Figure 44-4. We have moved the first integer of each discrete set—beginning with the sets in ascending numerical order—to the end of the series in order to *close* the series and show all of the intervals found between the adjacent integers. These intervals, expressed in cardinal nomenclature, are 4, 3, and 5 in (a) and 1, 1, 1, 7, and 2 in (b). The intervals formed by the integers 10 up to 3 in (a) and integers 4 up to 11 in (b) are the largest intervals found between any adjacent integers. Therefore, it follows that the intervals formed by the integers 3 up to 10 in (a) and 11 up to 4 in (b) represent the smallest numerical differences between the first and last integers of any permutations of the two sets. The prime orders of the two sets are as expected: [3, 7, 10] and [11, 1, 2, 3, 4].

44-4

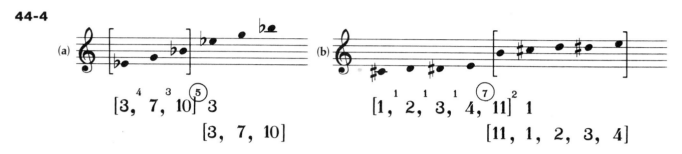

How can we further refine the process of finding
the largest interval between adjacent integers?

Because we know that the number of half steps expressed by the cardinal intervals produced by the adjacent integers of a discrete set add up to 12, we can simplify the procedure for determining the prime order of a set. The series of integers of a discrete set in ascending order does not have to be *closed* (Figure 44-4) in order to find the cardinal interval from the last integer up to the first integer. We need only to add the cardinal intervals produced by the adjacent integers and subtract the sum from 12, as shown in Figure 44-5a and b. In (a) the remainder is 5; in (b) it is 2.

44-5

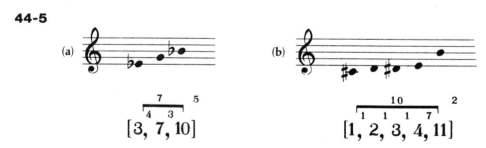

What is the total process for finding
the prime-ordered set?

Let us review the procedure for reducing a melodic shape, a simultaneously sounding collection, or any intelligible portion of a musicwork to a discrete set in prime order:

1. In Figure 44-6 a melodic shape is reduced to a discrete pitch collection. This, you will recall, is a fundamental procedure to be dropped as soon as it is no longer necessary.

2. In Figure 44-7, the discrete pitch collection of Figure 44-6 is reduced to a discrete set in ascending numerical order.

3. Figure 44-8 shows an interval 3 between integers 3 and 6 and also between integers 7 and 10. This means that, of the six possible permutations of the set, the smallest numerical difference between the first and last integers is a condition satisfied by two separate permutations: one with integers 6 up to 3 and another with integers 10 up to 7.

44-6

7 11 1 3 6 7 10

44-7

$$\left[1, \quad 3, \quad 6, \quad 7, \quad 10, \quad 11\right]$$

44-8

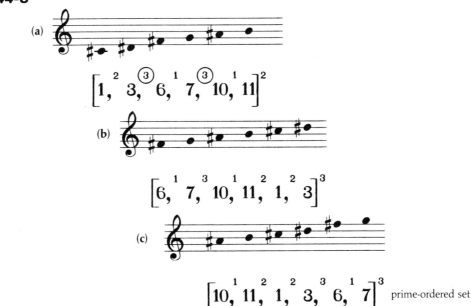

(a)

$$\left[1, \overset{2}{\quad} 3, \overset{\textcircled{3}}{\quad} 6, \overset{1}{\quad} 7, \overset{\textcircled{3}}{\quad} 10, \overset{1}{\quad} 11\right]^2$$

(b)

$$\left[6, \overset{1}{\quad} 7, \overset{3}{\quad} 10, \overset{1}{\quad} 11, \overset{2}{\quad} 1, \overset{2}{\quad} 3\right]^3$$

(c)

$$\left[10, \overset{1}{\quad} 11, \overset{2}{\quad} 1, \overset{2}{\quad} 3, \overset{3}{\quad} 6, \overset{1}{\quad} 7\right]^3 \quad \text{prime-ordered set}$$

4. Because *two* permutations satisfy the condition requiring the smallest numerical difference between the first and last integers, we must examine the difference between the first and second integers of the two permutations. In both cases the numerical difference between the first and second integers is 1 (Figure 44-8b and c).

5. We must, therefore, consider the numerical difference between the second and third integers of the two permutations. Here we find a numerical difference of 3 in (b) and of 2 in (c). Thus, the prime order of this discrete set is [10, 11, 1, 3, 6, 7]. **W164–165**

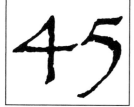

The Source Set and Complement Set

What is a source set?

A **source set** is any of the unique sets of intervallic relationships, arranged in ascending order from the pc C or 0 (zero), expressed in integer nomenclature and containing two to twelve integers. A source set is a prototype or archtype set that serves as a model for categorizing or comparing prime-ordered sets.

A source set is distinguished by two characteristics:

1. the relationship between the first and last integers represents the smaller (smallest) possible numerical difference, and

2. except in the case of "isometric" sets, the smaller (smallest) intervallic relationship(s) formed by adjacent integers occur(s) nearest the integer 0.

An **isometric source set** is one in which the intervallic relationships read the same in both directions (Figure 45-1).

45-1

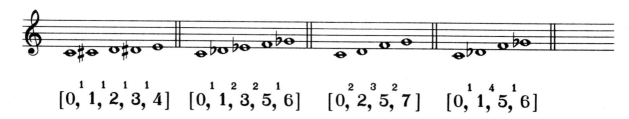

$$[0,\ 1,\ 2,\ 3,\ 4] \quad [0,\ 1,\ 3,\ 5,\ 6] \quad [0,\ 2,\ 5,\ 7] \quad [0,\ 1,\ 5,\ 6]$$

Both characteristics of a source set are seen in the set in Figure 45-2a. Just one of the characteristics is seen in the set in Figure 45-2b. The smallest numerical difference is between the first and last integers; however, the smallest interval occurs nearest the *last* integer. Thus, whereas [0, 1, 3, 5] is a source set, [0, 2, 4, 5] is not; it is a "complement" set.

45-2

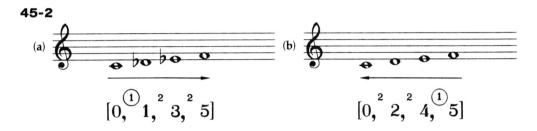

What is a complement set?

A **complement set** is a set of intervallic relationships in which the second characteristic of the source set is reversed; that is, the smaller (smallest) interval(s) occur(s) nearest the last integer of the set. For example, in Figure 45-3, the set [0, 3, 4, 6] is the complement set of the source set [0, 2, 3, 6]. When a prime-ordered set having one largest interval is transposed to 0 (zero), the result will be either the source set or the complement of the source set. An isometric source set obviously does not have a complement, because its intervallic relationships read the same in both directions.

45-3

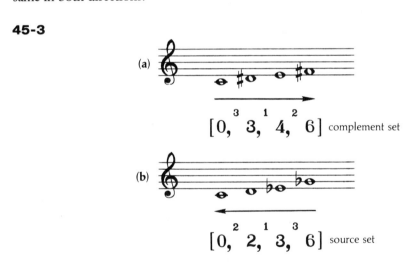

What is the precedent for one-of-a-kind prototypes?

In recognition of the concept that there is only one of any given shape—for example, there is one shape for a major triad, one shape for a minor triad, one shape for any given interval class—we recognize the E-flat major triad as a transposition of the **prototype** (model) of the major triad. The C major triad is probably recognized universally as the prototype for the shape of the major triad in the tertian system of chord spelling. In dealing with pc sets we must realize that each source set is a prototype for a number of other discrete sets. Though it is not necessary to do so, transposing a prime-ordered set to 0 (zero) is a useful intermediary step in determining the source set of a prime-ordered set. Transposition by integers is useful in several operations dealing with pc sets.

What is the procedure for transposing with integers?

To demonstrate transposition with integers, the previously discussed prime-ordered sets will be used: [3, 7, 10], [11, 1, 2, 3, 6, 7], and [10, 11, 1, 3, 6, 7]. Although there are a number of procedures that can be used, the following one is preferred. The first step is to determine the cardinal intervals between the integers of the prime-ordered sets; see Figure 45-4a, b, and c. Because all source sets begin with the integer 0, we can transpose the prime-ordered sets by projecting integers (above 0) that have the same cardinal intervals between adjacent integers; see Figure 45-4d, e, and f. A step-by-step demonstration of the procedure

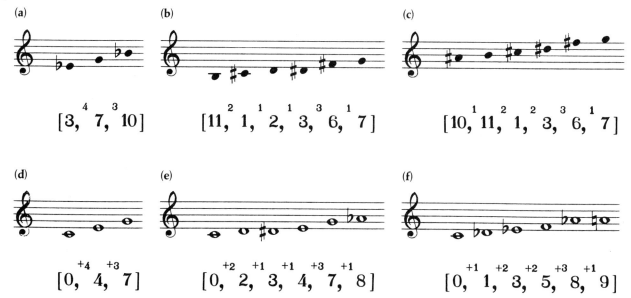

using the prime-ordered set [11, 1, 2, 3, 6, 7] is shown in Figure 45-5. As demonstrated there, the integers above 0 are determined by adding each successive cardinal interval to the sum of the previous ones.

45-5

$$[11, \overset{2}{1,} \overset{1}{2,} \overset{1}{3,} \overset{3}{6,} \overset{1}{7}]$$

(0 + 2 = 2)

0, 2

(2 + 1 = 3)

0, 2, 3

(3 + 1 = 4)

0, 2, 3, 4

(4 + 3 = 7)

0, 2, 3, 4, 7

(7 + 1 = 8)

[0, 2, 3, 4, 7, 8]

The pc set resulting from the transposition of a prime-ordered set to 0 cannot be regarded as a discrete set, because its pitch-class content is different from the pitch-class content of the original musical shape (the melody or chord). A prime-ordered set that already has 0 as its first integer obviously does not need to be transposed. A set of this nature remains a discrete set.

You should discontinue transposing prime-ordered sets to 0 as an aid in determining source sets as soon as you are able.

What is the rationale for accepting the concept of a source set and its complement?

Accepting the concept of a source set and its complement set requires the exercise of an argument that is supported in part by a rationale related to the way we read music. For us to accept the concept as reasonable, we must understand the conventions that have developed concerning how we read music as a process associated with performance and how we read music as a process associated with nomenclature and analytical comparisons.

How do the conventions associated with music reading differ?

When we read a notated melody during performance, we read from left to right without concern for ascending or descending order. When we read the notation of simultaneously sounding pitches, we regard them as a single entity without concern for ascending or descending order. However, for the purpose of spelling or identifying collections of pitches, we read *successions of pitches*—such as scales and pc sets—from left to right in ascending order, and we read *simultaneously sounding collections*—such as chords—from bottom to top. Thus, when we read for the purpose of identifying pitches, we read in ascending order.

How do reading conventions relate to the logic of design?

Let us begin with some examples. If you were asked to describe (read) the diagram shown in Figure 45-6, you would probably express the idea that dashed lines either project from, pass through, or converge on a point represented by the small oval. Because reading the diagram does not involve reading words or musical notation, you are not hampered by any conventions; you may simply read the diagram in terms of the basic logic of its visual appearance.

45-6

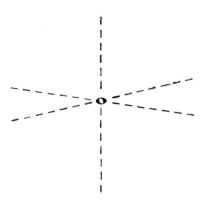

If you were to read the pitch collections in Figure 45-7 in the manner that music is performed, you would read collection a as "G, E flat, C," collection c as "C, E flat, G," collection d as "F, A, C," and collection f as "C, A, F." You would read collections b and e as simultaneously sounding pitches without respect to ordering. On the other hand, if you were to read the collections in Figure 45-7 for the purpose of spelling or identifying them *as pitch collections*, you would read collections a, b, and c as "C, E flat, G," and collections d, e, and f as "F, A, C."

45-7

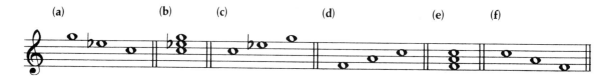

Now, visualize the six collections of Figure 45-7 as superimposed on the dashed lines (Figure 45-8). The pitch C would be a point (pitch) common to all six lines (collections) and the point from which the other pitches *project*. If we were to read the intervallic relationships projecting outward from the pitch C, we would read each of the collections as "zero, three, seven," that is, as [0, 3, 7]. See Figure 45-9.

45-8

45-9

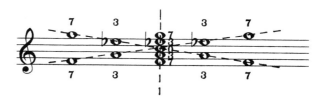

How do we reconcile the logic of design with the established convention for spelling and identification?

For the purpose of spelling and identification, it is conventional to read both successions of pitches and simultaneously sounding pitches in ascending order. Any collection of intervallic relationships that is expected to satisfy the second characteristic condition of a source set must read in ascending order from 0 (zero). Therefore, our mode of reading the pitches in Figure 45-9 would not suffice except in the case of C, E flat, G. We cannot read downward from C—that is, C, A, F; if we are to retain the established convention, we must read the collection as F, A, C. F, A, C, which is the prime-ordered set [5, 9, 0], yields the set [0, 4, 7] when transposed to 0 (zero).

In terms of what is required of a source set, [0, 4, 7] conforms to the first characteristic condition but not to the second one. Reading from left to right in ascending order from 0 (Figure 45-10a), we find intervallic relationships between the adjacent integers expressed in cardinal nomenclature as 4 and 3. If, however, we read from right to left in descending order from the integer 7 (Figure 45-10b), we find the succession of intervallic relationships to be 3

45-10

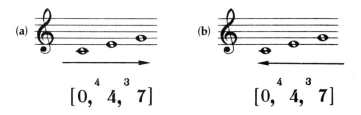

and 4. By projecting this succession of intervallic relationships in ascending order from 0 (Figure 45-11), we have the source set [0, 3, 7]. The set [0, 4, 7] is the complement set of the source set [0, 3, 7].

45-11

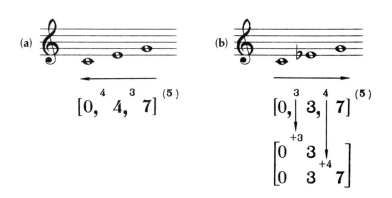

If a prime-ordered set is transposed to 0 and only one larger or largest interval is formed by its adjacent integers, it is either a source set or a complement set. If the smaller (smallest) interval(s) occur(s) nearest the first integer (Figure 45-12a), the set is a source set. If, on the other hand, the smaller (smallest) interval(s) occur(s) nearest the last integer (Figure 45-12b), the set is the complement of a source set. The source set of a collection known to be a complement set can be determined by projecting integers (above 0) that have the cardinal intervals between the adjacent integers, which are found by reading the intervals of the

45-12

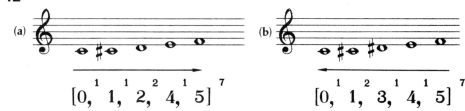

complement set inversely; that is, from right to left (Figure 45-13). Except for reading the intervals inversely, Figure 45-13 illustrates the same basic process used in Figure 45-5.

45-13

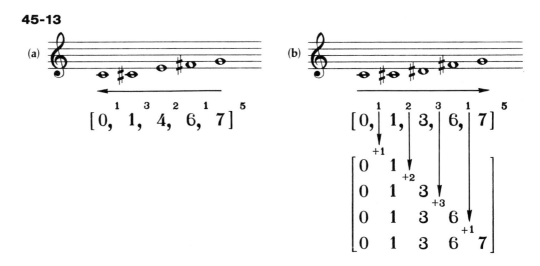

How do we order a transposed set having *two* largest intervals formed by two different sets of adjacent integers?

When a prime-ordered set with *two* largest intervals between adjacent integers is perceived not to be a source set when transposed to 0, we cannot assume that an inverse reading from the last integer will yield an arrangement of intervallic relationships that produce a source set. We must also read inversely from the lower integer of the other largest interval to determine which integer is nearer to where the smaller intervals occur. Refer to Figure 45-14. The intervals formed by reading from the last integer of the transposed set yield the intervallic arrangement 1, 1, 2, 3, 1, 1 (part a). The intervals formed by reading inversely from the lower integer (integer 2) of the *other* largest interval yields the arrangement 1, 1, 3, 1, 1, 2 (part b). The series 1, 1, 2, 3, 1, 1 provides the intervallic arrangement needed to conform to the second characteristic

45-14

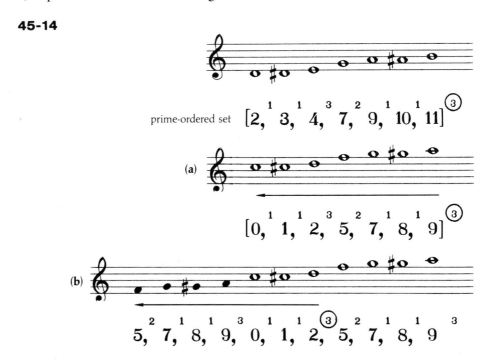

condition of a source set. The source set, therefore, can be determined by projecting the series 1, 1, 2, 3, 1, 1 in ascending order from 0 (Figure 45-15). Thus the source set of the prime-ordered set [2, 3, 4, 7, 9, 10, 11] is [0, 1, 2, 4, 7, 8, 9]. When transposed to 0, the prime-ordered set [2, 3, 4, 7, 9, 10, 11] forms the complement set [0, 1, 2, 5, 7, 8, 9].

Now refer to Figure 45-16. The intervals formed by reading inversely from the last integer of the transposed set yield the intervallic arrangement 1, 3, 1, 1, 2, 1 (part a). The

45-15

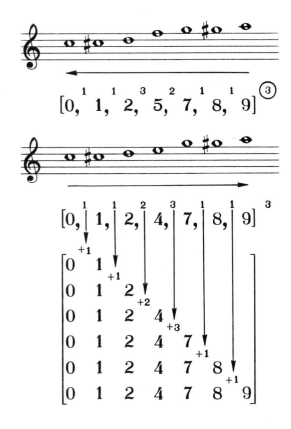

45-16

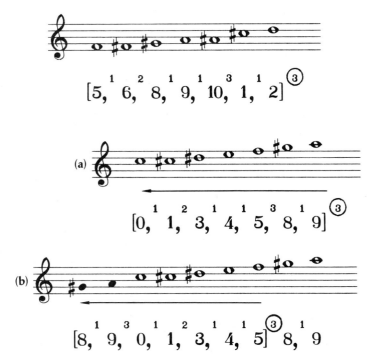

intervals formed by reading inversely from the lower integer (integer 5) of the *other* largest interval yield the arrangement 1, 1, 2, 1, 3, 1 (part b). The series 1, 1, 2, 1, 3, 1 provides the intervallic arrangement needed to conform to the second characteristic condition of a source set. The source set, therefore, can be determined by projecting the intervallic series 1, 1, 2, 1, 3, 1 in ascending order from 0 (Figure 45-17). Thus the source set of the prime-ordered set [5, 6, 8, 9, 10, 1, 2] is [0, 1, 2, 4, 5, 8, 9]. The inverse reading from part b of Figure 45-14, when projected from 0, forms the complement set [0, 1, 2, 5, 6, 7, 9].

When you have become more familiar with discrete sets and source sets, you will be able to reduce one to the other without transposing.

45-17

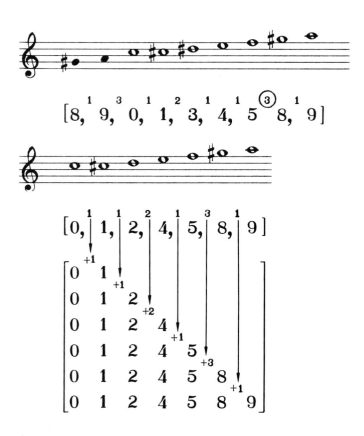

How can we determine a source set without transposing a prime-ordered set to 0 (zero)?

You may have noticed already that there really is no need to transpose a prime-ordered set to 0 (zero) before determining the source set. The intervallic relationships formed by the adjacent integers of a prime-ordered set are obviously the same as those of the same set transposed to 0.

To demonstrate a simple method for determining the source set of a prime-ordered set without using an intervening transposition to 0, we will use the prime ordered set [5, 6, 8, 9, 10, 1, 2]. Refer to Figure 45-18. The intervallic relationships formed by the adjacent integers, in ascending order from integer 5, read 1, 2, 1, 1, 3, 1 (part a). You may or may not perceive that this arrangement will not produce a source set if projected from 0. If you are sure it does not or simply suspect it does not, you must then move on to the next steps in the procedure.

45-18

The arrangement of intervallic relationships is 1, 3, 1, 1, 2, 1 when we read inversely from the last integer of the set (part b). Reading inversely from integer 10 (part c), the arrangement is 1, 1, 2, 1, 3, 1. Of the three arrangements of intervallic relationships produced, the arrangement 1, 1, 2, 1, 3, 1 best satisfies the second characteristic condition of a source set. When projected from 0, the series produces the source set [0, 1, 2, 4, 5, 8, 9] (Figure 45-19a). The complement set [0, 1, 3, 4, 5, 8, 9] is the prime-ordered set transposed to 0 (Figure 45-19b). **W166–173**

45-19

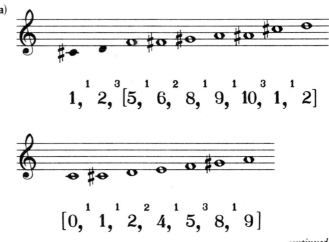

continued

45-19, *continued*

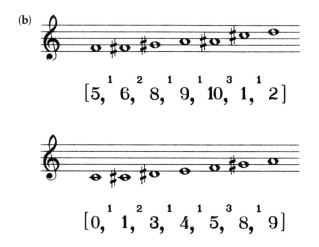

(b)

$$[5, \overset{1}{6}, \overset{2}{8}, \overset{1}{9}, \overset{1}{10}, \overset{3}{1}, \overset{1}{2}]$$

$$[0, \overset{1}{1}, \overset{2}{3}, \overset{1}{4}, \overset{1}{5}, \overset{3}{8}, \overset{1}{9}]$$

**MINI
PROJECT
19**

Using the pitch content of a five-member, prime-ordered set as your basic pitch material, compose a melody for your own instrument or voice (provide a text for the voice). The melody should be structured in the following manner:

1. Begin by using the pitch material of the prime-ordered set.

2. Provide tonal contrast by using a discrete complement set that utilizes one of the five pitches of the prime-ordered set as the first pitch member; see Figure 45-20.

45-20

$$[7, 8, 9, 0, 2]$$

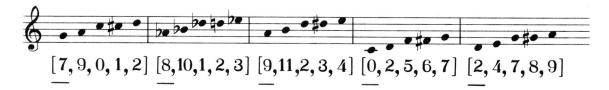

$$[7, 9, 0, 1, 2] \quad [8,10,1,2,3] \quad [9,11,2,3,4] \quad [0,2,5,6,7] \quad [2,4,7,8,9]$$

3. Conclude the melody with a return to the pitch content of the prime-ordered set.

When constructing the melody, remember that many mappings, projections, and modifications of the basic melodic shape(s) are possible; see Figure 45-21. The contrast provided by the complement set serves a function similar to that of the dominant triad in a I V I structure or a neighboring/passing chord between two tonic triads. The strength of the contrast will depend on the number of pitches common to each set.

Your notation should include all of the qualifying markings required to convey the expressive intent of the melody.

45-21

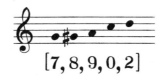

$[7, 8, 9, 0, 2]$

46 Generating Pitch Materials from Chordal and Melodic Structures

How is a chordal structure or melodic shape a "bountiful limitation"?

Considering the prospect of generating a musicwork out of a single chordal structure or melodic shape, we might have some concern for our ability to produce a sufficient number and variety of pitch materials and pitch relationships. An initial reaction to such a seemingly limited resource, for example, might be to believe that the musicwork would suffer from a paucity of pitch materials and pitch relationships. Actually, the amount of pitch material in the two-, three-, four-, and five-member pitch collections we can generate from the melodic configuration in Figure 46-1 represents what can only be described paradoxically as a bountiful limitation when we examine it.

46-1

Before we can use the resources of the source set to which the melodic shape in Figure 46-1 would reduce, we need to consider the variety of possible sonorous voicings within the five-member discrete set; see Figure 46-2. The various voicings of the five-member collection in Figure 46-2 demonstrate but a few of the many distinct sonorous qualities contained in the discrete pc set produced from the melodic configuration. The total number of possible voicings would be in the hundreds.

It must be emphasized that these hundreds of voicings are of only one set of distinct pitch classes of a single discrete set. Adding to this the number of sonorities that could be

46-2

permuted from the two-, three-, and four-member subsets we can extract from a five-member discrete set, the number of possibilities is staggering.

A total count of the many distinct sonorous voicings of the chordal structure *plus* the countless number of melodic shapes that also could be generated from this single discrete set would require an extremely complicated and, for our purpose, pointless permutation involving differing registers, pitch repetitions, and pitch deletions. Because of this, we will make no attempt to go beyond this one brief acknowledgment of the magnitude of the possibilities. The permuting we do here presents only the available two-, three-, four-, and five-member source sets, their complements, and the eleven transpositions of each that can be generated from one discrete set.

What five-member sets are available?

All of the distinct voicings shown in Figure 46-2a and b are reducible to the prime-ordered set [2, 4, 5, 9, 10], which reduces to the source set [0, 1, 3, 7, 8]. See Figure 46-3. The complement set [0, 2, 3, 7, 8] is a transposition of the prime-ordered set to 0. (Remember that the adjacent intervallic relationships of the prime-ordered set are read inversely from the integer 5 to produce the source set.) With these two sets—the source set and its complement—and their respective 11 transpositions, 24 five-member sets are available from which to produce sonorous voicings of chordal structures and melodic shapes.

46-3

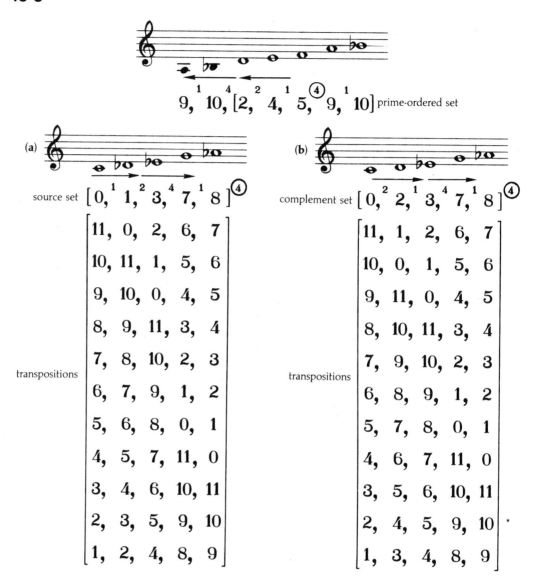

What four-member sets are available?

It is possible to extract five separate and distinct prime-ordered sets having four members each; see Figure 46-4a. In part b of that figure the five prime-ordered sets are reduced to the appropriate source sets. The possible complement sets are shown in part c. The complement set [0, 4, 6, 7] results from transposing the set [10, 2, 4, 5] to 0. The set [10, 2, 4, 5] is the one extracted discrete set whose adjacent intervallic relationships must be read inversely from the integer 5 to produce a source set. Thus we have a total of 9 distinct four-member sets (5 source sets and 4 complement sets) plus the 11 transpositions of each from which to produce sonorous voicings of chordal structures and melodic shapes. The total number of possible four-member discrete sets is 108.

The prime-ordered set [4, 5, 9, 10], being isometric, has no complement set. The ascending, numerically ordered set [2, 5, 9, 10] shown as the prime-ordered set [9, 10, 2, 5] in Figure 46-4 produces the same source set when the adjacent intervallic relationships are read in either ascending order from the integer 9 or in descending order from the integer 10.

46-4

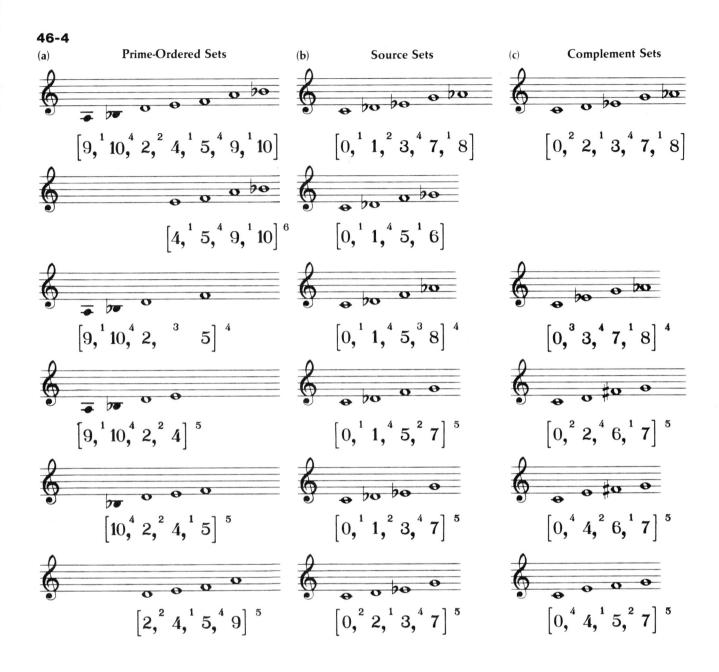

(a) Prime-Ordered Sets

(b) Source Sets

(c) Complement Sets

What three-member sets are available?

Refer to Figure 46-5. We are able to extract 10 separate and distinct prime-ordered sets having three members each. However, we find that the ten prime-ordered sets reduce to only 6 different source sets. (Within the 10 source sets there are 3 [0, 1, 5] sets, 2 [0, 1, 6] sets, and 2 [0, 3, 7] sets.) In reducing the prime-ordered sets to source sets, five of the reductions require reading the adjacent intervallic relationships of the prime-ordered sets inversely. When these 6 prime-ordered sets are transposed to 0, they produce 6 separate and distinct complement sets. With these 12 discrete sets (6 source sets and 6 complement sets) plus the 11 transpositions of each, a total of 144 distinct three-member sets are available for producing sonorous voicings of chordal structures and melodic shapes.

46-5

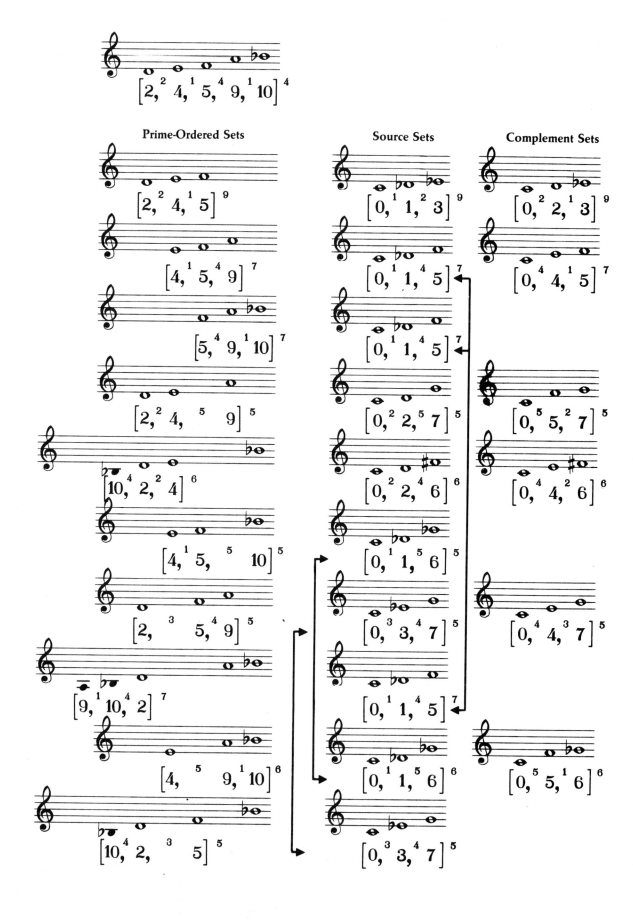

What two-member sets are available?

Figure 46-6 shows the 10 separate and distinct two-member prime-ordered sets. In reducing the prime-ordered sets to their respective source sets, we find that there are 2 [0, 1] sets, 2 [0, 4] sets, and 3 [0, 5] sets. Thus there are 6 distinct two-member source sets. Six is the maximum number of two-member source sets because there are only 6 interval classes; an interval class and a two-member source set, for all practical purposes, are the same thing. There are 72 available two-member sets from which to produce harmonic or melodic fragments, representing the 6 distinct source sets plus the 11 transpositions of each.

If you wonder why there are no complement sets for the two-member source sets, consider the fact that there are no other combinations of two pitches that can yield new pitch combinations. A re-examination of the complement sets having five, four, and three pitch-class members will reveal that each one contains a set of pitch relationships not represented by any of the source sets or their transpositions. Though two-member source sets and interval classes are practically the same, they are different in what they denote. Regardless of the fact that a source set represents a unique intervallic relationship, when it is used as a discrete set in a musicwork, it must be regarded as a set of pitch classes rather than as an interval class.

46-6

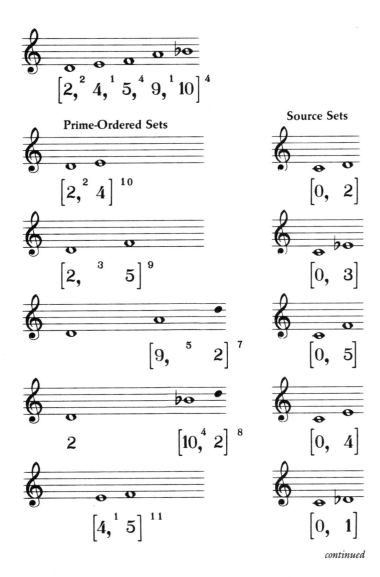

continued

46-6, *continued*

So how many discrete sets can be generated from the prime-ordered set [2, 4, 5, 9, 10]?

Considering the 72 two-member sets, the 144 three-member sets, the 108 four-member sets, and the 24 five-member sets, 348 separate and individually discrete sets can be generated from the prime-ordered set [2, 4, 5, 9, 10]. **W174–177**

Can a segment of the diatonic system be treated as a discrete pitch-class set?

When pitch-class sets are discussed, we are inclined to think in terms of nondiatonic pitch collections. We generally fail to consider segments of the diatonic system or pitch collections extracted from the natural diatonic system or its transpositions as collections to be described in terms of pitch-class sets. Any pitch collection can be identified in pitch-class-set nomenclature. It follows that any segment of the diatonic system or pitch collection extracted from any of its versions can be identified as a pitch-class set when it is appropriate to do so. The prime-ordered set for any octave segment of the natural diatonic system is [11, 0, 2, 4, 5, 7, 9]—an ordering that is coincidental with the segment of the natural diatonic system identified as the Locrian scale. The source set of this collection and any of its transpositions is [0, 1, 3, 5, 6, 8, 10].

When is pitch-class-set nomenclature appropriate for describing segments or collections from the diatonic system?

Though it would be possible to use pitch-class-set nomenclature as descriptors for any music produced from the pitch resources of the diatonic system, it would be pointless to do so with most music produced before the twentieth century. Pre-twentieth-century music, for the most part, is amply described by an existing nomenclature that is in accord with the describable sonic structures employed by pre-twentieth-century composers. Some musical examples, however, primarily in musicworks of the late nineteenth century, contain ambiguities that are better explained in terms of pitch-class sets. For example, some of the configurations found in Chopin's etudes for piano and in the works of Wagner lend themselves to pitch-class-set nomenclature.

In much of the twentieth-century music that utilizes the pitch content of the natural or transposed diatonic system, we seldom find tertian chordal structures or other manifestations of an established principle of organization related to the diatonic system (such as tonic-dominant tonality). When we do find tertian chordal structures, they are seldom from the same version of the diatonic system and they often result in the formation of aggregate sets that are nondiatonic. Most often, we find chordal structures and melodic shapes that cannot be adequately described in tertian nomenclature.

What are some twentieth-century musicworks we can consider in terms of pc-set nomenclature?

Scattered among the six books of the *Mikrokosmos* (1926–1937) of Béla Bartók are a number of musical examples that are best described in terms of pitch-class sets. These are appropriate examples for use as short analytical problems. A sophisticated example is found in the *Dance of the Coachmen* from Stravinsky's ballet *Petrouchka*. The pitch-class content of the first 56 measures of the dance forms the discrete set [8, 9, 11, 1, 2, 4, 6], which is a segment of a transposition of the diatonic system. For the first 35 of the 56 measures, various combinations of woodwinds, brass, and timpani reiterate the configuration in Figure 46-7, which forms the

46-7

Dance of the Coachmen from *Petrouchka*

Stravinsky

subset [2, 4, 6, 9]. Periodically the strings play chordal structures in quarter-notes using that subset (Figure 46-8). Woven into this repetitious texture, either along with the strings or separately, are eight melodic shapes (Figure 46-9). The aggregate pitch-class content of these melodic shapes forms the discrete set [8, 9, 11, 1, 2, 4, 6] (Figure 46-10).

46-8

Dance of the Coachmen from *Petrouchka*

Stravinsky

46-9

Dance of the Coachmen from *Petrouchka*

Stravinsky

1. Vlns. 1, 2 and Vcl.

2. Vlns. 1, 2 and Vcl.

3. Vlns. 1, 2

4. All strings

5. Tbns.

6. Horns

7. All strings

8. Horns

46-10

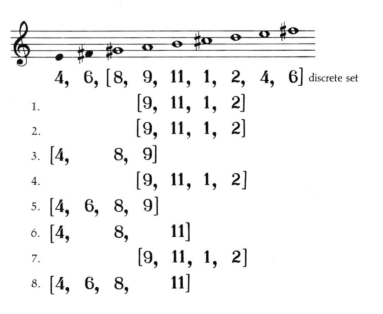

4, 6, [8, 9, 11, 1, 2, 4, 6] discrete set

1.   [9, 11, 1, 2]

2.   [9, 11, 1, 2]

3. [4,   8, 9]

4.   [9, 11, 1, 2]

5. [4, 6, 8, 9]

6. [4,   8,   11]

7.   [9, 11, 1, 2]

8. [4, 6, 8,   11]

An earlier example from music of the late nineteenth century, the second movement of Debussy's String Quartet Opus 10, has *melodic* structures that are best understood in terms of discrete sets and subsets. In the first 18 measures of the movement (14 of which are shown in Figure 46-11), the aggregate pitch-class content forms the discrete set [5, 6, 7, 8, 10, 11, 0, 2]. The first violin weaves a melody that uses the subset [5, 6, 7, 8, 11, 0, 2]. The second violin

46-11

46-11, *continued*

46-12

reiterates a brief melodic shape using the subset [11, 0, 2, 5]. The viola reiterates a more extended configuration using the subset [2, 5, 6, 7, 8, 10]. The 'cello reiterates a pitch configuration using the subset [7, 8, 11, 2]. The relationship of the four subsets to the discrete set is shown in Figure 46-12.

One last example, which uses tertian triads from differing versions of the diatonic system, is taken from Benjamin Britten's *Les Illuminations,* a musicwork for voice and string orchestra. Several of the songs in this musicwork utilize major triads in schematic relationships that are best described in pitch-class-set nomenclature. In the opening song, *Fanfare,* the aggregate pitch-class content forms the discrete set [10, 11, 0, 1, 2, 4, 5, 7, 8]. Throughout the first 32 measures, the first violins, using the E-major triad (subset [4, 8, 11]), alternate fanfarelike melodies with the violas, using the B-flat-major triad (subset [10, 2, 5]). This alternating occurs approximately thirteen times and takes place over an E to F trill, [4, 5], in the lower strings and a divisi tremolo of the alternating chords in the second violins. During this, the voice has one brief line using the E-minor triad (subset [4, 7, 11]). In measure 31, the C Mm⁷ chord (subset [10, 0, 4, 7]) is introduced over a C to D♭ trill [1, 2]. From measure 33 to the end, the solo first violin and accompanying arpeggiated harmonics use only the subset [10, 0, 4, 7]. Measures 24 through 35 are shown in Figure 46-13. The relationship of the subsets to the aggregate discrete set is shown in Figure 46-14.

46-13   *Les Illuminations, Op. 18, I. Fanfare*

Benjamin Britten

46-14

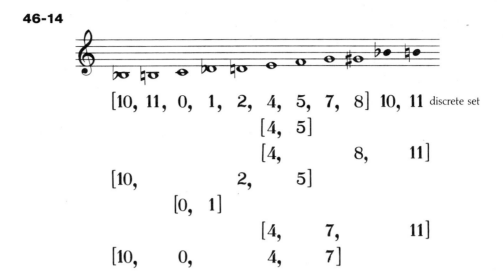

[10, 11, 0, 1, 2, 4, 5, 7, 8] 10, 11 discrete set

                      [4,   5]

                      [4,   8,   11]

[10,   2,   5]

          [0,   1]

                      [4,   7,   11]

[10,   0,   4,   7]

MINI PROJECT 20

Produce a brief homophonic musicwork for three instruments using the three-member subsets available from two discrete five-member pc sets. The first pc set can be any five-member prime-ordered set you select. The other set must be either a transposition of the original prime-ordered set or a transposition of its complement.

Discovery through trial and error is the best means of selecting the three-member susbsets you will use in the musicwork. Base your selection on what you believe produces the sonorous relationships you desire. All other aspects of the musicwork (expressive intent, choice of instruments, dynamics, articulation) should be part of your preparations and completion of the project.

Figure 46-15 is an example of what might be done for this mini project. The musical example (part c) is fashioned from the original discrete set [2, 4, 5, 9, 10] (part a) and from [7, 9, 10, 2, 3] (part b).

46-15

47 Interval-Class Indices

Is there a basis for determining the relatedness of pc sets?

After we have extracted the available three- and four-member subsets from the prime-ordered set [2, 4, 5, 9, 10] (Figures 46-4 and 46-5) and transposed each subset to 0 (zero), we must look for similarities and differences among the subsets with the same number of members. Which of the various similarities and differences can we compare and measure?

We must first eliminate the similarities and differences that cannot be measured objectively. For example, the similarities and differences of *quality* in the voicings of the sonorous chordal structure in Figure 46-2 do not relate to either the pitch-class or interval-class content of the prime-ordered set [2, 4, 5, 9, 10]. Matters of pitch placement, which result in an almost endless number of voicings, are further subjected to the inflective natures of such things as tone quality and amplitude. Such qualities, though not at all subtle, are difficult if not impossible to measure; they are best left to aesthetic judgment. This leaves one objective criterion upon which to establish a measurable comparison: the interval-class content of the subsets being compared.

What is an interval-class index?

An **interval-class index** (plural, *indices*) is a set of integers that indicates how many members of each interval class are contained in a source set, complement set, or subset when each pitch-class member is related to every other pitch-class member of the set. The interval-class index, therefore, serves as the instrument by which the interval-class content of source sets and complement sets can be compared. Sets having like numbers of members can be examined to determine the distribution of interval classes and to determine the degree of relatedness or unrelatedness of different sets.

In chapter 2, it was shown that one advantage of using the pitch class 0 (pc 0) as the first integer of integer nomenclature is that it permits us to interpret the pitch-class integer as an intervallic relationship (expressed in cardinal nomenclature) above the pc 0. Thus, as shown in Figure 47-1, the source set [0, 1, 3, 7, 8] can be regarded as a projection of intervals above 0 (zero) as well as a set of pitch classes. For example, the integer 1 is read as "interval 1 (i1) above the pc 0." Integer 3 is read as "interval 3 (i3) above the pc 0." Integers 7 and 8 are read as "interval 7 (i7) and interval 8 (i8), respectively, above the pc 0."

47-1

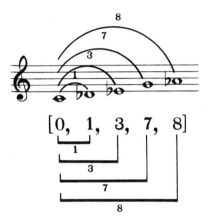

The integers 1, 3, 7, and 8 now represent the intervallic relationships above the pc 0. To find the intervallic relationships above the second integer of the source set (pc 1), we need simply to subtract 1 from the remaining integers—3, 7, and 8—to obtain the intervallic relationships 2, 6, and 7 (Figure 47-2). This process is continued until all of the intervallic

47-2

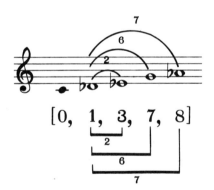

relationships are found: we subtract 2 from integers 6 and 7 to obtain integers 4 and 5, and subtract 4 from 5 to obtain integer 1, the final intervallic relationship (Figure 47-3). The composite of the intervallic relationships in Figures 47-2 and 47-3 is shown in Figure 47-4.

47-3

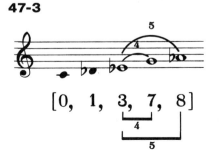

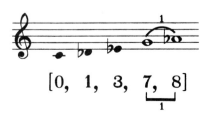

47-4

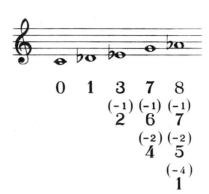

0   1   3   7   8
          (-1) (-1) (-1)
           2   6   7
               (-2) (-2)
                4   5
                   (-4)
                    1

We have now determined all of the available intervallic relationships projecting in ascending order above each of the first four integers of the source set [0, 1, 3, 7, 8]. What remains to be done is to put these intervallic relationships into an **interval-class index**. From the interval-class index we can determine the distribution of interval classes within the index. By an arbitrary standard of comparison, we can also determine the relatedness of two pc sets that have the same number of members.

In Figure 47-5 we see the results of the calculations from Figure 46-4 and the corresponding interval-class index. Among the intervallic relationships shown are two 7's, which are converted to the ic 5, and one 8, which is converted to the ic 4. The ic index is enclosed in parentheses. The numerals 1, 2, 3, 4, 5, and 6 appear above the ic index (*this time only*) to identify the six interval classes. The ic index of the source set [0, 1, 3, 7, 8] is (2 1 1 2 3 1).

47-5

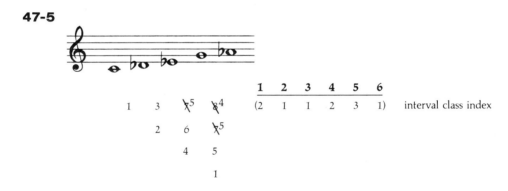

The ic index (2 1 1 2 3 1), indicates that the source set [0, 1, 3, 7, 8] contains two ic 1, one ic 2, one ic 3, two ic 4, three ic 5, and one ic 6. An ic index always contains six integers, each representing the number of interval classes of a set. When a particular interval class is absent, the interval class is represented by 0. Thus the source set [0, 3] would have an ic index of (0 0 1 0 0 0).

What are the ic indices of the four-member subsets (see Figure 46-4) **extracted from the source set [0, 1, 3, 7, 8]?**

The five four-member subsets extracted from the source set [0, 1, 3, 7, 8] are presented in Figure 47-6a along with the integers representing the intervallic relationships projected in ascending order from each of the first three integers of each set. The resultant ic indices of the five subsets are given (part b). Note that the index for subset [0, 1, 3, 7] indicates an even distribution of interval classes. The ic indices of complement sets are not given, because the ic index of a complement set is the same as that of its source set. The obvious differences between source sets and their complements appear with respect to other, generally subjective criteria.

47-6

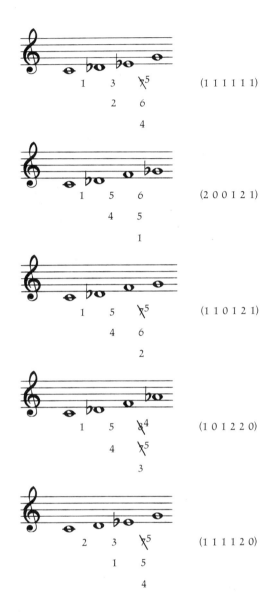

What are the indices of the three-member subset (see Figure 46-5) extracted from the source set [0, 1, 3, 7, 8]?

Figure 47-7 presents the six three-member subsets extracted from the source set [0, 1, 3, 7, 8] and the integers that represent the intervallic relationships in ascending order from the first two integers of each subset. The resultant ic index is given for each subset. Note that it is impossible to have an even distribution of interval classes with fewer than four pitch classes.

47-7

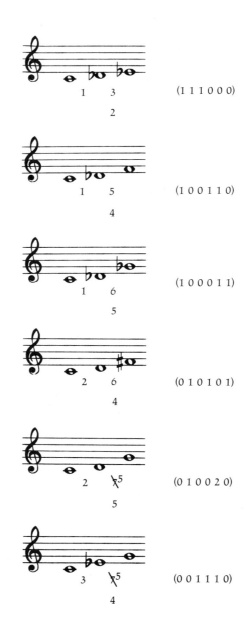

How is the ic index used for determining the relatedness of source sets and subsets?

The ic index cannot be used for comparison of anything but the interval-class content of sets. This kind of comparison is an objective measurement; it is not subjective. We will consider the following as some standard guidelines:

1. Sets with identical ic indices will be considered identical.

2. Sets with four interval classes in common in their ic indices will be considered related (would not apply to two-member sets).

3. Sets with three interval classes in common in their ic indices will be considered relatively unrelated.

4. Sets with less than three interval classes in common will be considered unrelated.

Examples of these categories are shown in Figure 47-8.

47-8

	Identical	Related	Relatively unrelated	Unrelated
1	(2 1 2 3 2 0)	(4 3 4 5 4 1)	(4 4 4 3 4 2)	(2 5 4 3 6 1)
2	(2 1 2 3 2 0)	(4 3 4 4 4 2)	(4 3 4 5 4 1)	(4 4 4 3 4 2)
	* * * * * *	* * * *	* * *	* *
				(3 4 3 5 4 2)
				(3 3 6 3 3 3)
				*
				(3 3 5 4 4 2)
				(2 6 2 6 2 3)

*indicates an interval class in common.

How do the ic indices of the four-member subsets extracted from the source set [0, 1, 3, 7, 8] compare?

Column a in Figure 47-9 lists the five ic indices representing the five different four-member subsets that can be extracted from the source set [0, 1, 3, 7, 8]. By comparing the first ic index with the other four, the second ic index with the remaining three, the third with the remaining two, and the fourth with the last one, we make the ten possible comparisons of the ic indices from this collection of four-member subsets. Column b presents the pairs that indicate the subsets are related. Column c lists the pairs that indicate the subsets are unrelated.

47-9

(a)	(b)	(c)
1 (1 1 1 1 1 1)	1 (1 1 1 1 1 1)	1 (1 1 1 1 1 1)
2 (2 0 0 1 2 1)	3 (1 1 0 1 2 1)	2 (2 0 0 1 2 1)
3 (1 1 0 1 2 1)	* * * *	* *
4 (1 0 1 2 2 0)	1 (1 1 1 1 1 1)	1 (1 1 1 1 1 1)
5 (1 1 1 1 2 0)	5 (1 1 1 1 2 0)	4 (1 0 1 2 2 0)
	* * * *	* *
	2 (2 0 0 1 2 1)	2 (2 0 0 1 2 1)
	3 (1 1 0 1 2 1)	4 (1 0 1 2 2 0)
	* * * *	* *
	3 (1 1 0 1 2 1)	2 (2 0 0 1 2 1)
	5 (1 1 1 1 2 0)	5 (1 1 1 1 2 0)
	* * * *	* *
	4 (1 0 1 2 2 0)	3 (1 1 0 1 2 1)
	5 (1 1 1 1 2 0)	4 (1 0 1 2 2 0)
	* * * *	* *

*indicates an interval class in common.

How do the ic indices of the three-member subsets extracted from the source set [0, 1, 3, 7, 8] compare?

Column a of Figure 47-10 lists the six ic indices representing the six three-member subsets that can be extracted from the source set [0, 1, 3, 7, 8]. Because the three-member subsets contain but three interval classes, the possibilities for identical and related sets are limited. In comparing the indices of the three-member subsets in the manner used for four-member subsets, we find only two pairs of indices that can be considered related. All of the remaining subsets would better be considered unrelated. The comparisons are shown in columns b and c.

47-10

(a)		(c)	
1 (1 1 1 0 0 0)	1 (1 1 1 0 0 0)	2 (1 0 0 1 1 0)	
2 (1 0 0 1 1 0)	5 (0 1 0 0 2 0)	5 (0 1 0 0 2 0)	
3 (1 0 0 0 1 1)	4 (0 1 0 1 0 1)	3 (1 0 0 0 1 1)	
4 (0 1 0 1 0 1)	5 (0 1 0 0 2 0)	4 (0 1 0 1 0 1)	
5 (0 1 0 0 2 0)	1 (1 1 1 0 0 0)	3 (1 0 0 0 1 1)	
6 (0 0 1 1 1 0)	2 (1 0 0 1 1 0)	5 (0 1 0 0 2 0)	
	1 (1 1 1 0 0 0)	3 (1 0 0 0 1 1)	
(b)	3 (1 0 0 0 1 1)	6 (0 0 1 1 1 0)	
2 (1 0 0 1 1 0)	1 (1 1 1 0 0 0)	4 (0 1 0 1 0 1)	
3 (1 0 0 0 1 1)	4 (0 1 0 1 0 1)	6 (0 0 1 1 1 0)	
2 (1 0 0 1 1 0)	1 (1 1 1 0 0 0)	5 (0 1 0 0 2 0)	
6 (0 0 1 1 1 0)	6 (0 0 1 1 1 0)	6 (0 0 1 1 1 0)	
	2 (1 0 0 1 1 0)		
	4 (0 1 0 1 0 1)		

*indicates an interval class in common.

How does the comparability of ic indices relate to the comparability of other quantitative measurements of sets?

We cannot assume that two pc sets with identical ic indices are identical or even related in other ways. For example, in Figure 47-11, the source sets [0, 1, 3, 7] and [0, 1, 4, 6] both have the same ic index of (1 1 1 1 1 1). Also, the quantitative differences between a source set and its complement must be recognized, even though they, too, have the same ic index.

A comparable relationship exists with words. For example, we easily recognize that the words *tone* and *note* contain the same number of the same letters. On this basis *alone*, the two words are identical. However, the order of the letters in the words is different, and this produces two words that differ in both sound and definition.

47-11

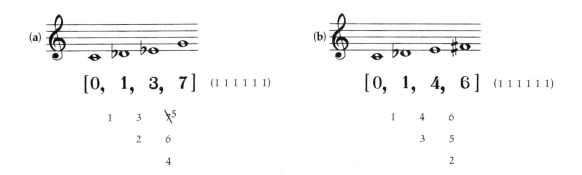

In comparing two source sets, a source set and its complement, or two complement sets, we can learn only the degree of their relatedness in interval-class content. No two sets are identical quantitatively *or* qualitatively. A **source set**, by definition, is a unique arrangement of intervallic relationships. By implication, the same is true of a complement set. A unique arrangement of intervallic relationships would necessarily result in a unique quality of sound as well.

What is the significance of an interval-class index, and what does a comparison of interval indices represent?

As was shown in chapter 46, the subsets available in a five-member source set, for example, are many. In this chapter subsets with the same number of members are regarded as having the same, related, or unrelated interval indices when compared with each other. Figure 47-11 illustrates that it is possible for two pc sets to have the same interval indices but yet differ in their pitch-class relationships and in the setup of their adjacent intervals. The two pc sets in Figure 47-11 do not sound the same. These circumstances leave us with a number of questions about the significance of an interval index and what a comparison of interval indices represents—questions that cannot be answered in objective, concrete terms. As with many other aspects of the musical art, there are no definitive answers; there are only understandings that evolve through circumspection, empathy, and experience.

Perhaps a clue to our understanding can be found in the illusive term *value* that artists use in evaluating colors. Value, we may suppose, is a subjective response to the component makeup of colors and their response to light and shadow. With all external conditions equal, the relative aesthetic compatibility of colors is determined in part by their values. If we translate the term *value* to music, we can recognize that, with all external conditions equal, the relative aesthetic compatibility of the simultaneously or successively sounding members of a pitch collection is a response to the collection's intervallic makeup. Because we deal with musical sounds within a time frame, value comparisons are a function of memory and are based on an intuitive impression of what we might call "a residual aura of sound." Such an intuitive impression is the result of a collective and comparative evaluation of our responses to expectations.   **W178–180**

How can we demonstrate the relatedness of subsets used in a musicwork by interval indices?

The first of Stravinsky's *Three Songs from William Shakespeare*, *Musick to Heare*, provides an example of four four-member subsets extracted from a six-member "parent" discrete set, [7, 8, 9, 10, 11, 0]. The first seven measures of *Musick to Heare* are shown in Figure 47-12 along with the appropriate identification of the various set forms used. What is not shown by Figure 47-12

47-12

Three Songs from William Shakespeare, I. *Music to Heare*

Igor Stravinsky

1 sounds as notated
* "parent" discrete set
** transposed parent set
‡ discrete subset
complement subset
§ source set

is the distinct possibility that the "parent" discrete set is the cumulative result of two four-member melodic configurations, the second of which is the inversion of the first (Figure 47-13). The probability that this is a factor in the basic design of the song is born out by the many repetitions of four-member pitch collections in the subsequent accompanying melodic configurations, all of which reduce to the source set [0, 1, 2, 4]; twelve of the twenty-plus configura-

47-13

from *Three Songs from William Shakespeare,* I. *Music to Heare*

Igor Stravinsky

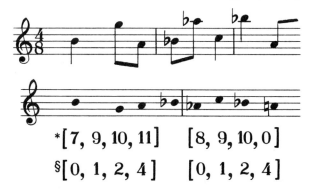

*[7, 9, 10, 11]   [8, 9, 10, 0]

§[0, 1, 2, 4]   [0, 1, 2, 4]

* discrete sets in prime order
§ source sets

tions are shown in Figure 47-14. The diatonic subsets found in the first seven measures of *Musick to Heare* are shapes that are easily extracted from the six-member source set; the two diatonic subsets do not occur again until the last six measures of the song. The relationship of the four four-member source sets to each other and to the six-member source set is shown in Figure 47-15. Our pointing out the organization of the pitch-class materials in this manner should not be construed as an analysis of the musicwork.

47-14

excerpts from *Three Songs from William Shakespeare*, I. *Music to Heare*

Igor Stravinsky

47-15

<table>
<tr><td>

MINI PROJECT 21

</td><td>

Produce a brief musicwork from a five- or seven-member discrete pc set (one not coincidental to a segment of the diatonic system) for piano solo, piano with a solo instrument or voice, or five instruments not including piano. The musicwork must be structured in a manner similar to that of Mini Project 20—that is, one means of obtaining tonal contrast will be a transposition of the prime-ordered set or a complement set whose first pitch is the same as one of the pitches of the prime-ordered set.

</td></tr>
</table>

Whichever of the three performance combinations you use, there must be at least one solo line that includes all of the pitch content of the prime-ordered set when it is in use and all of the pitch content of the contrasting set when it is in use. The accompaniment material will consist of chordal structures or configured chordal structures (such as shown in Figure 47-16) produced from the available three-member subsets (if a five-member set is used) or the available four-member subsets (if a seven-member set is used).

As always, you must carry out the precomposition "routine" to decide on your expressive intent, the function, and similar issues.

47-16

[2,4,9]   [5,9,10]   [4,5,10]

48 Spatial Cognition in Music

How are spatial cognition and acoustical phenomena related?

Space, the limited or limitless physical dimension within which all material things are contained, is another aspect of nature that becomes a factor in musical perception through various acoustical phenomena. Music, of course, does not occupy space; it is not a physical object. However, the acoustical effects of confined and unconfined space upon sound-producing waveforms are perceivable, and they provide us with an audible awareness of the nature of space.

Though music does not occupy space in the way physical objects do, the illusion that it does can be created. Such spatial connotations as the highness and lowness of pitch, the omnidirectional nature of hearing, and the resulting capacity of humans to perceive the subtle effects of an acoustical environment on the behavior of pressure waves contribute to this illusion.

In what ways are seeing and hearing similar?

Our first response to this question might be to question whether there *are* any similarities. Because the concept of space is more typically associated with seeing and because differences in the effects of seeing and hearing are so profound, we may fail to recognize the similarities in the way seeing and hearing function.

For us to perceive the location of an object visually, the object must reflect light. For us to perceive the location of an object aurally, the object must reflect pressure waves. Though we humans use vision as our principal means of spatial sensing, we use hearing for this purpose more than we realize. Some forms of animal life do not perceive visually and thus do all of their spatial sensing by means of reflected, sound-producing pressure waves.

Another area of similarity is associated with the fact that seeing and hearing both depend on vibration: seeing requires vibration at the receiving end; hearing requires vibration at the source. We receive reflected light rays into our eyes, which themselves are the vibrating physical bodies. The vibration of the eye is very slight, but it is essential to seeing. We receive reflected, sound-producing pressure waves into the ear from a vibrating source. The sense of hearing, therefore, is functionally similar to the sense of sight.

The functional similarities in hearing and seeing are not such that we are consciously aware of them. They are among the many involuntary functions of the human body that we hardly notice. A person's appreciation for the mutually supportive functions of seeing and hearing in spatial cognition is often not fully realized until one of the senses is lost or becomes impaired.

What are the spatial implications of the pitch continuum and the proximity of the sources of sound?

In the discussion of timbre in chapter 10 we pointed out that a number of frequencies are combined to form a complex waveform that is perceived as a single tone having a distinct pitch and timbre. Once we have perceived tones as intelligible information made up of frequency data, we organize this "intelligible information" into discernable patterns. In this chapter, our interest is in how the combining and separating properties of space and the sense of hearing interact to assure our clear perception of whatever homogenous combinations and heterogenous separations of patterns are important to musical coherence.

The listener cannot be expected to join together or to separate, in a perceptual sense, what the music maker has not joined or separated in accordance with the acoustical properties and behavior of sound-producing waveforms. Although individuals vary in their capacities to hear and perceive, no one can exceed the capacity of the human hearing mechanism. Before dealing with the combining and separating of patterns in time, let us first examine the simple matter of the relative homogeneity and heterogeneity of simple pitch collections.

What we want to be perceived as a homogenous sound must be made up of the same or similar tonal elements joined together by their positions in the pitch continuum and by the close proximity of their sources. For example, a **homogenous pitch collection** is one that is produced by instruments or voices of identical or similar tone qualities. The pitch members are voiced as closely as possible within the pitch continuum, and the various sound-producing waveforms emanate from sources that are in close spatial proximity to each other. The pitch collection scored for piano in Figure 48-1a would satisfy the conditions for homogeneity extremely well. Scoring the same collection for a string quartet (Figure 48-1b), woodwind quartet, or other collection of similar instruments could also produce a homogenous sound, providing the players were seated near each other.

48-1

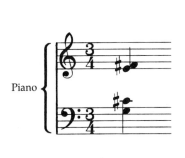

A **heterogenous collection of pitches**, on the other hand, is produced by instruments or voices of dissimilar tone qualities. Its pitch members are often voiced openly within the pitch continuum and emanate from sources that are not in close proximity to each other in space. Assigning the pitch collection used in Figure 48-1 to the players of four distinctly different instruments and also separating the players physically (Figure 48-2), would produce a heterogenous pitch collection. What is physically joined and meant to be heard as a homogenous sound will be perceived as such; what is physically separated and meant to be heard as a heterogenous collection of sounds will be perceived as such.

These, as apposing or contrasting conditions, permit all manner of variations and degrees of similarity and difference that permit us to regard a pitch collection, perceptually, as more or less homogenous than heterogenous. The manner and degree to which a pitch collection is perceived as more or less homogenous than heterogenous might be regarded as infinitely variable.

48-2

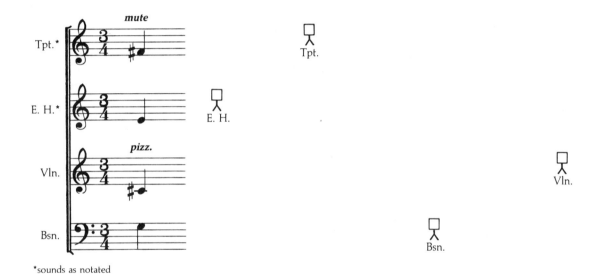

*sounds as notated

Of what concern has the physical proximity of sound sources been to composers?

Until recently, composers have shown little concern for the physical separation of sound sources. Two notable but seldom-heard exceptions are the antiphonal singing of plainsong (Gregorian chant) in the early years of the Church, and the polychoral music—also antiphonal and originating in the Church—produced in the late sixteenth and the seventeeth centuries. Early instrumental music made some use of the spatial effects of the antiphonal (polychoral) devices of the vocal conventions of the times. The more characteristic instrumental conventions were those typified by the seventeenth-century consorts (ensembles of similar instruments) of viols and recorders. The instrumental conventions were directed toward the concept of one point of focus and the homogeneity of sound, both of which culminated in the eighteenth-, nineteenth-, and very early twentieth-century orchestra, string quartet, and similar ensembles.

Though the epitome of the homogeneity of sound as an aesthetic ideal came at the very end of the nineteenth century and in the early twentieth century, the direction away from homogeneity came at about the same time. The movement toward heterogeneity as a rediscovered ideal was seen in such tendencies as: (1) the coloristic separation of sounds resulting from the increased use of instrumental combinations known for the dissimilarity of their tone qualities; (2) the increased contrast resulting from differences of texture, pitch range, dynamics, and other differentiating devices; and (3) the general search for new means of tonal organization. The last of these resulted in relationships that countered the homogenous effects of tonality as expressed in the tonic-dominant relationships of the seventeenth through the nineteenth centuries.

Until the advent of electronic recordings, spatial cognition was still confined to the acoustical limitations of the concert hall. The concert hall, in all of its varied shapes, is based principally on the concept of the megaphone; the sound source is at the small end, and the audience extends toward the large end. A well-designed hall has been the one that projects the clearest and most even distribution of sound to each member of the audience.

With the development of stereophonic sound recording, the origin of a sound source again became a factor in the nature of music and made possible the full exercise of spatial cognition as an aural function. What was conceived as a limited expression of spatial cognition and called *heterophony* by the ancient Greeks can be said to have reached its full realization during the last half of the twentieth century. A comprehensive discussion of spatial cognition is not the goal of this chapter; let us continue with those aspects of it that will help you complete the unit project that follows.

In what way is pitch a dimension of spatial cognition?

Pitch, as we have defined it, is a perceptual term for an audible frequency produced by a voice or instrument. The pitch continuum represents the entire range of audible frequencies. It extends from approximately 20 Hz (the lowest) to approximately 20,000 Hz. The pitch continuum is a frame within which the physical relationship of high and low provides one illusory dimension of spatial cognition.

The number and relationship of pitch increments within the pitch continuum are a matter of systems. The increments of *the diatonic system* form one of the most common systems. The half-step relationships of *the dodecaphonic system* form another. *The all-frequency, nonincremental continuum* of electronic music is yet another system. These three pitch systems are probably the most commonly used. However, several other systems that divide the octave into various numbers, sizes, and arrangements of pitch increments have been used.

Does the conventional stratification of pitches in voices and instruments contribute to spatial cognition?

The tessituras common to the human voice and represented by the terms *soprano, alto, tenor, baritone,* and *bass* provide a natural stratification of pitches within the pitch continuum. The tessituras of orchestral and band instruments also provide another natural stratification of pitches. *Tessitura,* generally defined as that portion of a voice's or instrument's range within which we may sing or play with the greatest ease and finest tone quality, provides the characteristics of tone and articulation that tend more to minimize the effect of high and low than to focus attention on it. Even though we may be fully aware of the natural stratification of pitch produced by the use of normal tessituras, stratification of this type contributes relatively little to our spatial cognition.

What are the expressive effects of using the extended ranges of voices and instruments as aids to spatial cognition?

We are all familiar with the physical strain that results when we stretch up or down to grasp something that is beyond our normal reach. In such cases our sense of high and low is stimulated beyond what it is when we reach for objects easily. Our sense of high and low is also stimulated when we hear an instrument or voice at the extreme ends of its range. An A-440 Hz sung by a tenor will appear as a high pitch, whereas the same A-440 Hz sung by a soprano will appear low (Figure 48-3). The tenor would be near the top of his range; the soprano would be in a very comfortable area of her range. An A-880 Hz played on a 'cello will sound high compared to the same A-880 Hz played on a violin (Figure 48-4). In contrast, the A-220 Hz scored for the trumpet in C will sound low compared to the same A-220 Hz played on the trombone (Figure 48-5).

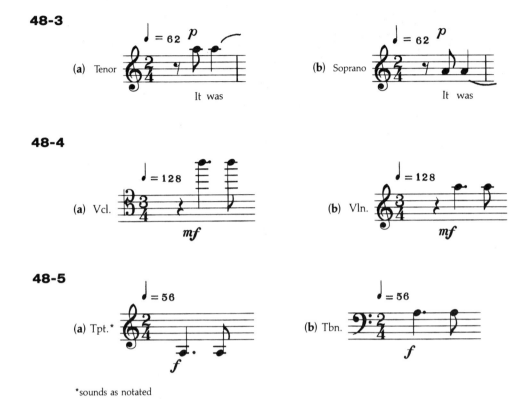

*sounds as notated

The expressive effects of high and low within the pitch continuum are best achieved when instruments and voices are used in the areas of range that give the illusion of tension or physical strain. If the trumpet part of Bach's Second *Brandenburg Concerto* were played on the violin or flute, the feeling of its being high within the pitch continuum would be greatly diminished. It would, in fact, lose the qualities that presently give it its spectacular expression.

Even though the top and bottom ranges of the human voice and some instruments convey qualities that emphasize high and low spatial dimensions, these qualities are not necessarily a physical strain or difficult to employ. The qualities that make the extended ranges of some voices and instruments appear high or low are more a matter of formant and the number, distribution, and intensity of the harmonics that make up the timbre of their sounds.

How do we describe the sensation of texture?

Texture, which is derived from the same Latin word as *textile*, originally had to do with the structure of the weave of a fabric. It is primarily associated with the sense of touch. This is born out by the adjectives we typically use to describe textures: *rough, smooth, lumpy, creamy, soft, sandy, mealy, gritty*.

The general inference to be drawn from any definition of texture is that an object or material (in this case, a musicwork) has consistency and surface characteristics (in this case, impressionable auditory differences) that permit us to differentiate between its components and the relationships they create. In translating the concept of texture from *tactile* impressions to *aural* impressions, we are once again borrowing an illusory impression of a concept from another sensory function—in this case, the sense of touch. Such borrowing of sense impressions among the various senses are common; they serve to enrich and expand our sensitivity to and understanding of sensations. "A quiet scene," "a loud color," "a smooth melodic line," and "a bright sound" are examples of descriptions of textural sensations. Such descriptors are foreign to the sense they describe, but they are nonetheless expressive.

What constitutes texture in music?

Texture in music refers to the degree of contrast and complexity associated with the rhythmic organization (the consistency) of a musicwork considered along with the shapes and relationships of its linear and chordal components (the surface characteristics). By associating rhythmic organization with the idea of textural consistency, we draw an easily perceived parallel between the effects of aural sensation and tactile sensation. A musicwork with subtle rhythmic contrasts that result in smooth (a tactile expression) differentiations in the placement of sound patterns in time produces an aural sensation we can mentally associate with the tactile sensation we experience when we touch a smooth, fine-grained surface. The bold rhythmic contrasts of a musicwork can be likened to bold contrasts in the feel of a very rough surface. Poorly conceived, erratic rhythmic contrasts result in inconsistencies of texture and mar the effect of a musicwork in the same way that poorly conceived, erratic textures mar the effects of a tactile sensation.

The surface characteristics of musicworks are as varied as the surface characteristics of physical objects. The surface characteristics of a musicwork may present a texture having such bold contrast as found, for example, between the soli violas and the hushed tremolos of the remaining strings in the opening Fanfare of Benjamin Britten's *Les Illuminations* (Figure 48-6). The sensation of spatial relief provided by the foreground of the soli violas and the back-

48-6

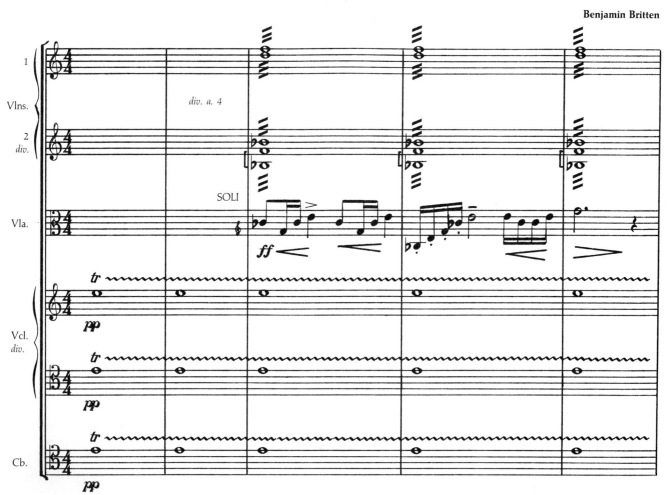

Les Illuminations, Op. 18, I. *Fanfare*

Benjamin Britten

ground of the tremolos is as pronounced as the raised letters of a bronze plaque are to our sense of touch.

The surface characteristics of a musicwork may, on the other hand, provide few and only slightly contrasting shapes, which in turn provide but the slightest sensation of relief in terms of foreground and background. A surface characteristic of this nature is demonstrated by the portion of the Gigue of Bach's fifth *English Suite* in Figure 48-7. The sixteenth-note and eighth-note patterns offer slight contrast because of their regularity. The three lines weave a rather tight fabric of sound, and because the lines compete with as well as complement each other on much the same level, there are only vague suggestions of relief.

48-7

English Suite No. 5, Gigue

J. S. Bach

What are some of the common descriptors associated with texture in music?

Some of the older adjectives conventionally used to describe musical textures are *monophonic, homophonic, polyphonic, contrapuntal, chordal,* and *polychordal.* Newer adjectives such as *thin, thick, sparse, smooth, clear, clean, pointillistic, muddy,* and *angular* have their origins in other, nonmusical forms of sensory perception. Even though such newer, nonmusical terms can be used to describe pre-twentieth-century music, the older, musical terms tell us a great deal about the music that generated them. The similarities in the approach to texture taken by most pre-twentieth-century composers permitted the use of such stereotypic terms as *homophonic, polyphonic,* and the like. It would be difficult to categorize the textures of much twentieth-century music with such limited descriptors.

Of what value are verbal descriptors of musical textures?

The use of a descriptor to identify the texture of a musicwork or any portion of a musicwork, if it serves no other useful purpose, provides a simple indication as to whether or not the music has representative, identifiable textural consistencies and surface characteristics. If the textural qualities of a musicwork are such that we cannot describe them in words, it is possible that it has some rhythmic inconsistencies and some nondescript linear and chordal shapes that mar it and make it difficult to comprehend. The use of verbal descriptors, however, should be regarded only as an *aid* to understanding. Use of them does not constitute proof of understanding, nor does it prove the existence of textural consistencies and surface characteristics that contribute to the quality of a musicwork. On the other hand, the textural quality of a musicwork should not be faulted for the limitations that exist in our own verbal abilities. As with all other evaluations, this kind of evaluation is only as good as the judgment of the person making it.

In light of the advantages and disadvantages of using verbal descriptors, they should be accepted as useful and relatively accurate when employed within the controlled circumstances of the classroom, where assessments can be tempered by collective judgments. A verbal descriptor used in this manner is no different from any other descriptor; it serves to convey information about a sensory impression to another person or group of persons.

How does color contribute to spatial cognition?

Color, along with shape, allows us to differentiate physical objects. This in turn, because of the nature of vision, enhances or hinders spatial cognition. Because color is reliable and important to the visual perception of shapes in nature, it can be used with equal effectiveness as camouflage. Some animals (through natural biological processes) and humans (by imitating nature) use color to nullify or confuse other animals' and humans' visual perception of shapes. Camouflage, as a negative factor, is a convincing, natural validation of the effectiveness of color as a shaping force in its own right.

How are coloristic differentiation and melodic highlighting used in a musicwork?

Just as color can serve both to define and to obscure our visual perception of physical shapes, tone color—a useful illusory expression that is a colloquialism for "timbre"—can serve either to define or to obscure our aural perception of musical shapes. For example, by means of instrumental tone color, we can highlight a melodic line so as to separate it more clearly from its surroundings, thereby creating a **coloristic differentiation**. Coloristic differentiation is achieved simply by using those tone colors which, because of differences in physical makeup, continue to be perceived as separate tone colors when they are used together. Though homogeneity of sound characterized the aesthetic ideal of the eighteenth and nineteenth centuries, coloristic highlighting of melodic lines was commonly used to create the relief necessary for spatial cognition.

The clarinet line from Schubert's Eighth Symphony shown in Figure 48-8 would still be heard if it were played by a stringed instrument. It would be heard also if placed somewhat in relief from other strings because of pitch range and rhythmic differences. However, the line, being highlighted as it is by the tone color of the clarinet, is placed in greater relief from its surroundings.

48-8

Symphony No. 8 in B minor, Mov. II

Franz Schubert

The relative values of color and line in music can be likened, in some instances, to the values of color and line in the visual arts. For example, black-and-white photographs of paintings by French Impressionists such as Degas, Renoir, Monet, and Manet permit us to perceive the shapes of the objects painted. However, black-and-white photographs cannot convey the substance of such paintings, because color, rather than line, is their substance. Color is what Impressionistic paintings are all about. A painter living during the time of Schubert, however, used color as Schubert did in music, as a means of highlighting lines and shapes.

Having observed a typical example of tone color used to highlight a rather lengthy melodic line, let us examine an application of tone color that obscures, if not nullifies, our aural perception of a continuous melodic line. In Anton Webern's Symphony Opus 21 we are confronted with a double canon that, it is assumed, was not intended to be heard as such. The double canon is made up of two two-voiced canons. In each canon, the *leading* voice is answered in contrary motion (mirror inversion) by the *following* voice. Rather than highlight each of the four lines with a distinctive instrumental tone color to enable the listener to perceive the double canon, Webern used color to break up the lines into single pitches and groups of two to four pitches. (See Figure 48-9.) The fragmented lines are connected in the reduction (canon 1 and canon 2) so as to point out the opening pitch series of each voice of the double canon. Because the pitch series is used melodically, four versions of the series are in use at all times. Webern's orchestration of the six-part ricercare from J. S. Bach's *Musical Offering* provides another example of how tone color can be used to obscure our perception of a melodic line. The individual lines of the ricercare are broken up into small melodic shapes, each of which is colored by an instrument or combination of instruments to distinguish it from the contiguous melodic shapes of the line.

What is tonal context, and how does it relate to spatial cognition?

Tonal context refers to the relative meaning engendered by each pitch of a musicwork as it fulfills the expectancies generated by the ordering of the pitches that precede it. The meaning of a single pitch in a composition is drawn from its place in order of pitches—the context of the tonal framework within which it functions. The idea of tonal context, rhythmic context, or any other organizing or formalizing framework within which something can fit and be understood in music is really no different in principle from the idea of context in a verbal language. Until words are used in the context of sentences, they have no meaning; they have only the definitions found in a dictionary. These definitions are the compendia of common usage that suggest a range of applications, which in turn may lead to similar or expanded usage. Until a pitch is used in a musical context, it means nothing; it can be defined, however, in terms of its frequency, letter name, or integer name.

Tonal contexts become important to spatial cognition when two or more tonal contexts are used simultaneously. Anton Webern's simultaneous use of four mappings of a pitch series in his Symphony Opus 21 (Figure 48-9) provides four simultaneously sounding contexts. Aaron Copland's use of a succession of two separated but simultaneously sounding chords creates two separate tonal planes in the music for the film *Our Town*. Bartok's manner of imitating a melodic line a half-step higher in *The Diary of a Fly* from volume VI of the *Mikrokosmos* creates two separate but tightly drawn together tonal planes. And finally, the two relatively independent lines in Josquin des Prez's Agnus Dei (Figure 27-1) provide tonal contexts that aid spatial cognition.

48-9

Symphonie, Op. 21, Mov. I

*Klingt wie notiert ("sounds as notated")

UNIT PROJECT 9

Music for Film or Video Tape

Description

Construct a musicwork of four to six minutes' duration to accompany: (1) a commercially made or student-made animated film, (2) a Marcel Marceau film from the *Art of Silence* series, (3) a commercially made or student-made nature film, or (4) a commercially made or student-made video tape of a nature subject. Draw the pitch materials from a source set derived from an initial melodic shape or chordal construct. The pitch-class content of the source set should not be coincidental to the pitch content of the natural diatonic system or any of its transpositions. Score the musicwork for at least five orchestral instruments available in your class plus piano (if desired) or for two pianos. Construct the musicwork so that it will be characterized by the following attributes:

1. An illusion of movement suitable for expressing the dramatic situation presented in the film or video tape.

2. Concern for the spatial demands of the film or video tape by incorporating such meta-idiomatic considerations as: (a) the expressive use of the nonidiomatic, extended pitch ranges of instruments; (b) the illusion of differing sound planes by varying the textures, tone colors, pitch levels, and tonal contexts; and (c) the physical placement of performers.*

3. An adherence to the formalizing demands of objective time (real time) imposed by the fixed duration and pace of the film or video tape.

Depending on the visual medium you use, your project may be self-contained and separate from all others or it may be part of a longer, cooperatively produced project of eight to eighteen minutes' duration for which each member of the group will produce four to six minutes of music. The exact amount of music produced by each student assigned to a group will necessarily be determined by the internal structuring of the film or video tape selected.

Notes

Before beginning this project, the entire class must consider a number of matters. Attention might best be given first to those elements of the project that you expect to be the least flexible—those established by a circumstance that would be difficult or impossible to change.

If, for example, you are to use a commercially prepared animated film, a Marcel Marceau film, or a video tape, the dramatic situation is generally established by the film or tape. It would be impractical to select a dramatic situation first and then seek a commercial film or tape that exploits that situation. Because of the limitations on your time and available films, it is much more practical to first find a film or video tape whose dramatic situation appeals to you and then prepare music for it.

If you will be using a commercially prepared film or video tape, bear in mind that few films and tapes have durations of only four to six minutes. Therefore, many films and video tapes would require the cooperative efforts of two to five students. Whether the project is to be approached individually or collectively should not affect the nature of your responsibilities or the quality of your music. Whether what you make is a small but complete, stand-alone musicwork or a small but complete portion of a larger work does not change the manner in which you make musical choices.

A list of animated films that have been used successfully for this kind of project and a list of Marcel Marceau films follow. Student-made animated films provide opportunities for cooperating with art or film students. Computer graphics provide a technical means of approaching such student works. Video tapes on any aspect of nature are easily made by students and are encouraged.

Because most students are unfamiliar with the available films and tapes, the first order of business is to hold one or two classroom or library viewing sessions for the entire class. The films and tapes must be viewed *without sound* at all times!

---

*Consideration (c) presupposes a "live" performance.

The methods used to establish how students are to work with the films and how the performing resources of the class are to be used should be worked out by the instructor and students. The more important decisions concern: (1) what films or tapes are to be used, (2) which students are to work together on one film or tape, (3) what viewing schedule will enable students to view the film or tape enough times so they can complete a timing chart and obtain a good feel for the expressive intent of the film.

After the films and tapes are selected and the expressive intent of the film is deduced, the student(s) working on each project must select the particular pitch collection or melodic shape that will form the prime-ordered set for the musicwork. The prime-ordered set is the material "stuff" of which all the melodic and chordal patterns will be generated. The *quality* of the prime-ordered set should relate well to the quality of the dramatic situation of the film or video tape. Ideally, the selection of the sound materials will be based on an intuitive, spontaneously sensual response to the visual stimulus of the film or tape.

You should then spend time with the film for the purpose of defining and then timing the various dramatic episodes or sections of the film. These timings should be charted in some manner to indicate their nature—that is, whether they are initiating something, developing something, or bringing something to a conclusion, and what these "somethings" are. After that, work on the music can begin. If you are working with other students, you need to decide which sections of the film will be done by each of you. Make the divisions in accordance with the logical divisions of the dramatic situation.

After the music writing stage is completed, the music should be rehearsed with the film or video tape to rectify any timing problems. Each student can be responsible for the performance of his or her own music, or one student can be appointed to conduct all of the music. Such a decision may depend on the particular needs of good instrumentation—a need that may require all of the instrumentalists in the class. If the music is made for two pianos, the performance problem is no less difficult but much less complicated.

After the music is rehearsed and the tempos are established, record the music. Once that is completed, the projects can be presented in a public performance using the taped music with the film or video tape. It is advisable to use the same film projector, video tape player, and tape recorder/reproducer for performance as you used for producing the work. Slight variations in projectors and recorders' reel speeds can result in unexpected timing problems if different equipment is used for the performance. Of course, you do have the option of performing the music "live" with the film or tape.

Film List

Cages. 9 min., sd., b/w
  Sparse line drawings present a philosophical exercise about an imprisoned man and his jailers. Illustrates man's dependence on authority and the consequences of breaking accepted rules.

Cria. 5 min., color
  A Michael Whitney computer production.

The Emperor's New Armor. 6 min., sd., color
  A humorous animated film that comments on consumerism and the arms race. An emperor is persuaded by three glib salesmen to buy a suit of armor made of soft metal.

The Fly. 9 min., sd., color
  A symbolic animated film without narration. A man is increasingly tormented by a fly that expands to many times the man's size.

Joshua in a Box. 4 min., sd., color
  An animated film that uses the situation of a boy being trapped in a box as a basis for a study of man's needs, emotions, and values.

Machine. 10 min., sd., color
  A deftly animated allegory on man and his inventions.

Permutations. 8 min., sd., color
  A computer-made art film that demonstrates the graphic art potential of the computer. Presents a set of permutations of a geometric equation.

A Place in the Sun. 6 min., sd., color
  Uses animation to satirize two figures competing for fame and immortality, noting human foibles as they win or lose.

The Refiner's Fire. 6 min., sd., b/w

> Squares and circles take on human characteristics as they portray the conflict that arises between an established society and its idealistic members who discover and preach a new truth. Demonstrates the tragic fate of the pioneers of social change.

Toys. 8 min., sd., color

> Examines the possible effects of modern war toys on children. A fantasy about a deadly battle fought by war toys in a store window at Christmastime.

Trends. 9 min., sd., color

> Uses animation to show how the future is developing different areas of human life—communication, reproduction, tools, nutrition, medicine, and war.

Up Is Down. 6 min., sd., color

> Presents through animation a direct treatment of some of the most central themes of intolerance, conformity, and the generation gap.

The Wall: Zid. 4 min., sd., color

> Animated story of an opportunist who lets another man expend all his energies blowing a hole in a wall. The opportunist walks through the wall over the body of the first man. The process begins again when he approaches another wall.

Some Titles from Marcel Marceau's
The Art of Silence Series

Bip as a Skater. 8 min., sd., color. "Bip" is Marcel Marceau's other self. Time includes introductory narration.

Bip as a Soldier. 18 min., sd., color

Bip at a Society Party. 14 min., sd., color

Bip Hunts Butterflies. 10 min., sd., color

The Creation of the World. 11 min., sd., color

The Hands. 7 min., sd., color

The Maskmaker. 9 min., sd., color

The Painter. 8 min., sd., color

The Side Show. 8 min., sd., color

U N I T

SEVEN

TWELVE-TONE SERIALISM

Introduction to Twelve-Tone Serialism

What is serialism?

Though twelve-tone serialism is a meta-idiomatic convention of the twentieth century, the underlying principle of serialism is relatively old. **Serialism**—the compositional use of a recurring pitch series or durational configuration—is seen in the isorhythmic motets of the fourteenth century and in the chaconnes and passacaglias of the eighteenth and nineteenth centuries.

Because the early applications of serialism were not identified as such and because the early applications were so unlike twelve-tone serialism, the connection is seldom made. Thus the concept remains a new and generally misunderstood principle to most musicians. In defense of this misunderstanding, we must realize that the strong meta-idiomatic conventions that have provided musicians with the basic principles of organization for most of the prevailing music literature have also provided them with a strong (often prejudicial) resistance to new and challenging conventions. Though tonic-dominant tonality was once a new and challenging convention, at least it shared a principle with modality—the principle of referentialism.

What is the dodecaphonic system?

Perhaps the most jarring reality of twelve-tone serialism was the final establishment of the **dodecaphonic system**—the twelve-tone system. The dodecaphonic system grew out of the chromaticism of the diatonic system. During its developing years in the early twentieth century it formed the pitch material for music that is characterized as *panchromatic* (that is, using all tones of the chromatic scale), and the system is still anchored to diatonicism. In the established dodecaphonic system, each of the twelve pitches within the octave is a separate, distinct entity that is not a member of a hierarchy of pitches. For the most part, the concept of referentialism was replaced with a different organizing principle, one based on pitch ordering.

How have principles been confused with style and practice throughout history?

One of the enduring myths surrounding twelve-tone serialism results from the confusion of style and practice with principle. This kind of confusion has occurred throughout the history of music theory. Because Schoenberg composed his early serialized musicworks during the period his music was considered "Expressionistic," it became common to consider Expressionism and twelve-tone serialism as one and the same. Schoenberg's aesthetic and technical application of the principle of serialism is (as is anyone's) a special case and it should not be confused with the principle itself. We must remember, the principles of tonal organization in music (like other principles that govern natural phenomena) are natural laws that are discovered and used; they are not invented. It is as possible to realize any particular expressive intent in a musicwork with twelve-tone serialism as it is with any previously discovered and used principle of tonal organization.

How have rules and special-case practices increased the confusion surrounding twelve-tone serialism?

Another aspect of this confusion of style and practice with principle is the establishment of rules and procedures (based on special-case practices) for governing students' applications of principles. Thus, a number of *do's* and *don'ts* concerning the application of twelve-tone serialism have found their way into the printed and voiced "mythology." These rules are irrelevant to the application of the principles of twelve-tone serialism, as were their counterparts to the application of the principles of tonic-dominant tonality and modality by composers of previous generations. There are many and varied applications of twelve-tone serialism. Each application must be judged in reference to the quality of the music produced, not by comparison with theoretical deductions based on the single or collective practices of composers. This is not to say that studying earlier applications of a principle is not helpful; it is immensely helpful. Past practices serve to offer avenues of approach, to influence, and to stimulate students to develop different, personal applications.

Another enduring problem is that the uninitiated are often unable to understand how composers can think intuitively and creatively in twelve-tone serialism. Probably all of us can remember our reaction when we heard an exotic foreign language for the first time: we wondered how anyone could possibly make sense out of that "unintelligible gibberish." It is equally difficult for many, upon hearing twelve-tone-serial music for the first time, to realize that it is completely intelligible to those who are familiar with it and that composing twelve-tone-serial music is basically no different from what composing music has always been.

As with using any principle of tonal organization, a limited number of basic functions and operations are exercised, and a limitless number of personalized applications are possible. In the chapters that follow, these basic functions and operations will be described and demonstrated, at times with examples from literature. The principles involved, rather than particularized applications, will be emphasized.

50 Physical Properties of the Twelve-Tone Series

What is a twelve-tone series?

A **twelve-tone series** is an *arbitrary ordering* of the twelve pitch classes of the dodecaphonic system; the pitch-class members of the series are considered *related only one to another*.

An arbitrary ordering of pitches is an ordering based on the composer's personal choice rather than on an external, prescriptive model. The word *arbitrary* is often misused to characterize something as being done in an unthinking, indiscriminate manner; proper usage denotes a decision based on *personal preference*. The ordering of pitch classes in a twelve-tone series is at the discretion of the composer. Using the word *arbitrary* expresses the point that no particular ordering or series of orderings is required and that any ordering of pitch classes produced by a capable serial composer will work.

The concept that pitch members are related "only one to another" means that no pitch class is considered a reference pitch. Theoretically, the pitch classes of a twelve-tone series are considered equal in importance. Thus, isolated from all other considerations, nothing about the ordering of pitch classes (or the pitch classes themselves) and their application in a musicwork should make any pitch class more important than any other pitch class. Though this is acceptable as a theoretical premise, it was very likely intended, when first expressed, more as a desired outcome than as a guaranteed, physical reality. Whereas the uniform neutrality of pitch classes in a twelve-tone series is desirable, it is not a condition achieved by chance; uniform neutrality must be a built-in condition of a twelve-tone series.

What are the inherent resources of a twelve-tone series, and how can they be shown?

A maximum of 48 twelve-tone series can be generated from a single series: the 4 mappings of the series beginning on each of the 12 pitch classes of the dodecaphonic system. These additional series are easily shown in the form of a matrix; see Figure 50-1.

The *original series* extracted from the musicwork from which it is taken is highlighted. The series representing the *original mapping* are found by reading the matrix horizontally from left to right. The *inversion mappings* are found by reading from top to bottom. The *retrograde*

50-1

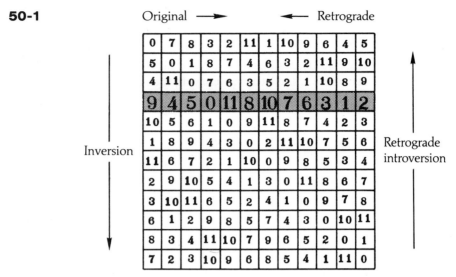

mappings are found by reading horizontally from right to left. The *retrograde-inversion mappings* are found by reading from bottom to top. Notice that the original mapping shown at the top of the matrix begins on the integer 0 and that a series of zeroes extends diagonally from the upper left corner to the lower right corner. This characterizes matrices of all twelve-tone series.

How is a matrix produced?

The matrix in Figure 50-1 was produced from an original series beginning on pc9. Because the top row of integers of a matrix must begin with 0, any series that begins with an integer other than 0 must be transposed. See Figure 50-2a. In this case, transposition is achieved

50-2

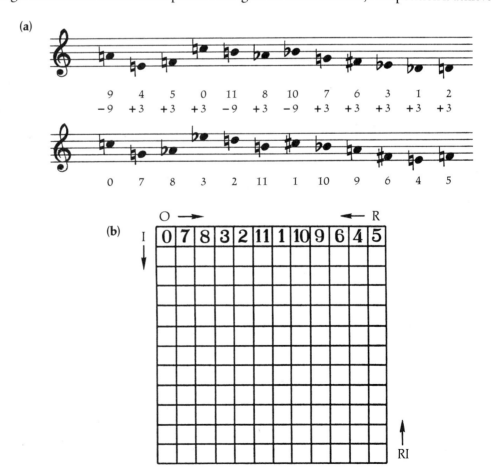

by subtracting 9 from or adding 3 to the original series. The series transposed to pc0 is then placed on the matrix (Figure 50-2b). The next step is to produce the inversion beginning on pc0. This is achieved by subtracting each integer of the original mapping on pc0 from 12 (Figure 50-3a) and projecting the result down the left column of the matrix (Figure 50-3b). The matrix is completed by following the process demonstrated in Figure 50-4a–d.

50-3

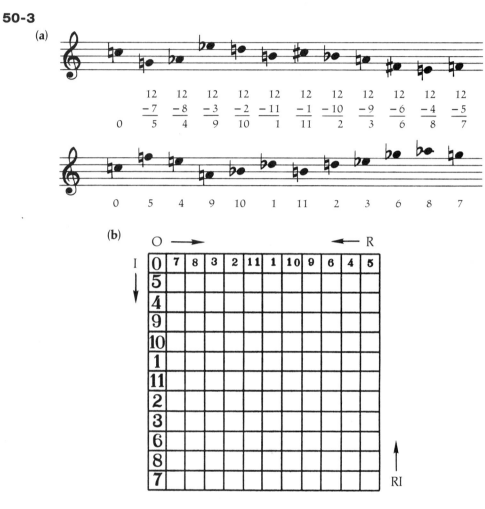

50-4

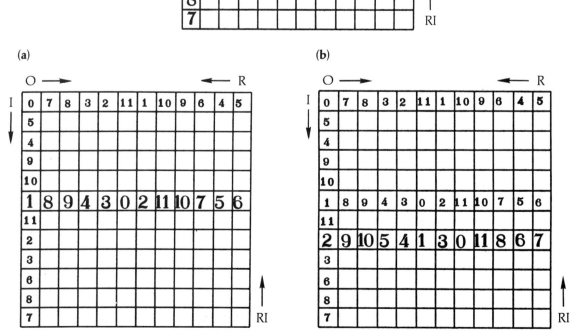

50-4, *continued*

(c)

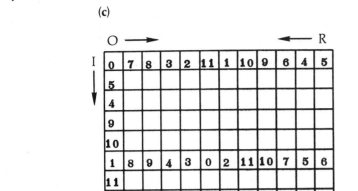

I↓	O →									← R		
0	0	7	8	3	2	11	1	10	9	6	4	5
5												
4												
9												
10												
1	8	9	4	3	0	2	11	10	7	5	6	
11												
2	9	10	5	4	1	3	0	11	8	6	7	
3	10	11	6	5	2	4	1	0	9	7	8	
6												
8												
7												RI

(d)

I↓	O →									← R		
0	0	7	8	3	2	11	1	10	9	6	4	5
5												
4	11	0	7	6	3	5	2	1	10	8	9	
9												
10												
1	8	9	4	3	0	2	11	10	7	5	6	
11												
2	9	10	5	4	1	3	0	11	8	6	7	
3	10	11	6	5	2	4	1	0	9	7	8	
6												
8												
7												

How is the ordering in a twelve-tone series established?

At the outset, we are dealing with a question that has no single, correct answer. Ideally, a serial composer should be thoroughly at home with his or her particular application of serialism and should be able to deal with it intuitively as the basic principle underlying a personal musical language. A personal, intuitive application of a conventional musical language has been required of the composer throughout the history of music.

Some serial composers begin a musicwork without much preparation beyond the normal, conventional preplanning composers have carried out for centuries. In such cases, a twelve-tone series unfolds as the composer intuitively establishes the opening gesture of the musicwork. The opening gesture, in such cases, may be entirely or almost entirely melodic, such as the one in Figure 50-5, which produces the series shown below it. Or, it might be a gesture in

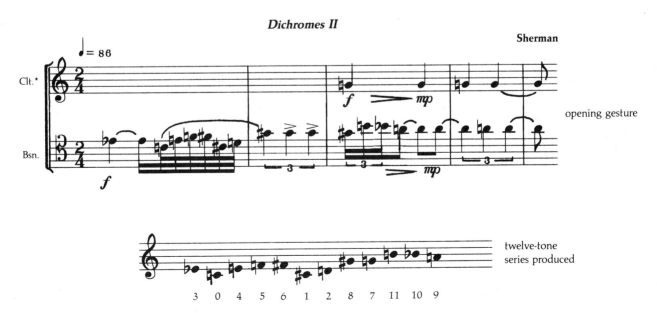

Dichromes II

Sherman

♩ = 86

Clt.*

Bsn.

opening gesture

twelve-tone series produced

3 0 4 5 6 1 2 8 7 11 10 9

*sounds as notated

which the series is generated by a melody combined with a chordal structure, such as the one in Figure 50-6, or a two-part dialog, like the one in Figure 50-7.

50-6

opening gesture

twelve-tone
series produced

0   4   5   11   10   7   6   8   9   2   3   1

50-7

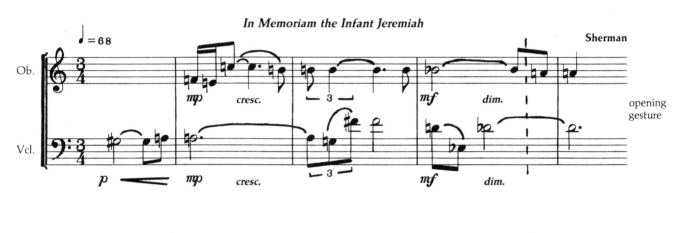

In Memoriam the Infant Jeremiah

Sherman

opening
gesture

twelve-tone
series produced

8   9   5   4   0   11   7   6   10   2   3   1

   Some composers begin a musicwork with a twelve-tone series they have spent much time developing. It is the result of a great deal of preplanning and is especially designed to enable them to achieve particular predetermined, compositional objectives. The opening gesture of Webern's *Variationen*, Opus 27 (Figure 50-8), utilizes canonic imitation, a device that requires foreknowledge of how the canon is to unfold, what the ensuing pitch relationships will be, and what manner of series is best suited for the intended purpose. The series used for this musicwork appears below the opening gesture. One factor of this predetermined series that contributes to Webern's control over the intervallic relationships between the voices of the canon is that each half of the series contains the pitch content of one-half of the octave (see Figure 50-9). This device is not unique to serialism, but it is compositionally useful to serial composers.

50-8

Variationen, Op. 27, Mov. I

Anton Webern

4 5 1 3 0 2 8 9 10 6 7 11

50-9

4 5 1 3 0 2   8 9 10 6 7 11

[0 1 2 3 4 5]   [6 7 8 9 10 11]

How does the ordering of pitch classes in a twelve-tone series affect expectations?

In Unit Five we learned that our aural comprehension of modality and tonic-dominant tonality is the result of the expectations created by the ordering of pitches in a musicwork. It was important that composers not violate the principles of modality or tonic-dominant tonality by introducing pitch elements that produce misleading or contradictory expectations. Likewise, it is important that the ordering of pitches in a twelve-tone series not result in misleading or contradictory expectations. There are 479,001,600 distinct twelve-tone series. They represent all of the possible linear permutations of the pitch content of the dodecaphonic system. Many of them contain pitch relationships that would, if used, result in misleading or contradictory expectations. Therefore, not just *any* pitch series is suitable for a musicwork. The pitch series in Figure 50-10 is one of them. It contains pitch relationships that lead to contradictory expectations that cannot be fulfilled.

50-10

1 11 5 9 0 3 7 10 2 4 6 8

A serial composer must understand the ways a twelve-tone series can be treated compositionally. Whether a series is generated intuitively or determined with much conscious thought, its makeup must be the result of a composer's knowing how the series and its various mappings are to be used. A series produced by an intuitively designed musical gesture must, nonetheless, be evaluated with respect to its usefulness in designing gestures for subsequent movements and for a host of other compositional concerns. Often it is necessary to modify the ordering of pitch classes in an initial gesture so that the series will better serve the general needs of the musicwork.

What is an isometric twelve-tone series?

An **isometric series** is one in which the retrograde mapping or the retrograde-inversion mapping of the series has the same ordering of interval-class relationships as the original mapping. The series in Figure 50-11 is from Anton Webern's Sinfonie Opus 21. Note the interval-class content: (3 1 1 4 1 6 1 4 1 1 3). In both its ordering and its directional relationships, it reads the same in both directions. Now look at the matrix for the series. Because of what is true of the interval-class content of the series, the pitch-class content of the retrograde on any given pitch class reads the same as the original on the same pitch class. For example, the retrograde on pc9 (R_9) is identical to the original on pc9 (O_9). Also, the retrograde inversion on pc9 (RI_9) is identical to the inversion on pc9 (I_9). The resulting effect is that an isometric series has only two distinct mappings, the original and its inversion.

50-11

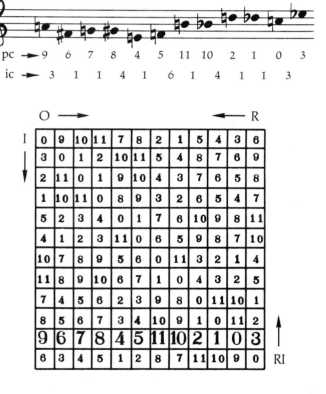

To demonstrate a series in which the retrograde-inversion mapping has the same ordering of interval-class relationships as the original mapping, we will use the first half of the Webern series used in the Sinfonie but will change the ordering of pitch classes in the second half of the series as shown in Figure 50-12. As the matrix shows, the retrograde inversion on pc0 (RI_0) is identical to the original on pc0 (O_0). The retrograde on pc0 (R_0) is identical to the inversion on pc0 (I_0). Again there are only two distinct mappings, the original and its inversion.

50-12

pc →	9	6	7	8	4	5	2	3	11	0	1	10
ic →	3	1	1	4	1	3	1	4	1	1	3	

O →   ← R

	0	9	10	11	7	8	5	6	2	3	4	1
I	3	0	1	2	10	11	8	9	5	6	7	4
↓	2	11	0	1	9	10	7	8	4	5	6	3
	1	10	11	0	8	9	6	7	3	4	5	2
	5	2	3	4	0	1	10	11	7	8	9	6
	4	1	2	3	11	0	9	10	6	7	8	5
	7	4	5	6	2	3	0	1	9	10	11	8
	6	3	4	5	1	2	11	0	8	9	10	7
	10	7	8	9	5	6	3	4	0	1	2	11
	9	**6**	**7**	**8**	**4**	**5**	**2**	**3**	**11**	**0**	**1**	**10**
	8	5	6	7	3	4	1	2	10	11	0	9
	11	8	9	10	6	7	4	5	1	2	3	0

RI

What procedures can be used to form isometric series?

To form the kind of isometric series used in Webern's Sinfonie, we begin by dividing the pitch-class content of the dodecaphonic system into two six-member sets (Figure 50-13). The second step is to order the pitch-class content of the first six-member set to produce the desired pitch-class and interval-class relationships. Because each ordering is but one permutation of the linear permutation of a six-member set, a total of 720 orderings are available from which to produce the kind of isometric series used in Webern's Sinfonie. Webern's ordered pattern is shown in Figure 50-14. Beginning on pc5, the arrows show that the ordering of pitch

50-13

[0, 1, 2, 3, 4, 5]   [6, 7, 8, 9, 10, 11]

50-14

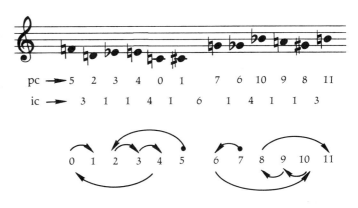

pc →	5	2	3	4	0	1		7	6	10	9	8	11
ic →	3	1	1	4	1	6		1	4	1	1	3	

0 1 2 3 4 5   6 7 8 9 10 11

classes is 5 2 3 4 0 1. To produce the ordering of the second half of the series, we begin on pc7 and reverse the order of the first half of the series, to get: 7 6 10 9 8 11. We began on pc7 because it coincides, in terms of its position, to the last integer (pc1) in the ordering of the first six-member set. The resulting series, 5 2 3 4 0 1 7 6 10 9 8 11, is found to be an original mapping on pc5 as well as a retrograde mapping on pc5 on the matrix in Figure 50-11. Additional examples of this type of ordering and the resulting series are shown in Figure 50-15.

The type of isometric series demonstrated in Figure 50-12 is produced the same way, except that the ordering of the second six-member set is reversed (Figure 50-16). The resulting series is 5 2 3 4 0 1 10 11 7 8 9 6. Not all such halves of an isometric 12-tone series must be confined to the half-octave. By transferring pitch classes from one hexachord to the other (Figure 50-17a), we arrive at the ordered collection 0 2 3 4 6 10 11 9 8 7 5 1, from which we produce the isometric series 3 0 4 2 10 6 5 1 9 7 11 8 (Figure 50-17b). Another isometric series made from the same ordered collection is shown in Figure 50-18. Two different pairs of pitch-class transfers are shown in Figure 50-19, along with the resulting ordered collections and the isometric series made from each collection. Though the transfer of two pitch classes from each hexachord was used in the examples in Figures 50-17 through 50-19, it is possible to use the transfer of 1, 2, or 3 pitch classes. Transferring four pitch classes, in effect, would be the same as transferring two. Figure 50-20 presents a matrix produced for the isometric series produced in Figure 50-19b. Notice that, as expected, only two mappings are possible: the original and the inversion.

50-15

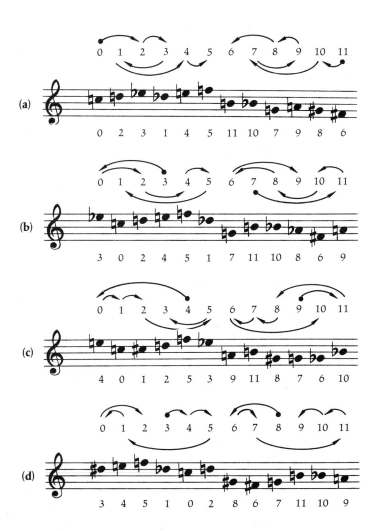

50-16

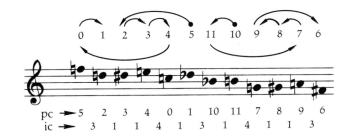

50-17

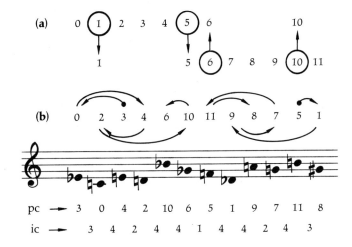

50-18

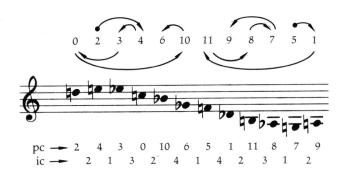

50-19

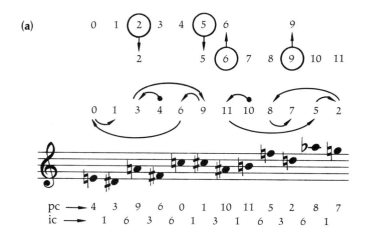

(a)

pc ⟶ 4 3 9 6 0 1 10 11 5 2 8 7
ic ⟶ 1 6 3 6 1 3 1 6 3 6 1

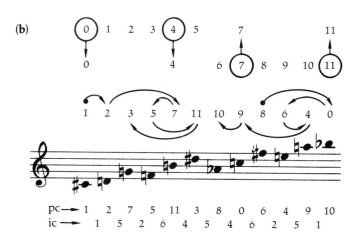

(b)

pc ⟶ 1 2 7 5 11 3 8 0 6 4 9 10
ic ⟶ 1 5 2 6 4 5 4 6 2 5 1

50-20

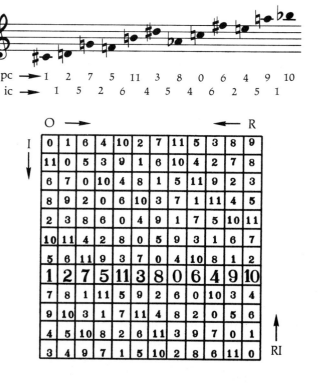

pc ⟶ 1 2 7 5 11 3 8 0 6 4 9 10
ic ⟶ 1 5 2 6 4 5 4 6 2 5 1

O ⟶										⟵ R	
0	1	6	4	10	2	7	11	5	3	8	9
11	0	5	3	9	1	6	10	4	2	7	8
6	7	0	10	4	8	1	5	11	9	2	3
8	9	2	0	6	10	3	7	1	11	4	5
2	3	8	6	0	4	9	1	7	5	10	11
10	11	4	2	8	0	5	9	3	1	6	7
5	6	11	9	3	7	0	4	10	8	1	2
1	2	7	5	11	3	8	0	6	4	9	10
7	8	1	11	5	9	2	6	0	10	3	4
9	10	3	1	7	11	4	8	2	0	5	6
4	5	10	8	2	6	11	3	9	7	0	1
3	4	9	7	1	5	10	2	8	6	11	0

I ↓   RI ↑

What is a combinatorial* series?

The combinatorial properties of a twelve-tone series are determined by the pitch-class content of the hexachords rather than the pitch-class ordering of the series. A series can be either partially combinatorial or all-combinatorial. The **partially combinatorial series** shown by the matrix in Figure 50-21 has only two transposed mappings, O_{10} and RI_{10}, in which the corresponding hexachords have the same pitch-class content. The hexachords do not have the same ordering. At the other extreme, the matrix in Figure 50-22 portrays an **all-combinatorial series**, in which all of the mappings and transpositions are produced from the same two hexachords. All of the hexachords in the second (upper left) quadrant and the fourth (lower right) quadrant of the matrix have the same pitch-class content. Also, all of the hexachords in the first (upper right) and third (lower left) quadrants have the same pitch-class content. Though the combinatorial properties of a twelve-tone series are not at all dependent on the ordering of pitch classes in a series, the pitch-class content of the hexachords in an all-combinatorial series can be arranged to produce an isometric series. For example, if the two orderings of the

50-21

0	11	8	1	2	7	3	4	6	10	9	5
1	0	9	2	3	8	4	5	7	11	10	6
4	3	0	5	6	11	7	8	10	2	1	9
11	10	7	0	1	6	2	3	5	9	8	4
10	9	6	11	0	5	1	2	4	8	7	3
5	4	1	6	7	0	8	9	11	3	2	10
9	8	5	10	11	4	0	1	3	7	6	2
8	7	4	9	10	3	11	0	2	6	5	1
6	5	2	7	8	1	9	10	0	4	3	11
2	1	10	3	4	9	5	6	8	0	11	7
3	2	11	4	5	10	6	7	9	1	0	8
7	6	3	8	9	2	10	11	1	5	4	0

O →   ← R
I ↓ O_{10} RI ↑ RI_{10}

50-22

0	2	6	10	8	4	1	3	11	7	9	5
10	0	4	8	6	2	11	1	9	5	7	3
6	8	0	4	2	10	7	9	5	1	3	11
2	4	8	0	10	6	3	5	1	9	11	7
4	6	10	2	0	8	5	7	3	11	1	9
8	10	2	6	4	0	9	11	7	3	5	1
11	1	5	9	7	3	0	2	10	6	8	4
9	11	3	7	5	1	10	0	8	4	6	2
1	3	7	11	9	5	2	4	0	8	10	6
5	7	11	3	1	9	6	8	4	0	2	10
3	5	9	1	11	7	4	6	2	10	0	8
7	9	1	5	3	11	8	10	6	2	4	0

O → 2   1 ← R
I ↓   RI ↑
3   4

*The term is attributed to Milton Babbitt.

hexachordal set used to produce the series represented by Figure 50-22 are in prime order (Figure 50-23a), the isometric series shown by the matrix in Figure 50-23 will result.

      There are only six hexachordal sets from which all-combinatorial series can be produced. When each of the hexachordal sets is used in prime order to form a twelve-tone series, the resulting series will be isometric as well as all-combinatorial. The hexachordal set [0, 2, 4, 6, 8, 10] was used in Figures 50-22 and 23. The remaining hexachordal sets are [0, 1, 2, 3, 4, 5], [0, 2, 3, 4, 5, 7], [0, 2, 4, 5, 7, 9], [0, 1, 2, 6, 7, 8], and [0, 1, 4, 5, 8, 9]. Each of these hexachordal sets can be arranged in 720 orderings by linear permutation. Because the ordering of the second half of a twelve-tone series produced from one of these hexachordal sets can also be arranged in 720 orderings, 1,440 distinct orderings of an all-combinatorial series are possible. The matrix in Figure 50-24 portrays an all-combinatorial series in which the two orderings of the hexachordal set are different. Hexachords that have the same pitch-class content are identified by letters outside the matrix; for example, all hexachords labeled *A* have the same pitch-class content.

W181—184

50-23

(a)   [0,2,4,6,8,10]   [1,3,5,7,9,11]

(b)   O ⟶   ⟵ R

I ↓

0	2	4	6	8	10	1	3	5	7	9	11
10	0	2	4	6	8	11	1	3	5	7	9
8	10	0	2	4	6	9	11	1	3	5	7
6	8	10	0	2	4	7	9	11	1	3	5
4	6	8	10	0	2	5	7	9	11	1	3
2	4	6	8	10	0	3	5	7	9	11	1
11	1	3	5	7	9	0	2	4	6	8	10
9	11	1	3	5	7	10	0	2	4	6	8
7	9	11	1	3	5	8	10	0	2	4	6
5	7	9	11	1	3	6	8	10	0	2	4
3	5	7	9	11	1	4	6	8	10	0	2
1	3	5	7	9	11	2	4	6	8	10	0

RI ↑

50-24

A = [0,1,4,5,8,9]   C = [1,2,5,6,9,10]

B = [11,0,3,4,7,8]   D = [2,3,6,7,10,11]

	A	A	B	A	B	B	D	C	D	D	C	C	
B	0	4	11	8	7	3	2	9	10	6	5	1	C
B	8	0	7	4	3	11	10	5	6	2	1	9	C
A	1	5	0	9	8	4	3	10	11	7	6	2	D
B	4	8	3	0	11	7	6	1	2	10	9	5	C
A	5	9	4	1	0	8	7	2	3	11	10	6	D
A	9	1	8	5	4	0	11	6	7	3	2	10	D
C	10	2	9	6	5	1	0	7	8	4	3	11	B
D	3	7	2	11	10	6	5	0	1	9	8	4	A
C	2	6	1	10	9	5	4	11	0	8	7	3	B
C	6	10	5	2	1	9	8	3	4	0	11	7	B
D	7	11	6	3	2	10	9	4	5	1	0	8	A
D	11	3	10	7	6	2	1	8	9	5	4	0	A
	D	D	C	D	C	C	A	B	A	A	B	B	

To gain practice in producing matrices for twelve-tone series, do the following:

MINI PROJECT 22

A. 1. Beginning on the pitch classes 3, 5, 6, and 10, produce four twelve-tone series, each with a different ordering.

   2. Transpose each series to 0 (zero) and produce a matrix for each series.*

B. 1. Produce two isometric series whose R_0 and O_0 mappings are identical when matrices are made for them.

   2. Produce two isometric series whose RI_0 and O_0 mappings are identical when matrices are made for them.

C. 1. Produce two all-combinatorial series from orderings of the pitch-classes in the hexachordal set [0, 1, 2, 6, 7, 8] and produce a matrix for each.

   2. Identify the hexachords that have the same pitch-class content with the letters *A, B, C,* and so on, outside the matrices you made for C. 1.

*Matrix forms should be made available by the instructor.

51 | Melodic Design

How is the invention and development of melody served by the design of a twelve-tone series?

Regardless of how a composer approaches the composition of a serialized, twelve-tone musicwork, there are only two basic ways the series can be used. The series, in any of its mappings, can be used in its entirety as melody, or it can be used as the source of all pitch materials—in which case the melodic elements are extracted arbitrarily from the series. These two basic applications of serialism can be used individually or combined; in either case, two or more mappings of the series can be used at the same time. This chapter will contrast the melodic application of the intuitively produced series and the preplanned series.

None of the meta-idiomatic conventions we have discussed (modality, tonality, pitch-class sets) or those we have not discussed is predicated on a consideration of pitch ordering. In all of these conventions, melody is extracted from or superimposed on the pitch content of the convention; it is not a built-in design element in the sense that a particularized ordering is required. For example, a musicwork in the key of D major does not require the pitch elements of the D-major scale to be ordered in any particular manner for the purpose of melodic design. Twelve-tone serialism *does* require particularized ordering. Regardless of how a series is used, melodic elements are commonly based entirely or in part on the ordering of pitch classes.

Therefore, whether a series is produced by an intuitively produced musical gesture or a preplanned ordering based on a particularized compositional imperative, serialism is basically a melodically oriented convention.

If a twelve-tone series is the result of an intuitively produced, totally melodic gesture, it is *very likely* to be serviceable for all the melodic needs of the musicwork. Note that this is *not* a guarantee. Historically, an inherent possibility has always existed that a melody can be "too precious" to lend itself to motivic manipulation. Twelve-tone serialism—generally characterized as *perpetual variation*—requires motivic manipulation as one of its conventional design principles. Like a precious jewel, a "too precious" melody cannot be broken up and rearranged; it can only be placed in different settings. A "too precious" twelve-tone melody might be one that produces a series having no distinguishable internal motivic shapes that relate either to one another or to the overall shape of the series. Such melodies only permit repetition; they do not permit manipulation.

Refer to the twelve-tone series (part b) generated by the melodic gesture (part a) in Figure 51-1. An obvious balance is built into the melodic gesture by the two rhythmic configurations made up of five sixteenth-notes. Even though the melodic gesture contains all of the pitch-class content of the twelve-tone series, a great wealth of distinguishable pitch-class configurations is built into the series that is not apparent in the rhythmic shaping of the gesture. The recurring three- and four-member configurations formed by adjacent pitch classes in the series are shown in Figure 51-2a. These and similarly shaped three- and four-member configurations can be extracted from the series (Figure 51-2b). Other viable melodic configurations can also be extracted from the series; see Figures 51-3 and 51-4. Each of these distinguishable configurations presents a vast potential for melodic invention and development when used in any of the available transpositions of the four mappings and when given a particularized rhythmic shape.   **W185–186**

51-1

51-2

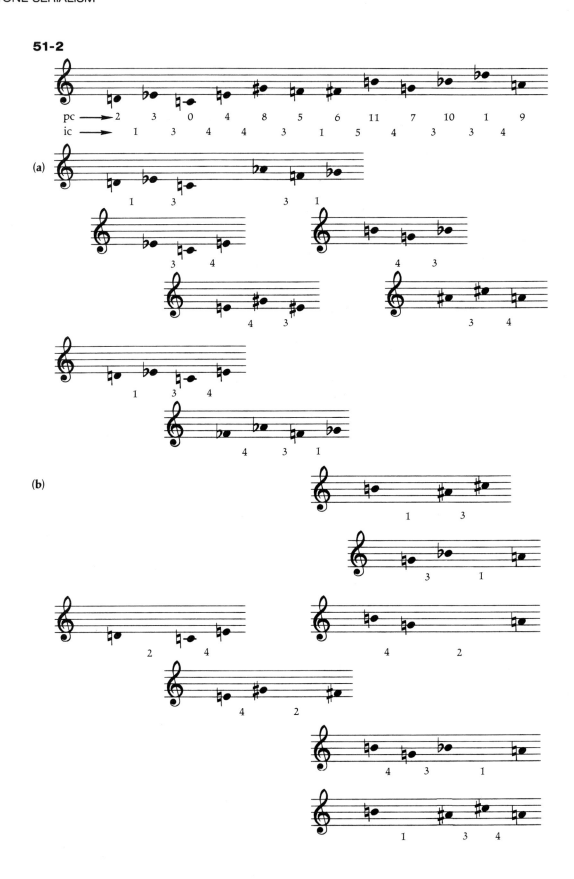

51-3

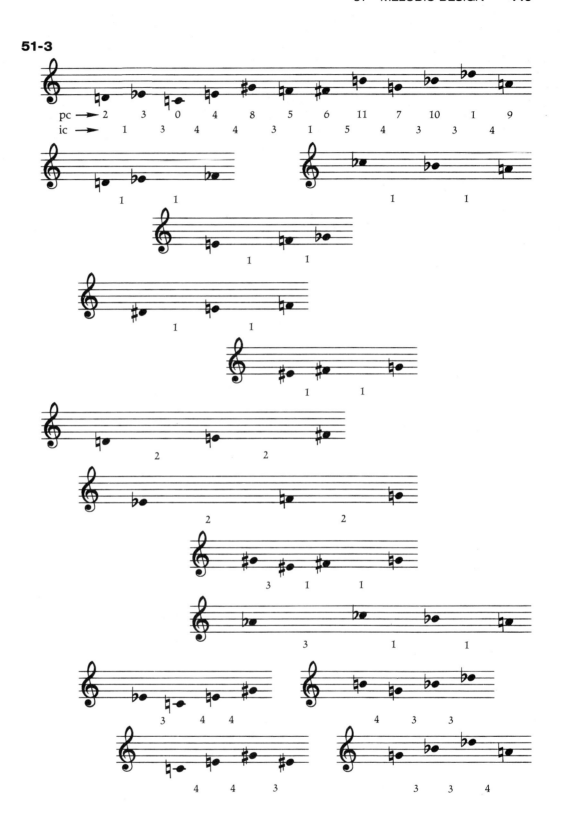

51-4

| pc → | 2 | 3 | 0 | 4 | 8 | 5 | 6 | 11 | 7 | 10 | 1 | 9 |
| ic → | | 1 | 3 | 4 | 4 | 3 | 1 | 5 | 4 | 3 | 3 | 4 |

How are rhythmic emphasis and pitch goals used to achieve melodic shaping?

The theoretical a priori equality of the pitch class content of a twelve-tone series provides a neutrality that makes rhythmic emphasis and pitch goals essential to melodic shaping. All of the three-, four-, and five-member shapes identified in Figures 51-2 through 51-4 remain conveniently buried within the series until they are brought forth by rhythmic shaping and the establishment of pitch goals. Though identified separately, pitch goals and rhythmic shaping are the *what* and the *when* of the intelligible relationships that can be brought forth from a fertile but uncommitted ordering of pitches. This process differs little from the process composers have employed from the beginning of the musical art; it differs only in what the serial composer begins with as basic pitch material.

If the series in Figure 51-1, in any of its transposed mappings, is used in its entirety as melody (alone or in conjunction with one or more other versions), any of the shapes in Figure 51-2a can be brought forth. This is demonstrated in Figure 51-5. The shapes in Figure 51-2b can be brought forth by manipulation. This is demonstrated in Figure 51-6. Notice that the shapes extracted from the series are presented on one pitch level, and the other pitches are presented either on a different pitch level or as unaccented ornamental pitches. This is simply an extension of a very old practice that was particularly common during the Baroque period. Its application was most effective in musicworks for unaccompanied stringed instruments. The melodies shown in Figure 51-6 are fashioned from the shapes identified in the examples in Figure 51-3. Rhythmic shaping and differing pitch goals can result in an infinite variety of melodic lines from a single series. A few examples are shown in Figure 51-7.

51-5

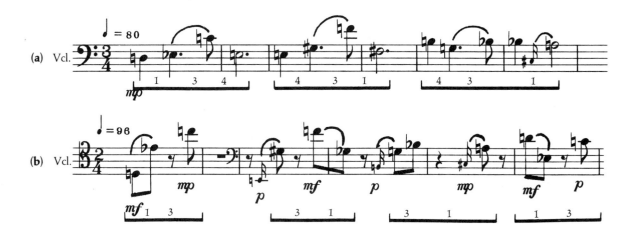

51-6

continued

51-6, *continued*

How do the melodic shapes in a preplanned twelve-tone series differ from those in an intuitively produced series?

In considering this question, we cannot assume there is or should be an inherent difference between an intuitively produced series and a preplanned series. Though we might believe that isometric series and all-combinatorial series as well as other highly organized series are preplanned, it is possible to arrive at an isometric or all-combinatorial series intuitively during the course of creating a melodic gesture. We must bear in mind that in composing, intuition is as much the handmaiden of the preplanner as it is of the intuitionist. In truth, we are differentiating between two approaches to producing a musicwork. The difference is not qualitative; it is a difference in mental process. The intuitionist is neither disorganized nor bereft of foresight. The preplanner, during the act of preplanning, must use a fair amount of intuition. The only difference between the intuitionist and the preplanner that we can deal with is that the preplanner, having an idea of the kind of musicwork he or she wishes to produce, designs a series that contains the kinds of shapes and relationships that are necessary for achieving the intended objectives.

In creating a preplanned series, it might be the intent of the composer to produce a musicwork that could be described as a "mosaic" in sound; that is, a work made up of seemingly isolated one-, two-, three-, and four-member sound "images." Anton Webern's *Concerto for Nine Instruments*, Opus 24, is dependent on the four basic shapes of the series. These four basic shapes serve as the basic motivic material of the musicwork. The opening gesture of the concerto (Figure 51-8a) is produced from the series in Figure 51-8b. Note that each three-member segment of the series is one of the four possible mappings of the three-member configuration. Sets that have different intervallic relationships but the same kind of internal organization—that is, four mappings of a given three-member configuration—are shown in Figure 51-9. Assuming these series represent the kind of highly organized twelve-tone series that are designed to achieve a compositional imperative, the series in Figure 51-9b is used in Figure 51-10a to demonstrate the recurring three-member configurations formed by adjacent pitch classes. Parts b and c of Figure 51-10 are the recurring three-member configurations that can be extracted from the series.

51-8

from Konzert, Op. 24, Mov. I, opening gesture

(a) Etwas lebhaft ♩ = c. 80

Anton Webern

Flöte

Oboe

Klarinette

Horn   *immer mit Dampfer*

(b) twelve-tone series

pc → 11 10 2   3   7   6   8   4   5   0   1   9
ic →   1   4   1   4   1   2   4   1   5   1   4

51-9

(a)

pc →	0	1	3	2	4	5	11	10	8	9	7	6
ic →		1	2	1	2	1	6	1	2	1	2	1

(b)

pc →	1	0	3	2	5	4	10	11	8	9	6	7
ic →		1	3	1	3	1	6	1	3	1	3	1

(c)

pc →	1	4	3	8	7	11	9	5	6	1	2	10
ic →		4	1	5	1	4	2	4	1	5	1	4

51-10

pc →	6	7	1	0	3	2	5	4	10	11	8	9	6	7	1	0
ic →		1	6	1	3	1	3	1	6	1	3	1	3	1	3	1

(a)

51-10, *continued*

(b)

(c)

Another objective a composer might work out in the preplanning process is to limit the number and size of the interval classes. The series in Figure 51-9a contains six interval-class ones, four interval-class twos, and one interval-class six. The melodies in Figure 51-11 are designed to emphasize the predominant interval classes. A contrary objective that might be

51-11

worked out during preplanning is to provide an even distribution of all the interval classes such as in the series in Figure 51-12a. Melodies produced from this series are shown in part b of the figure. An interesting aspect of this series is that of the twelve three-member source sets produced by the adjacent pitch classes, there are two each of the source sets [0, 1, 2], [0, 1, 3], [0, 1, 4], and [0, 1, 5] and four of the source set [0, 1, 6].

51-12

The various series presented in Figures 51-8 through 51-12 and similarly organized series are useful in the making of musicworks in which composers utilize canonic imitation. The Sinfonie Opus 21 and Variationen Opus 27 are two of a number of musicworks by Anton Webern in which canonic imitation is used. Each of the twelve-tone series employed in these musicworks is structured so as to imply preplanning (Figure 51-13).

A composer can build a great variety of special design elements into a twelve-tone series to enable him or her to achieve particular compositional objectives. The twelve-tone series used in Alban Berg's Violin Concerto is a celebrated example of including compositional imperatives in a series by preplanning the design. One of the imperatives is the incorporation of the pitches of the open strings of the violin (G, D, A, E)—they are shown as whole notes in Figure 51-14. Another imperative is the inclusion of the first four pitches of Bach's choral melody *Das ist Genug* as the last four pitches of the series—shown in half notes in the figure. It should be noted, however, that the Violin Concerto is not serialized, even though a series is used.

51-13

Webern, Op. 21:

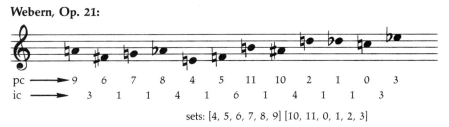

pc ——▶ 9   6   7   8   4   5   11   10   2   1   0   3

ic ——▶   3   1   1   4   1   6   1   4   1   1   3

sets: [4, 5, 6, 7, 8, 9] [10, 11, 0, 1, 2, 3]

Webern, Op. 27:

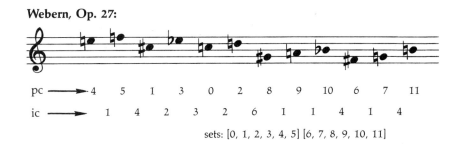

pc ——▶ 4   5   1   3   0   2   8   9   10   6   7   11

ic ——▶   1   4   2   3   2   6   1   1   4   1   4

sets: [0, 1, 2, 3, 4, 5] [6, 7, 8, 9, 10, 11]

51-14

Berg, Violin Concerto:

7   10   2   6   9   0   4   8   11   1   3   5

MINI PROJECT 23

The first part of this mini project provides practice in recognizing recurring pitch-class configurations in a twelve-tone series produced intuitively as a melodic gesture. A good way to prepare for this is to improvise a number of melodies at the piano or on your instrument, taking care to include all of the twelve pitch classes. This, of course, may take a considerable amount of practice and concentration if you have had no previous contact with twelve-tone serialism. The focus of your practice in producing an intuitive, twelve-tone melodic gesture should be to arrive at the point at which your melody represents the realization of an expressive intent.

When you feel prepared to proceed with the project, do the following:

1. Create a suitable twelve-tone melodic gesture that is complete with respect to tempo, dynamics, articulation, instrumentation, and any other consideration necessary to its expressive intent.

2. Identify any recurring three- and four-member pitch-class configurations made by the adjacent pitch classes and present them in the manner shown in Figure 51-2.

3. Identify any recurring three- and four-member pitch-class configurations that can be extracted from the series and present them, also, in the manner shown in Figure 51-2.

The second part of the mini project provides practice in producing a twelve-tone series *after* you have decided what the intended musicwork is to be. In preparing for this hypothetical musicwork, ask yourself the following kinds of questions. Does one particular three- or four-member pitch-class configuration seem necessary for expressing my dramatic or other aesthetic intent? Is there an interval I'm particularly fond of and want to exploit for dramatic reasons? How can I describe in words (verbal descriptors) a compositional objective that calls for preplanning and that I can translate into a design element of a twelve-tone series?

After you have thought about the compositional imperatives you would like to incorporate in a musicwork that you believe would require preplanning, do the following:

1. Describe at least two compositional imperatives—primary objectives—to be achieved in the hypothetical musicwork you are planning.

2. Construct a twelve-tone series having within it a recurrence of whatever pitch-class configuration(s) or interval(s) you have decided are useful for achieving your intended objectives for the hypothetical musicwork.

3. Identify the special design elements you have built into the series, those produced by adjacent pitch classes, and those that can be extracted from the series by skipping one or two pitch classes, as shown in Figure 51-2.

4. Using the twelve-tone series you have made, create three different melodic lines that feature its built-in design elements. The melodies should be complete with respect to tempo, dynamics, articulation, instrumentation, and any other considerations necessary to your expressive intent.

52 Multiple Series in a Contrapuntal Texture

A typical way in which an entire twelve-tone series is used as melody in a contrapuntal texture exists in canonic imitation. In **canonic imitation** a *leading voice* is imitated in some manner by a *following voice*. The word *canon* denotes a law or a body of laws; as a descriptor of a form of imitation in music, the term implies the existence of a body of restrictive or prescriptive conditions. There are indeed such conditions. They specify such things as when the following voice begins, what relationship its beginning pitch bears to the beginning pitch of the leading voice, and the mapping of the following voice in relation to that of the leading voice.

How is a twelve-tone series used in canonic imitation?

Canonic imitation produced with a twelve-tone series is not subject to the "cadential" formulas and tonal frameworks and goals common in the practices of modality and tonality. Thus, serialized canonic imitation does not require any special concessions that alter the flow of the imitation. Because of this, we might consider canonic imitation as having "come of age" in twelve-tone serialism. Regardless of the prescription a composer formulates for a musicwork using canonic imitation, we can expect that the canonic imitation, for as long as it is used, will unfold without distracting interruptions.

Several measures of simple canonic imitation that uses the preplanned twelve-tone series in Figure 51-9b are shown in Figure 52-1. The leading voice is the trumpet, which, because it is first, is considered the original mapping beginning on the pitch $D\flat_4$. The following voice is the trombone, which uses the original mapping beginning on the pitch $D\flat_3$. As the leading voice progresses through the O, RI, R, and I mappings of the series, the last pitch class of each mapping becomes the first pitch class of the next mapping. The following voice in the trombone proceeds in the same fashion. A musicwork for two instruments composed entirely of canonic imitation is called a **two-voiced canon**.

52-1

To demonstrate that it is possible to produce canonic imitation from a twelve-tone series resulting from an intuitively produced melodic gesture, the several measures of canonic imitation in Figure 52-2 were produced from the twelve-tone series shown in Figure 51-1. The leading voice is again the trumpet; it begins on the pitch D$_4$. The following voice is again the trombone. This time, the following voice uses the inversion mapping, which begins on the same beginning pitch as the trumpet. Also, this time the following voice enters a measure and a half after the leading voice, rather than after two measures as it did in the previous example. As the trumpet line continues, the last two pitches of the original mapping on the pitch D$_4$ are the first two pitches of the retrograde inversion on the pitch D$_4$. In the following voice, the last two pitches of the inversion mapping on the pitch D$_4$ are the first two pitches of the retrograde mapping on the pitch E$_4$. A musicwork composed in such a manner is called a **two-voiced inverted canon**. Another, more complicated use of canonic imitation is shown in Figure 52-3. The music in this figure is the opening portion of a **double inverted canon**—that is, two two-voiced inverted canons. These two canons use the same mapping of the series.

52-2

*sounds as notated

52-3

*sounds as notated

What consideration must we give to intervallic relationships formed by using two or more series simultaneously?

With twelve-tone serialism came what was called the "emancipation of dissonance." To some, this means that pitch relationships once considered dissonant are no longer considered dissonant. To others, it means that dissonance still exists but need not be given special treatment with regard to preparation and resolution. To yet others, the traditional concern for consonance and dissonance is an aesthetically misplaced concern. Because of the age-old emphasis on the treatment of dissonance in all homophonic music, we may have developed a simplistic view that greatly exaggerates the importance of the intervallic relationships between voices (melodic lines) in the contrapuntal music of all historical periods. Intervals, so formed, are important residual effects; but far more important and more to the point of any aesthetic consideration of music is the logic of the dramatic unfoldment and formalizing elements of melodic design. If a melodic line is ambiguous in its expressive intent and faulty in its design, it will not be improved by placing it in a contrapuntal texture with one or more other melodic lines or in any kind of musical texture—regardless of how "proper" the placement of consonant and dissonant pitch relationships is.

Consonant and dissonant relationships, in themselves, are like words: they have definition but no intrinsic meaning. The musical meaning of such relationships in a musicwork is cumulative in effect, and dramatic and unique in nature. We might say, that they are the "designed accidents" of motion between voices.

We should note that present concerns for the nature and function of dissonant and consonant relationships in all previous musics have been after-the-fact assumptions that may not have been a matter for consideration by any of the composers. There is nothing available to demonstrate that what has come to be thought of as a regulatory function of intervallic relationships has a genuine basis in principle. Whatever assessments were made concerning the practices that formed the conventions of the past, they are principally documentations of special-case practices that indicate what some one composer or what some few composers did. Nowhere do we find or should we find any documentation of the aesthetic and dramatic reasons for what was done.

It is appropriate, therefore, to reaffirm that

intervallic relationships produced by the voices of a contrapuntal musicwork
are a consequence of the dramatic and aesthetic interaction of melodic lines,
not a generating or regulatory force in the creative process of making music.

On the other hand, we cannot say that composers have never cared about intervallic relationships or that composers of twelve-tone serial music care less about intervallic relationships than their historical counterparts did. Intervallic relationships become what they are as a result of the design habits of composers, habits formed within the context of accepted conventions. Intervallic relationships can be likened to the agreement and disagreement in a verbal discourse between equals. The tone of the verbal discourse may be regarded in terms of the agreement or disagreement; but the discourse itself, if it is to be considered valid, must be based on credible assertions and responses, which in turn, are based on the principles of verbal discourse. There are no basic rules concerning intervallic relationships between the voices of a contrapuntal musicwork to which the composers of any historical period were, are, or will be obliged to adhere. When composers accept a given meta-idiomatic convention as a framework for their creativity, they are confronted with aesthetic principles and workable limitations for which they develop a "feel" and within which they can exercise their dramatic intent. Out of this grows an aesthetic awareness of which intervallic relationships "work" as part of the total texture of a twelve-tone musicwork and which ones "do not work." **W187–190**

How can multiple series be used in a noncanonic texture?

A noncanonic application of two or more transpositions or mappings of a twelve-tone series sounding at the same time provides a more flexible approach to texture than does canonic imitation. Even though there is an "air of polite conversation" exhibiting the give and take of musical discourse in canonic imitation, all of the voices of a canon are equal in importance and all of them sound in the foreground. There is no background in a canon; there are no principal lines or accompaniment. Everything is up front, on the surface.

In a noncanonic texture—even in one that is completely contrapuntal—there may be a principal melodic line in the foreground and supportive melodic lines or a less active chordal accompaniment in the background. The principal sounding line may be divided among several instruments, or there may be several principal lines. The point is that both a foreground and a background exist. Put another way, a distinction is made between the principal line (or lines) and the musical setting. Whereas canonic imitation can be likened to verbal discourse between equals, a texture having a foreground and a background can be likened to a painting in which principal objects are placed in an enhancing setting.

The musical example in Figure 52-4 uses the series from Figure 51-2. A solo oboe line is supported by a two-voiced string accompaniment. The oboe melody is produced from an inversion mapping beginning on the pitch E♭5; the accompaniment is from the original mapping beginning on the pitch C₃ and C₄, respectively. The series in the accompaniment is staggered so that the first half of the series is sounding with the second half of the series. Notice that, even though the oboe melody is the principal line, the strings are involved in a contrapuntal texture. Note also that the oboe line is perceived as the principal line because of its tone color and because it sounds above the strings. If the example were scored for three muted strings, we could not regard it so simply.

52-4

With the appropriate kind of twelve-tone series, it is possible to produce three- and four-member chordal structures that are useful in producing an accompaniment. The series and matrix in Figure 52-5 demonstrate the use of differing transpositions and mappings of a series in producing a chordal accompaniment for the melodic line in Figure 52-6. The trumpet melody is produced from the original mapping beginning on the pitch B_4. In the accompaniment, the violin line is made from the retrograde mapping on E_4; the viola line, from the original mapping on C_4; and the 'cello line, from the retrograde mapping on F_3.

52-5

pc →	0	5	11	4	8	3	4	9	1	6	7	10
ic →	5		6		5		4		5		1		5		4		5		1		3

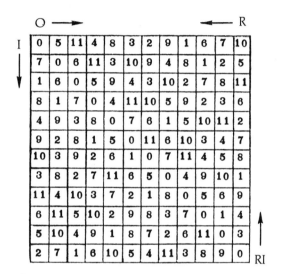

52-6

continued

52-6, *continued*

*sounds as notated

MINI PROJECT 24

The two activities of Mini Project 24 will provide you with practice in using two or more transpositions or mappings of a twelve-tone series in a contrapuntal and a homophonic texture.

Produce a contrapuntal texture using canonic imitation or nonimitative counterpoint.

1. Design a twelve-tone series (and produce a matrix) having the kinds of three- or four-member melodic configurations you believe are useful in developing a contrapuntal texture.

2. After deciding on the instrumentation and other elements that will achieve your expressive intent, do *one* of the following:

   a. Produce a two-voiced musicwork of 45 to 60 seconds' duration using canonic imitation. Each voice must complete a version of the series before repeating it or moving on to a transposition or another mapping.

   b. Produce a three-voiced musicwork of 45 to 60 seconds' duration using a nonimitative contrapuntal texture. Each voice must complete a version of the series before repeating it or moving on to a transposition or another mapping.

   Produce a homophonic texture using combined versions of a twelve-tone series.

1. Design a twelve-tone series (and produce a matrix) having the kinds of internal pitch relationships that, when combined with differing transpositions and/or mappings, will produce three-member chordal structures.

2. After deciding on the instrumentation and other elements that will achieve your expressive intent, complete a musicwork of 45 to 60 seconds' duration in which a principal melodic line is accompanied by chordal structures such as those described in item 1.

The two musicworks you produce should be performed in class and then discussed and evaluated. Important considerations include the logic of the dramatic unfoldment and the design of the melodic lines. Evaluate the compatibility of the melodic lines with each other in the contrapuntal musicworks; evaluate the effectiveness of the accompanying chordal structures and principal melodic line in the homophonic musicwork.

53 | Simultaneity

What is simultaneity?

In music, **simultaneity** refers to the sounding of two or more pitch classes of a twelve-tone series at the same time. This implies that any version of a twelve-tone series—that is, any transposition or mapping—can supply all of the pitch materials sounding at any given time in a musical texture. Because of this, it is possible for all of the pitch classes of a particular version of a series to be sounded within a portion of a musicwork as brief as a single measure or less (Figure 53-1). We can categorize the many, varied ways a composer utilizes simultaneity as either intuitive or preplanned—just as we did with the formation of a twelve-tone series. Although these two approaches may not appear clear-cut to us when we are considering the music of others, they are clear-cut to the ones, ourselves included, who produce the music.

As stated in chapter 51, the series that is used as a melodic entity may be combined with the same or a different version of that series to achieve simultaneity. When combining two or more series in such a manner, some of the pitch classes of the series used for the melody may serve "in common" with those of the version being used for simultaneity (Figure 53-2).

W191

53-1

Schoenberg, String Quartet No. 4, Op. 37, meas. 3

53-2

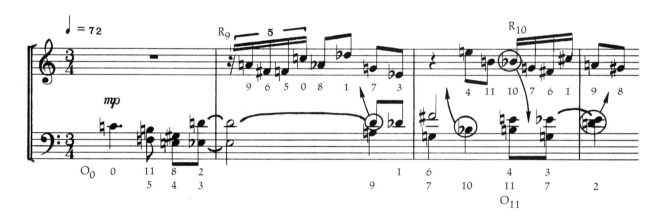

How can simultaneity result in the creation of a new twelve-tone series?

In a multivoiced texture, the pitch-class content of a series can be manipulated when simultaneity is used so that a new ordering of pitch classes results in the creation of a new series; see Figure 53-3. The new series is presented in both voices in this example, but each voice starts at a different point in the series. Theoretically, it is possible to produce a multivoiced musicwork from a twelve-tone series that never appears in its entirety as a melody by treating the series in such a way that one new series after another is generated as melody.

53-3

It is possible, also, for two voices that function similarly to those in Figure 53-3 to be used in conjunction with another version of the series that is used to create melody or to achieve chordal structures by applying simultaneity; see Figure 53-4.   **W192**

53-4

How does simultaneity serve in the dramatic unfoldment of an opening gesture and in the creation of new gestures?

The differing transpositions and mappings of a series combined with the flexibility provided by simultaneity make it possible to produce any number of melodic shapes, textures, and chordal structures. These can serve the dramatic unfoldment of a musicwork logically and effectively and they make it possible to create any number of new musical gestures for the various movements of a multimovement musicwork. Using simultaneity permits the extraction and expansion of a basic melodic configuration featured in a series. For example, the primary three-member configuration formed by the first three pitch classes of the twelve-tone series in Figure 51-2a is shown in Figure 53-5. It is possible to extract the transpositions and the various

53-5

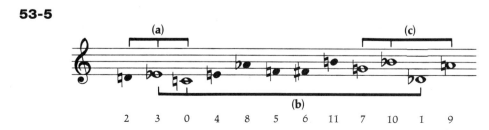

mappings of this and similar configurations from the series by bypassing one, two, or more pitch classes in the series. These extractions are made easy by using simultaneity. In Figure 53-5, a transposed retrograde-inversion of the three-member configuration is labeled with *b*, and a transposed retrograde of it is labeled with *c*. Using simultaneity, these and similar extracted mappings of a configuration might appear as melodic shapes in a two-voiced and a three-voiced musicwork as shown in Figure 53-6a and b, respectively.

53-6

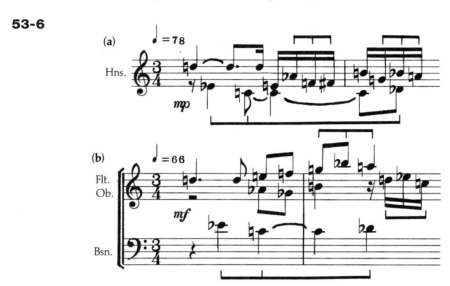

The three-member configuration in Figure 53-5 is shown with interval expansion as a result of extraction in Figure 53-7a, and as a transposed extension in Figure 53-7b. We can assume, therefore, that many of the techniques presented in Unit Three for transforming melodic configurations can be achieved by applying simultaneity. Figure 53-8a shows another mapping of the same three-member configuration. Part b of that figure shows a two-voiced realization, and part c shows a three-voiced realization of the extracted configuration. In each realization, the three-member configuration is presented in a transformation utilizing interpolation in a texture achieved through using simultaneity.

53-7

53-8

In contrast to the idea of extracting familiar basic shapes, simultaneity can be used to create new musical gestures containing basic shapes considerably different from those produced by the adjacent pitch classes of the series. In many instances, melody is not a primary concern in the design of a musical gesture. A gesture may be a rhythmic articulation of sonorous chordal structures. When orchestrated, the various chordal structures may or may not provide relationships in the various voices that reflect the basic shapes or even the characteristic intervals of the series used.

To demonstrate the production of new musical gestures from a single twelve-tone series, we will use five opening gestures from the author's *Thirteen Additional Ways of Looking at a Blackbird.* The twelve-tone series—generated from an intuitively produced opening gesture—and the resultant matrix are shown in Figure 53-9. Though the opening gestures (Figure 53-10) only occasionally use basic shapes from the series, characteristic intervals are often reflected in the outer voices of the chordal structures. Considerable use of the melodic shapes of the series occurs within the individual songs of the musicwork.

---

*Settings of H. David Eshleman's "Thirteen Ways of Looking at a Blackbird."

53-9

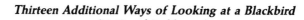

53-10

Thirteen Additional Ways of Looking at a Blackbird
(H. David Eschleman)

Robert W. Sherman

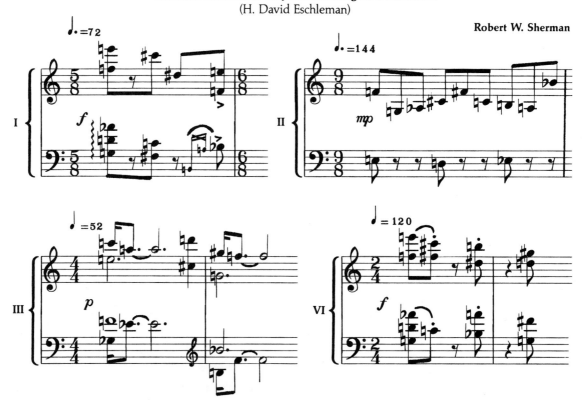

53-10, *continued*

How does simultaneity contribute to the formation of chordal constructs?

Our emphasis thus far has been on using simultaneity to achieve melodic goals. Nonetheless, many of the figures we have used to demonstrate melodic applications of simultaneity also demonstrate chordal constructs that can be formed by the simultaneous sounding of the adjacent pitch classes of any segment of any transposition or mapping of a series. It is also possible to form chordal constructs by the retention of pitch classes. Refer to Figure 53-11. Part a presents the twelve-tone series for the examples of pitch-class retention presented in part b.

53-11

Using simultaneity in this manner, there is more potential for variety in cumulative chordal constructs than can be used effectively in one musicwork. Regardless of whether chordal constructs are formed by using three or four versions of a twelve-tone series simultaneously, by sounding the adjacent pitch classes of a series simultaneously, by retaining the pitch classes in a series, or by combinations of these three means, the question of how we are to regard the chordal constructs remains.

Is the chordal construct a compositional entity or a consequence of linear motion?

When we dealt with a similar concern in our study of tonic-dominant tonality, we were confronted with the difference between a chord as a *compositional entity* and as a *theoretical construct*. This difference in the concept of chord is important to the analytical procedures of tonic-dominant tonality. In twelve-tone serialism, differences in the formation and use of chordal constructs are important for aesthetic reasons.

In tonic-dominant tonality, by convention, the possibilities for incompatibility between tertian, quartal, and other chordal constructs available within the diatonic system are relatively self-limiting. In twelve-tone serialism, chordal constructs are formed by the coincidence of pitch soundings of multiple series, by adjacent pitch classes of a series, and by retained pitch classes of a series. Because of the incredible number of chordal constructs made possible by these methods, the possibilities for aesthetic incompatibility are many. Obviously, if chordal constructs are presented as compositional entities, it is reasonable to assume that the aesthetic effectiveness of each chordal construct is in large part determined by its relationship to the others. It is reasonable to assume, also, that chordal constructs that result from linear motion—whether they are due to using multiple series or to some application of pitch-class retention—must be compatible with the chordal constructs formed by simultaneously sounding adjacent pitch-class members of a series. The key word here is *compatible; compatible with* does *not* mean "identical to." Therefore, the relationship is a matter of aesthetic judgment.   **W193–194**

MINI PROJECT 25	Since the beginning of notated music and probably before, composers have been faced with the need to "elucidate" or "expound" musically on the idea they express in the opening gesture of a musicwork. In other words, composers need to present musical ideas in a notated configuration, which in turn must evolve into a musicwork that is logical, dramatically satisfying, and formally complete. To do this, composers use the conventional techniques of their times that are appropriate to their specific needs. In a multimovement musicwork, there is also the need to produce an opening gesture for each movement that relates materially and aesthetically to the first movement and to the opening gestures of the other movements.

The purpose of this project is to provide practice in using simultaneity in the production and development of a musical gesture and in the production of new musical gestures.

1. By whatever means you find most effective, do *one* of the following:

   a. Utilizing simultaneity, produce what could serve as an opening gesture of a musicwork for an instrumentation (piano and voice included) available in your class. Produce what you believe is the best twelve-tone series from the gesture and produce a matrix.

   b. Produce a twelve-tone series as a preplanning operation for a musicwork and produce a matrix. Produce what could serve as the opening gesture of a musicwork for an instrumentation (piano and voice included) available in your class.

2. Utilizing simultaneity and the twelve-tone series you established in exercise 1, produce five examples of music that could serve to extend (develop) the gesture you produced.

3. Utilizing simultaneity and the twelve-tone series you established in exercise 1, produce five new gestures that could serve to initiate five different movements of a multimovement musicwork. The gestures should be different in such aspects as character, texture, rhythmic design, and tempo.

54 Segmental Partitioning of a Series

What is segmental partitioning?

Segmental partitioning is the practice of dividing a twelve-tone series into four segments of three adjacent pitch classes, three segments of four adjacent pitch classes, or some similar division. Segmental partitions are not a characteristic peculiar to a series; they are a characteristic peculiar to the way in which a composer chooses to use a series in producing a musicwork.

A composer using partitioning as an approach to a series will very likely preplan a series. A preplanned series, on the other hand, is not necessarily used for partitioning. The compositional reasons for partitioning are varied; when it is used, however, partitioning is usually the central activity on which all other developmental procedures depend.

How is segmental partitioning used melodically?

In general, segmental partitioning is used to define melodic configurations or chordal constructs. The melodic configurations so defined will very likely hold throughout the musicwork. In a purely contrapuntal musicwork, a series may be partitioned into three- or four-member segments that are related in some manner, such as in their basic shapes or in their pitch-class content when reduced to source sets. In Anton Webern's *Concerto for Nine Instruments*, Opus 24—the opening gesture of which is shown in Figure 51-8—each three-member segment forms a melodic configuration that is related to the others. The series from Webern's opus 24 shown in Figure 54-1 is made up of the four mappings of a three-member configuration that reduces to the source set [0, 1, 4]. (This particular series is similar to the several combinatorial series shown in Figure 51-9.)

A series similar to the one in Figure 54-1 is shown in Figure 54-2. Segmental partitioning of this series demonstrates two interesting characteristics of its organization:

54-1

(11 10 2) (3 7 6) (8 4 5) (0 1 9)

Prime-ordered sets: [10,11,2] [3,6,7] [4,5,8] [9,0,1]

Source sets: [0,1,4] [0,1,4] [0,1,4] [0,1,4]

54-2

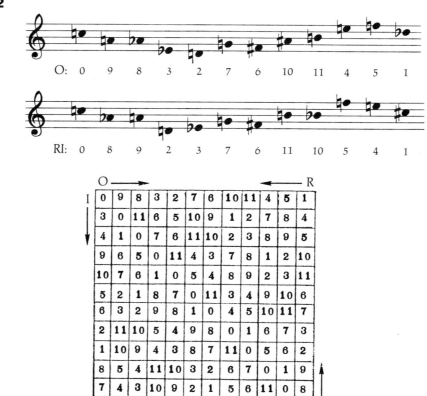

O: 0 9 8 3 2 7 6 10 11 4 5 1

RI: 0 8 9 2 3 7 6 11 10 5 4 1

O →									← R		
0	9	8	3	2	7	6	10	11	4	5	1
3	0	11	6	5	10	9	1	2	7	8	4
4	1	0	7	6	11	10	2	3	8	9	5
9	6	5	0	11	4	3	7	8	1	2	10
10	7	6	1	0	5	4	8	9	2	3	11
5	2	1	8	7	0	11	3	4	9	10	6
6	3	2	9	8	1	0	4	5	10	11	7
2	11	10	5	4	9	8	0	1	6	7	3
1	10	9	4	3	8	7	11	0	5	6	2
8	5	4	11	10	3	2	6	7	0	1	9
7	4	3	10	9	2	1	5	6	11	0	8
11	8	7	2	1	6	5	9	10	3	4	0

(I ↓ on left; RI ↑ on right)

1. When it is divided into four three-member segments, each segment forms a different configuration, but two of the segments, (0, 9, 8) and (4, 5, 1), reduce to the source set [0, 1, 4], and the remaining two, (2, 3, 7) and (6, 10, 11), reduce to the source set [0, 1, 5].

2. Each three-member segment of the original mapping on the pitch-class C (O_0) contains the same pitch-class content as the corresponding segments of the retrograde-inversion mapping on the pitch-class C (RI_0) but in a different order.

The opening gesture of Arnold Schoenberg's Fourth String Quartet, Opus 37, is a vigorous statement by the first violin that is accompanied by three-member chordal constructs in the remaining strings. The series is divided into four three-member segments (Figure 54-3a), which are used in the opening statement (Figure 54-3b). The melodic line in the first violin presents the complete series beginning on the pitch D_4. However, while the first violin plays

54-3

Fourth String Quartet, Op. 37, Mov. 1

Arnold Schoenberg

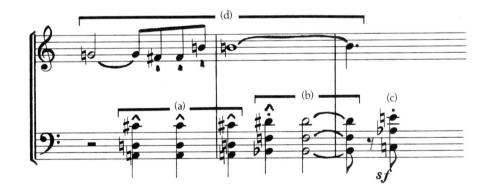

segment a, the remaining strings play segments b, c, and d as chords. While segment b is presented melodically, segments c, d, and a are presented as chords. While segment c is presented melodically, segments d, a, and b are presented as chords. And finally, while segment d is presented melodically, segments a, b, and c are presented as chords. By the end of the statement in measure six, the series has been used four times. An examination of the musicwork will reveal other ways partitioning is used, two of which are shown in Figure 54-4.

54-4

Fourth String Quartet, Op. 37

Arnold Schoenberg

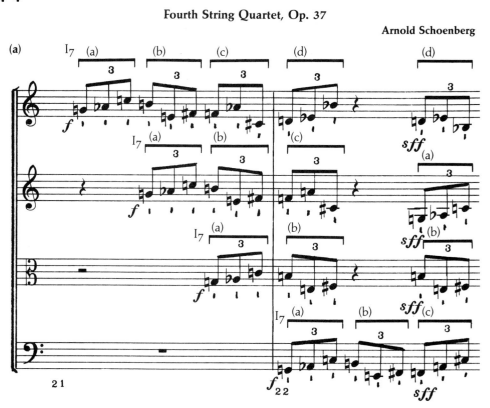

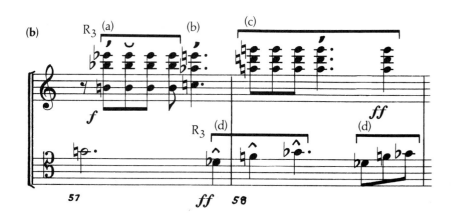

The matrix of the series Schoenberg used in this quartet (Figure 54-5) reveals characteristics similar to those demonstrated in Figure 54-2. For example, if we compare the original mapping on the pitch class C (O_0) with the retrograde-inversion mapping on the pitch class G (RI_7), we find segments a, b, c, and d of the original mapping corresponding to the segments a, c, b, and d of the mapping of the retrograde inversion. Varying the order of the segments and the order of pitch classes within the segments offers a wealth of possibilities for variety in melodic configurations and the contextural location of chordal constructs. Another observation to be made concerning the matrix is that the first six and second six pitch-class members of the original mapping on the pitch class C (O_0), for example, are found as the last six and first six pitch-class members, respectively, of the inversion on the pitch class F (I_5) but in a different order.

54-5

(a)

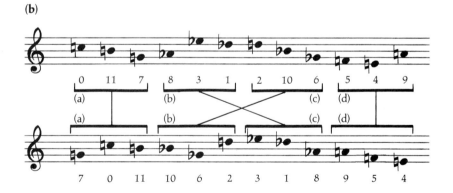

(b)

How can segmental partitions be treated as unordered sets?

Treating segmental partitions as unordered sets is primarily a means of achieving an effect similar to that of nondirected motion in tonic-dominant tonality. If we extend the practice of pitch retention beyond the simple notion of holding a pitch as the subsequent pitch classes of a series are introduced, we arrive at the following variation in the application of a basic principle. The practice of pitch retention can be extended to include the idea that once a partitioned segment of a series is introduced into the texture of a musicwork, it may be treated in any manner and any ordering.

Sommermüd, number 1 of Schoenberg's *Three Songs*, Opus 48, provides a marvelous example of partitioning a series into three four-note segments and treating an occasional segment as an unordered pitch-class collection. The series for the song and the matrix for the series are shown in Figure 54-6. The piano accompaniment in *Sommerüd*'s opening statement (Figure 54-7) uses only the last four pitch classes of the original mapping of the series beginning on the pitch class C♯ (O$_1$).

Pitch retention was demonstrated in chapter 53 using sustained note values. The practice of pitch retention can be extended to include the kind of rhythmically articulated pitch permutations demonstrated in Figure 54-7. Because the accompaniment is for piano, a more rhythmically active treatment than sustained or reiterated chords is demanded. It should be noted, also, that the treatment of the partitioned segments and the partitioning itself are the operant developmental principles in the song.

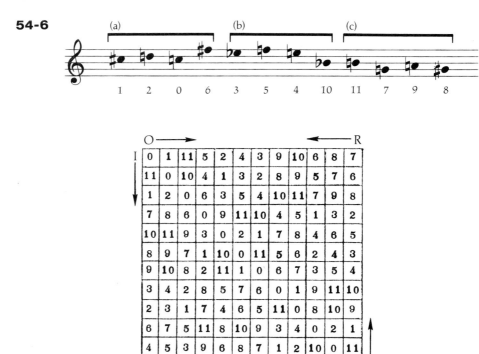

54-6

54-7

Three Songs, Op. 48, *Sommermüd*

Arnold Schoenberg

What are some less common applications of partitioning and unordered treatments of segmental partitions?

In describing an application of partitioning or an unordered treatment of a partitioned segment as less than common, unusual, or in any way out of the ordinary, we do not imply that the application is less valid or less appropriate. We must realize that with any functioning principle of music composition there is, and must be, ample latitude for invention. Artistic invention is like scientific invention except for the finished products. Principles may be applied but not denied. They may be offsetting but they may not be set aside. Principles, artistic and scientific, provide the delimiting framework within which the inventive mind can function freely.

A composer might, as a common practice, partition a series into four three-note segments, and then, as a less common practice, rearrange segments to form new series for subsequent movements of a musicwork such as shown in Figure 54-8.

54-8

Such a practice can result in:

1. a difference in the interval classes joining the adjacent partitions,

2. a difference in the makeup of chordal constructs formed by the adjacent pitch classes of the series except the four three-note segments themselves, or

3. a number of interesting relationships between the melodic shapes in a contrapuntal texture and between the melodic shapes and chordal constructs of a more homophonic texture.

Because of the retained ordering within each three-note segment, much of the intervallic content and the general aural impression of the series would be retained. This would yield 24 possible orderings from which to select a series for a given movement.

Given the series in Figure 54-8, a composer might choose to retain the order of the four three-note segments but treat the pitch-class content of each segment as an unordered set. The segment (0, 1, 11) might then be used, for example, in any of the three orderings made possible by a cyclic permutation or any of the six orderings made possible by a linear permutation

54-9

(a)

(0,1,11)   (1,11,0)   (11,0,1)

(b)

(0,1,11)   (0,11,1)   (1,11,0)   (1,0,11)   (11,0,1)   (11,1,0)

(Figure 54-9). Carried to completion, this treatment of the segments results in 144 different orderings. It is unlikely that any composer could or would use all or even a majority of them. Because the ordering of the three-member segments would be retained and because there could be no more than three interval-class types within each segment, the general aural impression of the series would not change appreciably.   **W195—196**

<table>
<tr><td>

MINI PROJECT 26

</td><td>

This mini project provides practice in forming a twelve-tone series that is suitable for partitioning into three- or four-note segments and in using the partitioned series in varying musical textures. Before establishing the series, however, you need to think about your expressive intent and the kinds of partitioned segments that will serve to produce both the desired melodic configurations and the chordal constructs necessary to your expressive intent. When you have finished experimenting with shapes and chordal constructs, do the following:

</td></tr>
</table>

1. Produce a twelve-tone series and its matrix.

2. Establish an appropriate instrumentation (including voice and piano if you wish) based on what is available in your class.

3. Using the series you produced, establish three opening gestures, each intended as the opening gesture for one movement of a three-movement musicwork. Make one entirely contrapuntal, one a melody with chordal accompaniment, and one entirely chordal. Use them in any order you like. In each case the gesture should be constructed so as to utilize the partitioning you have established. The gestures should vary in tempo, character, rhythmic design, and dynamics.

4. Using one of the gestures you have constructed, produce three examples of what could serve as internal episodes that develop the gesture. Exploit variations in the use of segments produced by other mappings of the series.

5. Perform the gestures and episodes in class. Evaluate the effectiveness of the partitioning and how well the gestures and episodes relate to each other.

55 Directed and Nondirected Motion and Miscellaneous Anomalies

How do the concepts of directed and nondirected motion relate to twelve-tone serialism?

Typically, directed and nondirected motion are not discussed in conjunction with twelve-tone serialism, but it is appropriate to do so. Twelve-tone serialism has usually been described in terms ("continuous variation" for one) that imply the concept of constant directed motion. Treatments of series that relate to the concept of nondirected motion have been considered individually as anomalies. Nondirected motion, of course, is *not* an anomaly in twelve-tone serialism; it simply has been treated as one. Any extended serialized musicwork contains considerable use of nondirected motion. Without some nondirected motion, a serialized musicwork takes on kaleidoscopic attributes, which in aural terms, might be described as "kaleidosonic"; that is, it is made up of constantly changing, nonrepeating patterns of sound.

Nondirected motion, within any conventional practice, could also be described as "arrested" motion. One of the procedures described in chapter 54, the unordered treatment of a segmental partition, has the effect of arrested motion. Regardless of how long the unordered treatment is sustained, the progression through the series is at least partially arrested. Directed and nondirected motion are fundamental to all musical design; it is unreasonable not to consider them within twelve-tone serialism.

What is the effect of a repeated pitch or collection of pitches in creating nondirected motion?

Repetitions can occur as uninterrupted repetitions of a single pitch or chordal constructs (Figure 55-1a and b). Pitch repetitions can occur as part of a sustaining configuration such as a tremolo or trill (Figure 55-2). Another form of pitch repetition occurs in melodic configurations as either structural elements or ornamental figures (Figure 55-3). And finally, pitch repetitions are typical in the use of unordered collections of pitches not associated with segmental partitioning (Figure 55-4). **W197—198**

55-1 (a)

Fourth String Quartet, Op. 37, Mov. III

Schoenberg

(b)

Quintet for Clarinet and Strings

Sherman

55-2

Fourth String Quartet, Op. 37, Mov. I

Schoenberg

55-3

Fourth String Quartet, Op. 37, Mov. IV

Schoenberg

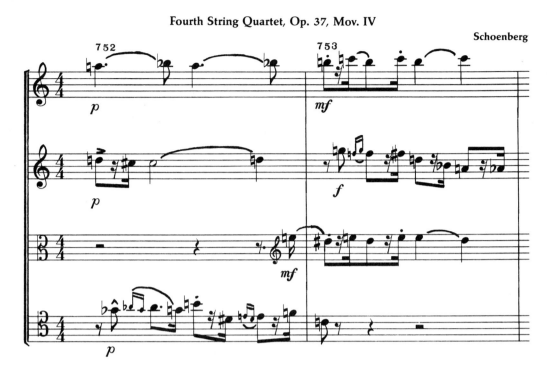

55-4

In Memoriam the Infant Jeremiah

(from the prophecy of Jeremiah)

Sherman

*sounds as notated

What constitutes an anomaly in twelve-tone serialized music?

An anomaly in twelve-tone serialized music is generally an application of a series or portion of a series that is germane to a given musicwork but not likely to appear in any other musicwork. Two such anomalies occur in Luigi Dallapicolla's *Goethe-Lieder:* a repeated pitch and a unique application of a portion of a series. (The series and matrix are shown in Figure 55-5.) In the third measure of the opening statement by the clarinets in the first of the seven

55-5

| 3 | 4 | 2 | 0 | 6 | 11 | 9 | 10 | 5 | 8 | 7 | 1 |

O——→   ←——R

	0	1	11	9	3	8	6	7	2	5	4	10
I	11	0	10	8	2	7	5	6	1	4	3	9
	1	2	0	10	4	9	7	8	3	6	5	11
↓	3	4	2	0	6	11	9	10	5	8	7	1
	9	10	8	6	0	5	3	4	11	2	1	7
	4	5	3	1	7	0	10	11	6	9	8	2
	6	7	5	3	9	2	0	1	8	11	10	4
	5	6	4	2	8	1	11	0	7	10	9	3
	10	11	9	7	1	6	4	5	0	3	2	8
	7	8	6	4	10	3	1	2	9	0	11	5
	8	9	7	5	11	4	2	3	10	1	0	6
	2	3	1	11	5	10	8	9	4	7	6	0

RI

songs (Figure 55-6), there is a repetition of the fifth member of the series (pc6). This repetition is unlike any of the repetitions found elsewhere in the seven songs. At first glance it appears to be a pointless repetition. On second glance, however, we can see that the three-note configuration containing the repetition (pc6) is an inversion of the opening three notes of the voice line shown in the fourth measure of Figure 55-6. A repetition of this kind may not occur often, but when it does, it should be viewed as a compositionally appropriate anomaly.

55-6

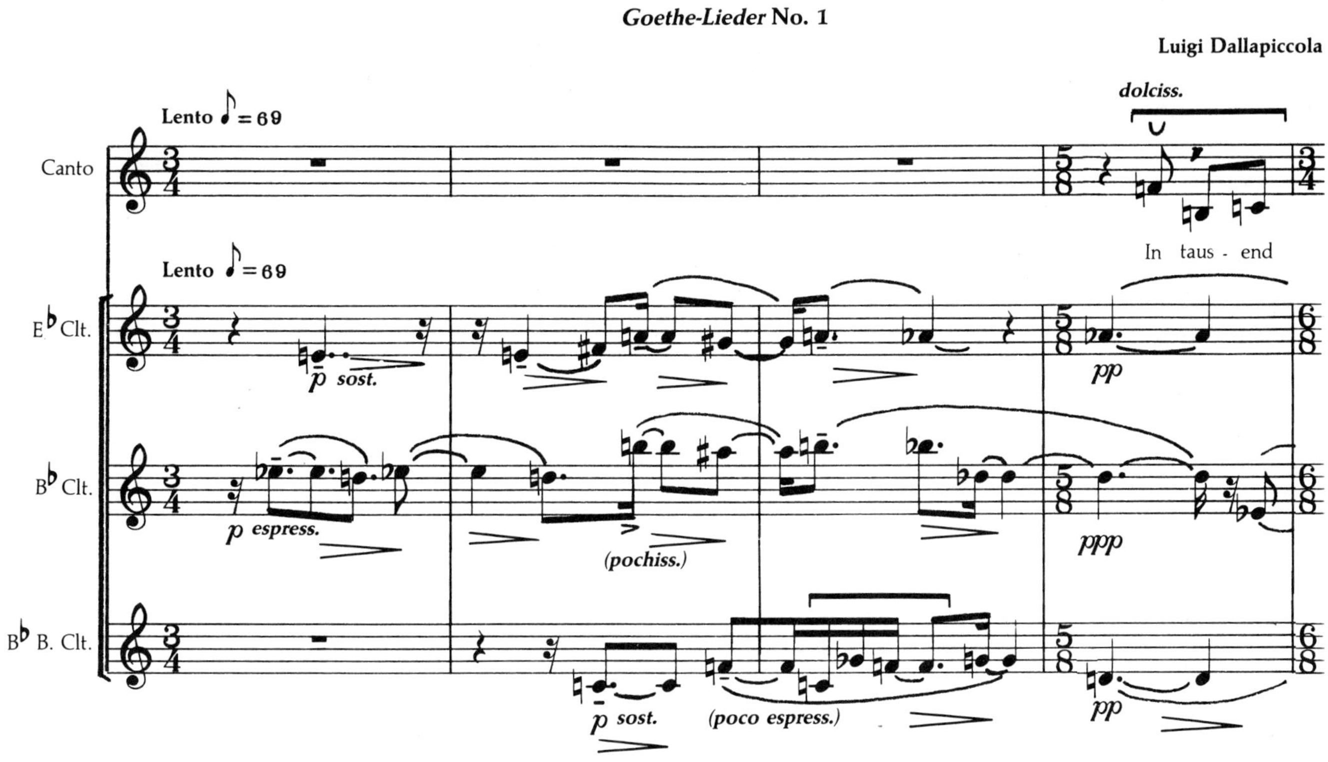

Goethe-Lieder No. 1

Luigi Dallapiccola

The other anomaly in the *Goethe-Lieder* is one that occurs often in several of the songs but it is probably unique to this musicwork. It involves using various mappings and transpositions of the first three members of the series to create a new series. This anomaly first appears in measures ten through fourteen of the first song (Figure 55-7). Two other examples of this unique application of the three-note configuration are shown in Figure 55-8.

55-7

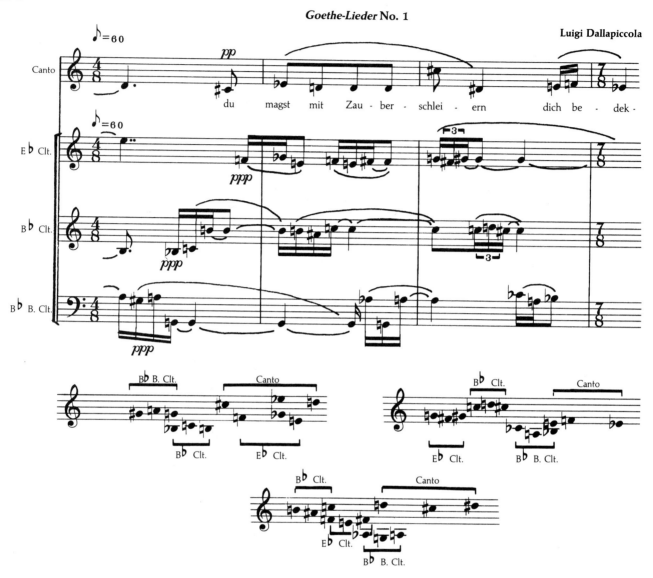

Goethe-Lieder No. 1

Luigi Dallapiccola

55-8

(a)

Goethe-Lieder No. 6

Luigi Dallapiccola

55-8, *continued*

(b)

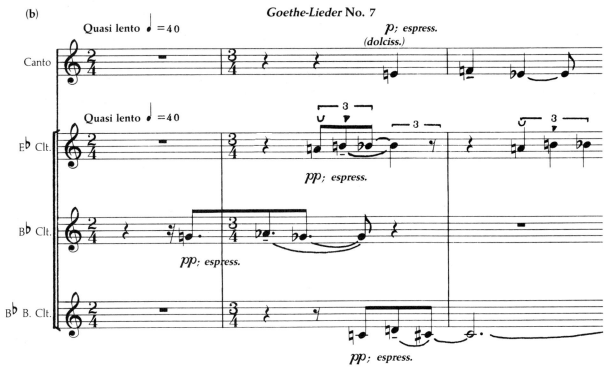

The first movement of Wallingford Riegger's Third Symphony provides a number of anomalous applications of a twelve-tone series. To enable us to relate some examples to a given series, Figure 55-9 provides the matrix for the first movement of the symphony. As the matrix shows, the series is combinatorial and provides a number of interesting relationships. First, note

55-9

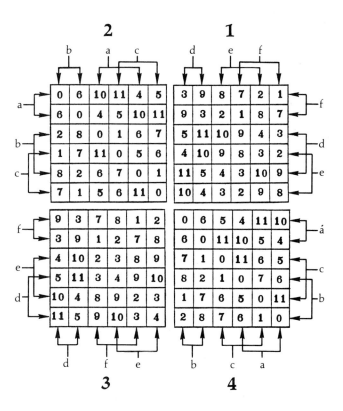

that the pitch-class content of the hexachords shown in the second quadrant (upper left) duplicates the content of those shown in the fourth quadrant (lower right). The same duplication exists between the first quadrant (upper right) and the third quadrant (lower left). Also, every hexachord labeled *a*, for example, has the same pitch-class content. This is also true for hexachords labeled *b, c, d, e,* and *f.* Because of the particular combinatorial aspect of the series, any hexachord labeled *a* can be used with any hexachord labeled *f*, for example, to form a twelve-tone series. Each series so formed would contain corresponding hexachords with the same pitch-class content but with a different ordering.

Upon examination of the score, it appears that the composer was either not interested in exploring the special combinatorial aspects of the series or was not aware that the series had combinatorial aspects. The combined use of a portion of the O_5 and O_{11} mappings hints that Riegger might have noticed at least one minor aspect of combinatoriality. This application of the initial hexachords of the O_5 and O_{11} mappings (Figure 55-10) is one of the several means the composer used to create a sense of nondirected motion. Other repetitions of portions of the O_5 mapping of the series are shown in Figure 55-11. These repetitions, also, create moments of nondirected motion.

55-10

Symphony No. 3, Mov. I

Wallingford Riegger

55-11

Symphony No. 3, Mov. I

Wallingford Riegger

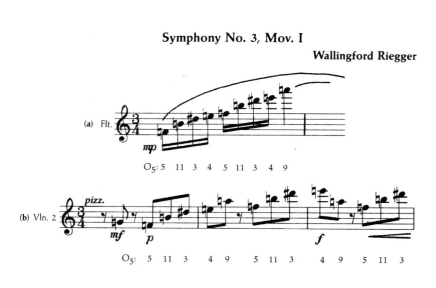

In a general sense, there is reason to consider nondirected motion as an anomaly exploited in this musicwork. For example, the first twenty-five measures are produced from numerous repetitions of the O$_5$ mapping. The repetitions of a single twelve-tone series over nearly one minute's time tends to establish nondirected motion as a basic premise of the musicwork.

How are anomalous, nonserialized pitch relationships utilized in the first movement of Riegger's Third Symphony?

Another anomaly found in the first movement of Riegger's Third Symphony is the occasional injection of nonserialized pitch materials. The first of these is a chromatic movement joining the pitch-class collection 11, 0, 5 to the collection 5, 6, 11 (Figure 55-12a). The second is

55-12

Symphony No. 3, Mov. I

Wallingford Riegger

a chromatic movement joining the pitch-class collection 11, 0, 5, 6 to another distribution of the same collection (Figure 55-12b). The third appears three times in as many measures (Figure 55-12c). In this third example, a diatonic movement joins the pitch-class collection 0, 6, 7 to the collection 4, 5, 10. Each of these sweeping gestures seems to serve as a connector between repetitions of short melodic statements or between differently textured sections of the movement. Lest we close the book on further developments in twelve-tone serialism, we must consider the possibility that today's anomaly may be the centerpiece of tomorrow's convention.

W199

What conclusion might we draw from this introduction to twelve-tone serialism?

This study unit has presented some of the more common conventional practices of twelve-tone serialism. Arnold Schoenberg described his concept of the principle as "composition with twelve tones which are related only one to another." This description does not suggest or support the rigid, uncompromising views set forth as "rules" by many who first attempted to explain it. As is true of all viable principles of tonal organization, twelve-tone serialism does not require the imposition of any external restrictions for it to survive as a principle. Nonetheless, twelve-tone serialism demands much of those who use it. In a general sense, it is a musical language for which the composer must create both the structure and the vocabulary for each musicwork produced. Twelve-tone serialism is not subject to the redundancies of chordal and melodic structures that characterize such earlier conventions as tonic-dominant tonality. Like tonic-dominant tonality, it will accommodate any expressive intent a composer may have. Considering the *millions* of available series and the options they provide, it is an extremely "deep well" from which we can draw. As with other such fruitful principles, we will tire of it long before we exhaust its resources.   **W200**

What is the future of twelve-tone serialism?

Viewed from the perspective of history, twelve-tone serialism is just one of the principles of tonal organization that has been developed. Because it was developed relatively recently, the controversy surrounding it is still fresh in people's memories. Time has dissipated many such controversies in the past. A new principle in any field of endeavor is intended to replace one whose usefulness is waning. Thus it is common for the applications of a new principle to be subjected to criticism and comparisons with the status quo. Such trials are simply natural challenges that serve to "filter out" those creative ventures that, in the case of music, lack the substance necessary to interest composers and listeners. Those that survive evolve into viable principles. Twelve-tone serialism has survived this critical review, and we can expect that someday it will encounter, be absorbed by, and eventually be replaced by some other principle of tonal organization.

What is the future of music?

One thing is certain, humankind will never come to "the end of the road" in how music is defined, organized, and produced. Though the history of music attests to periodic revivals of interest in past attitudes and aesthetic values, the techniques and tools of the art always go forward into the future. We can be certain that computers or computerlike tools will become widely accepted as instruments for making music. As it once was in the past, the composer and performer will again become one. And to suggest a distant and perhaps inevitable probability, the composer, performer, and listener may become one.

UNIT PROJECT 10

Introduction

In this last major project, you will encounter more options demanding more critical and inventive decisions than were required by the previous unit projects. Except for the twelve pitch classes of the dodecaphonic system, all that you produce or elect to use will be a product of your own invention or choice. The need for aesthetic discipline in what may appear to be an exercise in unbridled freedom is greater than ever.

The design of your twelve-tone series, though not your first major decision, will be one of the most critical decisions you make. As you well know, your options are exceedingly numerous, but not all permutations of the pitch-class content of the dodecaphonic system are useful for making music. The ordering of pitch classes in a twelve-tone series is an arbitrary decision based on personal choice; it is not a thoughtless, "grab-bag" selection.

Because the approaches to the internal structure of a twelve-tone series and the techniques for treating a series are numerous and varied, several types of projects will be described. Study all of them and select the one that best suits your creative skills and aesthetic temperament and the performance capabilities of you and your classmates.

Description

Complete and perform (in a public concert if possible) one of the following projects:

1. A two- or three-movement, two-voiced canon for two instruments.

2. A one-movement, four-voiced double canon for four instruments.

3. A two- or three-movement musicwork for a solo instrument and piano, preferably for you as a soloist.

4. A one-movement, a cappela setting of a text of your choice for three voices.

5. A setting of a relatively extended poem for voice and piano.

6. A setting of three very brief but related poems that can be treated as a song cycle for voice and piano.

As a class, develop an evaluation instrument (containing criteria pertinent to twelve-tone serialism) to be used by class members during the performance. The evaluations should be discussed in a class session.

Notes

Before you even think about producing a twelve-tone series, you must consider all of the usual precompositional decisions and procedures. Among other things, you must consider the function, expressive intent, instrumentation, performance site, capabilities of performers, and the duration of the musicwork.

Before you produce your twelve-tone series, you must consider how you will use it. Some of the more common options are

1. using multiple mappings of the series simultaneously (necessary in but not restricted to canonic writing)

2. partitioning the series into three- or four-member collections to satisfy melodic or chordal needs

3. partitioning the series to provide three- or four-member nonordered collections

4. ordering the series to satisfy the expected needs of simultaneity as well as the needs of melodic shapes

5. combinations of these options to meet special needs.

The treatment you select will in turn impose conditions on the design of your series. Your design may require:

1. a partial *or* all-combinatorial series *or* an isometric series,

2. specific intervallic relationships,

3. availability of special chordal constructs, *and*

4. special melodic shapes.

The importance of precompositional planning cannot be overemphasized; the success of any musicwork is dependent on it, not the least a twelve-tone-serialized one. You must plan what you will do in the composition. Composition is also a process of search and discovery. It is appropriate, therefore, that you work at the piano as you investigate the various possibilities that exist. Your own personal judgment is the standard of acceptability that you must satisfy; you have been cultivating this personal judgment in all of the mini projects and unit projects you have completed. Informed judgment and the skills to exercise it are the real end products of this course.

Credits

Index

A 8
B 9
C 0
D 1
E 2
F 3
G 4
H 5
I 6
J 7